Western Expansion and Indigenous Peoples

World Anthropology

General Editor

SOL TAX

Patrons

CLAUDE LÉVI-STRAUSS
MARGARET MEAD
LAILA SHUKRY EL HAMAMSY
M. N. SRINIVAS

MOUTON PUBLISHERS · THE HAGUE · PARIS
DISTRIBUTED IN THE USA AND CANADA BY ALDINE, CHICAGO

Western Expansion and Indigenous Peoples

The Heritage of Las Casas

Editor

ELIAS SEVILLA-CASAS

MOUTON PUBLISHERS · THE HAGUE · PARIS

DISTRIBUTED IN THE USA AND CANADA BY ALDINE, CHICAGO

Distributed in the United States of America and Canada
by Aldine Publishing Company, Chicago, Illinois
ISBN 90-279-7510-8 (Mouton)
0-202-90052-5 (Aldine)
Jacket photo by Nina S. de Friedemann
Cover and jacket design by Jurriaan Schrofer
Indexes by John Jennings
Printed in the Netherlands

General Editor's Preface

This book has a quality and a purpose logically independent of, but sentimentally tied to, its interesting historical origin in the celebration of the 500th anniversary of the birth of Fray Bartolomé de Las Casas. It is about the survival of the indigenous people who were the first (since the days of the Roman Empire) to be colonized by Europeans. Whether or not they are the heritage of Las Casas' humanity, and whether today they are Indians or peasants or proletariats — or all three at once — they have survived and can no longer be subjugated. This volume is also about the anthropologists who are not satisfied to be only sympathetically protective. They proclaim a "liberation anthropology," which in a class-structured world must be to a greater or lesser degree revolutionary. There could have been no atmosphere more suited to these subjects than the International Congress organized in Chicago in 1973.

Like most contemporary sciences, anthropology is a product of the European tradition. Some argue that it is a product of colonialism, with one small and self-interested part of the species dominating the study of the whole. If we are to understand the species, our science needs substantial input from scholars who represent a variety of the world's cultures. It was a deliberate purpose of the IXth International Congress of Anthropological and Ethnological Sciences to provide impetus in this direction. The *World Anthropology* volumes, therefore, offer a first glimpse of a human science in which members from all societies have played an active role. Each of the books is designed to be self-contained; each is an attempt to update its particular sector of scientific knowledge and is written by specialists from all parts of the world.

Each volume should be read and reviewed individually as a separate volume on its own given subject. The set as a whole will indicate what changes are in store for anthropology as scholars from the developing countries join in studying the species of which we are all a part.

The IXth Congress was planned from the beginning not only to include as many of the scholars from every part of the world as possible, but also with a view toward the eventual publication of the papers in high-quality volumes. At previous Congresses scholars were invited to bring papers which were then read out loud. They were necessarily limited in length; many were only summarized; there was little time for discussion; and the sparse discussion could only be in one language. The IXth Congress was an experiment aimed at changing this. Papers were written with the intention of exchanging them before the Congress, particularly in extensive pre-Congress sessions; they were not intended to be read aloud at the Congress, that time being devoted to discussions — discussions which were simultaneously and professionally translated into five languages. The method for eliciting the papers was structured to make as representative a sample as was allowable when scholarly creativity — hence self-selection — was critically important. Scholars were asked both to propose papers of their own and to suggest topics for sessions of the Congress which they might edit into volumes. All were then informed of the suggestions and encouraged to re-think their own papers and the topics. The process, therefore, was a continuous one of feedback and exchange and it has continued to be so even after the Congress. The some two thousand papers comprising *World Anthropology* certainly then offer a substantial sample of world anthropology. It has been said that anthropology is at a turning point; if this is so, these volumes will be the historical direction-markers.

As might have been foreseen in the first post-colonial generation, the large majority of the Congress papers (82 percent) are the work of scholars identified with the industrialized world which fathered our traditional discipline and the institution of the Congress itself: Eastern Europe (15 percent); Western Europe (16 percent); North America (47 percent); Japan, South Africa, Australia, and New Zealand (4 percent). Only 18 percent of the papers are from developing areas: Africa (4 percent); Asia-Oceania (9 percent); Latin America (5 percent). Aside from the substantial representation from the U.S.S.R. and the nations of Eastern Europe, a significant difference between this corpus of written material and that of other Congresses is the addition of the large proportion of contributions from Africa, Asia, and Latin America. "Only 18 percent" is two to four times as great a proportion as that of other Congresses;

moreover, 18 percent of 2,000 papers is 360 papers, 10 times the number of "Third World" papers presented at previous Congresses. In fact, these 360 papers are more than the total of ALL papers published after the last International Congress of Anthropological and Ethnological Sciences which was held in the United States (Philadelphia, 1956).

The significance of the increase is not simply quantitative. The input of scholars from areas which have until recently been no more than subject matter for anthropology represents both feedback and also long-awaited theoretical contributions from the perspectives of very different cultural, social, and historical traditions. Many who attended the IXth Congress were convinced that anthropology would not be the same in the future. The fact that the next Congress (India, 1978) will be our first in the "Third World" may be symbolic of the change. Meanwhile, sober consideration of the present set of books will show how much, and just where and how, our discipline is being revolutionized.

Other books in the World Anthropology series which are closely related to the present volume concern migration, urbanization, ethnicity, economic development and exploitation, and a variety of social problems related to race, sex, and minority group discrimination; Indians of North and Latin America; and anthropological fieldwork and applied anthropology in "Third World" areas.

Foreword

It is most appropriate and significant that the papers presented during the session dedicated to Fray Bartolomé de Las Casas at the IXth ICAES focused on the theme "Western Expansion and Indigenous Peoples."

Government people working with indigenous groups often criticize the anthropologists who receive titles, honors, and careers from their studies of Indian communities, but who seldom do anything to help resolve the problems. Another criticism is that knowledge gained by anthropologists is used by world powers to keep certain groups at their inferior social and political status.

It is not enough for us to exalt, to study, to write books about the great Friar Las Casas — it is not in his spirit nor was it his aim. We should also try to finish the work he started but could not complete, many of his ideas being far ahead of his time. What would he say about the horrible killings in the war in Asia which did not stop in spite of peace declarations mostly intended to mislead the world.

Many of us admire the cultural aspects of the Indians and agree it would be good to preserve their way of life. Many lament the impact our civilization has on their way of life today. On the other hand, we must nevertheless avoid trying to force indigenous people to stay within their culture. I prefer to see them in their beautiful traditional costumes and to admire their way of life, but I have no right to try to prevent them from living the way we do or the way they choose — and I must help them if asked to assist. I might tell them that we also must change, that we must learn to live again with fewer cars, fewer gadgets, and less frenzy, rushing in superfast cars and airplanes going nowhere — all those things which actually are forced upon us by an economy based on greed and which wastes the resources of our planet. If we stop this crazy way of life, then the Indians will have no need to make the same errors made most of the time in imitation of a stronger power.

Fray Bartolomé de Las Casas wrote many books which cannot be read easily, but he also wrote eloquent treatises which could be published for the general public. He wrote against discrimination, intolerance, disrespect for other civilizations, exploitation, and the lack of international understanding: topics which are not only easy to understand, but necessary to expose, for we still suffer from all those evils.

In spite of the fact that he is little known, Fray Bartolomé is one of the greatest figures in human history. Historians and very highly educated people know of him; the average person has no idea who he was. Tourists, for instance, visiting San Cristóbal de las Casas think that the name of the town has something to do with houses, not knowing that it is named for the first Bishop of Chiapas, Fray Bartolomé de Las Casas, who put up a brave fight against the exploitation of the Indians.

We must try to rectify his anonymity. The nefarious leaders of the world are better known than a man with ideals, ideals which could help make a better world. Popularizing his ideas could help us to realize his goals.

1974 is a good year to do just that. Five hundred years have passed since his birth, and the Patronato Fray Bartolomé de Las Casas is developing a program which can help make the great friar known and achieve some of his goals. It also will show that nothing is more incorrect than the idea that Fray Bartolomé created the Black Legend in Spain. What is true, however, is that he made Spain greater. The fact that he was able to talk openly without being silenced by the King of Spain about all the horrors of the Conquest, that he was able to fight against evils, and that his debate with Sepúlveda took place, are great examples of liberalism in the Spain of his time. Similarly, the United States' lifting the lid off the Watergate scandal should not vilify the United States but tell us that there is some health left in democratic institutions.

During 1974, many books about the friar will be published, many will be written to make his ideals popular, and many events in the world, especially in his town of San Christóbal de las Casas, will make a wide public aware of him as never before.

In January the theoretical foundation for these 1974 events was established with a symposium with the theme "Why are we honoring Fray Bartolomé de Las Casas?" Dr. Lewis Hanke from the United

States and Professor Ernesto Mejia Sánchez from Mexico were the principal speakers in the discussion. In February the members of the Patronato and a group of supporters were joined by Guatemalans on a trip to Copan, Vera Paz, for the commemoration of the friar's success in pacifying the Indians of that region. This was an act of fraternity and friendship between two countries in the spirit of Las Casas.

In March we shall come together to discuss colonial architecture and urbanism, trying to save in our colonial towns some of their past. In April governmental and private organizations as well as individuals who work with Indians will be brought together to discuss the problems of the Indian communities and possible solutions. At the end of July the ex-convent of Santo Domingo Church in San Cristóbal de las Casas will be inaugurated as a museum of Indian crafts. In October hundreds of Indians will gather in this city for the congress organized by the Bishop of San Cristóbal, Dr. Samuel García, with the colaboration of the State Indian Department and the Patronato Fray Bartolomé de Las Casas. In November ecologists will discuss problems of our planet with the idea in mind that no program can help Indians if we are unable to stop the destruction of our earth. In December a symposium on international law will be held. Fray Bartolomé was the first protagonist of international law, and today, more than ever, few problems can be solved only on a national basis. To conclude the year of Fray Bartolomé de Las Casas, our friends from Guatemala will come so we can evaluate what we achieved during 1974 and how we shall orient the future work of putting into practice the ideas of Fray Bartolomé de Las Casas.

There was never a status quo in any society which survived. What we need to achieve is a merging of the existing cultures with a view to saving, morally and ecologically, our perishing planet.

I am honored to write this foreword for a book which will help a great deal in directing our efforts.

San Cristóbal de las Casas, Chiapas
February 1974   Gertrude Duby Blom

Table of Contents

Introduction

ELIAS SEVILLA-CASAS

1. This volume has been compiled with the intent to present, in written form, the wealth of ideas expressed in Session 643 of the IXth International Congress of Anthropological and Ethnological Sciences. This session brought into focus the American aboriginal minorities, particularly the situations in which they are subject to forced cultural modification, exploitation, and physical extinction.

In preparing this introduction, three categories of potential readers come to my mind: first, the increasing number of indigenous leaders and activists around the world who are awakening to a critical perception of the dehumanizing living conditions of their people, the solidarity between all brothers confronted with injustice, and the formidable possibilities of building more equitable social relations for themselves and for others; second, the numerous persons from contemporary intellectual, technological, and political circles who have passed the stage of simply deporing "the fate," or mourning the extinction of the aboriginals and have decided to do something for them and WITH THEM; third, the fellow *lascasistas*, that is, the scholars and nonscholars who study, admire, or follow the ideas of Bartolomé de Las Casas.

In reference to this last group, I think that it is of more than passing significance that the session was linked to the five hundredth birthday of Las Casas. This man was, indeed, during his lifetime, a courageous

I want to thank particularly Señora Gertrude Duby Blom, Professor B. Keen, John Collier, the fellow anthropologists of the Research Unit of the Community Mental Health Program at the West Side Medical Complex of Chicago, and my wife, Martha, for their assistance in preparing the session. I am also grateful to Jay Schensul and Liz Cameron for their help in preparing this introduction.

defender of the American natives. To those who know the history of the sixteenth-century European expansion into the New World, Las Casas figures prominently in the efforts made to foster equitable social relations between Spaniards and Indians. Such efforts entailed for him a lifelong struggle against any type of oppression of the natives, and particularly against the exploitative conditions of the *encomienda* system.

In his struggle, Las Casas was adamant, incisive, and uncompromising. He won for himself among certain Hispanophiles the reputation of being a traitor to the Spanish cause, and was considered the individual chiefly responsible for the rise of the Black Legend regarding the Spanish conquest and colonization of America. Many of Las Casas' foes do not recognize, however, that he not only condemned and indicted; he also made positive contributions. Considering the European presence in America a *fait accompli*, he made serious attempts to present to the Spanish Crown alternatives that would recognize and uphold the right of the Indians to be treated *as human beings in no way inferior to the Spaniards*.

Looking back on Las Casas' life and work, it is sensible to celebrate him as the *Defensor de los Indios*, a title bestowed on him by Charles V and recognized unanimously by history. It is also proper to consider his ideas and activities as the basis of the modern *movimiento indigenista*, which attempts to regain for the Indians their pride, their freedom, their land, and their bread. Finally, it is equitable to commemorate him as the *Doctor de la Americanidad*, a title earned by his intellectual endeavors regarding the human condition of the native Americans.

The human condition, both of the aboriginals of America and of other nonwhite peoples of the world, is the kernel of Las Casas' political philosophy. His famous motto, "All nations of the world are men," was at the core of his rigorous attacks on the Spanish colonial policies. Fortunately, today this theme again is gaining deep significance.

The idea of doing something about Las Casas' centennial year at the IXth International Congress of Anthropologists came from the Patronato Fray Bartolomé de Las Casas (San Cristóbal de las Casas, Chiapas, Mexico). From the beginning the idea had a warm welcome among the organizers of the Congress. By mutual agreement, a session was planned in which the world anthropologists (1) would be informed of and invited to the celebrations of Las Casas to be held in Mexico during 1974, and (2) would discuss some ideas concerning the oppressive conditions of contemporary native peoples, particularly of Spanish

America. Gertrude Duby Blom, *presidenta* of the Patronato, was in charge of the first part of the program. The participants of the session were responsible for the second part.

Shortage of time prevented me, as the organizer of the session, from inviting colleagues around the world to write papers specifically designed for the session. Instead, a sort of conceptual framework for discussion was formulated, which helped to select from the titles and abstracts already submitted to the Congress those papers that would satisfy the general goals of the session. The authors of the selected would-be papers were formally invited to participate in the session. We were lucky enough to receive a representative number of answers, and even luckier in realizing how these papers, so artificially assembled, surpassed our initial expectations and opened immense perspectives for future work.

The most salient points of the conceptual framework used in the selection of the papers, and later in their discussion, were as follows:
a. Las Casas was in his time an intellectual who unmasked and denounced the ideologies and mechanisms of oppression characteristic of the Spanish conquest and colonization. He was at the same time deeply involved in the political and social arena, to bring about better living conditions for the natives. It seems reasonable that the best way of celebrating his memory is to reflect on his political and ideological practice in order to continue with renewed force his noble pursuit.
b. There are at present many people, some of them intellectuals, who are sincerely concerned with the "culture of oppression" in which contemporary American natives are living. Different ways have been proposed to put this concern into practice, and it would be hypocritical if they remained only in their planning stage. One of these ways is not only to denounce, but to make a critical analysis of past and current situations of injustice concerning the natives. Ideologies and mechanisms of oppression and of liberation could be identified and subjected to theoretical analyses which would provide a solid basis for direct political action. The results of these analyses should go directly and primarily to the subjects of the Indian libertarian efforts, that is, to the Indians themselves.

In the session we wanted to advance some steps in this direction. We attempted also to join our efforts to the ongoing projects of direct assistance to the natives, particularly in collaboration with the International Work Group for Indigenous Affairs.

The results of our efforts were encouraging, not only for the insights brought in by the individual papers, but for those stemming from the dialogue actually held during the Congress. In the following pages I will briefly introduce these papers. I will conclude with some comments on four major themes that arose in the exchange of ideas and that seem to characterize the current situation of the Indian peoples.

2. The papers presented in the session can be grouped in three sets which deal respectively with (1) general theoretical considerations of the mechanisms and ideologies of oppression and liberation, (2) studies of the situation of the Indians in the colonial past, and (3) case studies of contemporary Indian communities.

2.1. The first set of papers is introduced by my own work on the ideological and political activity of Las Casas concerning the American Indians. It is concerned mainly with the life of Las Casas and the nature of his philosophy and strategy of political involvement. A line of evolution is found in Las Casas' work in which he shifted gradually from a verbalist and voluntaristic approach to direct political action. Along with this transformation, there was also an increasing radicalization in his alternative proposals. The discussion of the above points is made in the light of the present need for having social scientists effectively involved in aiding the cause of the Indians.

Bodley's contribution is a critique of the explicit and implicit ethnocentrism that has characterized all previous forms of cultural modification, including those favored by anthropologists as alternatives to ethnocide. They are usually assimilationist policies presented under the name of integration, planned acculturation, or modernization. The above approaches indeed justify, with various arguments, the call for integration of cultural minorities into state political systems, and predicate their complete assimilation. The author states that these masked forms of ethnocide have harmful consequences, particularly ecological deterioration and relative deprivation of natural resources. As a viable alternative to the current forms of cultural modification, Bodley proposes cultural autonomy for tribal peoples that would be enacted in the form of autonomous, unsupervised tribal regions.

Forced cultural change, outrageous forms of dominance, and environmental deterioration are also the consequences deplored by Binder in his assessment of current policies of aid, development, and induced change among indigenous minorities. The author states that both Christian-capitalist and Marxist-communist approaches to aid and development are ways of incorporating minorities, by force or by deceit, into the fatal process he denounces. Partnership among cocultures, constructive cooperation, and intercultural symmetrical communication are positive suggestions the author offers in the cases he analyzes.

2.2. The implications of the above general considerations acquire a more pungent character when applied to concrete cases showing the dynamics of historic colonization methods. Markman makes a study of the physical layout of the early urban binomies, *pueblos españoles* and *pueblos de indios* specifically, as they reveal the racial and caste segregations created by the colonists. He points out that, once the physical and spiritual conquest of the natives by the Spaniards was consummated, the interaction of new historical forces signaled the disruption and deterioration of this caste and race organization. The two processes identified by Markman as responsible for this disintegration are the biological conquest of the Spaniards by the natives (*mestizaje*), and the socioeconomic transformation that established material wealth as a major indicator of social status.

The dynamics of colonization were also operative at the symbolic level of artistic and religious expression. Kelsey studies the persistence of baroque forms in the life-style of some Mexican and Peruvian communities, now observable in the celebration of pageants and processions. She concludes that in such cases the baroque expressions survive only in the form of fixed and unalterable rituals. It is suggested that because these rituals lack the meaning which is characteristic of the early forms, they may constitute a formidable barrier to cultural change.

In a third paper, Jácome and Llumiquinga focus on another important aspect of the colonization process — the exploitative character of the *tributo*, which was required from the natives by the Spanish rulers. *Tributos* are looked at in close connection with other forms of exploitation existing in colonial Ecuador, such as *obrajes*, mine labor, *encomiendas, haciendas*, and personal services. The authors point out the significance of the *tributo* as a drain of economic surplus going directly from the colonies to the metropolis. This significance is more apparent when the *tributo* is considered as an integral aspect of the global process that led to the rise and consolidation of modern Western capitalism.

The above three ethnohistorical studies deal specifically with the patterns of Spanish conquest and colonization. To offer a comparative perspective, Pope gives her interpretation of what she calls the "transculturation failure" of the Danish in their West Indies colonies (today's Virgin Islands). She indicates that there was a studied indifference on their part toward their subjects, as shown by the lack of interest in offering them citizenship, salvation, or education. This attitude and policy may explain why the colonized blacks failed to incorporate the colonizer's customs into their lives. Pope's study is also interesting in that it offers a point of comparison for Spanish colonial policies that is different from the traditional ones that focus on English or French patterns of colonization.

2.3.   The colonial past holds many lessons that may contribute immensely to the interpretation and analysis of contemporary native situations. The studies just mentioned regarding the Spanish colonial urbanization patterns, the persistence of baroque forms in contemporary peasant celebrations, the colonial *tributo* as a road to modern capitalism, and the Danish colonial policies shed much light indeed on what is occurring today in indigenous America.

The Mapuche Indians of Chile were successful in maintaining their independence *vis-à-vis* the white colonizers for over four centuries. They were defeated, however, when land, the most precious element of native self-assertion, passed gradually to white hands under the pressure of the modern capitalist social formation. Berdichewsky's paper deals with the land reform policies of Chile, as they have affected the Mapuches in the past, and as they reflect, respond to, or elicit significant transformations of Mapuche society in the present. The author devotes much attention to the current social and economic processes of Indian-peasant groups. This allows him to identify interesting aspects of the structural changes occurring now throughout Chilean society as a result of the land policies enacted by the late President Allende.

Ethnocidal land tenure policies have also impinged upon the Canelos Quechua Indians of lowland Ecuador. Such policies have sought to exert pressures which would eventually lead to total Indian disenfranchisement and ethnic annihilation. Whitten makes a detailed study of the oppressive mechanisms that are at work in the forced imposition of a national political culture. This policy overtly favors the territorial expansion of *blanco-mestizos* at the expense of the territorial encapsulation of groups such as the Canelos Quechua. Whitten also discusses the strategies developed by these Indians in response to these pressures. His conclusions emphasize particularly solutions to the problem which would incorporate the intensification of native ethnic consciousness, of bilingualism (Spanish-Quechua), and of adaptively successful patterns of land acquisition and territorial defense.

Unlike the case of the Canelos Quechua, the prospects for ethnic survival of the Jívaros of the Ecuadorian and Peruvian Montaña are particularly gloomy. Siverts, in his paper, states that the traditional head-hunting raids and corresponding ideological underpinnings of the Jívaros are the core of their ethnic identity, and a successful measure of tribal survival. In discussing the degree to which these raids are exponents of a structure that favors the formation of war corporations for territorial defense, the author points out the utter hopelessness of the Jívaros' survival. Headhunting is today proscribed by law, and the bulldozer and the machine gun have become current forms of territorial aggression against which the Jívaros are completely defenseless.

Moving from Jívaroland to the northeastern jungles of Colombia, we find that the Emberá Indians are also suffering, this time from a refined form of cultural aggression. Periodic religious practices of the neighboring white and black residents of the city of Quibdó have acquired an overt ethnocidal character. This provincial city is only one instance of a widespread pattern, discussed by de Friedemann in her paper, of exploitation of the natives in Colombia. The author tells us how the Emberás are encouraged to attend the Easter festivities of Quibdó. There the natives are "civilized" by means of "white" clothes and the wholesale consumption of alcohol. The consequent cultural and ecological disorientation of the Indians in its more amusing forms constitutes the chief derisive attraction of the festivities.

Two papers deal with cases of ethnic conflict drawn from Mexico. Both focus on the religious-magical realm, as it is affected or reflects the difficult conditions faced by the Indians. Iwańska studies the magical beliefs and practices of certain Mazahua groups whose malevolent crosses sometimes create veritable communal paranoia in the towns. These beliefs deviate from the point of view of the dominant syncretic Catholicism. The author puts their existence in causal relationship to the sword and fire methods by which sixteenth-century Christianity penetrated and sought domination in some Mexican Indian towns. On the other hand, Iwańska cites such factors as availability of modern medicine, creation of schools, and restructuring of land tenure patterns as producing perceptible changes in the whole system of beliefs and practices concerning the crosses.

Barabas' paper presents a case in which the crisis of a Chinantec community facing drastic change in its relationship to land (because of the construction of a dam) is manifested in the rise of a messianic movement. The secular and bureaucratic intermediaries have failed to carry the Indians' real concerns to the political elite of the country.

This has moved the natives to appeal to the prophet of the messianic movement as an alternative intermediary.

In his paper, Huizer applies his conclusions on peasant rebellions to the case of agricultural multinational corporations. The peculiar conditions of plantation economies which exert unbearable pressures on the peasants are added reasons for the rise and radicalization of their mobilization.

Finally, Kowalewski's paper analyzes the cyclical oscillation of Latin American rural communities between dependent marginalization and participant dependency in relation to the core of the capitalist social formation. The author suggests that the revolutionary guerrillas operating in certain countries of Latin America are very likely to be instrumental in altering, both culturally and politically, the above cyclical oscillation. This will end peasant dependency or marginality and promote radical structural changes in the global society.

3.   It is time for me to make some comments on the general themes that seem to run across the above papers and discussions. Undoubtedly, the papers present a selected view of the current scene of oppression of the Indians, although they seem to be fairly representative.[1] Their geographical variation and their range of issues testify to the fact that certain conclusions can probably be made concerning the contemporary situation and the importance of the session itself. In order to invite the readers to go further in the type of analyses initiated at this session, I will present tentatively some remarks on four of these themes.

3.1.   The relationship of the natives to their land and their reaction toward its invasion and conquest by foreign groups have always been a theme of primary importance for the study of social transformations. At the present time this importance is apparent not only on a theoretical level, but on an ideological-political level as well. The disruption by invaders of the Indian cultural and ecological balance is a major source of native afflictions (de Friedemann), and has proved to be a successful tactic for the invader in curbing otherwise independent tribes (Berdichewsky).

The above disruption of man-land relationship has been enacted gradually by the double-standard policies of "open frontiers" *(territorios baldíos)* which encourage or are favorable to the "colonization" of indigenous lands by *blanco-mestizos*. In this case the latter group is

[1]   Additional excellent material can be found in the documents periodically published by the International Work Group for Indigenous Affairs.

always thought of as "potential agriculturalists," while the Indians are denied even the elementary right of being considered in a similar fashion (Bodley, Whitten). In another familiar pattern, disruption is achieved drastically by launching government projects of modernization and industrialization in which the necessary channels of intercultural communication with the affected Indian communities are blocked by insensitive or incompetent bureaucracies (Barabas).

To the consequences of the above land policies for the Indian peoples as such, we have to add some other negative by-products. Unlike undisturbed Indian communities, we, the disturbed Indians and non-Indians, now face the threat of relative deprivation of natural resources and irreversible ecological deterioration (Bodley, Binder).

Land invasions, sharecroppers' rebellions, protests, and violent reactions against territorial aggression have occurred frequently in recent history, with peasants as enactors. These movements have acquired, on occasions, definite revolutionary overtones (Huizer). They also are becoming a locus for the merging of Indian and peasant forces and concerns. In these cases it is possible to talk of an emerging class consciousness that may have unforseeable consequences both for the Indian peasants and the larger society (Berdichewsky, Barabas).

Other types of responses also occur, not as overtly radical as the above ones, but also effective in terms of adaptation. One good example is the evolution of the Indian *comuna* from a "reservation-complex type" of territorial encapsulation to a corporate holding company (or communal cooperative of production). This would not be merely a defensive measure or protective mechanism, but a strategy of successful competition with other current non-Indian structures of production (Whitten, Berdichewsky).

3.2. A second theme that surfaced during the session was that of *mestizaje*, and the use of this concept as a weapon against the natives. Biological conquest was one historical response to the military and spiritual conquest of certain sectors of the New World population by the Spaniards (Markman). Today *ladinos, mulatos,* and *zambos* are an important component of the demographic panorama of Latin America, and their influence cannot be underestimated. This clearly indicates that *mestizaje* as a biological process has been successful and is an ongoing phenomenon with remarkable adaptive features. However, the *mestizaje* concept can be used as an ethnocidal weapon in the hands of a national political culture that condemns the unmixed and blesses the nondifferent. In this case many of the Indians to whom we are referring in this volume are treated as a serious threat to the national "progress" and assimilationist goals (Whitten). The disparagement of the natives and the perpetuation of dehumanizing stereotypes is an ongoing process. This appears to be a component of the programs of the dominant national culture, and is embedded in the current socialization patterns of the country — the people are explicitly or implicitly indoctrinated to prey upon the aboriginals (de Friedemann). Paradoxically this indoctrination reaches nonwhite people, such as *ladinos, mulatos, zambos,* blacks, and even certain natives (the *indios revestidos,* that is, the culturally *mestizo* blood Indians — Barabas). We come in this way full circle to a situation of complete exploitation and oppression. Not only does the white man continue his historic role as exploiter and dehumanizer but he teaches or forces nonwhites to do the same.

The ideology of *mestizaje* as a modality of vilification and affliction elicits in the indigenous groups an intensification of ethnicity by which the natives revive selectively certain themes of their culture, or create new ones (Berdichewsky). The accent on ethnicity does not necessarily block the emergence of a class consciousness (Barabas, Berdichewsky) nor hinder the formation of pan-Indian movements. This revival, other than signaling a return to the fossilized past, is a healthy adaptive effort that seems to acquire a dual character — the new Indian ethnicity is both "Indian and bicultural" (Whitten). The increase of Spanish-Indian bilingualism, and even of Spanish-Indian literacy, is a good example of how this revival is developing.

However, it must also be pointed out that for many Indians their survival as ethnic groups is not always a likelihood. Several groups do face extermination, especially those whose "core of Indianness" has been completely discarded, or who find themselves completely defenseless in the face of the mechanized advance of the white man (Siverts). From the above examples regarding positive and negative instances, we can see that "cultural pluralism" is not merely an anthropological concept to be celebrated in congresses and operas. It entails the physical survival of Indian and other ethnic minorities.

3.3. A third theme runs through our selections and emphasizes the urgency and importance of looking for new viewpoints and methodologies in our analyses. It is important, for instance, to place the study of mechanisms of oppression in the context of the Western capitalist social formation (Jácome and Llumiquinga). It is also necessary to formulate alternatives that seriously consider deeply rooted structural changes in the dominant national societies (de Friedemann, Kowalewski). At the same time we must run across national borders, if necessary, in order to study and denounce the current structure of "power domains" and channels of intercultural communication that are set up to maintain or further the exploitation of the Indians (Whitten, Barabas). Studying comparatively the forms of expansion, domination, and ethnic conflict that occurred during the formation and consolidation of pre-Spanish state political systems is also a good suggestion.

To the study of processes of political and socioeconomic nature should be added the study of the delicate areas of native religious and symbolic life. This has to be done keeping in mind, first, the givens of theological and "cultural" aggressions which occurred in the (colonial and precolonial) past, and second, the existence of sincretisms that have become themselves rigid structures (Kelsey, Iwańska). It seems clear that certain reactions of natives that are expressed in religious-symbolic language are in fact movements that have deep sociopolitical implications (Barabas).

Native reactions, as outlined above, tend ultimately to reject oppressive structures and to seek the creation of more just and humane alternatives. If this is the case we can expect strong repercussions within and between both the native and the dominant societies. These are destined to change, readapt, and redefine the basic assumptions of their mutual relationships. Certain native groups already appear to be moving in this direction, always retaining their self-respect and their own ethnic identity (Berdichewsky, Whitten). In contrast, the dominant society is reluctant to accept this as an alternative. The national elites seem to prefer pseudoindigenist policies that operate on the assumption that the native groups have only two options: to be assimilated or to die (Bodley).

3.4. I wish to conclude by commenting on a matter that was stressed several times during the Congress — namely, the forms of assistance offered to the aboriginals by the intellectual, social, and political elite of the dominant society. John White, a North American Indian present at the session, stated that the aspirations of the indigenous peoples can be expressed satisfactorily only by themselves, and that the help offered by non-Indian men of good will can best be directed to help Indians pull their forces together. In this statement was implicit an assertion that was made explicit by other participants: only the aboriginals themselves can bring about their liberation. This conclusion negates any form of interference with the efforts of autonomous Indian groups.

Interference can occur in the form of partisan capitalization of native efforts, alien ideological or religious proselytism, and "help" which would enhance or perpetuate patronage and dependency.

The role of the social scientist is important in this whole process, particularly in the form of presenting careful and fair analyses of oppressive situations and of furnishing coherent descriptions of Indian traditional life. The results of these studies should be made available directly and primarily to the native communities concerned. Siverts gave a good example of how this service can be done when he told us that his ethnography of certain Jívaro communities was used effectively by the native Shuara Federation for political purposes. A consistent model of assistance given to native groups is that of the International Work Group for Indigenous Affairs. It has features that respect the autonomy of the indigenous libertarian efforts and that are wholeheartedly welcomed by some active Indian groups, such as the National Indian Brotherhood of Canada.

Social scientists cannot avoid being involved in the contemporary social transformations. They certainly have specific responsibilities toward the native minorities, which were clearly indicated in the session. Studied indifference to the urgent needs of these brothers makes us irresponsible spectators to a phenomenon that ultimately will shake the totality of our society.

SECTION ONE

General Theoretical Considerations

Notes on Las Casas' Ideological and Political Practice

ELIAS SEVILLA-CASAS

It should not be considered unusual to celebrate the five hundredth birthday of Bartolomé de Las Casas, the Doctor of the Americas and Defensor of the Indians, in a congress of anthropologists. Although he is not even mentioned in the conventional histories of anthropology, the contributions of the Bishop of Chiapas to the discipline have been noted explicitly by outstanding scholars. The historian Hanke has a monograph (1949) partially dedicated to this subject. Sanderlin (1971), in his presentation of Las Casas' doctrines, refers to him as an "anthropologist." The above authors indicate that his contributions to the discipline are important not only in the area of first-hand ethnographic descriptions (particularly the *Historia de Indias*) but in the realm of theoretical-ideological discussion (particularly the *Apologética Historia*). Pérez de Tudela has called Las Casas' anthropology "the anthropology of hope" because the ultimate goal of his theoretical and descriptive efforts was to insist on the potential of "these Indian peoples" for being equally as HUMAN as their Spanish conquerors and colonizers (Pérez de Tudela 1957, I: cxvii). The Mexican anthropologist Comas has shown how the doctrine and activities of the Spanish Dominican form the basis of the modern *Movimiento Indigenista* (Comas 1953, 1971; see Friede 1971).

I do not want to repeat the above points but rather to analyze the work of Las Casas from a different perspective. Such a perspective is symbolically defined by the two titles that history has given to Las Casas, the DEFENSOR of the Indians and the DOCTOR of the Americas.

I will set this analysis in the light of two concerns that presently have extraordinary relevance for anthropologists: (1) the dehumanizing social relations existing between the still expanding Western civilization and non-Western peoples of the world, and (2) the increasing awareness of scholars, social scientists, and particularly of anthropologists of their social and political responsibility. My contention will be that in the PRAXIS[1] of Las Casas, as a SCHOLAR and as an ACTIVE FIGHTER for just social relations between Spaniards and Indians, we can find models that shed much light on the above concerns. In other words, I want to comment on the profound meaning of Neruda's verses from the *Canto General* regarding Las Casas' *regalo de cruda medianoche*:

... una luz antigua, suave y dura
como un metal, como un astro enterrado.
...
Pero tu prédica no era
frágil minuto, peregrina
pauta, reloj de pasajero.
Tu madera era bosque combatido,
hierro en su cepa natural, oculto
a toda luz por tierra florida,
y más aún era más hondo:
en la unidad del tiempo, en el transcurso
de la vida, era tu mano adelantada
estrella zodiacal, signo del pueblo.

In the following section (one), after a brief note regarding the life and personality of Las Casas, I will discuss the evolution of his work.[2] In section two I will comment on the two contemporary concerns I have mentioned above in order to draw some conclusions which will be presented in section three.

---

[1] Praxis and practice are given here a very precise meaning. Practice is taken in the Marxist sense, proposed by Engels, elaborated by Mao Tse Tung, and discussed extensively by Althuser. It is basically a process of production, of transformation, that has "raw material," "product," needs "human labor," and requires certain "means" of production. Social practice, the end product of which is a social formation, is the complex unity of practices existing in a determinate society and in which at least four essential levels are distinguished: the economic, the political, the ideological, and the theoretical (scientific) practices (see Althuser 1969:163–217). A further elaboration of these concepts is the Freirian concept of praxis, which is the "word" inasmuch as it transforms the "world" and is a synthesis of action and reflection. It stands in balance between the two extremes of verbalism and activism (see Freire 1970:75).

[2] In the review of Las Casas' work I have omitted exact historical references in order to free this article from an excessive bibliography. The discussion of Las Casas' activities is based mostly on the excellent work of Friede (1971). All citations of historical facts can be easily verified in the recent book edited by Keen and Friede (1971), where the reader may find further bibliographic references.

1. Bartolomé de Las Casas started his career in 1514 as one of the most
prominent and controversial intellectual and political figures of the Spanish colonization of America. In that year he renounced his estates in Cuba,
where he was an *encomendero,* and decided to put all his energies and
influence at the service of the new cause: the liberation of the Indians
from a subjection to the Spaniards that he considered inhuman. For more
than fifty years he fought with courage and lucid mind against an already
established oppressive system represented by the institution of *encomienda*[3], and against the ideology behind that system. He was then a
clérigo; indeed, he was the first priest ordained in the New World. In 1516
he was appointed by the King "Defensor of the Indians," and in 1523 he
became a Dominican monk. In 1544 he was offered the rich bishopric of
Cuzco (Peru), but he preferred the impoverished one of Chiapas in southwestern Mexico. His positions of official Protector of the Indians, of
religious man, and of bishop were effective elements of his total involvement, given the sociopolitical context in which he operated. (It was the
time of the Spanish Inquisition.)

Las Casas was a MAN OF ACTION, a vehement polemicist, a shrewd
politician. He carried out his work with the traditional *furia* of a Spaniard.
He was a pioneer in what has been called the "first social experiment in
America" (Hanke 1935). He crossed the Atlantic ten times, sailed the
Pacific, traveled incessantly in the Caribbean Sea. He particularly carried
out his humanistic work before the colonial *Audiencias,* and in the courts
of Ferdinand II, Charles V, and Phillip II.

Las Casas was, at the same time, a SCHOLAR, one of the most brilliant
ideologists of his time, who moved with ease and success in the intellectual
circles of his epoch. His numerous writings (the Soviet historian Afanasief
counts eighty significant works) make of him a historian, an autobiog-
rapher, a political thinker, an anthropologist, and a theologian (see
Sanderlin 1971). During four centuries his ideas have inspired struggles
for liberation and for equality among men in all the parts of the world.
Numerous critics consider him responsible for the rise of the Black
Legend concerning the Spanish Conquest of America. On the other hand,
a "white legend" has grown up around his writings concerning the
same Conquest (see Keen and Friede 1971). Las Casas' pamphlet, *Breví-
sima Historia de Indias,* is charged with fire and has been extremely in-

---

[3] The *encomienda* was a track of land or a town given to a Spanish settler. The Indians
of that region were entrusted to the settler, the *encomendero,* who in return for the
"evangelization" of the Indians in the Christian religion had the right to their forced
labor. The basic principle of the institution was that of domination of the colonist over
the Indian. Although theoretically the *encomienda* did not entail rights to the land,
these rights were often usurped by *encomenderos.*

fluential in many (anti-Spanish) subversive movements (see Afanasief 1971).

The Indians with whom Las Casas was in direct contact were those populating the Caribbean islands of Hispaniola, Santo Domingo, Puerto Rico, and Cuba as well as the northern coast of Venezuela, Central America (Guatemala and Nicaragua), and southern Mexico. His "ethnographic" work refers mostly to these Indians, but he was extremely well acquainted with secondary sources referring to other Indians of Spanish America. His peripatetic library (he usually traveled with all his books and papers) was virtually an archive of the Indies, full of letters, descriptions, petitions, memorials, and accusations coming from all corners of the colonies.

In the work of Las Casas we can distinguish an evolutionary process that is characterized by (1) a gradual transition from verbalism and voluntarism to direct action, and (2) a progressive radicalization of this political ideology. We can talk, using the above points, of four phases of his praxis.

PHASE 1 : MORALISTIC PREACHER   Soon after his conversion to the Indian cause (1514), Las Casas developed an ideology that substantially coincided with the doctrinal foundations of all defenders of the Indians in that epoch.

Las Casas maintained that the Indian, as a human being with all the human faculties, and despite the Conquest, retained all his natural rights, which included his personal freedom vis-à-vis the colonist and the freedom to freely dispose of his person, goods, and labor. The corollary of this was that Las Casas rejected all forms of Indian subjection to the white (*encomienda, naboría* slavery), and he sought a policy that would secure the full protection of the crown and the church for the Indian against the supposed rights which, by virtue of the Conquest, the Spanish colonist claimed for himself. The Indians, as vassals of the Crown, should be under its exclusive jurisdiction, which the King could not transfer or entrust to any private party — "nor commend them in such manner that any other might have direct dominion and lordship over them" (Friede 1971:158).

With the above ideas in mind Las Casas was ready to initiate a battle that would last over half a century. In its initial phase this involvement was essentially idealistic and moralistic. He sermonized to conquistadors, governors, *audiencias*, and royal councils of Spain, appealing to noble sentiments and supernatural sanctions. Soon Las Casas found out that this honest verbosity was completely ineffective. He was preaching to the walls.

PHASE 2: POLITICIAN   The failure of the moralistic approach originated a "second conversion" — to a struggle in the political arena. The change was not only in strategy but in theater. Pragmatically, he worked at the Spanish court. His theological discourses gave way to a realistic assessment of the means and possibilities of realizing his ideas. He did not reject, however, doctrinal discussions, which were often made, to attack the ideological justifications of the Indian oppression. If he said one day to Bishop Quevedo that Aristotle was burning in hell and that now the important thing was to save the Indians from extinction, this did not prevent him from conducting a thorough study of Aristotle in order to dismount the ideological machinery of Sepúlveda's *Demostenes II* and *Apologia*.

What disconcerted his opponents even more was that he was able to direct the battle to an arena where he was insuperable: the first-hand contact with the world of oppression. He used his American experience as an undefeatable weapon and as the framework for discussion. Abstract principles and arid philosophical speculations were neglected in order to operate from a basis of accurate accounts of events, from the living reality of oppression. In his battle he was pragmatic and utilitarian: his goal was less to construct laws than to make them effective. For this reason his rejection of the *Leyes de Indias* was based not on their content but on their unpracticability. He had a clear idea of what to propose, what to concede, what to reject uncompromisingly. Every issue regarding the creation of just social relations was considered and resolved in precise terms. The effectiveness of his approach had a glorious moment in the promulgation of the New Laws by Charles V in 1542. These regulations marked the culmination of the Lascasian and Indianist movement.

The New Laws enhanced substantially all the precepts of Las Casas. The most important regulations were those explicitly abolishing any type of Indian slavery and Indian personal service to the colonists. The *encomienda* system was practically abolished. Plans were made to convert the *encomienda* Indians into direct vassals of the King. The juridical principle of the colonists' dominion over the Indians was in this way substituted for an equal status before the Crown.

However, the victory of Las Casas' ideas was not secured simply by the promulgation of the laws. He knew, better than anyone else, that the social configuration of America was going to offer a strong resistance to the implementation of regulations that were aimed at overthrowing the privileges of an already consolidated oppressive class. He took measures of a strict political character before and after the promulgation of the laws. For instance, he suggested to the King a well-designed plan to bring twenty of the most powerful *encomenderos* "to inform your Majesty about the general situation." Once they had arrived in Spain, the King was to forbid their return to America, confiscate their colonial estates, and assign them revenues in Spain.

The fight over the implementation of the New Laws was intense. The force of a historical social process, in which the economic privileges of a new oppressive class were already settled and powerful, was stronger than the efforts of Las Casas and his followers. He lost his battle this time. The New Laws were revoked in 1545, and the new regulation on *encomiendas* re-established the juridical principle of Indian subjection to the colonizer.

Las Casas did not give up in his struggle, however. During those years, in the heat of the fight, his ideological position was sharpened. He become more radical in his demands. Friede (1971:80) summarizes these political ideas as follows:

Summing up the political ideas of the mature Las Casas with reference to America, we find: (1) denial of the right of the conquistador, and by extension all the Spanish colonists, to special economic and political privileges in the New World; (2) denial of their right to interfere in the life of the Indians; (3) the need to re-establish the pre-colonial Indian states, although under the sovereignty of the Crown; and (4) the grant of special rights over the Indian to the ecclesiastical authorities in America.

PHASE 3: DIRECT ACTIVIST   Las Casas, by his style of political-ideological practice, was ready to use all the available means that were in accord with his Christian beliefs to reach his cherished goal. After the failure of the New Laws, the current situation made him turn to a different weapon — one that for a sixteenth-century Spaniard was tremendously effective: the appeal to severe Catholic ecclesiastical sanctions. The Spaniards' treatment of the Indians would be judged by confessors and bishops according to precise standards set up by the church itself. Any unjust practice would be punished by strict penalties, those used traditionally to punish ecclesiastical misbehavior: excommunication, interdict, and denial of absolution.

With the new strategy Las Casas again changed the field of operations. He moved the center of his activity from the court to the colonies. He was a bishop, and had acquired enough theological and political prestige to make the strategy extraordinarily effective, up to the point of endangering the stability of the existing social order.

The reaction of the *encomenderos* soon became violent. They not only attacked the church and church officials in America, but financed the theologians, jurists, and intellectuals who opposed Las Casas' doctrines.

It was in the above context that the famous *Junta de Valladolid* (1550–1551) was called in order to hear the doctrinal debate between Las Casas and one of the most brilliant intellectuals of the time, Ginés de Sepúlveda. The theoretical framework of the debate was the Aristotelian doctrine of "natural slavery" applied by Sepúlveda to the Indians and rejected adamantly by Las Casas. The doctrinal clarity of Las Casas and the precision of his theoretical arguments based on his empirical perception of the American reality were decisive in the discussion. To the theoretical victory Las Casas added a political one. He still had the support of influential figures in the metropolis, and this was used to facilitate the publication of seven of his treatises in Seville in 1552 while the efforts of Sepúlveda to have one of his books published were completely unsuccessful.

The unrest caused by Las Casas' strategy grew rapidly in America, until it became a serious problem. Colonists attacked the church more and more openly. Even within the clergy itself a break formed between the supporters of the colonists and those following Las Casas. He was at the center of the battle, with his direct action and with his treatises, letters, and communications. These were designed as programs of action of sound practical and doctrinal foundation.

PHASE 4: THE DECLINE   The Crown initially overlooked the overriding intervention of the church in the political life of the colonies. After a while, however, the pressures of the colonists, the serious economic consequences of the above policy, and particularly the succession of Charles V by Phillip II marked the decline of the Lascasian movement. The change of climate, and, later on of policy, was reflected in the growing disinterest of the Council of the Indies in the Indian problems, and in the appearance of *Cédulas Reales*, which little by little revoked the existing pro-Indian regulations.

Certainly, Las Casas was given, by order of the King, the full consideration that "his quality" merited, but his influence was definitely dying. At the end of his life he was still firm and lucid in his ideological convictions, but more and more removed from the reality he was analyzing and attempting to change. By this time his position was completely radical. Until then he had made a distinction between the rights of the King, which he recognized, and those of other Spaniards, which he denied. At the end of his life even the King's privileges were subordinated to the welfare of the Indians. The *señorío* of the *caciques*, or "natural lords" of the Indians, was put before the *señorío* of the King of Castile who would have right to a symbolic tribute only on the basis of negotiations with the *caciques* once the Indians had been evangelized by PEACEFUL means. Even in regard to the missions he had a position that was sharp: he preferred a pagan Indian alive and free to a Christian Indian dead or slave.

Before closing this section, I want to comment on one aspect that is usually brought up when Las Casas' libertarian struggle is mentioned: the matter of black slavery in America. Las Casas made mistakes, perhaps not as many as his detractors claim, nor as few as his apologists would desire (see Comas 1971). The historical significance of his political ideas and activities was immense, given the prestige he had in the high decision-making circles of Spain. We cannot forget, however, that he was a man of his time and that to expect from him a "modern" approach to all social realities is a naïve attitude. The case of black slavery is precisely a case in point: he did not reject slavery as such, and he made a clear distinction between black and Indian slavery in the colonies. Moreover, he suggested in 1516 and 1518 the importation of certain African slaves, and in 1544 he obtained a license for these purposes (see Friede 1971:165). However, it is inaccurate to say that he was responsible for the institution of black slavery in America. He was simply using an approved and existing social practice of the Western world in order to alleviate the condition of the Indians. It is also fair to notice that his position on the matter was corrected in the last period of his life, when he defended the idea that "they [the black slaves] have the same right to freedom as the Indians" (see Comas 1971:505). In this he was obviously way ahead of his time.

2.   The shameful social relations against which Las Casas fought still persist and in our times are coming again to the focus of attention of many men of good will. The spectrum of abuse, manipulation, conquest, cultural invasion, ethnocide, and genocide of indigenous peoples is presently being displayed once more to the eyes of the Western man. Even the apparently innocuous practices of "planned acculturation," "integration," "assimilation," "evangelization," and "aid to the Indians" are shown to have the marks of refined or disguised oppression. It is unnecessary here to provide extensive references to the subject. The efforts of the International Work Group for Indigenous Affairs (IWGIA) and of similar groups such as the Amazon Indian Survival Action Group and the Minority Rights Group are well known. Bibliographic references and source material can be found in IWGIA documents and its bulletin (1972).

My purpose in this section is to examine briefly the covert ideology which attempts to justify these situations of injustice and relate it to (1) the work of Las Casas, (2) a genuine libertarian praxis, and (3) the social responsibility of anthropologists.

It is hard to decide how or when this covert ideology comes into existence. It can be as an afterthought developed by the man in power in order to hide the nakedness of his greed (Niebuhr 1948:8), that is, a *post factum* rationalization, or rather a living proof of the striking power of the "colonizer" who has the self-appointed mission of changing an abstract certainty (about "superior monkeys") into reality (Sartre 1968:15). In any case, racism in its various forms and the insatiable thirst for power and material resources, particularly land still in the hand of the oppressed, are its ultimate *raison d'être*

The ideology of oppression splits mankind into two species: the species of true men and the species of semihumans, underhumans or superior monkeys.

¿Cómo considera usted a los cuibas?
Para mí son animales, como los venados o los chigüiros. Claro está que los venaditos no nos dañan las cosechas ni nos matan los marranos. Además, para que lo sepa de una vez, desde hace mucho tiempo por estas regiones se hacen especies de excursiones para ir a cazar indios. Eso lo llamamos por aquí "Guahibiada." ... Los indios no son como nosotros. Son como los micos, que se nos parecen pero no son de los mismos. ..." (*El Espectador* 1968).

The above quotation refers to the massacre of sixteen Cuiva Indians that occurred in 1967. The perpetrators of this massacre confessed to their crime in trial, as well as to other raids in which about forty Indians were killed. They were acquitted because of their conviction that to kill a Cuiva was not a crime (see Arcand 1972:9–10). Their crude words reveal plainly the ideology hiding behind the oppression and cultural and physical extermination of the Indians. For this very reason it is understandable why Fanon (1968:36) says that decolonization is the veritable creation of new men.

In all cases of oppression it is the HUMAN CONDITION of the Indians that is questioned. It is amazing to find how this very point, presented almost in the same terms, was the leitmotif of Las Casas' ideology. Behind all his libertarian efforts one can find exactly this specific goal: to have the Indians recognized as human. As he said, his lifelong struggle was intended to implement his dream at all levels of sixteenth-century Spanish social structure:

To liberate my own Spanish nation from the error and very grave illusion in which they now live and have always lived of considering these peoples to lack the essential characteristics of men, judging them brute beasts incapable of virtue and religion, depreciating their good qualities and exaggerating the bad which is in them (in Hanke 1949:113).

Las Casas was, then, in his humanistic work operating from a basis that is the only basis for an effective job in promoting social justice. He was radical in his analysis and in his everyday practice. Indeed he seemed to have understood that any effort toward a restoration of just social relations between oppressors and oppressed has to be radical, that is, it must go to the roots of the situation. "Creation of new men" is a beautiful way of expressing this radical position.

The Brazilian educator Freire has developed a theory of liberation, a "pedagogy of the oppressed," which has exactly the above radical foundation (1970). He says that any true libertarian process is a return to humanity of those who have been raped and vilified by the oppressive situation, both the oppressors and the oppressed. Only the oppressed, with their revolutionary leaders, are in a position to carry out this task of rehumanization. This process is a praxis, a word transforming the world, a synthesis of two essential elements of any human practice: action and reflection (see Freire 1970; IDAC Documents 1973: Numbers 1 and 3).

It is in the above context that we have to examine the contemporary concerns of social scientists for their responsibilities toward society. They usually develop their practice on the side of reflection and look for ways of establishing a synthesis with a complementary social action. Let me discuss this point briefly.

The social scientific world is shaken nowadays by undercurrents of ethical and humanistic preoccupation. The myth of value-free research and apolitical science has been challenged more and more openly during the past two decades. Mills' programmatic concept of "sociological imagination" by which "reason is made democratically relevant to human affairs in a free society" has been followed by a host of debates, criticisms, and statements (1959). Anthropology, in particular, has been a field in which the issues of professional ethics and social responsibility and accountability to the different strata of society have been put in the spotlight.

The bitter words of Deloria (1969) about anthropologists being "forerunners of destruction" because they think they can find the key to human behavior, and his invitation to "come down from their thrones of authority and PURE research and begin helping Indian tribes instead of preying on them," reflect the new climate. This claim was echoed by the self-accusations of the *Declaration of Barbados* in 1972. It states that scientism, hypocrisy, and opportunism have characterized the irresponsibility of anthropologists in regard to their traditional "objects" of study — the Indian societies. Anthropology has been a device of colonial domination, a sophisticated instrument to disguise with "scientific" terms the practice of oppression and dehumanization.

It is proclaimed openly that it is a pernicious fallacy to "equate controversy, challenge, and change with the unscientific and political while equating consensus and support of the status quo with objectivity, scholarship, and science" (Berreman 1973:9). It is said that anthropology, by its very existence and by the nature of the data it produces, is a political activity (Weaver 1973:3). Students of social reality are warned of the danger of attempting a domestication of reality to their own truth while trying to understand that reality (IDAC 1973, Document 1:9).

Verbosity and voluntarism (IDAC 1973, Document 3) are the immediate traps for intellectuals obsessed with social change. This is the most favored way for intellectuals to domesticate reality to their own truth. It is not uncommon to hear in certain anthropological circles beautiful, truly radical programmatic statements coming from middle-class colleagues who by their very way of living are strong supporters of the economic system they proscribe. It is also frequent, and amusing, to see skeptical anti-intellectual and anti-elite intellectuals criticize intellectuals for not being involved, while their own hands are free of *el barro de las calles*. It is for this type of contradiction that the case of Las Casas, the intellectual-politician-activist, is illuminating. Let me close with some conclusive remarks in this regard.

3. In the case I have just presented we have a sort of revival of an old theme: the theme of oppression of the Indians that comes again to shake the social sensitivity of a portion of the dominant society. These oppressive social relations have existed since the first contact of "civilized man" with the Indians. Las Casas and his followers courageously fought this unjust situation in its early stages of development. We are now fighting the same oppressive system four centuries later. Las Casas was defeated, although not completely. However, from his strategies, successful or unsuccessful, as scholar and activist engaged in a struggle that is the same as ours, we can undoubtedly learn important lessons.

Las Casas was a realist, that is, his approach to the problem of the colonies conformed to a careful analysis of the "current situation" (to use a phrase of Lenin). In his approach, on the other hand, we can find a scheme made of the two essential elements that Freire says must be present in an effective libertarian process: action and reflection. In Las Casas we find these elements arranged in this way: action-reflection-action. Furthermore, Las Casas was right on target, from the beginning, in disclosing and attacking directly the true enemy: the dehumanizing ideology behind the oppressive practice of the colonies. This disclosure was the result of his reflection upon the "elementary perception" he had of the colonial situation. His realistic approach to the problem made him grow and evolve. We have identified in his praxis four phases that changed along the lines of progressive radicalization and transition, from a verbalist-moralistic approach to direct action.

To a contemporary observer Las Casas' early conception of the liberating process may look paternalistic, and for that reason doomed to failure. There is, however, a clear transformation of this approach, which had solid footing in his fundamental conviction regarding the full human potentialities of the Indians. He started with a moralistic preaching to the social class in power. He turned afterward to political maneuverings in the circles where high decisions were made. Then he entered the phase of direct involvement in the area of oppression, still intending to bring the oppressors to a reasonable position but without the Indians themselves participating in the liberating process. He did not have the opportunity to put into practice his late conviction that nothing could be expected from the Spaniards (including the King), and that the Indians had the right and the potential to take control of their own lives.

From the above remarks summarizing the first two sections we can draw some conclusions that are very relevant to our times.

a. First, we can point out that the mutually exclusive distinction usually made between the two elements of the libertarian praxis, theoretical-ideological practice versus political practice, reflection versus action, is untenable and harmful. A dynamic synthesis of these two elements is necessary, is possible, and is effective. Las Casas has proved that this is true. We may mistakenly confuse the heuristic distinction between these two aspects of human practice with another dichotomy that often paralyzes any well-intentioned effort: voluntarism versus activism. These are two pathologic deviations, characterized by a lack of action in the first case and a lack of reflection in the second. I have pointed out already that anthropologists, trained in the intellectual practice, have the tendency to remain in the ineffective realm of voluntaristic approaches.

b. The radical position acquired by Las Casas in the last period of his life seems to be the only one that was effective in the fight against oppression. On the one hand, the revolutionary history of the last decades has proved that only when one attacks the infrastructure of the oppressive situation, when one questions the whole socioeconomic system based on an ideology of exploitation of man by man, is success likely to come. Otherwise, we generate reformist solutions that only attack the effects of oppression leaving the causes unquestioned. Only at the end of his life, when he was old and physically unable to carry out his projects, did Las Casas come to this important conclusion. In any case, the historical context in which he operated made the implementation of such radical and revolutionary ideas utopian in his time.

c.   Marx once said that his analytical method did not start from man but from the economically given social period. This is the same message we discover in the scheme of Las Casas' praxis to which I have previously referred: action-reflection-action. Anthropologists, like other intellectuals, may be tempted to begin analysis of, and action against, oppressive situations from abstract speculations regarding the nature of man and his society. Their normative conclusions about what to do, and how, are marked in this way with failure, despite the titles and expertise their authors may claim. Only reflection upon the "current situation," upon the contradiction found at that precise historical conjuncture can provide a solid basis for political and ideological practice. Now, reflection on such contradiction has to be based on the "elementary perception" (IDAC 1973, Document 3) of oppression which is possible only when the person is immersed with the oppressed in their world. Otherwise, the possibility of "armchair revolutionaries" becomes, once more, a sad reality.

d.   Finally, we may ask: what about the "scientific responsibility" of anthropologists? Certainly, until now I have not stressed the distinction between theoretical and ideological practices. It is time now to indicate that there is an important distinction that is directly relevant to the practice of anthropology. Let me say that the product of theoretical practice is KNOWLEDGE, scientific knowledge. Ideological practice, on the other hand, has a product that is essentially of a PRACTICO-SOCIAL character. Ideology, says Althuser (1969:231) "is a system (with its own logic and rigor) of representations (images, myths, ideas or concepts, depending on the case) endowed with a historical existence and role within a given society." Science, the end product of theoretical practice, is also a system of representations with a function of knowledge, of understanding, submitted to an evolutive process "whose successive stages are characterized by an increasingly detailed and refined understanding of nature" (Kuhn 1970:170).

I leave open the question of whether Las Casas was or was not, strictly speaking, an ideologist or a scientist. The answer to the question is not so important. What is important is to notice that he used all his intellectual energies while fighting for just social relations between men.

In our case, if we recognize that both theoretical and ideological practices are necessary in any given society, that is, they are constitutive elements of the social practice of such a society, we can begin to define more specifically the role of a social scientist in that society. He has the job of developing a progressively more refined and detailed understanding of man in all his dimensions. How to use this knowledge, how to transform it into ideology for practico-social purposes and articulate it through ideology to the other levels of the current social practice is the key challenge for the ethical responsibility of anthropologists.

If ideologies of racism and oppression have in so many cases been PRESENTED as "scientific acquisitions" (and anthropologists have been involved in this practice!), it now seems appropriate to play the game in reverse, with the ideologies of humanization and liberation. The task would be not to PRESENT them as scientific acquisitions, but to MAKE them well grounded in scientific acquisitions. This is indeed the ultimate responsibility of social science: to provide a solid theoretical ground for just social relations.

REFERENCES

AFANASIEF, V.
1971   "The literary heritage of Bartolomé de Las Casas," in *Bartolomé de Las Casas in history: toward an understanding of the man and his work.* Edited by B. Keen and J. Friede. DeKalb, Illinois: Northern Illinois University Press.
ALTHUSER, L.
1969   *For Marx.* New York: Vintage Books.
ARCAND, B.
1972   *The urgent situation of the Cuiva Indians of Colombia.* International Work Group for Indigenous Affairs, Document 7. Copenhagen.
BERREMAN, G.
1973   "The social responsibility of the anthropologist," in *To see ourselves: anthropology and modern social issues.* Edited by T. Weaver. Glenview, Illinois: Scott, Foresman.
COMAS, J.
1953   "Razón de ser del movimiento indigenista," in *Ensayos sobre Indigenismo.* Edited by J. Comas. Mexico.
1971   "Historical reality and the detractors of Father Las Casas," in *Bartolomé de Las Casas in history: toward an understanding of the man and his work.* Edited by B. Keen and J. Friede. DeKalb, Illinois: Northern Illinois University Press.
DELORIA, V.
1969   *Custer died for your sins.* New York: Avon.
El Espectador
1968   Newspaper article. *El Espectador.* Bogotá. January 29.
FANON, F.
1968   *The wretched of the earth.* New York: Seabury Press.
FREIRE, P.
1970   *Pedagogy of the oppressed.* New York: Seabury Press.

FRIEDE, J.
1971 "Las Casas and indigenism in the sixteenth century," in *Bartolomé de Las Casas in history: toward an understanding of the man and his work.* Edited by B. Keen and J. Friede. DeKalb, Illinois: Northern Illinois University Press.

HANKE, L.
1935 *The first social experiments in America.* Cambridge: Harvard University Press.
1949 *Bartolomé de Las Casas: pensador político, historiador, antropólogo.* Havana: Sociedad Económica de Amigos del País.
1959 *Aristotle and the American Indians.* London: Hollis and Carter.

INSTITUT D'ACTION CULTURELLE
1973 Document Series. Geneva.

INTERNATIONAL WORK GROUP FOR INDIGENOUS AFFAIRS
1972 Document Series; Bulletin. Copenhagen.

KEEN, B., J. FRIEDE, *editors*
1971 *Bartolomé de Las Casas in history: toward an understanding of the man and his work.* DeKalb, Illinois: Northern Illinois University Press.

KUHN, T. S.
1970 *The structure of scientific revolutions.* Chicago: University of Chicago Press.

MILLS, C. W.
1959 *The sociological imagination.* New York: Oxford University Press.

NIEBUHR, R.
1948 *Moral and immoral society.* New York: Scribner.

PÉREZ DE TUDELA, J.
1957 "Estudio crítico preliminar," in *B. de Las Casas, obras escogidas.* Edited by J. Pérez de Tudela. Madrid: Biblioteca de Autores Españoles.

SANDERLIN, G., *editor*
1971 *Bartolomé de Las Casas: a selection of his writings.* New York: Alfred A. Knopf.

SARTRE, J. P.
1968 Preface to *The wretched of the earth.* By F. Fanon. New York: Seabury Press.

WEAVER, T., *editor*
1973 *To see ourselves: anthropology and modern social issues.* Glenview, Illinois: Scott, Foresman.

Alternatives to Ethnocide: Human Zoos, Living Museums, and Real People

JOHN H. BODLEY

The problem of ethnocide, or the forced modification of one culture by another, has again become a topic for anthropological concern. This concern is reflected in recent resolutions by anthropology organizations, the revival of the International Work Group for Indigenous Affairs and the attention ethnocide will receive at the IXth International Congress of Anthropological and Ethnological Sciences. While this new concern is distinctly more humanitarian than the frequently expressed concern for the loss of valuable data or "urgent anthropology," any search for alternatives to ethnocide will be hampered if it fails to consider the question from a viewpoint wider than that of industrial civilization. Significant alternatives might be disregarded if anthropologists do not recognize the bias in their own profession which, as some have recently acknowledged (Lévi-Strauss 1966: 126; Gjessing 1968: 399), is itself a product of industrial civilization and designed to serve its ends. In an effort to overcome some of this bias and as a stimulus for further discussion, this paper will briefly survey the general anthropological view of ethnocide, attempt to present it in larger perspective, and finally discuss "cultural autonomy" as a radical solution to specific ethnocide problems.

ETHNOCIDE, ACCULTURATION, AND MODERNIZATION

The current use of the term "ethnocide" represents a belated but explicit

This investigation was supported in part by funds provided by the Graduate School Research Funds from the National Science Foundation Institutional Grant through Washington State University.

recognition of the frequently destructive aspects of culture modification policies. Earlier terms such as ACCULTURATION (Redfield et al. 1936) and CULTURE CONTACT were widely used to cover all culture modification phenomena during the period when anthropologists were most frequently employed by colonial governments and were unanimously taking an ethically neutral position on their work. These terms served to legitimatize culture modification as a topic for scientific study and at the same time obscured both the unpleasant side effects of "change" and the actual causal factors involved, while the very neutrality of the terms reinforced a stand of scientific detachment. Enormous research effort has been devoted to acculturation but most anthropologists still scrupulously avoid any sort of value judgment on any aspect of culture change. During the postcolonial period anthropologists have largely replaced ACCULTURATION with such terms as MODERNIZATION and ECONOMIC DEVELOPMENT which, when applied to tribal peoples, refer to essentially the same phenomena, but again continue to obscure many of the realities of the change situation. Steward (1967: 16, 20–21) for example, called MODERNIZATION a value neutral term, and felt that the causal factors involved were still "not well conceptualized."

STATE ETHNOCIDE POLICIES AND ANTHROPOLOGY

Professing humanitarian motives and concern for progress, industrial states have always assumed that tribal areas must ultimately be fully assimilated or integrated with the national polity and economy at whatever cost to the peoples involved. This fundamental assumption seems to underlie all official state policies toward tribal cultures which are designed to extend administrative control over tribal areas, promote economic development, create national loyalties, and to modify or eliminate any cultural patterns considered as obstacles to these objectives. Expansive modern states have never questioned the ultimate rightness and inevitability of these policies, even though they must often be carried out in the face of obvious resistance. However, such policies are explicitly ethnocentric and must be considered ETHNOCIDE whenever they are opposed by tribal peoples. As participants in industrial civilization, anthropologists have directly supported such policies by attempting to reconcile the natives to the "inevitable" loss of their cultures and even by working to speed the process of their destruction. There has also been a clear tendency for anthropologists to disregard their own admonitions concerning ethnocentrism, cultural relativism, and the fundamental right of different life-styles to coexist, and to develop theoretical concepts and arguments that mask the realities of ethnocide.

ANTHROPOLOGICAL ETHNOCENTRISM AND CULTURAL RELATIVITY

Along with other members of industrial civilizations, many anthropologists have often taken the ethnocentric position that tribal cultures must be drastically modified because of their assumed inadequacies. At the same time anthropologists have long recognized the dangers of ethnocentrism, and urged that cultures be evaluated only in their own terms. This conflict places many anthropologists in a moral dilemma which is resolved by assuming an ethically "neutral" position, which has only recently come under attack (Berreman 1968; and Gjessing 1968; for example), or by rejecting cultural relativism as "romanticism." Goodenough (1963: 62) considers romanticism to be an overidentification with exotic peoples, or a "private compulsion" that is really ethnocentrism in reverse. Barnett (1956: 59–60) calls it a "quixotic fixation," and "emotional investment" which sometimes makes anthropologists object to "tampering with native life and evokes nostalgic laments over its passing." While Murdock (1965: 146) dismisses cultural relativism as simply unscientific "sentimental nonsense," many anthropologists consider it a positive hindrance to their profession. Foster (1962: 263) complains that "Anthropologists are indoctrinated to see the good in all cultures" and sometimes suffer "nostalgia over vanishing primitives." He advises that applied anthropologists not hesitate in making judgments "on the relative merits of the ways of life of other people" (1969: 136), and declares (1962: 263) that some cultures may be in such bad shape that "a major cultural overhaul for them would be the best possible thing in the world." Mead (1961: 367) has also warned anthropologists against "romanticism" and called cultural relativism an "overstatement." She declares "no forebodings about the effect of destroying old customs" (1961: 19–20).

Redfield explicitly proclaims his ethnocentrism as a justification for cultural modification. He finds modern civilization "more decent and humane" (1953: 163) than primitive cultures and feels that in view of our more humane standard a cultural relativist position will be difficult to maintain. After all, Redfield asks, what modern nation could permit its tribal peoples to carry on such inhuman practices as head hunting and cannibalism? According to Redfield, anthropologists were greatly relieved when the United Nations statement on human rights did not follow a strictly relativist position, thereby leaving nations free to suppress "disgusting" native customs. Unfortunately for tribal peoples, this "more humane standard" has been applied in a variety of ways even by other anthropologists to justify the abolition of various cultural traits. Elwin (1959: 250–251), for example, would interfere with customs that were "clearly and unnecessarily impoverishing the people," while ideally, British colonial policy would only allow customs to exist if "compatible with justice, humanity and good government" (Lindley 1926: 375). In many areas the "standard" has been stretched to its logical extreme, as for example in Australian New Guinea where:

The political autonomy, economic habits, religious practices, and sexual customs of organized native groups, in so far as they threaten European control or offend Western notions or morality, must be abandoned (Reed 1943: xvii).

Tribal cultures have been variously described by anthropologists as "backward" and "retarded" (Kroeber 1948), or simply "inferior" (Pitt-Rivers 1927: 17), while the not uncommon belief that tribal peoples are "sick" or mentally incompetent also finds support in the anthropological literature. Kroeber, for example, states:

When the sane and well in one culture believe what only the most ignorant, warped, and insane believe in another, there would seem to be some warrant for rating the first culture lower and the second higher (Kroeber 1948: 298).

Other anthropologists (Arensberg and Niehoff 1964: 4–6) refer to economic "underdevelopment" as a "sickness," speak of the "medicine of social change" and compare change agents to brain surgeons. Tribal economic systems are criticized more severely than virtually any other aspect of tribal culture. In spite of abundant evidence to the contrary, many anthropologists still feel that tribal economies are so unproductive and technologically inadequate that they are barely able to support life. Levin and Potapov (1964: 488–499) called the hunting and fishing economies of Siberia "a very poor support for life," and others have emphasized the assumed "precariousness" of tribal economies (Nash 1966: 22) or the "ever-present threat of starvation" (Dalton 1971: 27). One anthropologist even speaks of raising a tribal economy "up to the subsistence level" (Elwin 1959: 76).

THE INEVITABILITY ARGUMENT

Perhaps the strongest bias with which anthropologists view ethnocide is the familiar assumption that it is natural, inevitable, and probably even beneficial. This position seems to be almost unanimously accepted by anthropologists today and presents a serious obstacle to any real search for alternatives to ethnocide. Anthropological pronouncements on the "inevitable fate" of "primitive" cultures are virtually indistinguishable from similar statements made over the years by political leaders, development experts, and missionaries. We are told by anthropologists, for example, that the disappearance of traditional tribal life "simply seems to be an inevitable process" (Berndt 1963: 394), or that "changes cannot be prevented" (Elkin 1946). Some speak of tribal disruption as the "inevitable logic of events" (Manndorff 1967: 530), "facts of life" (Huff 1967: 480), or "destiny" (Hoernle 1934).

The forced modification of tribal cultures is still justified by anthropologists as a case of "survival of the fittest" in which maladapted cultures, those "out of harmony with the modern setting" (Keesing and Keesing 1941:259), or possessing a "life style which flies in the face of world trends" (Cunnison 1967:9), must either be changed or eliminated. This argument basically does not differ from the characteristic views of colonial writers who called tribal peoples "feeble survivals of an obsolete world" (Merivale 1861:510), who were "doomed to elimination" (Maunier 1949:716), and who must either "perish, or be amalgamated" (Merivale 1861:510). The same opinion is expressed by a recent writer on economic development: "Perhaps entire societies will lack survival value and vanish before the onslaught of industrialization" (Goulet 1971: 266). Pitt-Rivers represents a British functionalist who supported this view. He spoke (1927: 2) of the "rigid and ruthless process of selection" which operated in the culture contact situation and favored "higher" cultures over "lower." More recent anthropologists continue to support this view, as for example Ribeiro (1967: 115–116) who tells us that Brazilian Indian cultures "represent obsolescences in modern Brazil"; they are "anachronisms ... whose coexistence with an ever more homogeneous industrial civilization is not feasible." While the American applied anthropologists Arensberg and Niehoff (1964: 58) merely assure us that "people of different cultures are always in competition" and that superior technologies always conquer, modern evolutionary anthropologists following Leslie White's lead have elaborated "The Law of Cultural Dominance" to account for the "inevitable" disappearance of tribal cultures:

...that cultural system which more effectively exploits the energy resources of a given environment will tend to spread in that environment at the expense of less effective systems (Kaplan 1960: 75).

Most anthropologists still probably agree with Elwin (1959:59–60) that they do not want to stop the "clock of progress," and feel strongly that traditional cultures must make way for progressive evolutionary trends toward world cultural homogeneity which are considered to be "natural and necessary trends in human progress" (Ribeiro 1970).

There can be no disagreement with the fact that historically the expansion of industrial civilization has been at the expense of less powerful cultures, and it can be granted that tribal cultures are not at the same level of evolutionary complexity and energy consumption as industrial civilization, but we need not agree that therefore ALL cultures must inevitably follow these trends or even that it is beneficial that they do so. Progressive trends certainly occur in biological evolution without the loss of simpler forms, and likewise simpler cultures may not be "predestined" to extinction merely because they can be modified at will by an evolutionarily more "advanced" culture. The inevitability argument may well have become a self-fulfilling prophecy which has prevented serious consideration of alternatives to tribal extermination.

ETHNOCIDE AS RESOURCE EXPLOITATION

If examined in perspective, the disappearance of tribal cultures over much of the world in the past 150 years can be seen as the direct result of government policies designed to facilitate the exploitation of tribal resources for the benefit of industrial civilization. When viewed in this manner, rather than in terms of ethnocentric appeals to "inevitable progress" or evolutionary trends, the immediate causes of ethnocide become more apparent and possible alternatives become more realistic.

A wide comparative view of the official tribal policies of socialist, capitalist, and newly independent nations will show that more efficient exploitation of tribal resources has always been a prime concern of governments. In this regard, "tribal resources" must be interpreted to include not only tribal land, minerals, and other natural resources, but also tribal peoples themselves who have been considered valuable "human resources" for cheap labor, markets, military manpower, tax-paying citizens, religious converts and material for research projects and museums. Government concern for more efficient tribal exploitation can be seen first of all in official policies which have promoted "uncontrolled frontiers" where private citizens were permitted to harvest tribal resources without legal restrictions and at little government expense. When this process met tribal resistance governments resorted to military force and extended administrative control over formerly independent tribal regions so that resource exploitation could continue through legal means and at greater rates. "Administration," whether by "direct" or "indirect" rule, destroyed tribal sociopolitical autonomy and brought further measures that undermined their economic independence. Once under political control, tribal peoples were taxed and "educated" to create "new needs" and thereby encouraged to participate further in the national economy. More direct measures included official decrees requiring labor or the planting of cash crops, and the creation of "native reserves" designed to be inadequate to support the traditional economy. More recent measures are usually called "economic development" and involve many more forms of direct force and subtle persuasion to reach the same goals.

The critical significance of these policies is that they create conditions under which a tribal life-style can no longer be a viable alternative for those wishing to pursue it. On the contrary, in the absence of government policies to promote the exploitation of tribal resources, there is abundant evidence that tribal cultures can maintain contacts with other cultures on their own terms and still retain their own viability. There are many examples of cultures that have been in continuous communication with "higher" cultures, and merely borrowed selectively from them.

These facts must be emphasized because many anthropologists and development experts still argue from the ethnocentric position that mere CONTACT with a "superior" culture will cause tribal societies to reject their own cultures voluntarily. Then, assuming that it would not be possible to maintain any people in TOTAL isolation, ethnocide could therefore never be prevented.

According to this "demonstration effects" view, all people share our desire for material wealth and "prosperity" and have different cultures only because they have not yet been exposed to industrial civilization. The availability of the "better life" results in the "self-destruction" of traditional cultures, and "ethnocide" in the usual sense would therefore rarely occur at all. This position is clear in the writings of many development anthropologists (e.g. Foster 1969; Goodenough 1963; Arensberg and Niehoff 1964; Dalton 1971), and is represented in the following statements:

... men in every culture harbor unexpressed wishes to have more in order to be more. Once it becomes evident to them that it is possible to desire more, they will, by and large want more ... (Goulet 1971: 76).

The structure of traditional village society becomes undermined because its traditional functions become displaced once superior economic and technological alternatives become available (Dalton 1971: 29).

These arguments serve as rationalization for what is still essentially **a** process of "conquest" in which a single technologically powerful culture type forces other less powerful cultures to comply with its wishes.

ETHNOCIDE, ECOCIDE, AND RELATIVE DEPRIVATION

Ethnocide resulting directly in large-scale depopulation would not normally be defended as acceptable culture change policy today, but other long-range consequences of cultural modification which cannot always be foreseen but which may be fully as serious are still being disregarded. Attempts to prevent ethnocide continue to be opposed as the romanticizing of traditional culture and undue emphasis on the detrimental effects of cultural modification. We are told that "sentimental considerations must not be allowed to become an obstacle in the path of progress of indigenous peoples" (Métraux 1953:884), and cautioned against placing "undue stress" (Reed 1943:258) on the disintegrating effects of change. However, we are also warned that people should not suffer too much, or pay too high a price for progress, while it is frequently admitted that "progress" may not even make people "happy." It is felt that they must at least be made to think that whatever the cost progress will be desirable, as a recent government report from Papua New Guinea stated:

... there remains the task of awakening in the people such a desire for progress that they will be prepared to pay the price of major social change (Australia n.d.: 3).

Promoters of cultural modification evidently consider themselves competent to evaluate whether or not change will be worth the unknown "costs" that it is certain to involve, but it now seems particularly urgent to re-assess the "price" of cultural modification in view of recent concern for overpopulation, resource depletion, and environmental deterioration. At the same time economists warn that world development goals may well be unrealizable or may benefit only a small segment of any population (Ward et al. 1971). Anthropologists have long realized many of these problems, but have failed to take them seriously. Now it may not be considered too cynical or romantic to suggest that very often tribal peoples have been forced to accept unreachable goals, whose pursuit may in the long run bring more hardship than those goals originally promised to alleviate.

Tribal peoples have been quick to recognize the price of "progress," but have been powerless to do anything about it. In 1948 the Maya villagers of Chan Kom complained to Redfield (1962) over the shortening of their swidden cycles, which they realized was the direct result of population increase due to new health measures. They also complained that the new roads made them poor because of unfulfilled new "needs." Population pressure on Tikopia in the thirties prompted the Tikopians to suggest to Firth that infanticide be legalized (Keesing and Keesing 1941: 64–65). Some tribal writers have recently observed that environmental pollution may eventually invalidate treaties containing such phrases as "as long as the grass shall grow."

Ecological stability may well prove to be the most costly price tribal peoples will pay for cultural "progress." While no one would argue that all tribal cultures were in complete harmony with their environments, it must be acknowledged that tribal cultures are generally characterized by distinctive features which are notably absent from industrial civilization and which contribute to ecological stability. Among these features are: (1) a world view that makes MAN PART OF NATURE in contrast to the view that he must conquer nature (Meggers 1971: 1–2; White 1966); (2) a "LIMITED GOOD" concept (Foster 1969: 83) which kept wants from going unfulfilled and prevented relative deprivation; (3) WEALTH-LEVELING DEVICES, which in combination with a "limited good" concept lead to "no-growth" economies; and (4) local SELF-SUFFICIENCY, which as Rappaport (1971) and Meggers (1971:151–152) point out, prevents forces from being applied in local ecosystems which will be unresponsive to changes in those systems. As might be expected, all of these features are considered "obstacles to progress" by applied anthropologists and are slated for drastic modification. When these and other stabilizing factors are weakened, the way is opened for perpetual relative deprivation (i.e. "poverty") and rapid environmental deterioration. As wants and population increase, the resource base dwindles and people soon discover that the new goals that have been forced upon them remain just out of reach and are becoming progressively more difficult to reach. They are then told that they must abandon even more of their culture and that they have "no choice but to go forward with technology" as Redfield told the people of Chan Kom (1962). We should not be surprised that tribal peoples often feel angry and frustrated over the results of culture modification, and that as one observer from New Guinea has recently pointed out: "Inevitably they blame the purveyors of industrial civilization for their troubles" (Distroff 1971: 39–40).

THE INTEGRATION ALTERNATIVE

Over the past 150 years modern nations have consistently advocated the incorporation of tribal peoples into state political systems, and what may be called an "integration" policy is the only alternative to ethnocide which has ever been generally acceptable to anthropologists. This approach calls for the transformation of independent tribal populations into ethnic minorities within a nation, the goal being to institute "progressive" change, which ideally would be freely chosen by the population. In fact, the actual wishes of the people involved are completely immaterial. Integration policies usually anticipate the eventual loss of ethnic distinctions and in practice often merge imperceptibly into assimilation policies. Clearly this approach does not reject the necessity for cultural modification, and to the extent that coercion is involved it would condone partial ethnocide while leaving open the possibility of any ultimate retention of ethnic identity. In effect, "integration" as an official state cultural modification policy is not a real alternative to ethnocide at all, in spite of its wide acceptance and long history.

Since the early nineteenth century native peoples have generally been treated as "wards" of the state to be protected and gradually "improved" (i.e. integrated) by their guardians regardless of their possible wishes. For example, when British humanists became alarmed over the extermination of native populations in the wake of colonization, the 1836 House of Commons Select Committee on Aborigines was called upon to recommend ways to "promote the spread of civilization" and the "voluntary reception" of Christianity among tribal peoples with "justice and protection of their rights" (British Parliamentary Papers 1836: iii). The possibility that the natives might not desire "civilization" was apparently never seriously considered. Most individual nations took similar positions on their respective "native problems" and various international organizations have supported them. One of the earliest international statements of this type occurs in the *General Act* of the Berlin Africa Conference of 1884–1885 which calls on the fifteen signatory powers to support organizations designed for educating the natives "and bringing home to them the blessings of civilization." The Brussels Act of 1892, in article 2, called on the powers "to raise them [African tribal peoples] to civilization and bring about the extinction of barbarous customs." Similar views are expressed in the 1919 League of Nations Covenant (article 22) which gave "advanced nations" responsibility for "peoples not yet able to stand by themselves under the strenuous conditions of the modern world," thereby placing many tribal peoples officially under "tutelage" as "a sacred trust of civilization." Under the 1945 United Nations Charter, many of these same tribal peoples were identified as "peoples who have not yet attained a full measure of self-government" and their "advancement" was to be promoted by their guardians by "constructive measures of development" (Articles 73 and 76 United Nations Charter).

When discussing possible alternatives to ethnocide anthropologists usually set total ISOLATION and no change on one side and complete ASSIMILATION on the other as the unacceptable extremes, and then support INTEGRATION as a moderate middle position and the only rational alternative. Isolation is vigorously rejected as immoral and impossible, while assimilation is considered undesirable only if hurried too fast, and is expected to be the probable outcome of change in the long run. The middle course of integration has been in anthropological favor since at least the turn of the century when "indirect rule" began to be advocated as scientifically sound administrative policy. By 1929 Malinowski (1929) felt that indirect rule was supported by "all competent anthropologists" as the best means for "the control of Natives." Indirect rule has frequently developed into a policy of "selective emphasis" (Keesing and Keesing 1941:81–95) of tribal culture, or "growth from within" (Elwin 1959) which would at least temporarily preserve what is thought to be the best from the traditional culture and promises to combine "the best of both worlds," as in South Africa where:

The aim ... is to take from the Bantu past what is "good" and, together with what is "good" for the Bantu in European culture, build up a new distinctive culture (Schapera 1934: x).

As Elwin (1959: 44) puts it:

We believe that we can bring them the best things of our world without destroying the nobility and the goodness of theirs.

In the northeast frontier areas of India this approach has been applied in its most extreme form to purposefully create pleasing, tailor-made cultures. Very careful cultural modification policies were instituted under Elwin's guidance aimed at improving the "quality of human beings," bringing "MORE colour, MORE beauty," and "a wider view and a purer conception of God and man" (Elwin 1959: 136, 215–216). Of course, at the same time these tribal peoples were urged to become loyal Indian citizens and participants in industrial civilization. Where selective emphasis has been applied in other areas, it has been widely criticized as an attempt to keep the natives backward and subservient (Keesing and Keesing 1941:81–95; Mead 1961:369) and thereby facilitate their exploitation. At the present time most "realistic" anthropologists, concerned over possible racism charges, seem much less concerned with preserving and improving elements of tribal cultures, and instead appear to favor letting economic development follow its "natural and inevitable" course from integration to eventual full assimilation, because this is thought to be truly in the best interests of tribal peoples. The only difficulty with such a view is that it disregards the rights of the peoples really concerned to make the basic decisions.

Throughout the integration process "free choice" is generally called for. We are told for example that "choices must lie with the indigenous people themselves" and:

... it is the responsibility of the governing people, through schools and other means, to make available to the native an adequate understanding of non-native systems of life so that these can be ranged alongside his own in order that his choices may be made. (Keesing and Keesing 1941:84, citing the "pragmatic" view of a 1935 international seminar on education in colonial dependencies.)

Even the 1968 IUAES Resolution on Forced Acculturation calls for "just and scientifically enlightened programs of acculturation which allow the peoples concerned a free and informed basis for choice" (Sturtevant 1967:360). We are not told what to do in cases involving small, truly isolated tribal societies, such as those in Amazonia which are attempting to avoid contact with civilization and where the degree of contact necessary to provide them "a free and informed basis for choice" would unavoidably overwhelm them. In practice, of course, it becomes clear that there is really only one choice presently allowed to tribal people. Bulmer (1971: 18), for example, warns against doing anything that would prevent New Guinea tribal peoples from "exercising to the greatest extent possible their free choice in joining the modern world," and Métraux (1953) tells us that the members of any culture have the right to reject it outright "if they think fit." Tribal peoples are only given freedom to choose "progress":

For practical purposes, societies have little choice but to come to terms with development: they simply are not free to reject it outright (Goulet 1971: 93).

I take it for granted that in a complex society and a complex world it is utopian and unrealistic to assume that people can live without intervention (Foster 1969: 174–175).

Like a clever advertising agency for industrial civilization, much of applied anthropology has been devoted to supporting cultural modification policies with the techniques necessary to make sure that tribal peoples make the only correct choice. Change agents are advised to destroy self-esteem and create dissatisfactions among people so that they will come to desire change (Goodenough 1963: 219) which of course "must be accepted voluntarily" (Arensberg and Niehoff 1964: 3). This scientific "get the natives to do it to themselves" approach was anticipated by earlier colonial authorities:

By teaching and education you may subtly incline the natives to give up their ancient traditions without their feeling that they have done so under pressure (Maunier 1949: 506).

Anthropologists apparently continue to assume that those in other cultures realize their "obsolescence" and "inferiority" and eagerly desire progress toward the "better life" as defined by industrial civilization. Anthropologists seem unable to recognize the ethnocentrism and hypocrisy of the "choice" argument that permits only one choice. It is forgotten that peoples who have already chosen their major cultural patterns, and who have spent generations tailoring them to local conditions, may not even wish to consider adopting another life-style.

THE CULTURAL AUTONOMY ALTERNATIVE

While discussing a specific ethnocide problem in Amazonia this author (Bodley 1972) recently called for government support of tribal efforts to retain a traditional life-style. It was proposed that development programs and other outside intrusion into traditional areas be halted, and that official recognition be given to tribal rights to land and continued cultural autonomy. This radical proposal, which could be called the CULTURAL AUTONOMY alternative, might perhaps be extended to specific ethnocide problems in many parts of the world. The cultural autonomy solution would specifically recognize a tribal culture's right to remain permanently outside of any state political structure and to reject further "development" along the lines that would otherwise be forced upon it by outside powers. Three specific points are involved:
(1)   the recognition and support, by national governments and international organizations, of tribal rights to traditional land, cultural autonomy, and full local sovereignty;
(2)   the responsibility for initiating outside contacts must rest with the tribal people themselves: outside influences may not have free access to tribal areas;
(3)   industrial states must not compete with tribal societies for their resources.
   In actual application this proposal will undoubtedly involve many serious difficulties which cannot be discussed in detail here, but will need to be treated individually with reference to specific cases. However, broad

outlines for its operation can be suggested. Cultural autonomy would perhaps best be implemented through the United Nations, which would be authorized to designate Tribal Autonomous Regions to be permanently withdrawn from the sovereignty of the nations which now happen to claim control over them. Border defense would be handled by international peace-keeping forces and health assistance could be supplied to tribal peoples requesting it by the World Health Organization. While many criticisms will be raised against a cultural autonomy approach, it seems to offer the only clear alternative to ethnocide and if put into effect would permit many tribal peoples to carry on their traditional life-styles.

The cultural autonomy alternative has been consistently misunderstood and rejected by anthropologists who have obscured it under the misleading category of "isolation policies" where it could be ridiculed with false emotional arguments about "human zoos," and "living museums." As a so-called "human zoo policy," cultural autonomy has been criticized as "sheer cruelty" (Williams-Hunt 1952: 79) because it would "deny them the chance to progress"; and has been labeled "inhuman and inefficient" and "morally wrong" because it would perpetuate famine, disease, and ignorance (Goulet 1971: 208, 249); and a "retrograde step" that would stifle "the right of people to mould their lives according to their light" (Ghurye 1963: 193, 172–173). It has also been called simply "impossible" (Elwin 1959: 59) and those who would propose it are accused of not believing the tribals capable of "advance" or wishing to keep them in their place, or else their sanity is questioned and they are accused of other inhuman motives:

No reasonable person could suppose that it would be possible to turn vast areas of the world into preserves for the protection of native cultures (Métraux 1953: 883–884).

No sane, humane and well-informed scientist or scholar could possibly argue that in the interests of the ethnological or cultural record any part of New Guinea should be preserved as a cultural museum or human zoo ... (Bulmer 1971: 18).

In the first place it must be emphasized that cultural autonomy would permit tribal peoples to choose the degree of isolation they wished to maintain, it would not lock them in cages. It could hardly be considered a human zoo approach unless people were deliberately confined against their will for display and scientific observation. Such criticisms might be expected from those who have difficulty viewing different cultures as something other than objects for study and who are too ethnocentric to recognize that other peoples might actually wish to maintain their own life-styles.

Some will feel that the principle of cultural autonomy may have merit, but that it is too late to apply "because of potent changes in native life and desires" (Keesing and Keesing 1941:81–82). This argument about the supposed futility of attempting to "turn back the hands of the clock" (Smith 1934) has been used for years, even when there were still very large populations of essentially "untouched" tribal peoples. In 1956 Barnett (1956:62) stated that anthropologists "appreciate the futility of advocating a restoration of an extinct way of life." That may be, but the critical question is: at what point are changes caused by outside intrusion irreversible? It must not be forgotten that there are numerous examples of people "reverting" to traditional patterns even after major changes have occurred. This was the case for example in many areas of the Pacific when people were forced to rely on their subsistence economies during the economic depression of the thirties (Thompson 1940:92); in the Philippines when political upheaval left tribal peoples on their own (Keesing and Keesing 1934:74); in the Peruvian Amazon when in 1742 the Campa revolted after intensive Franciscan domination and were left to enjoy more than a hundred years of full autonomy (Bodley 1970:3–7); or in the recent case of Canadian Cree "returning to nature" (Anonymous 1972). Judging from these and other similar cases, it might be well to let tribal peoples decide for themselves when their way of life is "extinct."

Those who recognize the validity of a cultural autonomy approach, but who argue that it would be impossible or impractical to carry out, may be reminded that it has already been applied in a *de facto* fashion in several parts of the world in recent times. Any areas that have effectively remained outside of government control either because they were too remote or because they contained no valuable resources are, *de facto*, Tribal Autonomous Regions. Cultural autonomy has also at least temporarily been official policy in some areas, as for example the "inner line policy" of the British in the northeast frontier areas of India (Elwin 1961: 43–44); the "uncontrolled areas" policy in Australian New Guinea (Reed 1943: 168–169); and the 1822 Native Code of Czarist Russia, which provided a category for Siberian tribal peoples "not completely dependent on the government" (Levin and Potapov 1964: 804). When autonomy has been official policy, it has only existed for a limited time and for the convenience of the state. These examples demonstrate, however, that tribal autonomy is neither impossible nor impractical when it is thought desirable.

Another line of argument which has been raised against the cultural autonomy approach would deny the uniqueness of tribal peoples. According to this view, tribal peoples are no different from any other citizens and should deserve no special treatment. This may be expressed as: "None of the present day needs of Aboriginals are exceptionally 'special'" (Barnes 1968: 46), or as in the following reference to a small group of hunter-gatherers in Borneo:

However, at no time have the most "primitive" Punan nomads been treated as a special class of person. They are just inland citizens, with allowances made for the facts of remoteness (Harrison 1967: 345).

This kind of argument is a complete denial of the true uniqueness of tribal peoples, and of their right to be different. Some will no doubt argue further that a major weakness of the cultural autonomy policy is that tribes have never existed in isolated pristine purity. Ghurye (1963: 169) takes this view and others agree. Kunstadter (1967: 42) argues that the traditional model of tribal society which emphasized uniqueness, isolation, stability, and homogeneity "is no longer acceptable." He feels that minorities are not defined by cultural differences, but rather by "THE PATTERNS OF RELATIONSHIP WITH DOMINANT MAJORITIES." This position sounds very much like the old French colonial method of abolishing tribes by denying their existence:

French courts laid down that the tribes were in no sense collective bodies as understood by French law; consequently they possessed no personality; from a legal point of view, they did not exist (Maunier 1949: 572).

The important point that must not be forgotten is that tribal societies are composed of REAL people who are pursuing a unique life-style which they have given every indication they wish to continue to pursue. They should have that alternative.

Perhaps the most important reason for a cultural autonomy approach, however, is not simply that many tribal peoples have shown repeatedly by their actions that that is what they desire; it may well be that real global cultural diversity will be as critical for the long-run survival of mankind as some suggest (Meggers 1971: 166; Watt 1972; Dubos 1965; Rappaport 1971). This argument must be taken with special seriousness now that cultures which specifically reject many of the values resulting in our present worldwide environmental problems are themselves about to disappear. We should not forget Tax's recent warning:

I am certain that there is something for us ... industrialists to learn from the values associated with the tribal life and with the determination of these peoples to preserve this way of life at all costs (Tax 1968: 345–346).

If industrial civilization cannot exploit tribal cultures without destroying them and degrading their environments, then perhaps it should leave alone those that remain. Anthropologists, at least, might do well to acknowledge their complicity in the destruction of tribal cultures, and to re-examine the question of alternatives. We might remember that even Alan Holmberg came to regret his "adventures in culture change" with the Siriono:

Today I am frequently disturbed by the fact that I had a hand in initiating some of the changes which probably ultimately overwhelmed them and over which neither I nor they had control. Indeed, when I contemplate what I did, I am not infrequently filled with strong feelings of guilt. MAYBE THEY SHOULD HAVE BEEN LEFT AS THEY WERE (Holmberg 1954: 113. Emphasis added).

REFERENCES

ANONYMOUS
1972   Back-to-wild movement attracting more native people in Alberta. *Akwesasne Notes* 4(3):36.
ARENSBERG, CONRAD M., ARTHUR H. NIEHOFF
1964   *Introducing social change: a manual for Americans overseas.* Chicago: Aldine.
AUSTRALIA
n.d.   *Report for 1967–1968.* Department of Territories, Territory of Papua.
BARNES, JOHN A.
1968   Australian Aboriginals? or Aboriginal Australians? *New Guinea* 3(1): 43–47.
BARNETT, HOMER G.
1956   *Anthropology in administration.* New York: Row, Peterson and Company.
BERNDT, RONALD M.
1963   "Groups with minimal European associations," in *Australian aboriginal studies.* Edited by Helen Sheils, 385–408. New York: Oxford University Press.
BERREMAN, GERALD D.
1968   Is anthropology alive? *Current Anthropology* 9:391–396.
BODLEY, JOHN H.
1970   *Campa socio-economic adaptation.* Ann Arbor: University Microfilms.
1972   *Tribal survival in the Amazon: the Campa case.* International Work Group for Indigenous Affairs. Document 5.
BRITISH PARLIAMENTARY PAPERS
1836   *Report from the select committee on aborigines* (British settlements). Imperial Blue Book, volume eight, p. 538.
BULMER, RALPH
1971   Conserving the culture: an institute of New Guinea studies. *New Guinea* 6(2):17–26.

CUNNISON, IAN
1967   *Nomads and the nineteen-sixties*. Hull: Hull University.

DALTON, GEORGE
1971   *Economic development and social change: the modernization of village communities*. Garden City: Natural History Press.

DISTROFF
1971   The confusion of cultures: if prosperity is the objective then something has to give. *New Guinea* 6(4):39–42.

DUBOS, RENE
1965   *Man adapting*. New Haven: Yale University Press.

ELKIN, A. P.
1946   Conservation of aboriginal peoples whose modes of life are of scientific interest. *Man* 46(81):94–96.

ELWIN, VERRIER
1959   *A philosophy for NEFA* (second edition). Shillong: J. N. Chowdhury.
1961   *Nagaland*. Shillong: P. Dutta.

FOSTER, GEORGE M.
1962   *Traditional cultures, and the impact of technological change*. New York: Harper and Row.
1969   *Applied anthropology*. Boston: Little, Brown and Company.

GHURYE, G. A.
1963   *The scheduled tribes* (third edition). Bombay: G. R. Bhatkal.

GJESSING, GUTORM
1968   The social responsibility of the social scientist. *Current Anthropology* 9(5):397–402.

GOODENOUGH, WARD H.
1963   *Cooperation in change*. New York: John Wiley and Sons.

GOULET, DENIS
1971   *The cruel choice: a new concept in the theory of development*. New York: Atheneum.

HARRISON, TOM
1967   "Tribes, minorities, and the central government in Sarawak," in *Southeast Asian tribes, minorities, and nations*. Edited by Peter Kunstadter, 317–352. Princeton: Princeton University Press.

HOERNLE, R. R. ALFRED
1934   "Race-mixture and native policy in South Africa," in *Western civilization and the natives of South Africa*. Edited by I. Schapera, 263–281. London: George Routledge and Sons.

HOLMBERG, ALAN
1954   "Adventures in culture change," in *Method and perspective in anthropology*. Edited by R. F. Spencer, 103–113. Minneapolis: University of Minnesota Press.

HUFF, LEE W.
1967   "The Thai mobile development unit program," in *Southeast Asian tribes, minorities, and nations*. Edited by Peter Kunstadter, 425–486. Princeton: Princeton University Press.

KAPLAN, DAVID
1960   "The law of cultural dominance," in *Evolution and culture*. Edited by

Marshall E. Sahlins and Elman R. Service, 69–92. Ann Arbor: University of Michigan Press.

KEESING, FELIX M., MARIE KEESING
1934 *Taming Philippine headhunters: a study of government and of cultural change in northern Luzon.* London: George Allen and Unwin.
1941 *The South Seas in the modern world.* Institute of Pacific Relations International Research Series. New York: John Day.

KROEBER, A. L.
1948 *Anthropology.* New York: Harcourt, Brace and World.

KUNSTADTER, PETER
1967 *Southeast Asian tribes, minorities, and nations.* Princeton: Princeton University Press.

LEVIN, M. G., L. P. POTAPOV
1964 *The peoples of Siberia.* Chicago: University of Chicago Press.

LÉVI-STRAUSS, CLAUDE
1966 Anthropology: its achievements and future. *Current Anthropology* 7:124–127.

LINDLEY, M. F.
1926 *The acquisition and government of backward territory in international law.* London: Longmans, Green and Company.

MALINOWSKI, BRONISLAW
1929 Practical anthropology. *Africa* 2(1):22–38.

MANNDORFF, HANS
1967 "The hill tribe program of the Public Welfare Department, Ministry of Interior, Thailand: research and socio-economic development," in *Southeast Asian tribes, minorities, and nations.* Edited by Peter Kunstadter, 525–552. Princeton: Princeton University Press.

MAUNIER, RENE
1949 *The sociology of colonies,* volume two. London: Routledge and Kegan Paul.

MEAD, MARGARET
1961 *New lives for old.* New York: New American Library.

MEGGERS, BETTY J.
1971 *Amazonia: man and culture in a counterfeit paradise.* Chicago: Aldine.

MERIVALE, HERMAN
1861 *Lectures on colonization and colonies.* London: Green, Longman and Roberts.

MÉTRAUX, ALFRED
1953 "Applied anthropology in government: United Nations," in *Anthropology today.* Edited by Alfred Kroeber, 880–894. Chicago: University of Chicago Press.

MURDOCK, GEORGE P.
1965 *Culture and society.* Pittsburgh: University of Pittsburgh Press.

NASH, MANNING
1966 *Primitive and peasant economic systems.* San Francisco: Chandler.

PITT-RIVERS, GEORGE H.
1927 *The clash of culture and the contact of races.* London: George Routledge and Sons.

RAPPAPORT, ROY A.
1971   The flow of energy in an agricultural society. *Scientific American* 224(3):117–132.

REDFIELD, ROBERT
1953   *The primitive world and its transformations.* Ithaca: Cornell University Press.
1962   *A village that chose progress.* Chicago: University of Chicago Press.

REDFIELD, ROBERT, RALPH LINTON, M. J. HERSKOVITS
1936   Memorandum on the study of acculturation. *American Anthropologist* 38:149–152.

REED, STEPHEN W.
1943   *The making of modern New Guinea.* Philadelphia: The American Philosophical Society.

RIBEIRO, DARCY
1967   "Indigenous cultures and languages of Brazil," in *Indians of Brazil in the twentieth century.* Edited by Janice H. Hopper, 77–165. ICR Studies 2. Washington, D.C.: Institute for Cross-Cultural Research.
1970   Précis of *The civilization process. Current Anthropology* 11(4–5):419–421.

SCHAPERA, I.
1934   *Western civilization and the natives of South Africa.* London: George Routledge and Sons.

SMITH, EDWIN W.
1934   Anthropology and the practical man. *Journal of the Royal Anthropological Institute* 64:xxxiv–xxxvi.

STEWARD, JULIAN
1967   *Contemporary change in traditional societies.* Urbana: University of Illinois Press.

STURTEVANT, WILLIAM C.
1967   Urgent anthropology: Smithsonian-Wenner-Gren Conference. *Current Anthropology* 8(4):355–361.

TAX, SOL
1968   "Discussion," in *Man the hunter.* Edited by Richard B. Lee and Irven De Vore, 345–346. Chicago: Aldine.

THOMPSON, L.
1940   *Fijian frontier.* New York: Institute of Pacific Relations.

WARD, BARBARA, J. D. RUNNALS, LENORE D'ANJOU, *editors*
1971   *The widening gap: development in the 1970's.* New York: Columbia University Press.

WATT, KENNETH E. F.
1972   Man's efficient rush toward deadly dullness. *Natural History* 81(2):74–82.

WHITE, LYNN
1966   "The historical roots of our ecological crisis." Paper presented at the 133rd meeting of the American Association for the Advancement of Science.

WILLIAMS-HUNT, P. D. R.
1952   *An introduction to the Malayan aborigines.* Kuala Lumpur: Government Press.

The Right of the Third World to Develop in Its Own Way and Remarks on the Idea of "Change"

TEODORO BINDER

The term "development aid" has become fashionable. Individuals and groups of all kinds are seduced by its fascination. Just as previously one went to work in a mission, now people go into development aid. Why is this so? Looking for the answer to this question I have asked innumerable development aid people for their motives and aims. On the surface, one often finds a romantic disposition to help others. But underneath, one mostly discovers that what is considered the essential help to be given is offering or even forcing upon the recipients of the aid, using all means of persuasion, the accepted cultural values of the giver, in all their materialistic, spiritual, or ideological features.

The key word is PROGRESS, which has brought penicillin, the tractor, the airplane, the refrigerator, as well as the gun, atomic weapons and poisonous gas, bacteriological warfare, an increasing number of traffic deaths, threatening pollution and wasting of the environment, nationalism and many other "isms" which pit one section of mankind against another more dangerously than ever before. These characteristics of the aiding culture are usually not mentioned.

Neither the Third World as a whole nor any of its individual nations has had any part in the fast development, the positive and negative results of which I have just enumerated. It has been thought that the goals of the aid are achieved more successfully when the results of the operation show that the recipient people have accepted, either in fact or ostensibly, the values of the donor's civilization, in the process abandoning to a greater or lesser degree the values of their own native culture. The fact remains that our Christian-Western culture (including its legitimate daughter, the Marxist-Communist) understands that the development of other peoples involves the complete surrender of their culture to ours and the ultimate abandonment of their values. In this day and time, when we hear so much about de-mythologizing and sociological ideologizing, nothing has changed regarding the disgraceful treatment of the peoples and ethnic minorities in the Third World. It is true that in some Christian churches there has been argument about this concept now and then, and its fairness has been questioned. The aftermath of the activities of the so-called heathen mission prove that this concept has had fatal results for the cultures involved. Nevertheless, the peoples of Africa, South America, and Asia stand today in the cross-fire of the attacks of the fundamentalists, the political ideologists, and, recently again, certain Catholic groups.

In comparison to this fundamental destruction by members of ideological groups supported by foreign cultures, a few people teaching reading and writing or the operation of some modern machinery is of secondary importance.

However, on the inspiration of the most outstanding of their stock, these nations have not contributed less than the West to the intellectual and spiritual wealth of mankind. The philosophies of the Orient, the dances of Bali, the artistic instinct which is so natural to the so-called primitives, come to mind. And so does the world of the Navaho Indians, who experience a reality of beauty and harmony that permeates their worship and their medical art, and is also decisive in shaping the daily labor of this nation of sheep-raisers. There are the Hopi Indians, an old peasant folk who call themselves "the peaceables." Who, besides a few initiated people, mostly anthropologists, knows their wisdom? They have survived up to now almost unspoiled in the middle of a civilization that for centuries has tried all means of aggression to "integrate" them, that is to say, to destroy them.

Few people accept as a matter of course those who differ from themselves, be it through their way of thinking or feeling, their creed, or the color of their skin. It seems to me that this inability, with its consequent feelings of superiority, insecurity, envy, or aggression, creates the dangerous tensions existing in today's world more than social differences. There are certainly shocking social inequalities that must and will be balanced (though not through bloody revolutions). I know from experience that the fundamental motives of those who preach violent changes or development aid out of ideological fanaticism are hatred for those who are different and a grudge against the still unbroken spirit with which some peoples of the Third World face life. (There are such people contrary to what some people might think.) If the motives are not hatred and resentment, at least utter contempt and rejection of a different way of life are the moving factors. Any activity among other cultures is meaningful and fair only when its dominant feature is the acknowledgment of their values and the strictest respect for the differing way of life.

We can no longer afford to limit mankind's concern to our own species. It is obvious that we will always worry first about our own kind, but the struggle for human dignity and equality of changes for all must continue. Individuals and groups must be delivered from oppression, injustice, and discrimination. The sharp division of mankind into power groups confronting each other ruthlessly — especially the United States and her allies on the one hand, and the Soviet Union and her satellites on the other — appears almost irrelevant when we realize the danger threatening not only man but all living things on our planet. And I am not thinking of the possibility of a worldwide atomic war, for even the most fanatical nationalists and ideologists of today concede that such a war would destroy them as well. I am thinking rather of the increasingly reckless exploitation of the natural reserves, including even the oxygen in the air.

If we analyze the ideological backgrounds of the two power groups of our time, we find — just as Ludwig Klages did in comparing idealism and materialism — that in practice, these groups, which for brevity's sake we will call capitalism and communism, do not in the least differ from each other in their attitude toward the biosphere. We need cite only one example: the supersonic airliner. Both groups reflect the basic attitude that man enjoys an exceptional position in the universe, and has an absolutely superior value in comparison to all other living things, as is formulated frightfully in the Biblical text: "Fill up the Earth and make yourself the master of it."

Capitalism can only be understood as the logical consequence of the Protestant puritanical way of thinking. It derives its peace of mind about the reckless exploitation of the earth's resources from the Biblical command, on the illusion that the resources are inexhaustible. On the other hand, there is no indication that the founding fathers of communism, such as Hegel, Marx, Engels, and Lenin, ever had any idea, as philosophers and revolutionaries, of modifying the Jewish-Christian approach to non-human nature. The mastering of the earth by man with the help of a "planned" science (namely Marxism) is the ultimate goal of a much sought-for change. In the capitalist-liberal world, on the contrary, this goal is pursued without a special program, but with the same suicidal consequences.

This might sound as if we were neglecting our original scientific subject. So let us go back to it and try to look at it against the background of what we have just said. Let us consider the catchword "change," which is in such vogue today and heard most loudly, though not exclusively, from the New Left. Let us not worry about deepening our psychological or sociological considerations any further than we have already. Let us analyze what the aims of this change in the Third World are and what it really means for the ethnic minorities.

Simply and plainly, or rather bluntly, this change attempts to incorporate into the capitalist or communist orbits of power as many African, Asian, Polynesian, or Latin American countries as possible. Both power groups emphasize either individual or collective issues, thus appearing different. But the difference is only on the surface, for the practice is all the same. It calls for forced and urgent industrialization, thus expanding and intensifying the plundering of our planet, the poisoning of its atmosphere, and the ruining of the environment. Whoever knew Mexico City twenty-five years ago and goes back today to suffer the noise and smog now prevailing can easily understand by these shocking conditions what the meaning of development really is. What is the difference, if this development is promoted and financed by the United States, as it is in Brazil, or by the Soviet Union, as it was in Chile, or elsewhere, always on a nationalistic basis and with the same disastrous consequences?

And as far as ethnic minorities go, what is the difference for them, if this development is carried on by the underlings of big business, or from a socialist state headquarters? What is really important for them is that their living space gets restricted and their right to their own way of life and to development in accordance with their individuality is restrained. The first stage of the process is the wretched proletarization, and the next, provided that physical survival is possible, is the active participation in the suicide of the species. Our colleague Andreas Lommel, an authority on Australian native cultures, has called this process "the progress into nonentity."

Once a country is infected by the germ of the faith in unchecked and glamorous progress and in the endlessness of natural resources and industrial possibilities, it reaches, as has been the case in some Third World countries, such a speed in its "industrial revolution," that it becomes a deadly dangerous place for ethnic minorities to live in. These minorities have to face the same perilous attitudes that are faced by minorities living within the boundaries of the capitalist or communist powers. This overpowering faith in progress, as it is fostered and carried out in the name of "change," apparently entitles the powerful in developing countries to oppress their minorities.

I would readily admit that many people, especially ethnologists, acting in good faith, try to help the situation without realizing that the final result of it is to include the minorities in the suction range of the machinery of progress. I have known others who do not hesitate to eliminate ruthlessly groups that resist the voracious advance of progress or just stand passively in its way. I have myself reported previously the fact that certain missionary groups act as pioneers and comrades-in-arms of the above-mentioned progress, thus helping in the process of destruction.

This is not the place to mention even the most important economic aspects and consequences of my thesis. But I would like to mention briefly some of the consequences for our scientific field of applied anthropology.

1. Because Western civilization, with its aim of controlling and exploiting nature as much as possible, has proved to lead to the extermination of innumerable nonhuman and co-living species, and this attitude, within a predictable period, will bring about the impossibility of life for our species as much as for others, it is criminal to try to include in the process of destruction those human groups that as yet still stand outside of it, be it by force or by persuasion or by outwitting them, regardless of whether this is done out of the best convictions.

2. The origin and the spiritual weapons of an attitude that elevates man, either in a religious or in a secularized context, to the absolute central position of life on earth (and even in the universe) are to be found in the Jewish-Christian religion. However, there are still many ethnic groups, within and outside the current spheres of power of the two main representatives of this attitude — the Christian United States and the communist Soviet Union — who still know and accept that man is only a part of living things and not their master. Therefore, all attempts to sow uncertainty among these groups by offering them philosophies — mainly Christian, Islamic, or Marxist — that alienate them from nature and destroy their sense of certainty in their instinct, thus diminishing their chance for survival, should be blocked.

3. There is no doubt that sympathetic, gentle, and patient help can and should be brought in from the outside in most cases. However, this help should be offered keeping in mind what we have just stated. We do not intend in saying this that rationality should be given up, but we mean, on the contrary, that rationality should stop human greed for power and expansion from getting the upper hand. So rationality would lead to the service of all living things in order to allow them to have life in all its fullness.

4. In our encounter with other cultures the term "partnership," in its full meaning, should not be restricted to contact between men, but be understood as the sharing of all the forms of life embraced by the cultures involved. Partnership means reciprocity and full mutual acknowledgment.

I know from my own experience that even now members of some ethnic minorities still offer their whole acceptance to us. This is so even when they have had the most bitter experiences in their contacts with representatives of our civilization.

5.   An ethnologist who is not a narrow-minded specialist and who cares for more than collecting material for museums or scientific journals, will care constantly about new aspects of man's nature and possibilities, as well as his responsibilities. If he is especially critical of the situation in the world today, he will have more enriching and enlightening human experiences. And he who has had the chance, as I have, to witness religious ceremonies of relatively simple groups (such as Amazon Indians or Congo blacks) or of old peasant nations (such as the Hopi) will lose his sneer. And this will happen even to those who do not care for religion at all. They will be inclined to protect such religiosity instead of suppressing it, for it rests upon the responsibility of the living toward all other living beings. Among these peoples enlightenment will develop too, but their basic attitude will remain and will express itself in a technology quite different from ours at the present time. And it is to that basic attitude that we have to return, even with pain, if we want to survive. Their technology will ignore the unhealthy gain of supply and demand and will afford a considerably simpler life and simpler aims, much simpler than the ones we are used to now. It will reveal and create new values that will allow us to give life its meaning again.

In this mutual effort — in which our civilization will have to reorient itself in relation to other cultural groups, including the ethnic minorities — ethnology has its decisive place and perhaps its most noble function.

SECTION TWO

The Colonial Past in Spanish America

The Gridiron Plan and the Caste System in Colonial Central America

S. D. MARKMAN

Because they have been isolated for centuries and thus conserve many pristine colonial traits, a number of cities and towns of Central America, especially some small villages of present-day highland Chiapas and Guatemala, serve as an assemblage of urban artifacts by means of which the early stages of the history of urbanization in Hispano-America may be reconstructed. And even in those cities of Central America that have been swept into the mainstream of the twentieth century, recent developments are hardly commensurate with the changes, both physical and socioeconomic, that were witnessed in Bogotá, Quito, or Lima, let alone such truly megalopolitan centers as Mexico City or Buenos Aires.[1] For the historian of the urbanization process in the New World, it is a fortunate circumstance, therefore, that in Central America there still exist towns that have preserved in various degrees the physical aspect of their pristine colonial character.

The Spaniards became urbanization experts well before the middle of the sixteenth century in Central America. By 1553 the majority of the colonial urban centers were already in existence, exclusive of the uncounted number of establishments which were later extinguished or moved to other sites — and all this barely twenty-five years after the first Spanish permanent settlement at Ciudad Vieja in 1527. This was actually the

---

[1] Morse (1965:42) observes that only eight "second-echelon" metropolitan centers developed with commanding positions in their own regional spheres, but not on an international scale: Mexico City, Lima, Guatemala City, Bogotá, Quito, Buenos Aires, Havana, and Rio de Janeiro. Only three are truly metropolitan today: Mexico City, Buenos Aires, and Rio de Janiero.

second site for the city, the first being an abortive attempt at Iximché in 1524 in the vicinity of a pre-Columbian urban grouping.[2]

[2] Vásquez (1944, volume one: 128 ff.), quoting a communication of the first bishop of Guatemala, Francisco de Marroquín, says that by 1553 most of the Indians had already gathered into towns, especially through the efforts of the Franciscans, of which order both he and Marroquín were members. The same may be said for Honduras; see Lunardi (1946:67ff.), who lists the towns and their founding dates as follows: Trujillo by 1525 (p. 68); Puerto Cortés (Puerto Caballos) by 1524 (p. 73); San Gil de Buenavista (Nito), 1524 (p. 74); Triumfo de la Cruz, 1524, which was soon extinguished (p. 76); Naco in 1524 (p. 78); Toreaba, 1524 (p. 80); Villa de la Frontera de Cáceres, 1526 (p. 81); Villa de la Buena Esperanza, 1533–1534, extinguished in 1536 (p. 81ff.); Choluteca, 1535 (p. 84); San Pedro Sula, 1535 (p. 84); Gracia a Dios, 1536 (p. 84); Comayagua, 1537 (p. 84); Villa de Nueva Salamanca, 1543(?) (p. 88). He derives these dates from contemporary accounts, which he does not always cite.

Other Central American towns founded in the sixteenth century are: Ciudad Real (San Cristóbal de las Casas) in April of 1526 and Chiapa or Chiapa de Indios (Chiapa de Córzo) in March of 1526 (Markman 1963:7, Note 1); Santiago de los Caballeros de Guatemala (Ciudad Vieja) in 1527 (Markman 1966a:11); the same moved in 1541 (Antigua Guatemala) (Markman 1966a); the first Spanish settlement, founded by Pedro de Alvarado, at the Cakchiquel ceremonial center of Iximché, established in July 1524 and abandoned in August of that same year — see ASGH (1965, volume thirty-eight:79), *Libro Viejo* (1934:281), the second letter of Alvarado to Cortes in which he reports that he founded a town for Spaniards. The letter is actually dated 27 July 1533 and he does not specify where the site was or the date of its founding. See also Recinos (1949:57 ff.), also *Libro Viejo* (1934:5) for the *cabildo*, in fragmentary condition, recording the establishment of the city under the advocation of Santiago dated July 25, 1524, and Pérez Valenzuela (1960:32–33); also Guillemín (1959:22), identifying Iximché with the pre-Columbian site where Alvarado established the town referred to as Guatemala as well as Santiago. See also Szecsy (1953a) for a report of the preliminary excavations at the site and its identification with Santiago Guatemala.

Other towns in Central America also founded in the sixteenth century may be listed as follows: Granada in Nicaragua in 1527 (Juarros 1936, volume two: 132; de Remesal 1932, volume two: 310; López de Velasco 1894:321 ff.; Ponce 1873, volume one:365); San Miguel in El Salvador, before 1550, according to López de Velasco (1894:297); Realejo in Nicaragua in 1534 (Juarros 1936: vol. 1, p. 43); Nueva Segovia (El Ocotal) in Nicaragua by Pedrarias Dávila early in the century (López de Velasco 1894: 326); Léon, Nicaragua, first established in 1527 (Juarros 1936: vol. 2, p. 133; López de Velasco 1894:318; Diez de la Calle 1646:129ff.); San Miguel in El Salvador before 1550 (López de Velasco 1894:297); San Salvador by 1543, when it received its official title from Carlos V, according to Vásquez de Espinoza (1943:26ff.); Cartago in Costa Rica in 1573 (AGG: A 1.23 [1573] 1512–334); Tegucigalpa, Honduras, also in 1573, as a *real de minas* in 1579 (Bonilla 1945:242).

Hardoy and Aranovich (1967:354 ff.) give a ranking of the cities of Latin America reported by López de Velasco (1894) for 1580 and by Vásquez de Espinoza (1943) for 1630, eighteen of which are in the former Reino de Guatemala, out of a total of 260. The towns are ranked in numerical order according to the number of *vecinos* reported in 1580 for each as follows: Antigua Guatemala, 6; Sonsonate, 9; Chiapa (probably San Cristóbal de las Casas), 25; Granada, 25; León, 36; San Salvador, 36; San Miguel (in El Salvador), 41; Valladolid (Comayagua, Honduras), 45; Trujillo (give its location as in Veraguas, but there is also a Trujillo in Honduras), 45; Cartago, 70; Gueguetlán (Huehuetán), 70; Gracia a Dios, 79; San Pedro (not specified where — there are a number of San Pedros in sixteenth-century Central America), 79; San Jorge de Olano (possibly Olancho in Honduras, no longer existing), 90; Nueva Segovia (Ocotal), 90;

The fervor of urbanization in sixteenth-century Central America was motivated by a two-fold purpose reflected in the two types of towns founded hard upon the Conquest. Though essentially the same as regards plan and spatial extension, they were quite different institutionally: *pueblos de españoles* for the conquistadors-turned-settlers and *pueblos de indios* for the recently conquered natives (Markman 1971: *passim*). *Pueblos de españoles* were established primarily as centers for political, ecclesiastical, and economic control of the hinterland, whereas *pueblos de indios* served as sites for the concentration of the Indian population who were to be controlled the more readily politically, ecclesiastically, and economically. However, many of these sixteenth-century foundations lost their original juridically segregated character with the eventual disintegration of the caste system. The historical, economic, and social forces at play during the course of the colonial period also served to transform the pristine physical character of many of the two original types of towns. By the eighteenth century strictly monoracial towns were rare, except in remote highland villages of Chiapas and Guatemala. The caste system ultimately became a *de jure* vestige or fossil once the physical and spiritual conquests of the natives were consummated by the Spaniards, who in their turn were overwhelmed by a biological conquest. The most visible consequence of the biological conquest was the formation of a vast segment of colonial society that did not fit into the racial categories by means of which the population had originally been divided into castes.[3]

The Spanish cultural institutions brought to America and especially the neomedieval social structure into which the European Spanish population was organized in *pueblos de españoles* are reflected in the location on the grid plan of building plots assigned to the governing bodies, the church authorities, and the settlers themselves, both the leaders and the rank and file. That towns reserved exclusively for Spaniards were primarily centers of control is reflected in the layout on the ground of a physical paradigm in space, a visible table of organization of Spanish society in the New World.

Choluteca, 103; Realejo, 103. Ranks are given towns from 1 to 4. None in Central America is ranked in the first category, in fact only the capital city, Antigua Guatemala, is ranked 2, the rest are either in category 3 or 4.

See also Chueca Goitia et al. (1951, volume one: viiff.) for a brief and eulogistic statement relative to the urban creativity of Spain in the New World.

[3] For the history of the caste system and the population of colonial Central America see especially Barón Castro (1942: *passim*). For a bibliography on the caste system in colonial Central America and elsewhere in the New World, see Note 25 dealing with mestization.

The residents of the *pueblos de indios* were objects of control and were all members of the same caste. Because its residents were forced to live in what for them was a contrived, exotic urban environment, more frequently than not against their will, with social distinctions and ranks of former days proscribed, and to be members of a single class in colonial society as a whole, the physical layout of Indian towns could hardly serve as a paradigm for ranking the inhabitants. The location of the sites assigned for dwellings did not reflect any social distinction. The church and/or *convento* and the government house on the plaza represented external authorities rather than any internal power structure. Because they were mainly engaged in agricultural pursuits, it was extremely difficult to force the Indians to live in the towns founded for them. Some, especially in contemporary highland Chiapas, eventually became no more than places of residence for the "*cargo*-holders" (officials) who changed periodically, so that the towns became religious and market centers in a manner not too different from what had been common before the Conquest.[4]

The earliest intimation that the layout of the *pueblos de españoles* founded in the sixteenth century was conceived of as a physical paradigm for locating the different classes of Spanish society destined to live in these towns comes from Jorge de Alvarado, brother of Pedro de Alvarado, in the act of founding the first permanent settlement in Central America, in the valley of Almolonga, now Ciudad Vieja, Guatemala, on November 21, 1527.[5] The organization of colonial society is clearly indicated by the

[4]   See Markman (i.p.a.: *passim*, 1963:21ff.) for the problems of gathering the Indians into towns in the early sixteenth century. See also Vogt (1969, volume seven:150, Figure 3) for the "vacant town" type. For Tzotzil settlement patterns, the vacant town, see Laughlin (1969, volume seven:170). Also see Note 21 below.

[5]   For the text of Alvarado's order see *Libro viejo* (1934:29), ASGH (1927–1928: 106), and Pérez Valenzuela (1960:32–33): "Asentá escribano que yo, por virtud de los poderes que tengo de los gobernadores de su magestad, con acuerdo y parecer de los alcaldes y regidores que están presentes, asiento y pueblo aquí en este sitio la ciudad de Santiago, el cual dicho sitio es término de la provincia de Guatemala.

"Primeramente ante todas cosas mando que se haga la traza de la dicha ciudad, poniendo las calles norte sur, leste hueste.

"Otro si mando que sean señalados cuatro solares en cuatro calles en ellas incorporados, por plaza de la dicha ciudad.

"Otro si mando que sean señalados dos solares junto á la plaza, en el lugar más conveniente, donde la iglesia sea edificada, la cual sea de la advocacción de del Señor Santiago...

"Otro si mando que se señale un sitio para un hospital, á donde los pobres y peregrinos sean acorridos y curados...

"Yten mando que se señale un sitio cual convenga para una capilla y adoratorio...

"Otro si mando que se señale un sitio cual convenga, donde á suplicación desta ciudad, su magestad mande hacer una fortaleza, o su gobernador en su real nombre, para la guarda y seguridad de la dicha ciudad.

explicit location, in the very heart of the town, of the plaza which was laid out first, giving it a spatial preeminence in the grid of streets emanating from it north-south and east-west. The civil and ecclesiastical authorities also were located on the plaza.

Jorge de Alvarado's pointed remark that the rest of the plots should be distributed according to the manner and customs in which this was done in the rest of New Spain would seem to indicate that the organization of the space of the town, a grid of streets surrounding a plaza, and the placement of the *vecinos* along those streets had already been formulated in fact, if not yet in official regulations or directives from Spain. In other words, the plaza and the town represent the germinal unit, the nucleus or center from which the surrounding countryside may be conquered and brought into the Spanish realm. Pedro de Alvarado had said as much in his second letter to the Crown, regarding the first short-lived Spanish settlement at Iximché in 1524, "donde para mejor conquistar y pacificar... hize y edifiqué una ciudad de españoles...."[6]

This act of Alvarado, bringing into existence a town conceived of as a base from which first to conquer and then to control the country, could hardly have been original with him. Efficacious methods of conquest and settlement seem to have been arrived at almost at once and, though of extremely recent origin, are referred to as if they had been long-standing methods well seasoned by years of experience. For example, only

---

"Otro si mando que junto a la plaza sean señalados cuatro solares, el uno para casa de cabildo, y el otro para la cárcel pública, y los otros para propios de la ciudad.

"Señalados los sitios y solares de susocontenidos, mando que los demas solares sean repartidos por los vecinos que son y fueren de la dicha ciudad, como y de la manera que se haya hecho en las ciudades, villas y lugares que en esta nueva españa estan poblados de españoles, no excediendo ni traspasando la orden acostumbrada. Jorge de Alvarado."

It was three years before this permanent site was picked. The first Spanish town was founded July 25, 1524, at Iximché, a small pre-Columbian ceremonial center of postclassic origin. The hostility of the local Indians forced the Spaniards out the following month. The city then existed on the paper of the *cabildos* held from time to time until the site at Almolonga, after some debate, was finally selected. For Iximché see ASGH (1965, volume thirty-eight:79) and Recinos (1952:164); also the second letter of Alvarado, dated 27 July 1524, in which he says, "...donde para mejor conquistar y pacificar esta tierra tan grande y tan rezia de gente hize y edifique en nombre de su majestad una ciudad de españoles del señor Santiago..."(*Libro viejo* 1934:281); also Villacorta (1925–1926: *passim*). For an excavation report on Iximché see Szecsy (1953a) and Guillemín (1959: *passim*). For some excavations carried out at the first permanent settlement at Almolonga, Ciudad Vieja, see Szecsy (1953b: *passim*). The lesson was well learned and never again were populated indigenous sites picked for Spanish towns because most of these were either well fortified by nature or by man-made works. See Díaz del Castillo (1933–1934, volume two:106 ff.) speaking of Utatlán, and Ximénez (1929–1931, volume one:122) with regard to Chiapa (Chiapa de Córzo, Chiapas).

[6] See *Libro viejo* (1934:281); also references in Note 5 above.

three years later, 1527, and but five or six after the founding of Mexico, and a scant generation since the Spanish settlement at Santo Domingo, his brother Jorge already refers to an established custom to follow as a guide in the distribution of plots to the *vecinos*. To found a town was to create a practical tool for a specific purpose, the extension of the central authority of the Spanish Crown in the New World. The best means of achieving this end was a chain of cities, of power centers spread over the vast American continent, each link being a fixed point in space from which control — economic, political, ecclesiastical — radiated and interconnected with other units as part of an urban hierarchy of *caserios, lugares, pueblos, villas, ciudades,*[7] terms still employed in modern-day Guatemala.

The plaza of the Spanish town became the locus for the highest ranks or echelons of the power structure of colonial society — the church, the city hall, and the jail. Though Jorge de Alvarado makes no mention of distinction in rank as a basis for assigning plots to the *vecinos* at Almolonga, there is some evidence forthcoming elsewhere that the leaders, the elite of the Spanish forces, were indeed given special consideration in the choice of building sites, sometimes directly on the main plaza. For example, the house of the conquistador Montejo still stands on the main plaza of Mérida, and needs no further documentation. When Villa Real (later Ciudad Real and now San Cristóbal de las Casas, Chiapas) was laid out in 1528, "en forma de pueblo por barrios, cuadras y calles...,"[8] the *vecinos* who had been assigned plots were requested to come to the city council and sign for them in the official *libro de cabildo*.

Diego de Mazariegos, the leader of the conquistadors, asked for four *solares*, three for himself and one for his son, in recognition of his services. Though not identified with certainty, the house he built may be the one still standing on the southwest corner of the plaza of San Cristóbal.[9] De Remesal (1932, volume two: 386), usually a reliable reporter, goes

---

[7]   See Foster (1960:48) for a discussion of the plaza and the grid plan as the geographical and cultural center of the power structure. He rightly considers the plazas in the New World, not so much representing the diffusion of a material trait, as the utilization of an old idea for specific political, religious and economic goals. See also Stanislawski (1946:108 ff.), who recognizes the grid plan as reflective of a centralized power for military and political control.

[8]   De Remesal (1932, volume two: 385 ff.), writing at the beginning of the seventeenth century.

[9]   This house is traditionally identified as having belonged to Diego de Mazariegos (see Markman 1963: photograph between pages 94–95). It is quite possible, however, that Mazariegos' house no longer exists, and also that its site was on the south side of the plaza across from the cathedral, now occupied by some nondescript temporary structures. The present Casa de la Sirena, on the east half of the south side of the plaza (Markman 1963:108), may possibly have been built by his son Luis or have belonged to another conquistador, Andrés de la Tobilla.

on to say that for similar reasons of extraordinary service, choice plots were assigned to Pedro de Estrada, Francisco de Lintorne, and others. Once the plots in town had all been distributed the land in the country-side was parceled out "...por caballerías y peonerías a los vecinos de la villa." *Caballerías*, each 600 by 300 feet (*piés*), were used to measure out the land allotted those of the conquistadors who brought horses with them, and *peonerías*, each 100 by 50 feet, were the units employed for foot soldiers.

The location of the elite classes of conquest society in the center of the towns, either on or adjacent to the main plaza, may also have been customary among the indigenes before the advent of the Spaniards, if Bishop de Landa's description of some of the pre-Conquest urban centers of Yucatán may be accepted as reliable, and not a case of his interpreting the facts from the European point of view. He says that before the coming of the Spaniards the indigenes lived in very civilized fashion close to-gether in towns, in the middle of which there were the temples on plazas and around which were also the houses of the rulers and the priests; then beyond were the houses of the higher classes and still further away on the outskirts of town, those of the common people.[10]

Whether de Landa's description of the social stratification of post-Classic Yucatec society on the actual ground plan of towns is correct is not as pertinent as the question as to whether or not he was unwittingly de-scribing a tradition already implanted in Spanish cities in Mexico and Central America, whereby the choicest sites were considered to be those on the plazas or at least contiguous to it. For example, in 1541 when Antigua Guatemala, the new capital after the destruction of Ciudad Vieja, was laid out, it is reported that the building plots were distributed "...conforme a la calidad de los vecinos...."[11]

The elitist character of the sixteenth-century *pueblo de españoles* is further attested to by the fact that the plan itself, the *traza*, had a status in law. The very physical shape of the town with its plaza and grid of streets was established verbally by means of a legal instrument before a single foundation trench for any building was dug. And only Spaniards could be inscribed as official residents, that is, as *vecinos*. In the course

---

[10] De Landa (1966:28). For a good translation and a well-annotated edition see Tozzer (1941:62).
[11] De Remesal (1932, volume two: 45). "Primero edificaron la plaza y las cuadras que están cerca de ella y luego se extendieron a todas partes." This *traza* [plan] then en-larged before the plots were distributed according to the quality of the *vecinos*. This might be interpreted as implying that the highest ranks of the *vecinos* were given plots on the first streets laid out contiguous to the plaza, and only when these were extended were the rest of the *vecinos* in the lower echelons assigned plots.

of time, as the population of Spanish towns increased in size, usually because of the growth in the numbers of the members of racially mixed origin, the official physical town plan was extended in special acts of the city council, sanctioned by the Crown; as, for example, in the case of Antigua Guatemala in 1559, and again in 1641, and a number of times again during the eighteenth century.[12]

From the very first, those Indians required to serve as a labor force for the city were established in *barrios* outside the official *traza*, usually referred to as being *extramuros* of the city. By 1686, according to Fuentes y Guzmán, there were ten such wards on the outskirts of the central area of town, the original official *traza*. The plans of some were eventually integrated into the gridiron scheme, the streets of which had been extended as the racially mixed non-Spanish population grew.[13] The original intention was to segregate the Indians from the Spaniards. However, in the course of time, as people of neither of the two main original castes, *español* and *indio*, but *mestizos, mulatos* and mixtures of all, became more and more numerous, they naturally settled in the new streets opened up as the official *traza* was enlarged by the extension of the town plan. The original official *traza* around the plaza remained the particular preserve of the purely Spanish elements of society.

From the very first, satellite *pueblos de indios* were also established in the vicinity of *pueblos de españoles* in order to ensure the availability of a labor force on the farms of the surrounding countryside or for personal services for the Spaniards or for public works. Sometimes these satellite Indian towns were located on the very outskirts of Spanish towns, as, for example, Jocotenango to the north of Antigua, or Subtiava to the west of León. There were thirty-one such satellite Indian towns around Antigua Guatemala, some at a considerable distance away, most of which had been founded in the sixteenth century, and whose

[12]   Markman (1966a: 12–16). For the official status of the *traza*, the grid plan, see Markman (1971: Note 32) and Borah (1973: *passim*) for an extensive bibliography.
[13]   Fuentes y Guzmán (1932–1933, volume one: 136 ff.), and Markman (1966a:14). The ten *barrios* were as follows: (1) San Francisco, inhabited by Indians, probably one of the first *barrios* for Indians and established at the time the city was founded in 1541; (2) El Tortuguero, along the southern edge of town, about three squares below and to the east of the *plaza mayor*; (3) San Sebastián, to the northeast of the main *traza* and beyond the *convento* of La Merced; (4) El Manchén, further north still; (5) San Jerónimo, west of San Sebastián, inhabited by people of completely mixed and no especially definable racial caste; (6) Santiago, which Fuentes calls an *arrabal*, not identified today and probably a slum area; (7) Espíritu Santo, to the southwest on the edge of town; (8) Santo Domingo, the area near the Dominican *convento* to the northeast of the main *traza*; (9) La Chácara on the eastern edge of town; and (10) La Candelaria, a populous neighborhood to the northeast beyond the *barrio* of Santo Domingo. See Pardo et al. (1943) for plans of the colonial town.

inhabitants had originally been brought together from afar to serve as a labor force on the lands held in *encomienda* by *vecinos* of the city.[14] Some of these towns were actually held in *encomienda* by religious orders, especially the Franciscans who dervied a considerable part of their income from them.[15] Satellite Indian towns were established around every Spanish town, repeating with but slight variations the case of Antigua Guatemala. For example, San Cristóbal de las Casas (Villa Real or Ciudad Real in colonial times) had five Indian *barrios*. At first these were located a short distance from the main center, but eventually, with the growth of the city, they were incorporated into the grid of streets so that today they are almost indistinguishable, except for the church and plaza in each.[16] This particular type of *pueblo de indios*, the satellite town, was different from those established by the religious orders as part of their missionary activities, which were scattered far and wide in remote areas, frequently far from the major Spanish urban centers.[17]

The Spaniards were never a numerous caste in relation to the Indian and, eventually, to the *mestizo* and other castes, numbering some 2,300 *vecinos* in 1580 and about 2,900 *vecinos in* 1630 in all of Central America.[18]

[14] Juarros (1936, volume two:221 ff.), writing at the very end of the eighteenth century. All had been established as far back as the sixteenth as follows: to the east, Santa Inés, Santa Ana, Santa Isabel, San Cristóbal el Alto, San Cristóbal el Bajo, San Bartolomé Carmona (extinguished in his day), and San Juan del Obispo; to the south, Santa Catalina Bobadilla, San Gaspar Vivar, San Pedro (Huertas), San Lucas, San Miguel, and Almolonga (Ciudad Vieja); to the southwest, San Miguel Milpas Dueñas, Santa Catarina, San Andrés, San Antonio Aguascalientes, San Lorenzo (el Cubo), and Santiago; to the west, San Andrés Dean, San Bartolomé; to the northwest, San Dionisio Pastores and San Lucas de las Carretas; to the north, Jocotenango, Utateca, and San Felipe; and to the northeast, Santo Tomás, San Miguel, San Bartolomé Milpas Altas, Santa Lucía, and Magdalena. Most of these towns still exist today and may be located on the map, "Departamento de Sacatepéquez," scale 1:100,000, as well as in the gazeteer (Dirección General de Estádistica 1953:35ff.).
[15] Fuentes y Guzmán (1932–1933, volume one: 376), writing circa 1690, gives eight of the towns listed in Note 14 above as *encomiendas* of the Franciscan *convento* in Antigua.
[16] See Markman (1963:105). The five are El Cerrillo, Cuxtital, San Antonio, San Diego, and Mexicanos. See Juarros (1936, volume one:16); the names of the five *barrios* appear in a report dated 1785 concerning the damage caused by a flood (AGG: A 1.1 [1785] 17–1); see also Trens (1957:221), who also gives the names of the Indian *barrios*. Also at some distance from town, all originally held in *encomienda* by *vecinos* of San Cristóbal, are San Felipe Ecatepec, Chamula, Zinacantán, and Iluistán, among others.
[17] See Markman (1971: *passim*) for the type founded by religious orders.
[18] These figures are given by Hardoy and Aranovich (1967). By 1580 or so, according to a geographical report, Archivo de Indias, Sevilla: Audiencia de Guatemala, *Estante 2, Cajón 2, Legajo 4,* Tomo 1, Folio 57, "Pueblos... Audiencia de Guatemala, 1581," and López de Velasco (1894:284), there were but five *pueblos de españoles* in the province of Guatemala: Santiago (Antigua), San Salvador, Sonsonate, San Miguel, and Choluteca. Ponce (1873, volume one:344), says that in all the province of Honduras

In fact, the total population of the Reino de Guatemala near the end of the colonial period in 1776, by which time the difference between *pueblo de indios* and *pueblos de españoles* no longer had any significance, was estimated to be 805,000 inhabitants, plus 8,000 more for Guatemala City. The number of urban centers at that time totaled twelve *ciudades*, twenty-one *villas*, and 705 *pueblos* (Juarros 1936, volume one:66ff.; AGG: A 1.10 [1773] 18.773–244). By the early nineteenth century, circa 1839, of the twenty-nine cities in all Central America, only eleven were considered important from the point of view of a visitor from the United States (Montgomery 1839).

Many of the *pueblos de indios* became ghost towns when it was found that their locations were unsuitable for economic reasons or because of bad climatic conditions.[19] Also, in some cases, because of great distances from Spanish towns, control was difficult. The lines of authority and power were overextended in space, so that many of the Indians would run off and go back to their former life, especially in the Petén and in Verapaz, Guatemala (Cevallos 1935–1936; AGG: A 1.18.4[1650] 38. 300–4501). In El Salvador, in the eighteenth century, apparently not only Indians but even the *ladinos* preferred to live in the country rather than in towns.[20]

But unlike *pueblos de españoles*, the population of Indian towns by law lacked social stratification, the Indian having been forcibly settled there, and the class stratification of his former society extinguished.[21] The physical layout of the town, often hastily executed, was not conceived of as a paradigm for the social ranking of the inhabitants because they

---

there were five or six: Comayagua, Trujillo, Gracia a Dios, Olancho, San Pedro in Comayagua, and Agalteca. In all of the Soconusco, the Pacific littoral of Chiapas, there was but one Spanish town, Huehuetán (López de Velasco 1894: 302 ff.) Even more scant were the population and the number of Spanish towns in the rest of Central America, i.e. in Nicaragua, Costa Rica, and highland Chiapas, where San Cristóbal de las Casas (Ciudad Real) was the only Spanish town.

[19] In the seventeenth century, many towns near Comitán, Chiapas, were extinguished (Ximénez 1929–31, volume two: 199); also in the Golfo Dulce area and in the Alcaldía de Amatique, Guatemala (Fuentes y Guzmán 1932–1933, volume two: 289 ff., 295ff.).

[20] Cortes y Larraz (n.d.: folio 89), reports that three-quarters of the population of the parish of Chalatenango lived in *despoblados*, and that three-quarters of that population is *ladino*. In folios 112–113, he describes and laments the Indians' custom of living in solitude. To a Spaniard this was incomprehensible.

[21] For the gathering of Indians into towns see Markman (1963:21ff., also 1971: *passim*). See also a *cédula* of 1540 ordering that Indians be urbanized (AGG: A1.23 [1540] 1511–10, also A 1.2.4 [1540] 5752–54 *vuelto*). This *cédula* is cited by de Remesal (1932, volume one:220); Vásquez (1944, volume one:66ff.); and Fuentes y Guzmán (1932–1933, volume two:446). For gathering of Indians into towns see also de Remesal (1932, volume two:211, 244, 245). A similar *cédula* was emitted for Peru, 22 July 1595, according to de Remesal (1932, volume two:243, 244, 246).

were all indistinguishably members of one class, *indio*. As long as the Indian town remained solely a *pueblo* for Indians and was not invaded by members of other castes, it consisted of hardly more than a plaza with a church, the street plan remaining ever embryonic. Control of the Indian residents, except in satellite towns, was concentrated in the ecclesiastical authority as represented by the one monumental building on the only urban space in town, the church on the plaza.

If contemporary practice is any clue to colonial customs, the example of so many contemporary towns of highland Chiapas and Guatemala that are still not much more than a church plaza surrounded by corn fields, and are in fact "vacant towns" inhabited by alternating *cargo-holders*, as mentioned above, may be accepted as evidence of the original appearance of the *pueblo de indios* of the sixteenth century, both satellite and missionary.[22] The symbolic values associated with the plaza in *pueblos de españoles* were totally foreign to those of the *pueblo de indios*. The *plaza mayor* of Spanish towns was the location and seat of political authority, of the market and of commerce, and was the main religious center. To live in its proximity implied that one was either a member of the power structure or of the elite of local Spanish society. In the *pueblo de indios*, the plaza was just a vaguely defined vacant space dominated by a church,[23] its sole architectural distinction.

[22] See Markman (i.p.b. *passim*) for an analysis of this particular urban scheme; see also Note 4, above, for "vacant towns" in contemporary highland Chiapas.

[23] Ricard (1950: 325 ff.) rightly observes that the Hispano-American town is a plaza surrounded by streets, that the plaza is really a *plaza del estado*, that is a seat of authority. This is quite contrary to the Renaissance conception of the plaza (Zucker 1959: 140), a man-made order to establish definite spatial limits, a space unified by architectural means, space articulated by the buildings around it, in fine, an aesthetic interpretation current in Renaissance Europe. The city plan and the plaza of Antigua Guatemala were designed by an Italian military engineer-architect, Bautista Antonelli (Juarros 1936, volume two: 178).

The strict orthogonal layout with the open plaza as the center and the origin of the grid must not be taken at face value as being based on Renaissance theories of town planning. The question is one of answering whether Antonelli was continuing a practice already in use when Ciudad Vieja was laid out in 1527 and San Cristóbal de las Casas in 1528. Was he primarily concerned with aesthetic considerations expressed in the Italian theories of the "ideal city" of the time (Rosenau 1959), or was he guided by practical considerations? See Markman (1966a: 11, 56) for biographical data on Antonelli; also Angulo Iñiguez (1942), and Calderón Quijano (1953: 12–18) for Antonelli's activities in Mexico before going to Guatemala.

In the New World, however, the plaza becomes a sociopolitical instrument, at least in Spanish towns, which by the seventeenth and eighteenth centuries is embellished with fountains and arcades. But from the very first the architectural elements which define that space are directly reflective of the institutions or authorities they house — church, jail, city hall, government offices, mint, commercial establishments. None of these institutions, except that of the church, is a determinant of the architectural treatment of the plazas in *pueblos de indios*. Government buildings and commercial

The physical conquest of Guatemala and the rest of Central America was effected by a remarkably scant number of determined men and within a remarkably short space of time, most of the country having been pacified and controlled by the end of the sixteenth century. However, in the biological conquest that ensued, the victors turned out to be the vanquished. By the eighteenth century, the elite caste which had populated the Spanish towns had become almost extinct, by mixing not only with the indigenes to form the *mestizo* caste, but also with exotic racial elements from a distant continent, Africa. As a result of the intermixing of the three racial strains, the caste system itself, the juridical instrument by means of which society was organized, lost its meaning and usefulness as the racial qualifications for each social category, or caste, became blurred.[24]

This process of the mestization of the population was dramatically reflected in the changes that gradually took place in both Spanish and Indian towns in the Reino de Guatemala during the colonial period, not so much in the external physical aspect of the town plan, as in the symbolic values formerly attached to its various parts.[25]

In time, pure Spaniards were totally outnumbered in Spanish towns, as were Indians also outnumbered in many Indian towns. It would seem that the Indian population of satellite towns and *barrios* was not so much converted to Christianity and other European institutions as it was bred to them. Just as Indian towns were eventually invaded by *ladinos*, i.e. people of mixed racial ancestry, so were Spanish towns which, as a result, ultimately lost their elitist identity in the ever-increasing rise in the numbers of residents of mixed ancestry. The *mise-en-scène* of the mestization process in colonial Central America was primarily urban. The enormous growth of the racially intermixed and urbanized population was the cause of the repeated need to extend the street plan

---

establishments even today in Indian towns of highland Chiapas and Guatemala are largely nondescript, except for the schools in the last few years. For an excellent synthesis of the literature on the origin of the grid plan in America, see Borah (1973:*passim*).

[24] For a discussion of the term *casta* see Morse (1965:40ff.), who believes it is reminiscent of the Thomist-Aristotelian notion of a functional social hierarchy.

[25] There has been much interest in the history of race mixture — *mestizaje* — in recent years, particularly in colonial Central America. One of the best general works dealing with the caste system as a whole is Barón Castro (1942). See also Adams (1964); Magnus Mörner (1964); Samayoa Guevara (1960:63–106; 1962, 1966: 65–74); de Solano (1969:145–200); and Markman (1966b, volume four:189–194). Other works of a more general nature of interest to the problem of *mestizaje* are: Calderón Quijano (1971); Esteva Fabregat (1964:279–354); Konetzke (1953, 1946, Nos. 23–24:7–14, 215–237); Kubler (1966); Lipschutz (1967); Moreno Navarro (1969); Mörner (1960, 1967); Rosenblatt (1954, 1967); Salas (1960); Zavala (1971).

of Antigua, rather than any numerical increase of the elite caste of Spaniards, which actually decreased during the course of time.[26] As mestization increased, the traditional social hierarchy, which had been based on ethnic or racial origin, could no longer function. The only racially distinguishable castes by the end of the colonial period were still the Spanish, almost extinct by then, and the more numerous Indian. The *mestizo* and *mulato* castes had blended entirely. The five castes — *español, indio, mestizo, mulato, zambo,* the latter a mixture of Indian and Negro — were still employed for legal matters in the mid-eighteenth century.[27]

However, by the end of the eighteenth century the five were reduced to three — *español, indio,* and a racially indeterminate third, sometimes called *pardo,* or *mulato. Ladino* began to be employed with greater frequency by the beginning of the nineteenth century, because by 1800 the population was completely mixed, except for the larger nonurban-

[26] See Notes 12 and 13 above. By 1810, the majority of the urban population of the Reino de Guatemala were *pardos,* i.e. people of no particularly determined race, but a mixture of all three. See Larrazabal (1953–1954: 87 ff.), who gives the following statistics on the population: 646,660 *indios*; 313,334 *pardos y algunos negros*; 40,000 *blancos.* The term *pardo* was already in use by the end of the seventeenth century in Antigua Guatemala. The residents of the *barrio* of San Jerónimo were termed *pardos* at the time of an uprising or riot, which took place 15 September 1697 (Pardo 1944: 120). The term *ladino* was also commonly employed during the colonial period. For example, Fuentes y Guzmán (1932–1933, volume two: 242), around 1690, speaking of the town of San Cristóbal Cazabastlán (Acasaguastlán), gives the number of *indios* and *ladinos* resident there saying "...así llamamos en los pueblos de indios los que son españoles, mestizos, mulatos y negros, a diferencia de los indios que solo hablan su materna." *Ladino* may also mean an acculturated Indian. Vásquez (1944, volume four: 37), referring to the population of San Juan del Obispo in 1689 reports a "barrio de indios ladinos" as distinct from one of *indios*; also Fuentes y Guzmán (1932–1933, volume three: 448) says that those Indians who had been trained and educated were quite "cortesanos y ladinos, como los de Nicaragua, los mejicanos de San Salvador, los de Comayagua, Quetzaltenango, Huehuetenango, Chinautla, Petapa, Amatitlán, Santa Ynés Petapa, Mixco, Almolonga, y de los barrios de la Candelaria, Santiago, San Jerónimo, San Antón, Espíritu Santo, Santa Ynés del Monte Policiano, que son bastante ladinos..." Juarros (1936, volume two: 87), giving statistics on the population of some towns in El Salvador, uses the terms *pardo* for San Miguel and San Vicente, but for Sonsonate, he distinguishes between Spaniards and *indios* with a third classification, *mulato,* who outnumber the other two castes almost five to one. He uses this term also in giving the population figures for León and Granada, Nicaragua (1936, volume one:40ff.). But here he separates the population into four categories, *españoles, mestizos, mulatos, indios.* In the case of Realejo, Nicaragua, he says (1936, volume one:43) all are *mulatos,* and in El Viejo there are only fifty-nine Spaniards out of a total population of 2,968, the rest being *mulatos.* Even by mid-eighteenth century in the geographical report on the Valley of Guatemala (Antigua) the majority caste in the population was given as *mulato* (AGG: A 1.17[1740]5002–210).
[27] Pardo (1944:216); an ordinance prohibiting the use of firearms in Antigua Guatemala with punishment for infractions scaled according to the caste of the delinquent.

ized Indian population, i.e. nonurbanized in large towns or cities but still living in small villages.²⁸ From very early in the colonial period, as people of mixed ancestry began to outnumber the Spaniards in Spanish towns and also overflowed into Indian towns, the authorities tried to prohibit this movement by means of special decrees, the idea being to ensure the continued services of Indians for the Spanish elite caste on the one hand, and to control the *ladinos* who wished to be free of restraints imposed on them in Spanish towns.²⁹

The rise in the numbers of the *ladino* population brought with it the eventual decimation of the elite Spanish caste, which declined not only in numbers but also in economic power. By the end of the colonial period, the segregated urban centers, reserved exclusively for Spaniards, were overrun by non-Spanish elements of the population who, for them, were social inferiors.³⁰ Little by little, members of the indeterminate racial caste of *ladinos* began to occupy what had been the choice building sites

²⁸   In Honduras, Nicaragua, and Costa Rica three main castes are referred to by Juarros (1936, volume one: 32 ff.): *españoles, mestizos, mulatos*. In some cases, as for example, Quetzaltenango, he is rather vague as to caste denominations (1936, volume one: 49 ff.), and gives figures only for *indios* and *ladinos*. In the province of Escuintla (1936, volume one:20ff.), he speaks of twenty-three "*pueblos de indios*" and eleven "*pueblos de mulatos*." Cortes y Larraz (n.d.: folio 237), reporting in the third quarter of the eighteenth century on the Valle de las Vacas, where Guatemala City was eventually to be located, says there were 7,139 inhabitants, a mixture of Spaniards, *ladinos*, and Indians and that it was impossible to distinguish the three main castes. In 1765 in Honduras, the population was quite mixed (AGG: A 1. 17 [1765]13.999–1840), where it is reported there were two "*villas de españoles y mulatos*," five *minerales* inhabited by "*gente de otra jaez*," seventeen *pueblos de indios* and that in Tegucigalpa there were but seventy *vecinos*, presumably Spaniards. For the disintegration of the caste system in Antigua Guatemala, see Markman (1966a: 14 ff., 19, 46 ff., 49–50).
²⁹   García Peláez (1943–1944, volume two: 152 ff.) summarizes the history of the movement of *ladinos* into Indian towns and the legal measures enacted against this practice, which began as far back as the sixteenth and seventeenth centuries. The towns in the vicinity of Antigua where this had occurred were Mixco, Petapa, Amatitlán, San Andrés Itzapa, Escuintla, all mentioned by Fuentes y Guzmán (1932–1933, volume three: 448; see Note 26 above), where Spaniards and *mulatos* had appropriated Indian land. See also Juarros (1936, volume two: 215) and Fuentes y Guzmán (1932–1933, volume one: 411) for towns with a mixed racial population. See also Larreinaga (1857:266) for a *cédula*, dated 22 December 1605, prohibiting other castes from living in *pueblos de indios* and another *cédula*, of 26 April 1762, explicitly prohibiting *ladinos* from taking up residence in Indian towns.
³⁰   García Peláez (1943–1944, volume two: 217), writing between 1834 and 1841, laments that there were not thirty illustrious families left in Guatemala City. He mentions the extinction of certain noble families, and that some girls of good families were reduced to doing work formerly done by their slaves. The plebians are on the ascent "…decaecen las familias ilustres, se abaten los ánimos de los niños á barajarse, y tripularse entre negros y mulatos. Bien lastimoso ejemplo son algunas familias, a que no ha quedado más que el nombre mezclados por su probreza en el plebe."

in the vicinity of the *plaza mayor*. The original distribution of building sites according to the quality of the recipient was no longer the factor in determining the ownership of real property which could be, and was, sold by members of the Spanish caste, as their fortunes declined, to anyone, including *ladinos*. The location of real property, that is of individual houses on streets near the plaza, was no longer indicative of the caste of the owner, but rather of his position in the new society, now more often than not based on personal wealth instead of family lineage.

The offices of government and the church still dominated the plaza, but the other sides, at least one side and the central open space as well, were given over to commercial enterprises, a custom harking back to the very founding of the Spanish towns in the sixteenth century. But the *portál del comercio* became very valuable real estate and by the eighteenth century had passed through many changes of ownership since it had been first granted to the original *vecinos* when the cities were laid out. The sites on the corners of the streets leading away from the plaza, often occupied by the houses of the conquistadors and other meritorious settlers, also became valuable real property which could be and was sold to members of any caste so long as they had the means to pay.[31] *Mestizos* and *mulatos*, i.e. *ladinos*, eventually rose in social status, beginning with their admission to craft guilds, to the religious orders, and ultimately by intermarriage with members of the Spanish caste.[32]

The paradigm for ranking the social classes on the checkerboard plan of the Spanish town had lost its pristine symbolic meaning by the end of the colonial period and no longer reflected the original hierarchy of colonial society in Central America. The plaza remained the center of the religious, political, and commercial affairs of the city, but the location of private houses in its proximity now reflected the material wealth of the owners and not necessarily their position in the dead and fossilized caste system.

---

[31] For the history of the *plaza mayor* of Guatemala City, laid out after the destruction of Antigua in 1773, and the commercial establishments on the south side, see Markman (1966a: *passim*).

[32] See Samayoa Guevara (1960) for the admission of people of mixed ancestry to the craft guilds after 1750; also (1962) for an extended treatment of the craft guilds in the Reino de Guatemala. See also, Markman (1966b: *passim*). With regard to the religious orders, all castes, even Spaniards born in America, had been excluded at first. Spaniards born in Spain but who had arrived in Guatemala before the age of ten were also excluded from religious orders; see de Remesal (1932, volume two: 311–315). By the seventeenth century this policy changed and *criollos*, i.e. Spaniards born in the New World, were admitted and eventually *mestizos* were too.

REFERENCES

ADAMS, RICHARD N.
1964   La mestización cultural en Centroamérica. *Revista de Indias* 24 (95–96).

AGG
Archivo General del Gobierno de Guatemala, Guatemala, C.A.
Documents are classified as follows: section, date, *legajo*, *expediente*,
e.g. A 1.10 [1565] 33256–210.

ANGULO IÑIGUEZ, DIEGO
1942   *Bautista Antonelli, las fortificaciones americanas del siglo XVI.* Madrid:
Real Academia de la Historia.

ASGH
1924–   *Anales de la Sociedad de Geografía e Historia de Guatemala.* Guatemala,
C.A.
1927–1928   Fundación de la ciudad de Guatemala, 1527. *Anales de la
Sociedad de Geografía e Historia de Guatemala.* Guatemala City.

BARÓN CASTRO, RODOLFO
1942   *La población de El Salvador.* Madrid.

BCIHE
1964   *Boletín del Centro de Investigaciones Históricas y Estéticas.* Universidad
Central de Caracas. Facultad de Arquitectura y Urbanismo.

BONILLA, MARCELINA
1945   *Diccionario histórico-geográfico de las poblaciones de Honduras.*
Tegucigalpa.

BORAH, WOODROW
1973   La influencia cultural en la formación del primer plano para centros
urbanos que perduran hasta nuestros días. *Boletín del Centro de
Investigaciones Históricas y Estéticas* 15: 55–76.

CALDERÓN QUIJANO, JOSÉ ANTONIO
1953   *Fortificaciones en Nueva España.* Seville.
1971   *Población y raza en Hispanoamérica: discurso de ingreso a la Real
Academia Sevillana de Buenas Lettras.* Seville.

CEVALLOS, FR. BERNARDINO (fl. ca. 1750)
1935–1936   Visión de paz; Nueva Yerusalén. *Anales de la Sociedad de
Geografía e Historia de Guatemala* 12: 463–485. Guatemala City.

CHUECA GOITIA, FERNANDO, LEOPOLDO TORRES BALBAS, JULIO GONZALEZ Y
GONZALEZ
1951   *Planos de ciudades ibero-americanas y filipinas existentes en el Archivo
de Indias,* two volumes. Madrid.

CORTES Y LARRAZ, PEDRO (fl. 1711–1786)
1958   *Descripción geográfico-moral.* Biblioteca Goathemala. Guatemala
City: Sociedad de Geografía e Historia de Guatemala.
n.d.   "Descripción geográfico-moral de las diócesis de Goathemala."
Unpublished manuscript. Archivo de Indias, Audiencia de Guatemala
948, Seville.

DE LANDA, FRAY DIEGO (fl. sixteenth century)
1966   *Relación de las cosas de Yucatán* (ninth edition). Notes and introduction by Angel María Garibay K. Mexico City.

DE REMESAL, FRAY ANTONIO (fl. early seventeenth century)
1932   *Historia general de las Indias Occidentales, y particular de la gobernación de Chiapas y Guatemala* (second edition), two volumes. Biblioteca Goathemala. Guatemala City: Sociedad de Geografía e Historia de Guatemala.

DE SOLANO, FRANCISCO
1969   Aéreas linguísticas y población de habla indígena en Guatemala en 1772. *Revista Española de Antropología Americana* 4: 145–200.

DÍAZ DEL CASTILLO, BERNAL (fl. 1496–1584)
1933–1934   *Verdadera y notable relación del descubrimiento y conquista de la Nueva España y Guatemala*, two volumes. Guatemala City.

DIEZ DE LA CALLE, JUAN (fl. mid-sixteenth century)
1646   *Memorial y noticias sacras y reales de las Indias Occidentales.* Madrid.

DIRECCIÓN GENERAL DE ESTÁDISTICA: REPÚBLICA DE GUATEMALA
1953   *Departamentos, municipios, ciudades, villas, pueblos, aldeas y caseríos de la República de Guatemala.* Guatemala City.

ESTEVA FABREGAT, CLAUDIO
1964   El mestizaje en Iberoamérica. *Revista de Indias* 24 (95–96).

FOSTER, GEORGE M.
1960   *Culture and conquest.* New York.

FUENTES Y GUZMÁN, FRANCISCO ANTONIO (fl. seventeenth century)
1932–1933   *Recordación florida*, three volumes. Biblioteca Goathemala. Guatemala City: Sociedad de Geografía e Historia de Guatemala.

GARCÍA PELÁEZ, FRANCISCO DE PAULA (fl. 1785–1867)
1943–1944   *Memorias para la historia del antiguo reyno de Guatemala* (second edition), four volumes. Biblioteca Payo de Rivera. Guatemala City.

GUILLEMÍN, JORGE F.
1959   Iximché. *Antropología e Historia* 11(2): 22–64. Guatemala City: Instituto de Antropología e Historia de Guatemala.

HARDOY, JORGE, CARMEN ARANOVICH
1967   Cuadro comparativo de los centros de colonización existentes en 1580 y 1630. *Desarrollo Económico* 7 (27): 349–360.

JUARROS, DOMINGO (fl. 1752–1820)
1936   *Compendio de la historia de la ciudad de Guatemala* (third edition), two volumes. Biblioteca Payo de Rivera. Guatemala City.

KONETZKE, RICHARD
1946   El mestizaje y su importancia en el desarrollo de la población hispanoamericana durante la época colonial. *Revista de Indias* (23–24).
1953   *Colección de documentos para la historia de la formación social de Hispanoamérica, 1493–1810*, five volumes. Madrid.

KUBLER, GEORGE
1966   Indianismo y mestizaje. *Revista de Occidente* 4 (38): 158–167.

LARRAZABAL, ANTONIO (fl. early nineteenth century)
1953–1954   Apuntamientos sobre agricultura y comercio del reyno de Guatemala. *Anales de la Sociedad de Geografía e Historia de Guatemala* 27: 87–109. Guatemala City.

LARREINAGA, MIGUEL (fl. 1771–1847)
1857   *Prontuario de las reales cédulas ... del antiguo reino de Guatemala desde ... 1600 hasta 1818.* Guatemala City.

LAUGHLIN, ROBERT M.
1969   "The Tzotzil," in *Handbook of Middle American Indians*. Edited by Robert Wauchope, 152–194. Austin, Texas: University of Texas Press.

Libro Rotulado
1534   *Libro rotulado: Cartas barias antiguas.* Contains letters of Pedro de Alvarado, Bishop Francisco Marroquín, Bishop Fray Bartolomé de Las Casas, as well as others, all dating ca. 1534. Archivo General del Gobierno de Guatemala A 1.2.5 [1534] 1576–2202. Guatemala City.

Libro Viejo
1934   *Libro viejo de la fundación de Guatemala y papeles relativos a D. Pedro de Alvarado.* Biblioteca Goathemala. Guatemala City: Sociedad de Geografía e Historia de Guatemala.

LIPSCHUTZ, ALEJANDRO
1967   *El problema racial en la conquista de América y el mestizaje* (second edition). Santiago, Chile.

LÓPEZ DE VELASCO, JUAN (fl. sixteenth century)
1894   *Geografía y descripción universal de las Indias.* Madrid.

LUNARDI, FEDERICO
1946   *La fundación de la ciudad de Gracias a Dios y de las primeras villas y ciudades de Honduras.* Tegucigalpa.

MARKMAN, S.D.
1963   *San Cristóbal de las Casas.* Seville: Escuela de Estudios Hispanoamericanos.
1966a   *The colonial architecture of Antigua Guatemala.* Philadelphia: American Philosophical Society.
1966b   "The non-Spanish labor force in the development of the colonial architecture of Guatemala," in *Actas y Memorias del 36° Congreso Internacional de Americanistas*, volume four, 189–194. Seville 1964.
1971   Pueblos de españoles y pueblos de indios en el reino de Guatemala. *Boletín del Centro de Investigaciones Históricas y Estéticas.* Universidad Central de Guatemala. Facultad de Arquitectura y Urbanismo. Caracas.
i.p.a.   "Pueblos de españoles and pueblos de indios," in *Verhandlungen des 38 Internationalen Amerikanistenkongresses, Stuttgart, 1968.* Munich.
i.p.b.   El paisaje urbano dominicano de pueblos de indios en Chiapas colonial. *Revista de Indias.* Madrid.

MONTGOMERY, GEORGE W.
1839   *Narrative of a journey to Guatemala in Central America in 1838.* New York.

MORENO NAVARRO, ISIDORO
1969   Un aspecto del mestizaje americano. El problema de terminología. *Revista Española de Antropología Americana* 4: 201–218.

MÖRNER, MAGNUS
1960   *El mestizaje en la historia de Iberoamérica.* Stockholm.
1964   "La política de segregación y el mestizaje en la audiencia de Guatemala."
1967   *Race mixture in the history of Latin America.* Boston: Little, Brown.

MÖRNER, MAGNUS, *editor*
1970 *Race and class in Latin America.* Institute for Latin American Studies Series. New York: Columbia University Press.

MORSE, RICHARD M.
1965 Recent research on Latin American urbanization: a selective survey with commentary. *Latin American Research Review* (1): 35–74.

PARDO, J. JOAQUIN
1944 *Efemérides para escribir la historia de ... Santiago de los caballeros del reino de Guatemala.* Guatemala City.

PARDO, J. JOAQUIN, PEDRO ZAMORA CASTELLANOS
1943 *Guía turística de las ruinas de la antigua Guatemala.* Guatemala City.

PÉREZ VALENZUELA, PEDRO
1960 Ciudad Vieja. *Universidad de San Carlos de Guatemala* 32–33.

PONCE, ALONSO (fl. ca. 1586)
1873 *Relación y verdadera de algunas cosas de las muchas que sucedieron al Padre Fray Alonso Ponce en las provincias de Nueva España,* two volumes. Madrid.

RECINOS, ADRIAN
1949 La ciudad de Guatemala, 1524–1773. *Antropología e Historia de Guatemala* 1 (1): 57–62. Instituto de Antropología e Historia de Guatemala. Guatemala City.
1952 *Pedro de Alvarado, conquistador de México y Guatemala.* Mexico City.

RICARD, ROBERT
1950 La plaza mayor en España y en América española. *Estudios Geográficos* 11: 321–327. Madrid.

ROSENAU, HELEN
1959 *Ideal city: its architectural evolution.* New York: Harper and Row.

ROSENBLATT, ANGEL
1954 *La población indígena y el mestizaje en América.* Buenos Aires.
1967 La población de América en 1492. Viejos y nuevos cálculos. *El Colegio de México.* Mexico City.

SALAS, ALBERTO M.
1960 *Crónica florida del mestizaje de las Indias. Siglo XVI.* Buenos Aires.

SAMAYOA GUEVARA, HÉCTOR HUMBERTO
1960 "La reorganización gremial guatemaltense en la segunda mitad del siglo XVIII. *Antropología e Historia de Guatemala* 12 (1): 63–106. Instituto de Antropología e Historia de Guatemala. Guatemala City.
1962 *Los gremios de artesanos en la ciudad de Guatemala, 1524–1821.* Guatemala City.
1966 El mestizo en Guatemala en el siglo XVI, a través de la legislación indiana. *Antropología e Historia de Guatemala* 18 (7).

STANISLAWSKI, DAN
1946 The origin and spread of the grid pattern town. *Geographical Review* 36: 105–120.

SZECSY, JANOS
1953a *Iximché.* Universidad de San Carlos de Guatemala, Facultad de Humanidades. Guatemala City.
1953b *Santiago de los caballeros de Guatemala en Almolonga. Investigaciones del año 1950.* Guatemala City.

TOZZER, ALFRED M.
1941   Landa's "Relación de las cosas de Yucatán," a translation. Papers of the Peabody Museum 18. Cambridge, Mass.: Harvard University Press.

TRENS, MANUEL
1957   Bosquejos históricos de San Cristóbal Las Casas. Mexico City.

VÁSQUEZ, FRANCISCO (fl. 1647–ca. 1714)
1944   [1837] Crónica de la provincia del santísimo nombre de Jesús de Guatemala de la orden de n. seráfico padre San Francisco en el reino de la Nueva España (second edition), four volumes. Biblioteca Goathemala. Guatemala City: Sociedad de Geografía e Historia de Guatemala.

VÁSQUEZ DE ESPINOZA, ANTONIO (d. 1630)
1943   La audiencia de Guatemala. Primera parte. Libro quinto del compendio y descripción de las Indias Occidentales, por A.V.E., año de 1629. Guatemala City.

VILLACORTA C., JOSÉ ANTONIO
1925–1926   Las cartas relaciones de don Pedro de Alvarado. Anales de la Sociedad de Geografía e Historia de Guatemala 2: 215ff. Guatemala City.

VOGT, EVON
1969   "Chiapas Highlands," in Handbook of Middle American Indians. Edited by Robert Wauchope, 133–151. Austin, Texas: University of Texas Press.

XIMÉNEZ, FRANCISCO (fl. 1666–ca. 1722)
1929–1931   Historia de la provincia de San Vicente de Chiapa y Guatemala de la Orden de Predicadores, three volumes. Biblioteca Goathemala. Guatemala City: Sociedad de Geografía e Historia de Guatemala.

ZAVALA, SILVIO
1971   Las instituciones jurdicas en la conquista de América. Mexico City.

ZUCKER, PAUL
1959   Town and square from the agora to the village green. Cambridge, Mass.: M.I.T. Press.

The Persistence of the Baroque in Peru and Mexico

GLADYS H. KELSEY

The baroque we are to discuss is not a matter of Salomonic columns and gold filigrees, but of the life-style which produced those columns, since art does not arise in a vacuum. In particulaı, attention will be focused on the transmission of the life-style from Spain to the Spanish possessions in the New World and its persistence there today.

It is the baroque life-style centering today largely around pageants and processions, that sends thousands, men and women, young and old, tramping the highways and byways to carry out some obligation undertaken by a community so many decades ago that today its object may not be remembered, but the precise ritual is never forgotten and must be unvarying, as witness what happened in Papantla, Vera Cruz State. This is the home of the Flying Pole Dance, an intricate and difficult ritual. Not long ago one of the dancers fell to his death. The other dancers agreed that the god was angry, because an attempt had been made to hurry the action by leaving out a few details in order to commercialize the spectacle. To the participants this is not a spectacle but a ritual, every step of which must be blessed – the poles are taken to the church for blessing before each repetition.

There are other rituals apparently equally meaningful where even the participants have forgotten what the meaning is, but they are unanimous in their belief that any deviation from the accustomed procedure would bring disaster. One such is the fiesta, *Los Tastoanes*, which takes place every July in Tonalá, a short drive from Guadalajara. The Indians are vociferous in their insistence that no little detail ever be omitted, though they have forgotten exactly what it may mean.

Qualities of energy and movement are characteristic of the baroque, which colors the soul of Spain throughout its history. The baroque was not just a light that flickered momentarily at a particular time in European culture — toward the end of the 16th century; it is a "constant" phenomenon, with specific qualities... Baroque characteristics are found in all Spanish art, except for the brief and barren academic periods. One of these characteristics is the ability to portray pathos and pain. Never has human anguish in the face of death or martyrdom been expressed so poignantly as in the Christs, Mater Dolorosas and martyrs painted or carved in Spanish works of art. We have already pointed to the persistence in Spain of another baroque signpost — a realism that seeks truth in all its crudeness, showing decrepitude and ugliness, taking delight in emphasizing abnormalities and shortcomings (Juan de Contreras 1966:11–12).

The strong realism of the Spanish baroque was modified in the New World by the fervent interpretation, mystical, calculated to please at once the old gods and the new, given by the Indians who not only altered the iconography of Christ on the Cross and other biblical scenes but actually employed a new material for making religious statues — new, that is, to the Christian Fathers, but harking back to the most ancient practices of indigenous religions. "America brought the maize, her own autochthonous plant, into the service of God. The use of a light and pliable mixture based on the pith of the corn had a deep significance..." (Pál Kelemen 1967).

The use of such a light-weight material made it possible to depict elaborate biblical scenes in the processions which wound up and down narrow, treacherous paths. For the most part the holy figures were removed from their customary niches in the parish churches for only a brief time while the procession was in progress. There is, however, one highly revered Virgin who began making miraculous journeys in the middle of the sixteenth century, and carries them on even more extensively today.

Our Lady of Zapopan is known as "the evangelizer" to the Indians who live in the town where her shrine is, because her first appearance among them was the occasion of their conversion to Christianity. In 1542, these Indians settled the town of Zapopan and the statue was placed in their chapel, where she constantly worked miracles. In 1734, the newly founded city of Guadalajara was stricken by a pestilence, and the first pilgrimage of Our Lady of Zapopan to the nearby city took place. As the Virgin was borne from one suburb to another the pestilence was controlled.

The Virgin is credited with the bloodless accomplishment of independence in the town of Tlaquepaque, a suburb of Guadalajara, when she was taken there on the morning of June 13, 1821. She is also credited with restoration of the water level in Lake Chapala which had diminished in the decade from 1946 to 1956 until Guadalajara was threatened with a serious water shortage.

In 1734, it was decreed that the Virgin should visit the parishes of Guadalajara from June 13 to October 4 of every year. The high point of the year is reached when she is returned to Zapopan. In October, 1971, more than 600,000 people of all classes and from diverse localities jammed the Avenidas Alcalda and Avila Camacho leading from the cathedral in Guadalajara to the basilica in Zapopan. They came from as far away as Baja California.

There are some 600 miraculous Virgins in Mexico, the most famous of which is Our Lady of Guadalupe, designated Patron of Mexico by the Pope in 1754. In 1910, when Hidalgo led his troops into battle in the War of Independence, it was behind the banner of this Virgin, and the cry was "Guadalupe!" It is said that the Aztec dances which the Indians performed in the first procession of the Virgin to her chapel were those which the Indians had been accustomed to dance on that spot from time immemorial in honor of the mother of the Aztec gods, Tonantzin.

The intermingling of heaven and earth in the minds of the aborigines has retained religious overtones for every economic act or act of government, from the blessing of the seed corn on the fiesta of Candelaria (February 5) through a multitude of annually recurring difficulties.

An incredible parallel existed between the Spanish peninsula and the two most developed areas of the New World. The configurations of mountains and plains which led to isolation were amazingly similar. Both in Mexico and in Peru an absolute dictatorship prevailed but, especially in Peru, it was evangelical and intended to be benevolent — not too different from the rule of the Catholic Kings if analyzed deeply.

The hegemony of Spain was at its height coincident with the initial settlements made in the New World. Spain's greatness began in the reign of Alfonso el Sabio (1252–1284) and had waned by 1588 when the Invincible Armada was defeated. Alfonso X — the wise, the sage, they still call him when they speak of him — best loved to be known as the "troubador of the Virgin Mary," since his *cantigas*, over a hundred poems to be sung, each recounted some miracle attributed to the Virgin. Of paramount importance to posterity was his *Siete Partidas* (the seven books) treating of canon law, public law, persons, obligations, property, procedure, and maritime law. While they were modelled after Roman law they were more a statement of moral and ethical values with a strong tincture of Thomist thought, and were essentially an admonishment as to how the world ought to be rather than a confrontation with the world as it was.

The common law of Queen Isabella was based chiefly on this codification. The *Partidas* were particularly emphasized in the New World where their persistence in legal thought was remarkable. Ricardo Palma attested to the *oidores* of the *Real Audiencia* [city officials] in Lima, Peru, as late as the year 1801, using the law of the *Partidas* in order to decide a case in which equity would best have been served by "strict judicial doctrine".

While Queen Isabella was rebuking the Admiral of the Ocean Sea for enslaving her vassals, King Ferdinand was being singled out for attention by Machiavelli, receiving a sort of King of the Year award. "We have in our own day Ferdinand, King of Aragon, the present King of Spain. He may almost be termed a new Prince, because from a weak King he has become for fame and glory the first King in Christendom" (Machiavelli 1950:81–82). The profoundness with which Machiavelli shocked the Church with his reasons of state doctrine was due to the fact that it completely undermined the position of the Church on matters of fundamental importance, such as the concept of the "just war," to only name one. Thus the caravels that went to the Indies took with them a deepseated contradiction, a salient characteristic of the baroque life-style, which at times led to an almost dream-like sense of unreality.

When the conquistadors walked the streets of Cuzco they found a city laid out after the Spanish plan — streets meeting at right angles and the important buildings grouped about a central square. To be sure, in Spain the cathedral dominated the area whereas in Peru it was the Temple of the Sun. In one place many saints were prayed to and in the other subsidiary deities. It is doubtful if the Indians understood the distinction. Inca Garcilaso de la Vega tells of an instance where, for him, the Christian and the pagan religions were celebrated side by side with mutual satisfaction.

The Indian tunes having a kind of sweet air with them, the musick-Master of the Cathedral Church at Cuzco, in the year 1551 or 1552, composed an anthem and set it to one of their tunes, which he played on the organ, upon the Festival of the most Holy Sacrament, at which solemnity he introduced eight mongrel boys of mixed blood between Spanish and Indian... singing the songs which he had set according to the true air of the Inca musick... to the great satisfaction of the Spaniards and contentment of the Indians who were overjoyed to see the Spaniards so far to honor them as to practice dances and the musick when they celebrated the festival of their Lord God, whom they called Pachacmac... (Rycaut 1699: vol. 5, p. 124).

Between the Inca and Spanish religious calendars there was a deceiving similarity — the Inca fiestas and the Spanish feast days needed no forcing to merge quite naturally. The great festival of the Inca year, *Kapaj Raymi*, began with Christmas, December 25, and ended with Epiphany, January 6. The Corpus Christi fiesta of the Spanish Church took place some time between the end of May and the middle of June, and at precisely the same time that the Incas observed *Inti Raymi*, the annual harvest thanksgiving. To this day the procession in Cuzco is said to follow the same path and practices followed when Tawantinsuyu was the center of the Inca world (Valcárcel 1946:471–476).

Not only did the times of the religious observances coincide, but in some instances the prescribed ritual itself. Prescott notes that the Christian missionaries were not oblivious to the coincidence of some phases of the Inca rites with Christian observance — the distribution of bread and wine at the festival of *Raymi* or the practice of confession and penance. "The good Fathers were fond of tracing such coincidences which they considered as the contrivance of Satan, who thus endeavored to delude his victims by counterfeiting the blessed rites of Christianity..." (Prescott 1855:I;108).

The Fathers complained of a "most irregular form" used by the Indians. This is an excellent example of divergence in meaning between similar appearing rituals, as explained by an anthropologist:

Whereas the other South American Indians regarded disease as a natural catastrophe personified in the nature spirit, the Inca attributed it to disturbances in the socio-religious structure. The remedy for disease caused by sin was confession (Ackerknecht 1949: vol. 5, p. 634).

In March 1568 the first Jesuits arrived in Peru, thereafter advancing upon the Indians of Hispanic America, claiming many conversions and baptizing *en masse*. Eventually it became apparent that with little or no preparation the Indians carried their paganism into the Christian rituals.

A year and a half later the fifth Viceroy of Peru, Francisco de Toledo, from whose tenure in office the effective colonial government of Peru may properly be dated, arrived in Lima. By that time a cultural *mestizaje* was well advanced under the direction of the Jesuits — a mixture of Spanish and Indian characteristics.

Emilio Harth-Terré said that for the Jesuits the erection of sumptuous edifices to the glory of God was not an end but rather a means of achieving the end. Indian craftsmen, lacking a written language, were to be educated while working joyously and freely on the designs of the Jesuits. The result was a baroque in a new environment characterized by "Americanismo" which, developing through the seventeenth century, produced in the eighteenth century a true Peruvian baroque.[1] José García Bryce also finds in the development of colonial architecture in Peru the formation of a cultural *mestizaje*, pointing to Cuzco where the Dominican convent was built on the ruins of the Temple of the Sun as the symbol of this intermingling.

Was there a real intermingling? Or did the extensive resettlement ordered by Toledo and the *reducciones* [Indian settlements] established by the Jesuits, those indefatigable organizers of the pomp and circumstances of the Church, place the Indians in mental isolation? With pageant and pretense deep inner convictions that diverged sharply were covered by a thin outer veneer of similitudes.

The seventeenth century, according to Mariano Picón-Salas, was the period in which the baroque became a way of life in Peru, just as scholasticism had been. In fact it might be described as a repressed scholasticism attendant on the establishment of the Inquisition in Lima in 1570 and the subsequent activities of the Counter Reformation which made dissembling seem the wisest course and which plunged the white elite of Peru into two centuries of elaborate trifling. Picón-Salas defines the baroque as a "propensity to pair opposites or to superimpose one upon the other

[1]   Seldom has any great master been able to give to the world a complete vindication of his theory, but Harth-Terré has done this on the grounds of the Franciscan Academy on Carmelite drive in Potomac, Maryland. There stands the chapel of Our Lady of Guadalupe. The original design of chapel and altars is by Harth-Terré. Father Antonine Tibesar, O. F. M. directed the construction of the chapel, which was completed in 1961. Designer and director are close friends and their cooperation, along with that of the Indian artists, has produced something without counterpart in the U.S.A. — a faithfully reproduced mission chapel, of which even the wood came from Peru. There are three altars, the largest and central one being high baroque. Santa Rosa de Lima and Toribio, the second Archbishop of Peru, are here, as well as an overwhelmingly beautiful Our Lady of Guadalupe before whom there are always fresh flowers. Below Our Lady is a Christ on the Cross done by a full-blooded Indian circa 1647. Our Lady is flanked to the right by St. Francis Solena, who came from Europe to America, and to her left by St. Felipe de Jesús of Mexico who went from America to Japan. The wealth and beauty of the gold in the altar is enhanced by the twisted columns — Salomonic columns — the very essence of high baroque. To the right of the main altar, as one enters the chapel, is an eighteenth-century altar at the top of which is St. Francis d'Assisi, a copy of the famous statue by Pedro de Mena in the Cathedral of Toledo, Spain. Below him, St. Anthony of Padua is a copy of an equally famous statue in Rio de Janeiro, where he ranks as a general in the armies of Brazil. There is a neoclassical tendency in the altar itself, but large gold discs are superimposed on the wood. Most significant is the realism of the faces. In the altar to the left, St. Michael has the highest niche, and then Santiago de Campostela, the Patron Saint of Spain and of Spaniards in the New World. Below Santiago is a remarkable Cristo Ecce Homo designed especially for the place it occupies by Valentin and Domingo Rael Quinto, Lima 1963. It is the most completely baroque representation in the chapel, with a face distorted in agony. This is a copy of a seventeenth-century altar, inscribed, as are the other two, "Zaragosa *opus me fecit*, Lima, Perú, 1960."

[which] acquired, in some mysterious manner, the designation 'baroque'."
Again he says, "The Renaissance was a dialogue, a being together,
whereas the Spanish baroque was mostly a soliloquy" (Picón-Salas 1962:
93–94).[2]

At a time when all the rest of the Western world was turning to ration-
alism and technical pursuits, Spain and her colonies in the New World
became more deeply involved in the haunting unreality they had known
for so long, obsessed with the idea of death's universal domain. This is
a thought which runs through all baroque expression. Suárez, in his
argument for popular sovereignty, makes the statement that all men are
equal, but we must be wary of such a statement. It was meant strictly in
the sense of *memento mori*. All men are equal in being mortal.

Today in Mexico and Peru a plastic skull is an acceptable gift, displayed
for sale in gift shops. Today in Peru and Mexico there is no month of
the year lacking a variety of fiestas.[3]

The *mestizo* (of mixed Spanish and Indian blood) has been an example
of contradictions from earliest colonial times.

"Pray, be seated, *gentlemen*," a South American President is said to have requested the Minister of a neighbouring republic known for its predominantly
mestizo population. "But, I am alone, Mr. President." "Oh," smiled the President "you people of your country, you are always each at least two...." The
mestizo is always at least two: a White and an Indian (de Madariaga 1948:103).

The two men living together under the skin of the *mestizo* produce
almost incredible contradictions. When a Spaniard speaks to him it is the
Indian who answers, but let the Indian speak to him and he will answer
with all the Castilian disdain of the Spanish population. He is the
perfect protaganist of revolutions because in contrast to the Spaniard's
arrogant contentment and the passive indifference of the Indian, the
mestizo is a whole civil war all by himself.

Te Deums and *Pater Nosters* mark the rhythm played on llamabone
flutes, trumpets, drums and rattles. Anthropology, theology, and historical
science must join hands in an unprecedented manner if we are to understand one of the richest and most neglected phenomena of modern times.

---

[2] This soliloquy is embodied in Calderon's great baroque drama, *La Vida Es Sueño*,
whose hero, Segismundo, in his prison cell, contemplates the opposition of reality and
illusion until he is unable to distinguish one from the other.
[3] Lack of space compels us to neglect Peru where *El Señor de los Milagros*, dating
back to 1671, annually passes the *Plaza de Armas* (main square), where in 1971 the
President of Peru and his ministers waited on a balcony and white doves were released
from the roof of the palace. The Fiesta of Santa Rosa de Lima is peculiarly a product
of the country. See also Matos Mar (1950) for a different type.

REFERENCES

ACKERKNECHT, ERWIN H.
1949 "Medical practices of the Inca and earlier Central Andean Civilizations," in *Handbook of South American Indians*, volume five. Edited by Julian H. Steward, 633–643. Washington: Government Printing Office.

CALDERON DE LA BARCA, PEDRO
1955 *La Vida Es Sueño*. Santiago de Chile: Biblioteca Zig-Zag.

DE MADARIAGA, SALVADOR
1948 *The fall of the Spanish American empire*. New York: Macmillan.

GARCÍA BRYCE, JOSÉ
1965 Arquitectura religiosa colonial en el Perú. *Mercurio Peruano* XLIX No. 543:5–10.

JUAN DE CONTRERAS, MARQUIS OF LOVOZA
1966 "Introduction to the art of Spain," in *Spain: A history of art* by Bradley Smith, 11–12. New York: Simon and Schuster.

KELEMEN, PÁL
1967 *Baroque and rococo in Latin America*, two volumes. New York: Dover Publications.

MACHIAVELLI, NICCOLO
1950 *The Prince; Discourses*, one volume. New York: Modern Library.

MATOS MAR, JOSÉ
1950 La fiesta de la herranza en Tupe. *Mar del Sur* XII:39–53.

MILNE, JEAN
1965 *Fiesta time in Latin America*. Los Angeles: Ward Ritchie.

PICÓN-SALAS, MARIANO
1962 *A cultural history of Spanish America*. Translated by Irving A. Leonard. Berkeley: University of California Press.

PRESCOTT, WILLIAM H.
1855 *History of the conquest of Peru*. Boston: Phillips, Samson and Company.

RYCAUT, SIR PAUL
1699 *"Los commentarios reales de los Incas del Inca Garcilaso de la Vega"* rendered into English. London: Miles Flesher.

VALCÁRCEL, LUIS
1946 "The Andean calendar," in *Handbook of South American Indians*, volume two. Edited by Julian H. Steward, 471–476. Washington: Government Printing office.

Ecuador: The Indigenous Tribute System as a Mechanism of Exploitation During the Colonial Period and the First Years of Independence

NICANOR JÁCOME and INÉS LLUMIQUINGA

Our aim in the present study is to analyze the tribute system in Ecuador from its first appearance until the time of its legal abolition. Mere description, however, is not our objective; we intend to determine the relationship between the tribute-paying aspect of the indigenous population and the social system of the colonial period and the first years of the Republic.

By social system we mean the kind of union that exists between the economic, juridical, and political structures of a given territory. The first part of this study is devoted to clarifying this relationship in order to pinpoint the problems of the tribute system.

In the second part we examine the origin, development, objectives, evolution, and structural implications of the institution of tribute.

On the methodological level we have utilized the indigenous tribute system as the central point around which to reconstruct the successive stages during colonial domination and the first third of the independent period. Our intention is to arrive at the most objective exposition possible in order to shed light on the true character of the social system of Ecuador.

Finally we describe the process by which the indigenous tribute system gradually disappeared on the legal level. This did not mean, however, that the Ecuadorian Indian was free of the domination of white and *mestizo* groups. The oppression of centuries has provided the impulse for many social changes and will be crucial for the global transformation of our societies.

THE COLONIAL SOCIAL SYSTEM

Before undertaking the actual subject matter of this study, we must outline the theoretical concept which is central to its development. Without doing so, we would run the risk of falling into mere historiographical description, which is more or less informative and interesting, but which would not furnish the causal explanation of the colonial reality in which the indigenous tribute system assumes its singular importance.

In analyzing the tribute system, one must not approach it as an isolated segment of society. A detailed knowledge calls for viewing its social relationships within the totality of colonial life, as well as apprehending its significance in the evolution of what is now Ecuador.

Theoretically we must dissect the composition of the social system, considering its structure and the forces whose dynamic imbrication results in a given social formation. For the social totality is in effect a complex of structures: economic, juridico-political, and theological, each possessing specific functions in accordance with a historical stage within the abstract concept of production modes. Hence it is important to perceive the domain of each of these structures in order to pinpoint their interrelationships and the dominion of one over another. In this respect, "it is a matter in the first place of situating social relations in terms of the structures of a production mode and a social system" (Poulantzas 1969:70).

We must elaborate on this for a better understanding of subsequent developments. The three levels noted above (economic, juridico-political, and ideological) are categories that enable us to come to grips with contemporary and colonial society.

The ECONOMIC STRUCTURE is characterized by material relationships of production that divide men into those who possess the means of production and those who are subjugated by them. In order to exercise control, society must be organized and cohesive; it is the product of a whole complex of ideas and attitudes proper to an epoch and issuing from the nature of material relations. This social force, complementary to the economic level, is called the IDEOLOGICAL STRUCTURE. Finally, the apparatus of the State coordinates and centralizes the dynamics of these two domains and is either the cohesive force of the social system or the instrument for exercising control by one group over another. We call these functions the JURIDICO-POLITICAL structure.

It must be borne in mind that the State provides the focus for all activities of the ruling class (not necessarily in a mechanical way); the State is the integrating force of an entire social system and as such exercises a threefold function: economic, ideological, and political.

The economic function of the State consists of all that which is directed toward modernizing capitalist production systems with the goal of preserving the equilibrium of the system; it must eliminate all that is dysfunctional to the equilibrium even if a sector of the ruling class is adversely affected in the process. In other words, the State must assure the rationalization of the system, which never proceeds from economic needs but rather from the need to preserve the State.

The ideological function derives from the fact that the ideology which permeates State activity corresponds, in general, to the ideology of the ruling class; as a result, its ideology tends to benefit its own economic and political interests in such a way as to mask its true intentions. In fact, a specific characteristic of the ruling bourgeois ideology is the specific disguise of class exploitation, inasmuch as every trace of class rule is systematically absent from its language. Of course, given its nature, no ideology can present itself as that of a ruling class. Nonetheless, in the case of precapitalist ideologies the functioning of classes is always present in principle, being justified as "natural" or "sacred" (Poulantzas 1969: 275). On the other hand, the State undertakes to impart education, a function closely allied with the values and standards of the ruling class, i.e. it transmits the ideology of the system and all its values.

The political function of the State emerges on two levels, that of the systematization of class ideology and that of the exercise of physical coercion over actors in society (whether individual or collective). The role of the State is to create the organic infrastructure necessary to the exercise of political goals, i.e. to maintain class rule.

Thus, on principle, the State "represents all," but it disguises the juridico-political network which directly benefits certain dominant groups of society. It activates all its mechanisms of repression whenever members, escaping ideological control, adopt a critical attitude (thus endangering the social equilibrium, i.e. the status quo established by the dynamics of the material relationships of production in a given social system). "Order" is monopolized and maintained by the group in economic control, which directly or indirectly finds it necessary to direct and control the apparatus of the State to suit its own needs and political interests.

When we analyze the Latin American colonial reality in these terms and the Ecuadorian reality in this context, we perceive something totally different from and opposed to the analytic models produced by anthropological and sociological methodologies. These disciplines subscribe to the doctrine of social empiricism and, in an ideological way, do not describe the social whole as a basis of their interpretation; they fragment reality, attaining a high standard of minute description but no causal explanation of phenomena. Their studies remain on the surface of the facts and achieve merely a fragmented perspective, not necessarily mistaken, but incomplete. This methodological orientation reflects their subjection to cultural and ideological stereotypes, which do not benefit our exploited society; on the contrary, they reinforce the structural dependence of the people.

Working with an empirical methodology one would treat indigenous tribute directly, producing at the most a good description but without transcending it or relating it to other colonial and national realities. To avoid these pitfalls, we have chosen to approach our analysis on the level of the worldwide social form prevailing when tribute played an important part.

For the purposes of this study we have taken as the compass of the social structure the colonial territories of Spain and their cities, and within them, as the coordinating factor, the different modes of production which existed in this vast region. The reality of the tribute system is interpreted within the framework of this geographical whole, taking into account the socioeconomic processes which were coming to a head at that time in the rest of Europe, especially in England, France, and the Low Countries. With such a framework, both methodologically and theoretically, we can approach an analysis of the matter.

Marx explains the phenomenon of the accumulation of capital in the following terms:

To what result does primary accumulation of capital tend, that is, in its historical genesis? When it is not restricted to converting the slave and the serf of the glebe into a wage earner — thus determining a mere change of form — primary accumulation signifies quite simply the expropriation of the direct producer, or, what amounts to the same thing, the destruction of private property based on labor (1971:647).

At the time of the Spanish Conquest, the metropolis was engaged in a genuine transition from one mode of production to another, from feudalism to capitalism, through an intermediate stage of mercantilism. On one hand, we have the concentration of power in the hands of an absolute monarchy, which was a result of the Reconquest of Spain. On the other, "the Spanish peoples tended to a diversification of production accompanied by a rapid development of craftsmanship and of certain manufactures" (Barbosa 1971:28).

The metropolis at the end of the fifteenth century, besides constant agricultural expansion based on the systematic exploitation of this resource, showed a considerable development of the basis and spirit of capitalism. For example "Seville possessed 16,000 looms occupying 70,000 workers. Toledo produced 430,000 pounds of silk, which gave employment to 34,484 persons. Segovia possessed important manufactures of silk and textiles ..." (Sombart 1966:132, cited in Barbosa 1971).

In general there seems to have been a breakdown in feudal production, which in its turn produced new conditions of social, political, and intellectual life and which must have imposed a specific character on Spanish rule in the colonies.[1]

Nevertheless, the discovery of the West Indies prevented the metropolis from completing a process which would have allowed, "at a certain stage of development, the forces of material production to enter into conflict with existing production relationships or with that which is nothing other than their juridical expression" (Marx 1971:9).

The qualitative passage to capitalism would have meant a higher level of development of the productive forces, as well as that religion — the ideological skeleton of the system — would have ceased to provide one of the systematizing elements guaranteeing the perpetuation of existing production relationships.

Actually, the tendency was to pass to capitalism. This is more evident when we consider that the very discovery of Latin America was the result of the commercial interests of the Catalan bourgeoisie which, not being able to carry on trade with the Far East because of Muslim domination of the Mediterranean, sought a new route to the East Indies.

This process, which appeared to be largely a logical sequence in Spanish development, was held up by the discovery of America. In the view of certain scholars, this had the virtue of refeudalizing Spain, of arresting the development of the commercial bourgeoisie under whose auspices the discovery had been made, and of reinforcing archaic forms which were already crumbling but which now took on new life, as did the feudal forms of production radiating from Castille (Ramos 1969).

Consequently it is undeniable that the discovery of America took place when, historically speaking, a primary accumulation of capital based on

---

[1]   Spain's entrance into the modern era with the Catholic kings has been well demonstrated by Jorge Abelardo Ramos, who shows that in the face of the displeasure of the military nobility the kings favored a policy of protection for manufacturing industry in 1484. They granted facilities to Italian workers as well as to Flemish ones, exempting them from taxes for ten years so that they could become established in Spain and apply their mechanical arts. In the same spirit traditional industries were revived: the arms industry in Toledo, the making of paper and silk in Jaén, leather in Córdoba. Similarly, the importation of cloth to Murcia and of Neapolitan silk thread to Granada was prohibited for two years. In Barcelona industries recovered their energy; in Saragossa 16,000 looms were at work; and in Ocaña there was soap making and the celebrated glove industry. Politically, in order to moderate the growing power of the bourgeoisie and center it on the State, King Ferdinand undermined the autonomy acquired by the cities (Ramos 1969:16–19).

commerce was in progress, and when, in terms of economic theory, the basis was being laid for a mercantilism rooted in the accumulation of precious metals.[2] Hence "in her American possessions Spain built up a politico-economic complex centered on the mining and export of precious metals and producing up to the end of the eighteenth century from 80 to 85 percent of the world's output of silver" (Velasco 1972: 23).

Taking ourselves back to primary accumulation of capital, we find ourselves in a period in which the acquisition of precious metals by Spain aided the industrial development of other countries such as England and France through trade. In the case of England a number of changes followed one another, including a very considerable increase in population and changes from feudalism affecting the tenure of land and the forms of cultivation. During the seventeenth century, the most important mercantilist group achieved a type of parliamentary government which made it possible to carry out policies adapted to the concentration of capital and productive investment (cf. Stanley and Stein 1971:8–9).

By contrast, Spain showed herself incapable of transferring her wealth to manufacturing industries and very rapidly became a country economically dependent on other countries where capitalism had a considerable growth. As these countries had no colonies from which to extract the precious metals, they acquired the metals by the sale of manufactures to the country that possessed them.

Economically Spain played the role of mere intermediary in the development of European capitalism. As she could not provide herself and her colonies with manufactured products, she allowed a series of commercial networks to be formed extending from the most developed centers to the colonies. Under these circumstances, her internal structural weakness caused those commercial channels to become the best avenue

---

[2]   As to this we are told by von Humboldt that in the course of three centuries 5,445,000,000 silver *pesos fuertes* found their way to Spain, apart from what remained legally or illegally in private hands or was smuggled directly to the Philippines or to the East (Ramos 1969: 20–25).

Furthermore José de Ceitia Linage, in his *De las ordenanzas de comercio 1672*, confronting the trade that foreigners were carrying on with the Spanish colonies, says: "This kind of trade with the Indies, sending or transporting great cargoes for wholesale, or exchanging them for the fruits of those provinces ... does not degrade the nobility, neither, as he says, is he opposed to it, for it is in such a style that not only true gentlemen, but titled noblemen of Castille as well load ships for the Indies; what we should regret is our own carelessness, for not having known how to favor, encourage, esteem, and reward merchants, so that most of the trade is now in the hands of foreigners who have become masters of it, enriching and ennobling themselves by means of the very situation we have failed to take advantage of" (quoted in Stanley and Stein 1971: 47).

of escape for surplus from the colonies. In this way Spain as much as the colonies became the market for the manufactures of England, the Low Countries, and other dynamic European centers, where the development of production was in an advanced state thanks to internal structural reforms.[3] So real was this role of intermediary that it was said that Spain was merely the gullet through which passed the cargoes of gold, silver, and emeralds issuing from her colonies, and that these other European countries were the stomach where these riches ended up.

Trade with the Spanish colonies on the part of nonpeninsular agents began as soon as the continent was discovered. Charles V had to compensate the German bankers and traders for the innumerable bonds they accepted from him in return for enormous loans to meet the expenses of his many wars and the administration of his great empire on which "the sun never set." Such bonds issued to the merchants of the period were amply rewarded by permits for the working of mines, by the introduction of commodities into the Spanish colonies along with the slave trade, and by a number of official posts which were soon to open the doors to other traders, not necessarily German.

Thus in the Assemblies of Santiago and Corunna in 1520, just before the return of the King from the North, the deputies petitioned that in no circumstance should the House of Trade be transferred from Seville, nor any but natives of Castille serve as its officials. Charles V answered that he had made no changes in this sense, nor had any intention of doing so, a promise which he kept; but not having promised to respect the mercantilist monopoly enjoyed by the Castillians, in 1526 he dictated the edict alluded to by Oviedo, applicable to all subjects within the domains of the Hapsburgs.

Two transactions concluded before that year illustrated the new policy that the new government was to follow. Jacob Fugger got permission in 1522 for German ships to participate in the projected spice trade with the Moluccas Islands by way of the Magellan Strait; in 1525 the Welsers of Hapsburg were put on an equal footing with Spanish traders in America and immediately set up *factorías* [trading houses] in Seville and Santo Domingo, thus initiating an intense program of colonial activity. Three years later in the spring of 1528 and in association with another German house, the Ehnger of Constance concluded a whole series of pacts with the Emperor: in January, to transport fifty miners to instruct the Spanish colonists, in February to provide the West Indies with 4,000 slaves over a period of four years (Haring 1939: 124–125).

To this must be added the great advantages these traders obtained by

---

[3] Other students of situations somewhat similar to contemporary Ecuador have also opted for an explication of different modes of production which are coexistent and sustained by the capitalist mode of production. Rodrigo Montoya has made a study of Peruvian conditions in which he claims "to offer certain facts that demonstrate the predominance of capitalism in Peru and its ARTICULATION with noncapitalist modes of production which exist in the country" (1970: 12).

depositing their merchandise in the warehouses of the House of Trade: they were thus assured of ports for the loading and unloading of their goods, a supreme privilege in that age. Later when Spain could not provide its overseas territories with manufactures, other more developed European countries joined in the Latin American trade; this activity was constantly on the increase because of Spanish inability to adapt internal resources to industrialization. Thus in 1805 the value of English exports to Latin America amounted to 7,771,418 pounds sterling, and in 1809 this rose to 18,014,219 pounds sterling. This represented a fabulous market for England, greater than that offered by the United States and India (Ramos 1969: 114–115).

The great free bazaars organized periodically in some American plazas offered many means of carrying on trade, as did the Spanish trading companies which offered to lend their names to the export of English and French products (the latter on a smaller scale). Another great channel of commerce was smuggling, which by the beginning of the eighteenth century had attained such importance that participation in it was considered by merchants to be like "winning first prize in a large lottery" (Ramos 1969: 115).

When Marx speaks of the primary accumulation of capital, he is referring to the process of transition from the feudal to the capitalist modes of production. The latter gains its foothold by pauperizing the serf and by concentrating the means of production in the hands of a few while depriving the majority. If this is the phenomenon as it occurred in Europe, Spain and her colonies were for the most part favorable to it; the rise of world capitalism demanded a type of colonization and capital accumulation that would permit a better exploitation of resources. Nevertheless, if we look back on history we dimly perceive that capitalism was the mode of production guiding economic relations. This phenomenon is obscured by the flourishing of a series of events of an economic character which are not always identified with capitalism and which appear to be in opposition to it because they are coexistent modes of production which are coordinated by the capitalist mode.

This is self-explanatory if we view Spain and its colonies as a single unit in the context of the appearance of capitalism; also, it corresponds to the structural necessities of capitalism. We have formulated a tentative working hypothesis in this sense, namely that the dominant imperial mode of production was capitalism, even though it may have coexisted with other modes of production, such as slavery, "tribute despotism" (Semo 1972: 449), feudalism, a highly archaic tribal system, and a colonial mode. All these modes were articulated by a capitalist dynamics, which as it progressed tended to consolidate itself while causing the other modes to disappear. Development itself required a *sui generis* type of rule like that of the colonial period, based neither on slavery nor feudalism in the traditional sense, but rather on a different reality whose essential characteristic was the investing of many peculiar economic forms with the common denominator of capitalism.

This point is essential if we are to understand the whole of colonial development and from it the development of Ecuador up to our own time. The hypothesis we have formulated enables us to start from the total global picture in which the phenomena are explicable, rather than inversely, i.e. from the unit of production to the detection of the mode of production. The hypothesis has a meaning for the articulated whole, not for a small area of colonial territory which almost always distorts conclusions, since this theoretic problem must be solved in terms of the total picture.

Our hypothesis is not new or original; some investigators have suggested it as the basis of further research. Thus it has been affirmed:

Confronted with the parameter of the pure capitalist mode of production, the Latin American economy presents some peculiarities which sometimes are taken for inadequacies and others, which are not always distinguishable from the first, for deformations. Hence it is not accidental that the notion of "precapitalism" keeps cropping up in studies of Latin America. What can be said is that, even when we are dealing with an inadequate development of capitalist relationships, this notion is being applied to aspects of a reality which by reason of its global structure and functioning could never have developed in the same form as the so-called advanced capitalist economies. This is because what we have here is not so much a precapitalism as a *sui generis* capitalism, which only makes sense when we see it in the perspective of the whole (Marini 1972: 2–3).

Although the above refers specifically to the period between independence and the phenomenon of joining the world market, it is a fact that the colonial period was characterized by the organization of a series of economic, administrative, and ideological institutions, the nature of which corresponded to the necessities of accumulation and expansion of markets for a capitalism in the process of formation.

Indigenous tribute, founded on the right of conquest, was nothing more than forcing the indigenous population to pay a certain amount for each individual between the ages of eighteen and fifty. This economic mechanism was simply a way of extracting the aboriginal surplus, for in addition to utilizing the indigenous labor force, it plundered the Indians by obligating the community to an overexertion in order to achieve the amount of tribute due from its members. The money thus collected went directly to the metropolis, sometimes to the hands of the *encomenderos*, sometimes to feed the ever-hungry coffers of the Crown.

Money accumulated in this way becomes a significant contribution to primary capital accumulation, and thus signified the expansion and development of capitalism. If we take this as our focal point, the tribute system and other economic institutions which functioned in the various colonial territories of Spain take on a different character, that of production relationships of a peculiar nature, not explicable in themselves, but eminently explicable as the outcrop of capitalism.

These forms, which are very obvious, may appear to belong to slavery, to despotism, to feudalism, etc., if we look at them individually; they do not have the same meaning when considered in relation to the global totality of a social system, as outlined above. It must be admitted that they are only the concrete manifestations required by the system, by the development of productive forces as determined by the type of exploitation pursued in the colonial territories. In view of this, we do not endeavor to explain theoretically each one of the productive units, but rather all within the global tendency of the system.

We must point out further, in concluding these preliminaries, that there is no intention of simplistically affirming that the economic activities of our colony were either capitalist or feudal. Rather they corresponded to a specifically colonial mode with the characteristic of not being something independent, but coordinated by the capitalist form of production. In other words, the very existence of an organization of archaic economic forms has a modern *raison d'être* when seen in relation to the development of capitalism.

This leads to the conclusion that for the purposes of theoretical analysis the legal boundaries of the *audiencias* and the viceroyalties were inappropriate. Research within these limits could only lead to a view of each productive unit as separate, ignoring the Conquest and its repercussions. The energetic development of productive forces taking place in hegemonic circles would be unperceived, as would the reality of the conquered peoples, and the symbiosis between the mode of production of the conquerors and that of the conquered (a question which has not yet been fully defined or analyzed and which must be the subject of further study in depth). All of this presents us with a colonial mode of production which affords a coherent explanation within the development of world capitalism.

THE FUNCTIONING OF THE INDIGENOUS TRIBUTE SYSTEM

The Concept of Tribute

Tribute meant the legal imposition of an obligation, on every indigenous inhabitant between eighteen and fifty, to pay a given amount in money or goods as tribute and to recognize through this formality the vassalage he owed to the King of Spain. Vassalage was acquired by right of armed conquest and by right of the grant made by the supreme pontiff of these territories to the King of Spain.

Theoretically speaking, tribute constituted one of the mechanisms for extracting surplus value from the indigenous population. It was not enough to employ the Indians as servants or day laborers on the *haciendas*; all possibilities of accumulating capital had to be drained off, and to this end a certain rate of tribute was imposed as an efficient means of getting money from the peoples of the colonies.

Previously, with the Inca conquest, a basic economic structure had come into being which respected land and its ownership, the only modification being a more rational organization of production. The Inca utilized the labor force of the different conquered tribes for the construction of public works which greatly contributed to the productivity of the land as well as to the unification of an empire in the process of expansion and rendered accessible by numerous roads. Among the conditions imposed on the conquered peoples was the tribute which had to be given without fail to the Inca as a demonstration of submission and vassalage, and which was duly collected by the administrative authorities through the chief.

The Spaniards availed themselves, up to a point, of the administrative structure of the Incas; their modification consisted in the removal of the dominant elite from the apex of the power pyramid and the rearrangement of the system for their own benefit, especially through the *mita* [indigenous forced labor] and tribute, institutions existing before the arrival of the Spaniards which they oriented toward their own ends.

The institution of tribute meant that the indigenous community, or *ayllu*, acquired value as a sustaining force in an economy where tribute was possible because work was communal. Already in the time of the Incas the mode of organization was governed by the *ayllu*, which had become a community linked by ties of blood with a fixed form of communal property divided for the purposes of usufruct (Moreano 1972). The surplus product resulting from sedentary agriculture "took the form of tribute which finally came into the hands of the State and its representatives" (Semo 1972: 450).

The indigenous community based on common property in land underwent a complete transformation, not so much with regard to the communal
form, but rather to the distribution of the agricultural surplus. Land and
its products were organized on three levels:

THE INTIPACCHA   The product of the *Intipaccha* was reserved for the
outlay on worship and on a whole group dedicated to the rites, and to
the intellectual sector, the *Amautas,* who were charged with the ideological
process of the system. Work on this land was communal and usufruct
on the part of the personages mentioned above took the same form.

THE INCAPACCHA   Production of the *Incapaccha* provided for the
maintenance of the Inca's family and of the royal court, and also defrayed
the expenses of the army and the administration, especially that of the
Curacas [local chiefs appointed by the Incas as rulers of conquered
peoples]. Here work was also carried out collectively.

THE MAMAPACCHA   This was the common land, usufruct being for the
members of the community. Nevertheless in this category work was not
communal but was done by families. The parcel assigned to a family was
called a *tupu,* and it was to this that the members of the family applied
their labors.

As this last type will be an important element in the explanation of
indigenous tribute, let us pause here to analyze the *tupu* and its peculiarities.
The extent of the *tupu* varied. The Incas, who were expert agriculturalists,
fixed a portion of land in accordance with "the conditions of the soil and
the ecological conditions of the region; it was larger on high ground and
smaller in valleys, even smaller in warm regions" (Reyeros 1972: 832).

Besides these conditions, the size of the *tupu* depended on the number
of members in a family. The birth of another child meant adding another
tupu to the family land. Those pieces of ground for family labor over and
above what had to be done on the common lands of *Intipaccha* and
Mamapaccha were not subject to trade. They could not be increased as the
result of personal industry, nor could they be transferred by heredity. The
only possibility was usufruct; property rights extended solely to the fruits
obtained by "the labor and the capital of the land" (Reyeros 1972: 832).
In this way subjects had a material basis for their subsistence and in
exchange for this grant, the Incas and nobility obtained the service of the
various peoples.

The service that the Inca obtained from his vassals may be summed up
under the following divisions: the *yanaconas,* a "slave labor force"
(Moreano 1972), who worked in the mines, construction of imperial

hostelries, etc.; and in agriculture, (2) the *llactarunacuna*, who cultivated the royal portions and (3) the *llactacomayo*, who organized the work teams, stored the seed, and looked after the crops until the time of their transport to the royal storehouses of the districts and to the roadside lodgings. These buildings, besides serving as inns, also stored provisions for the Inca on his journeys and those of his army (Reyeros 1972:834), as well as for the royal delegates (*Tucuricu*) when they made one of their frequent visits to their various territories. Once they had completed the cultivation reserved for religion and for the Incas the families returned to their *tupus*.

This structure was utilized by the Spaniards. Lands previously dedicated to the service of religion and the Incas became the private property of the Spaniards; to the native community and *ayllu* were assigned lands in accordance with the number of families, though clearly not in accordance with the criteria used by the Incas for the distribution of the family *tupu*. Land was simply left for the community; its internal division according to families was not considered to be the business of the Spanish State but rather that of the respective chiefs.

In this way the family *ayllu* had access to the land, and when it had members between eighteen and fifty they had to pay the tribute either to the King or to the *encomendero*. There would be two possibilities: payment in kind from the fruits of the family allotment, or, if there was a *mitayo* [Indian in charge of the *mita*], payment to the person to whom this office had been assigned and who, according to the ordinances, received an average salary of fifteen pesos a year, from which seven to nine were deducted for the tribute. In both cases the economy of the community pulled its weight, quite easily in the first case; but in the second, although the member of the *ayllu* theoretically earned a salary, it scarcely sufficed for the payment of the tribute, and the native community had to help to support the *mitayo*.

The absence of a community economy would have rendered the imposition of tribute impossible. Its functioning is explicable only through the existence of communal economic activity. The community acquires contemporary meaning and importance when we see the problem of tribute in this light.

Moreover the adaptation of the existing structure to the ends of capital accumulation made possible a satisfactory intertwining of the old with the new, the native becoming enmeshed in the economic, juridical, political, and ideological framework of the colony.

MODALITIES OF TRIBUTE

The Encomienda

Indigenous tribute underwent modification with the times. At first, with the coming of Pizarro, it was the conquistador's administrative arbitrariness that predominated, ignoring almost completely the legislation concerning the conquered territories. Tribute was about to become in a very special manner a pervading institution for the remainder of colonial history, above all as far as the implantation of the *encomienda* was concerned. This was a right conceded by the grace of the King for services rendered to the Crown in the Spanish Indies. Royal favor consisted in being able to collect tribute from a given number of Indians and in being charged with indoctrinating them in the Christian faith and looking after their material well-being. The duration of the *encomienda* depended on the laws of inheritance and on the nature of the grace and favor; it was certainly for the lifetime of the *encomendero* and sometimes he could pass it on to a son as a legacy. This latter case rapidly disappeared, the majority of *encomiendas* being for "one life only."

It appears that at first in certain regions it was not only a matter of raising tribute from the *encomendados* ["commended ones," or subjects] who constituted the *encomienda*, but mingled with it was the utilization of their labor force. This can be gathered from certain studies on the subject, the sense of which is conveyed in a letter of 1524 to the Parliament:

He did not allow the Indians of an *encomienda* to be dragged from their houses to do labor, but ordered that a portion of his lands should be set aside where they worked for the *encomendero*, and the latter had no right to demand anything further (Zavala 1935: 219).

Although it is not clear whether the Spaniard had proprietary rights over that land or only the enjoyment of its fruits, he was evidently not absolute master in a territorial sense of the entire *encomienda*.

In the case of Quito the functioning of the *encomienda* was not properly regulated in the early days when the conquistadors were trying to implant feudalism (a project rejected by the Crown and which culminated in the battle of Iñaquito). It was taken for granted that the *encomendero* had the right, not only of collecting tribute but also of using the Indian for various tasks exactly as he pleased. Regarding this we are told:

We may well suppose that Pizarro was not behind hand in the use of licence to deliver *encomiendas*. As he penetrated into the Inca territory, he established garrison cities with men of war whom he endowed with lands and vast *encomiendas* ... .
   ... in their dominions the *encomenderos* could employ the *encomendados*

as laborers, practically without limit and on the conditions that they themselves laid down. They had likewise the right to collect personal tribute from them, with neither limits nor rates being determined in advance... (Roel 1970: 90–91).

We note that this was a kind of initial foray in which the aim was to get the greatest possible gain. This procedure was not peculiar to the territory conquered from the Incas; it was the same in Central America, to such an inhuman extreme that the health of the native population was rapidly undermined. It was contrary to the policy of the Crown, which strove to preserve the native manpower to a moderate degree, for without it there would be no labor force and that would seriously interfere with the possibilities of capital accumulation. Extermination in the West Indies, for example, reached exorbitant proportions; populations were dying *en masse*. "Las Casas and the Dominicans maintained that the mortality of the aborigines was the inevitable consequence of the *encomienda* system, invented by the insatiable cupidity of the Spaniards" (Konetzke 1971: 168).

This series of abuses endangered the very existence of the Indian population, the basis of the economy, and obliged Spain to concern itself with the general system of exploitation in its colonies even though it had to counter certain private interests. Thus the way was prepared for the first laws to protect the inhabitants of the Indies.

It is curious that the very defense of the Indian — the polemics of Las Casas and the Dominicans in favor of the Indian population, clothed in the garb of humanist-Christian ideology — was based on the advocacy not of an end to exploitation but only of a preservation of the indigenous labor force so as to allow a more rational and lasting exploitation of land and of natural and mineral resources. The accelerated elimination of manpower through excess of work and forced labor would logically bring about the accelerated disappearance of the indigenous population and lead to scarcity of cheap or gratuitous manpower for further development.

We must admit that in this protection of the Indian the State played its part very well. It was the State that appeared in the first instance as his defender, rejecting exploitation and thereby denying its own interests, but the situation was not as mechanical as it seems: the absolutist State[4]

---

[4] The absolute State, according to Poulantzas, is characterized by the fact that the titular head, generally a monarch, concentrates in his hands a power not checked by other institutions and the exercise of which is not restricted by any law, whether of the positive or natural-divine order; the holder of power is *legibus solutus*. Contrary to the feudal type of State, therefore, in which State power is limited by divine law, the State considers itself as the manifestation of the cosmic-divine order. Against the privilege of the medieval estates — insofar as feudal links were marked out in a hierarchy of exclusive powers of feudal lords over the land of which they were proprietors and over

represented "the specifically political unity of a centralized power presiding over a national complex. Subjects have fixed places in the political institutions of the State as private citizens, and the central power frequently shows respect for such laws" (Poulantzas 1969: 205). What we wish to point out is that the State was not the feudal State which looked after the interests of a few feudal lords. On the contrary it had converted itself into an absolute State, in which it was assumed to incarnate the general public interest, in which the problem of the nation seemed to have a central place in the system (Poulantzas 1969: 208–210).

In this sense the promulgation of apparently humanitarian laws for the protection of the natives was actually in opposition to the minuscule privileged groups of the first stages of the Conquest; this protection stood guard over the coherence of the system which was seen as consisting not of independent fiefs but as a nation of vassals of the King (not of the feudal lords), among whom were reckoned the natives of the West Indies (although the latter were vassals only in name).

One of the first indications of a policy that looked to economic interests was the first laws of Burgos of 1512. They commanded that the Indians be well treated; they considered them to be free persons, allowing them forty days rest every five months,[5] and prescribed a meat diet for them. As for the spiritual side, churches were to be constructed at convenient points (Vargas 1948: 11–12). And for ideological considerations, there was great insistence on Christian instruction, which constituted an element of cohesion for the whole system; it was the focal point on which

---

the men linked to the land — the absolute State appears as a strongly centralized State. One important feature is that even if the sovereign central power does not believe itself to be limited by any "law," in the feudal sense of the term, it is no less certain that as soon as it appears a written juridical system is substituted for medieval privilege. Concern is for the rules of "public" law, which present the characteristics of abstraction, generality, and formalism associated with the modern juridical system, and regulating the relations of the subject to the central power of the State. Another characteristic of the absolute State is the place of the army. Its system is determined by the central power; this power maintains its own army. Military service is not based on feudal ties, but on a mercenary army at the service of a political power relatively freed from feudal ties (Poulantzas 1969: 204–206).

[5]   This rest was not a holiday as in modern labor contracts. The time was devoted to agricultural work on one's land with the aid of one's family. Even though quite certainly some regulations were to all intents and purposes a dead letter, nevertheless during the first years of the Conquest the Indians fought for a return to work on their land at sowing and harvest times.

This includes at the present time small farmers of Chimborazo, Tungurahua, and Cotopaxi who are obliged to work as salaried agricultural laborers, since their small parcels of land do not yield a subsistence; they customarily leave the work gangs during the month of October for the sowing, a few months later for cultivation and hoeing, and finally for the harvest.

were centered the different social sectors, and at which the groups of exploiters and exploited tuned in with one another under the sign of a divine ordinance. Furthermore, the exploitation of the "commended" Indians was justified by a supposed Christianization which, in exchange for tribute, was carried out by the conquerors. The type of relation established was in itself peculiar: the community paid tribute to the *encomendero* either in money or in kind, and simultaneously there resulted a kind of personal relationship between the *encomendero* and his *encomendados*. In exchange for the quota of tribute, the *encomendero* provided for indoctrination, charging some parish priest-teacher of Christian doctrine with the task, who in his turn received pay from the *encomendero* for his services.

To summarize, the *encomienda* had two essential features: one was the extraction of the indigenous community's surplus value which made possible the survival of the *Firmas Agrícolas* of native production based on the *ayllu*. The surplus went to the Spanish *encomenderos* and the royal coffers.

Evidently the Indians had no money with which to pay tribute. As for precious metals, the Spaniards soon put a stop to that, and furthermore these metals were solely for a sumptuary use in which the Indian had no part, only the nobility. For this reason they paid in kind as a rule, including those occasions when foremen had to pay to the account of the *mitayos*' tribute destined for the *encomendero* or the tax office. Another method was the assignment of raw material by the *encomendero*, the "commended ones" providing labor and producing fabrics, so as to acquit themselves of tribute.

Tribute so collected had a limit; the *encomendero* could not consume all the products, especially since a considerable number of them resided in Spain. He had to turn that which he had received in kind into money, and for that a market was necessary. At first it was the royal officials themselves (Barbosa 1971: 89) who engaged in trade, playing the part of intermediaries between the tribute payer and the *encomendero*. These intermediaries got rid of their products in the little urban markets created for the mining centers, markets which in our present milieu are not very important but which were relatively significant in the early days of the Conquest.

In some parts where the native community was not well organized, the natives could not pay their tribute in commodities realizable in money. In regions of primitive culture, agricultural and craft products, which an *encomendero* could accept as a contribution, were not forthcoming. In this case only personal service had an economic value. Thus in remote districts we find the *encomienda* of personal service called *reparti-miento* [distribution], for it consisted in the distribution of Indians to the *encomendero* for purposes of work. Although from 1549 on this type of *encomienda* was in general prohibited, in fact it continued to exist until the seventeenth century in all places where the legal *encomienda* was not practicable (Konetzke 1971:176). Insofar as the legal *encomienda* was possible for the purposes of collecting tribute, personal services "were not considered as *encomienda* but as *mita*"; this was the prevailing situation in the first period and would disappear later. In densely populated areas the right of the *encomenderos* to get contributions in money or kind took first place, rates being fixed by the authorities.

It was not always easy to apply the institution of *encomienda*; this varied according to the degree of development of societies; in those in which there was no State organization it was impossible for this mecha-nism to function. Indeed, in eastern Ecuador, among peoples apparently subdued, the continual attack by Indians on settlers, or their retreat into the depths of the forest, rendered impossible the functioning of *encomien-das*. Where they did exist they were few in number and scarcely viable economically.

The second element of the *encomienda* was the search for an ideological cohesion between the conquered peoples and the cultural patterns of the conquerors. The most appropriate path to this unity was religion, and this was to play a double role: it would justify exploitation by philo-sophical and theological arguments, and it would cause the Indian to accept his new status.

In other words the system will endeavor to support itself on the idea — which is basic — of an inequality existing between its two initial components, to wit victors and vanquished, conquerors and conquered, rulers and ruled; and starting from this simplified polarization which it will endeavor to maintain unalterable, it will proceed to adaptations, adjustments, accommodations, to the extent that the dynamics of economic life and the mixture of races introduce gradations into human interrelations, thus complicating the initial scheme of social stratification (Guzmán and Loup Herbert 1972:48).

Clearly all this grading went on under the apparent principle of the union of all as children of the same God and of the King, His representative. Religious ministers transmitted this ideological content; any comment hostile to the King was forbidden. A decree reading as follows was issued:

Love, respect for the sovereigns, for the Royal Family and for the government is an obligation dictated by the fundamental laws of the State and taught to subjects as a grave question of conscience by Holy Scripture. Hence it is im-perative that ecclesiastical authorities in their sermons and spiritual exercises instil these principles in the people, and also with still more reason abstain on all occasions, and in familiar conversation, from declamation and criticism tending to denigrate members of the Government and arouse odium against them (Archivo Nacional de Historia 1786: folio 181).*

If even the possibility of private talk was excluded, it is not surprising that the circulation of books marginal to orthodoxy was prohibited. In 1768 things had gone so far that the work *"Incommoda probabilismi"* of Fray Vincente de Casavalle was prohibited because of the desire, it was said, "to destroy the pernicious seed of regicide and tyrannicide ... scattered by so many authors, as being destructive of the State and of public tranquility" (Archivo Nacional de Historia 1768).

Tribute Payment to the Treasury

Not all Indians were *encomendados*; a good portion of them depended on the Crown and for this reason had to pay directly to it, in their capacity as vassals, the sums fixed by the authorities. This tribute too was paid in part by the wage earned in the work of the *mita*, where the amount was deducted directly from the list of payments to be made.

As we have said, the Spaniards utilized the existing structure, i.e. the distribution by chiefs of the different districts, in order to facilitate the collection of tribute; all they had to do was to adapt the existing social organization to their purpose. As a matter of fact, the collection of tribute was carried out by the State administration. Collection of tribute for the *encomiendas* as well as for the King was a function generally discharged by the *corregidor* of each place; but he in turn made the chiefs responsible for the communities. The chiefs were obligated to collect the tribute of the land portions or *ayllus* assigned to them and to answer for the amount collected. It was not rare for chiefs to be put in prison for not having managed to collect the tribute.[6] This occurred

---

* Now part of the Casa de Cultura Ecuatoriana
[6] A sample of the collection of tribute by the chiefs of the different towns would be the instruction to the chiefs governing the *corregimiento* of Otavalo, which in one part directs as follows: "You the said principal chief of the Indians of the said towns of Otavalo, Cotacache, Tontaqui, Inta, Tulla, and San Pablo are to give to the said Royal Officials every year the following tribute: First you, the said chief of the Indians to whom have been entrusted the towns of Otavalo, Cotacache, Tontaqui, Inta, Tulla, and San Pablo must give and pay each year to the said Royal Officials, and to him who is *corregidor* of the said district in their name, 11,124 *patacones* [coppers] of the value of eight reales, half on St John's day and the other half on Christmas Day. In this way payment 'of the whole amount of the said tribute' must be made every six months" (Archivo Nacional de Historia 1750).

principally when, in spite of possessing the tribute census he found those in it dispersed through the service of the *mita*, which made collection difficult if not impossible. To add to the difficulty, there were also Indians, the so-called "vagrants," who went from place to place to free themselves from both the tribute and the *mita*.

In order to facilitate the collection of tribute, the custom developed of taking numerous censuses to bring up to date the number and location of the tribute payers. In spite of this, there were the *yanacona* and vagrant Indians. The vagrants passed from one town to another without taking up residence in any, thus eluding the payment of tribute. As a result, frequent ordinances were promulgated which were intended to control the displacement of the indigenous population so that the estimated amount could be met. In the tribute accounts of some cities we find groups qualified as vagrants figuring in the lists of tribute payers. Thus we encounter vagrants in the tribute accounts for 1691–1695 of Coto-collao, Calacalí, Perucho, Pifo, Tumbaco, Cumbayá, Zámbiza, San Roque, San Marcos, and Chimbacalle.

Tribute paid by the Indians was of the personal type, i.e. imposed on the vassals themselves without taking into account the goods they did or did not possess. In this respect, the *Itinerario para párrocas de Indias* 1691–1695 explains, there were various types of tribute: personal, royal, and mixed. The last two were connected with charges on the possession of properties, businesses, or industrial concerns. Obviously the Indians did not pay such tribute because they had no land; they paid only the personal type of tribute. In the same book we read:

They are so poor and have so little industry or business or even husbandry or cattle breeding that if our pitiful King and Lord came to know about it, he would relieve them of tribute, or would moderate it, for the majority pay each year more than the worth of all they possess.

Because we do not claim to explore all the ramifications of tribute in this study, but merely to propose certain guidelines for the interpretation of our history, a brief view may be given here of how tribute affects the economic and social evaluation of the total social system.

The Tribute System Before Legislation

We have already shown that at first what prevailed was the will of the conquistadors, then the Crown had to intervene directly to conserve the labor force which was in danger of disappearing from severe exploitation. We have also noted that the causes contributing to the State's preoccupation with the preservation of manpower were directly related to the economic aims of the Crown in keeping an eye on the demographic equilibrium of the indigenous population.

The Tribute System After Legislation

Once tribute had become subject to juridical norms and the administrative machinery established, the authorities proceeded to make up the censuses to assure its collection, as far as this pertained to the *encomienda* and to the King.

Two very different phases of native tribute must be distinguished within the territories of the Royal *Audiencia* of Quito, the first covering the time up to 1670, the other extending to the abolition of tribute in the 1850's. Let us take these two well-defined stages as a basis of study.

THE PERIOD OF 1550–1670   This was the stage when the tribute structure was consolidated and when the distribution and settlement of converted Indians functioned well. The economy was based on the production of textiles and certain foods for the mining center of Potosí, which gave a certain dynamism to the flow of cash and consequently a good collection of tribute. The payment of tribute functioned through two basic causes which promoted the smooth working of the economic network:

1.   The interlocking system of adjacent territories was drawn by the dynamic magnet of mining production in Potosí and caused a high demand for textiles, in which economic activity in the territory of Quito was specialized. The demand for its fabrics was all the greater because there was no competition from foreign manufactures of European origin. The bonanza made for good production and a high level of trade, and also enabled the *mitayo* Indians to pay the tribute in full in accordance with the established rates.

2.   The manner of accumulating wealth in this period, besides the *encomienda*, was to set up workshops, wool fulling mills, etc. (Jácome 1972). Land was not yet utilized as the principal means of accumulating value or as a source of riches. Despoiling the Indians of their lands had not yet reached the vast proportions which it assumed with the decay of the mining center of Potosí. This division of colonial labor allowed the Indians to carry on with their communal-style economy and to produce a surplus assigned in great part to the paying of members' tribute.[7]

---

[7]   The form of paying tribute was mixed, as often in money as in kind. Payment in shawls and fabrics was exacted, the *encomendero* providing the raw materials; payment was made also in hens, hogs, etc.

At this time we meet with doctrines which encompassed the tribute-paying Indians. These doctrines were professed by clerics and religious ministers who constituted "an entire colonizing-evangelizing-exploiting complex" (Guzmán and Loup Herbert 1972: 44) — Dominicans, Franciscans, Mercedarians, and Augustinians, and later on Jesuits. The doctrines created the nuclei of civic life which later became parishes. These teachers of Christian doctrine introduced the calendar of festivals accepted in the dioceses (Vargas 1948: 28). In this form they exercised their authority, justifying and disguising the oppressive action of the conquistadors: thanks to them acts considered blameworthy appeared as illicit cults, while at the same time they had the ideological power of suppressing what in their eyes had no justification.

The mode of collection was not separated from the *encomenderos'* share of what pertained to the Crown; the same administration undertook the collection, and from the amount collected expenses thereby incurred were deducted. Once the expenses were separated, a further sum was put aside for the service of the church of each town or village, for the indoctrinating priest, and for the pay of the *corregidor* and the chief and assistant in the collection. Of the remainder one part went to the *encomendero* and the other to the King, according to the source of the tribute.

Besides the paying of tribute, according to certain ordinances passed at the beginning of the seventeenth century, provision was to be made in the *repartimiento* for the service of the church in the capacity of sacristan and choir singer, who were exempted from the service of the *mita* and from tribute. Even if these Indians were exonerated personally, the community from which they came was responsible to the royal officers for the amount of their tribute.

Payments made by the Indians in the form of tribute were still incomplete, for districts or *ayllus* had to pay the expense of wax candles and decoration of the church during Holy Week and Christmas.

Each parish priest had an Indian as cook and another as baker; each served for a year, after which they were replaced by others. The priest had to feed them and see that they were relieved of the *mita;* the community of course would have to pay the tribute for these servants.

Furthermore, every priest had an Indian assigned to him from the group of elderly men who acted as groom. This servant was changed once a week, according to the order determined by the *ayllu.*

Tribute was also owed to the chief. Indians had to serve him in such activities as cultivating the growing crops for which *mitayos* were assigned to him. In the seventeenth century when the possession of land became more important than the possession of manpower, the collection of tribute by chiefs was prohibited because when they passed through the *hacienda* they were manhandled. As a result the government was obliged to appoint a white collector directly connected with the *audiencia*. It behooves us to ask who were those favored with indigenous tribute in this milieu? When we reconstruct colonial life in detail, we find that "the *encomenderos* were, for the most part, also the mayors and magistrates of Quito" (Bayle 1968).

The sector where the most tribute-paying settlements were found was the sierra, the historical place of settlement, which facilitated the grouping of converted Indians and the *repartimientos*. The most important locations for the majority of tribute-paying *encomiendas* were Quito and Riobamba,[8] prominent centers of colonial economy during the first years of conquest. In the case of Riobamba we find a multitude of towns

Table 1. Towns paying tribute in Riobamba

Towns	Encomiendas	Tribute, second half of 1642 (in pesos)
Chambo	*Mitimas* of the Crown	18
	Zizibies	14
	Indians of the Crown	43
Quimiac	Town of the Crown	47
Ligto	Of Pedro Cepeda	850
	Of the Crown	225
San Luís	Of the Crown	118
Penipe	Of the Crown	177
San Andrés	General Antonio López de Galarza	462
	Doña Tomasa de Larraspuro	754
Cubixíes	Antonio López de Galarza	191
Calpi	Doña Tomasa de Larraspuro	279
Langos	Doña Tomasa de Larraspuro	104
Lican	Doña Inés Fernandes de Aguicera	345
Punin	The Count of Monterrey	622
Macaxi	The Count of Monterrey	240
	Total	4,489 pesos

Source: Archivo Nacional de Historia (1642–1644).

[8]   Though Quito and Riobamba were the most dynamic centers during the colonial period, as time went on Riobamba receded to the secondary plane of economic importance, outstripped by other centers that appeared as the country developed. In the present century Quito has maintained its hegemony while Riobamba has had to yield to Guayaquil.

With regard to the process of growth and decay as it affects towns, attention should be paid to the phenomenon of the transfer of a country's surpluses to certain fixed centers in that country. This has received the name of "internal colonialism" and is beginning to disturb members of certain intellectual circles in Ecuador.

Table 2.   Encomiendas of the corregimiento of Quito, second half of 1691

Towns	Encomenderos	Semiannual tribute rate (in reales)	Number of tributary Indians
Pamacoto	Countess of Barajas	12	56
Conocoto	Dr. Pedro de Ozacta (Judge of Guatemala)	16	90
Guanalo	Dr. Pedro de Ozacta (Judge of Guatemala)	12	88
Chillogallo	Juan Sarmiento (Commissioner)	18	145
San Roque	Juan Sarmiento (Commissioner)	18	144
San Marcos (Chimbo Indians)	Juan Sarmiento (Commissioner)	20	101
Conocoto	Juan Sarmiento (Commissioner)	16	344
Alangasi	Juan Sarmiento (Commissioner)	16	150
Salgolqui	Juan Sarmiento (Commissioner)	20	92
Amaguaña	Juan Sarmiento (Commissioner)	20	860
Uyumbicho	Juan Sarmiento (Commissioner)	20	37
Mindo, Zambe, Tapo, and Tusa	Juan Sarmiento (Commissioner)	12	102
Chillogallo	Juan Sarmiento (Commissioner)	18	145

Total   2,354

Source: Archivo Nacional de Historia 1642–1644.
Note: Each peso is worth eight reales. Besides the money, every tributary had to pay a hen every six months.
To this group of encomiendas, which have been cited merely as examples, should be added other encomiendas of the same corregimiento of Quito, such as: San Antonio, Santa Prisca, Cotocollao, Cumbayá, Tumbaco, Quinche, Zambiza, and Mayon.

that customarily paid tribute every six months. Table 1 gives an idea of these towns. For example, the rate of tribute imposed on the encomiendas of San Andrés and Cubixíes was on the order of: (1) fifteen silver reales, (2) half a woven shawl, for which the encomendero provided the raw material, (3) five pounds, four ounces of worked sisal grass, (4) one hen, and (5) three almudes (twenty-five pounds) of potatoes. See Table 2 for Quito encomiendas on 1691.

The rate of tribute for the different peoples fluctuated between four and six pesos a year, plus two hens, and in some cases the obligation to give woven shawls, the encomenderos providing the raw material. It is no rare thing to find in some encomiendas the additional requirement of furnishing articles in kind such as potatoes, maize, and worked sisal-fiber. We get an idea of the high amount represented by this tributary rate if we compare it with the amount earned by the mitayo Indian as wages, and with the little or nothing that he received for his work. The mitayos as day laborers and agricultural workers earned less than anyone else, scarcely achieving a wage of fifteen pesos a year, and it is easy to see that 50 percent went to the payment of tribute.

The sums collected under the heading of indigenous tribute were an important percentage of the total intake for the royal treasury. For example, in 1648 the total intake in taxes amounted to 139,682 pesos, of which 39,513 were collected as tribute. And if we compare payments under their rubrics, the highest was that of tribute, surpassing excise in importance which provided only 19,000 pesos. Furthermore, we must take into account that the quantity of tribute taken up corresponded to the actual collected sum for the year. The nominal sum was higher, the difference arising from the cost of collection which was set aside (Archivo Nacional de Historia 1678).

This type of economic network, within which tribute was one of the mechanisms for the absorption of economic surplus in the community and above all was based on an organization peculiar to the Indians, functioned well while the flow of cash produced by the rich deposits of Potosí continued. Likewise the system itself of the *encomienda* had no problems; the *encomendero*, accepting the delay of the great ships in reaching Spain, received the products of his *encomienda*, which were immediately utilized in a courtier's life of ostentation.

THE PERIOD OF 1671–1822   Once there was a falling-off in the production of Potosí, the economy of adjacent territories became unbalanced. In the case of the *presidencia* of Quito, the principal center of its economy, factory production began to diminish noticeably, as much through lack of demand in the Lima market as through the introduction of European textiles of better quality and lower price. These were made by machine, not by hand like those of domestic factories. Furthermore, the King of Spain had to make a series of commercial concessions as a consequence of military defeats. These concessions were made to the English and certain groups of the Low Countries, and implied the use of persuasive means to squeeze the textile industry out of the colonies.

The value and possibilities of enrichment which before existed in factories now existed in land, as there was abundant manpower to work it. The problem was not very easy to solve; at these altitudes, the high rate of indigenous mortality had left the aboriginal population decimated, as much through constant maltreatment in the work of the *mita* as through plague, which had an atrocious effect on native populations. Practically speaking, manpower was scarce at the end of the seventeenth century. It was necessary to maintain this scanty population, capable of lending cheap service to the accumulation of riches, not in the mode of the *mita*, which after all was but the temporary assurance of a fixed number of workers (scarcely for a year, or little more). In view of the shortage of labor, the most adequate solution was to take advantage of the serious economic straits of the Indians, who had been victims of the whole process of land expropriation. Due to this system of "land compensation," the Indians were deprived of their land and obliged to work for someone else. To these Indians in their growing economic need, the landlords now gave advances, either in money or in kind, in return for work on their lands. The debts were to be acquitted by work on the land of the creditor landlord, but once he had set foot on the property, obligated by the debt he had contracted, the Indian saw it grow rather than diminish, owing to a system in the *hacienda* which kept him constantly in the position of debtor, the debt passing as a legacy to his descendants if he did not manage to pay it himself.

Through this new economic network, towns and villages were depopulated and the Indians remained ensnared on large agricultural properties. Tribute which had functioned within the framework of an organization for its collection from towns and villages, in which the indigenous population was easily located, lost its virtue as the Indians were scattered on various properties and it was extremely difficult to collect from them. Furthermore, they had nothing to pay with, and when the authorities had recourse to the master with whom it had been arranged that he should pay the tribute to the Indian, he argued that the man was not a *mitayo*, but was working for the debt he had contracted.

Such was the state of poverty in which the aboriginal population found itself when the King, to accelerate the collection of tribute, allowed it to be collected not only in money but in kind and in what could most conveniently be given (Archivo Nacional de Historia 1681–1685: folio 192). The Protector of Indians replied to this ordinance that the Indians had no money with which to pay tribute and that it would be worse if they had to pay in kind. At that date they had no land because they had been stripped of it. In the *corregimiento* of Riobamba, it was decreed by letter patent in 1685 that if the annual wage fixed in 1621 did not suffice for sustenance and payment of tribute, the latter must not be augmented (Landazuri Soto 1959: 26). Indeed, at the time the Indians could not even pay the amount of the previous tribute much less new impositions.

The commission of inquiry charged by the King of Spain with investigating what was going on in his dominions reported on the situation of land expropriation to which the natives were subjected and tardily demanded, when the process was irreversible, that at least a part of this land should be given back to the natives. This is what Juan y Santacilia y de Ulloa had to say on the matter:

Given that the greater part of the *haciendas*, and some in their entirety, were formed from lands unjustly taken from the Indians, from some with violence, from others by deception, and from others still according to the perverse principle that the Spaniards were free to dispose of them, it would be very desirable, in order that this nation should be given relief from the straitened circumstances in which it is living, and that its misfortune should in part be remedied, to order that all the lands that had belonged to them some years ago should be returned to them, or at least that restitution should be made of the half of those that have been taken from them in the last twenty years, which would be feasible in our view, without anyone being wronged, supposing what has been stated to be true (Juan y Santacilia y de Ulloa 1918, volume one: 324).

Indeed the registers of the collection of tribute by the *corregidors* showed the entry under this rubric to be poorer every year, enormous residues remaining irrecoverable because of the poverty of the tributaries, those of the *encomiendas* as much as those of the Crown. Highly corroborative of this state of affairs were the tribute accounts for 1691 to 1695: the total amounted to 111,029 pesos, of which it had been possible to collect almost 41,559 pesos, which left 69,470 pesos and three-and-a-half reales outstanding. This was only for the rubric of tribute to the King; the same thing happened with the tribute of the *encomiendas* (Archivo Nacional de Historia 1691c; volume thirteen, folios 67–69). For the latter, figures of tribute paying for the northern part of the *corregimiento* of Quito covering the period 1631–1685 may be of assistance: out of a total of 91,129 pesos, which was the theoretical amount of tribute for the *encomiendas*, scarcely 24,782 pesos and 7 reales were collected.

The change in economic relations which rendered difficult the collection of tribute broke up the *encomienda* system. It disappeared legally at the beginning of the eighteenth century; the "commended" Indians now came under the Crown. Because of its financial difficulties, the treasury decided to grant the tribute by towns to the highest bidder; in this way, obtaining or collecting the tribute became strictly the private business of the lessee who had been placed in charge of the particular area.

This situation based on the mercantile energy of the tribute farmers brought about a still greater deterioration in the condition of the Indians. The system itself was open to a series of abuses on the part of private collectors exceeding any arbitrary act of a despotic *corregidor*.

With the rise to power of the Bourbons in the eighteenth century, there was a movement to rescue the metropolis from its economic and social straits. Various men of liberal and enlightened opinion sought to bring about a kind of industrial revolution. The model proposed for development, if we may call it so, was that the metropolis should produce manufactured goods and the colonies raw materials, and that the colonies should be consumers. This process involved a great deal of money, and where could it better be obtained than from the efforts of the King's good subjects in the colonies; they must pay for the scheme of industrializing Spain. Naturally this policy, which began to make itself felt in 1750, involved a whole series of new attitudes toward the colonial inhabitants of Latin America, as did the raising of the rates of tribute assigned to the Indian population. In its wake followed a series of Indian revolts, not only in the *presidencia* of Quito, but in other colonial territories. There were indigenous uprisings in Latacunga in 1766; there were insurrections in Riobamba, Calpi, Cajabamba, San Luís, Lican, and Yaraquíes. Also in 1766, there was an uprising in Guano and in San José de Muliambato; in 1770 they revolted in Pillaro and Patate; in 1778 in Otavalo, Cotacachi, San Pablo Caranquí, and Tabacundo; in 1779 in Guamote and Columbe; in 1780 in Pelileo, Quizapincha, Píllaro, Patate, and Baños; in 1781 in Alausi; in 1784 in Calpi, Luisa, and San Juan; in 1791 in Cayambe; in 1794 in Riobamba and Cumbayá, etc. (Albornoz 1971: 21–31).

This succession of insurrections was evidence that the indigenous population would not tolerate heavier tribute charges and that an internal climate of independence was beginning to take shape. The series of coercive measures brought about a mobilization among the Indians that launched a number of movements toward political liberation. They were to culminate in independence.

The scheme of converting Spain into a manufacturing center so that she would be able to live on her colonies did not have the desired effect. The peninsular metropolis was far behind in the process of industrialization compared to England and France, and it was difficult to regain lost ground. To this was added a series of military disasters culminating in Napoleon's invasion of Spain, an event that unleashed the liberation movement in America which was to end in the secession of the colonies.

Republican Period up to 1860

Political independence had not brought any major change in the socioeconomic structure of the new nation. Cueva expresses fairly well the content of the change in the following analysis of the moment of separation between Spain and the territory which is now Ecuador (1973: 7):

Immediately after Ecuador obtained its independence, the people found the right phrase to describe the epoch that had begun with our emancipation from Spain. LAST DAY OF DESPOTISM AND FIRST DAY OF THE SAME THING were the words, and popular genius was not far wrong, inasmuch as the event did not signify for the exploited classes anything but the substitution for the metropolitan functionary of the colonial *encomendero* in the various departments of national life. And so it had to be, since Ecuadorian independence was not the product of an authentic popular revolution, but only the successful insurrection of colonial marquises against the Crown, and that was scarcely likely to generate a process of decolonization.

The indigenous population, which did not gain any economic or social advantage from independence, continued to provide the social basis supporting the production of the economic surplus value. The great liberal ideas — equality, liberty, and fraternity — were no concern of the group that brought about independence. Their objective was the control of the State by the territorial aristocracy, whose power was rooted in the tenancy of land and in the assurance of gratuitous Indian labor, which allowed a high index of accumulation.

It is clear that in principle the Indian was capable of all the rights given by national life. But as far as his obligations to the State were concerned, he was regarded in the same way he had been in the colonial epoch — he was still obligated to pay tribute. Thus we see that in the year 1854, thirty-two years after independence, he still had to pay tribute as in the days of Spanish domination because of the fact that he was an Indian.

The contribution of the Indians to national taxation under the name of tribute was so high that it occupied second place after the amount collected through customs. Indeed for the year 1854 the total collected in the tribute section rose to 150,558 pesos and 5 reales, which is equivalent to 12 percent of the country's entire revenue (Ministerio del Interior 1855).

At the end of the 1850's tribute was abolished. The ruling class advocated its extension, but the more progressive sectors were in favor of its disappearance.[9]

From the moment of independence, an ideological veil was drawn over the character of exploitation inherent in the continued demand for tribute from the Indians. That veil was a change of name. Tribute was now called CONTRIBUTION. The aristocratic landowning group thought it was changing the nature of tribute when it changed its name, making it appear not as a compulsory obligation imposed on a sector of the population but as a

[9]   The repressive mood in favor of collecting the tribute was so strong that Eugenio Espejo in his defense of the parish priests of Riobamba said that over a period of four years the amount collected was as much as 110,000 pesos and that the royal officials were so extortionate that "the parish priests know of widows of free Indians who died in debt being persecuted to pay the tribute of their dead husbands as though it were their own personal debt." On the other hand, colonial nobles were about to lose their titles of nobility because of debts owing to the Crown in the form of obligations they had not been able to meet.

personal and voluntary contribution from citizens of a free, democratic, and independent country. In that period, in reference to this mechanism for the extraction of surplus value it could be said:

Tribute, thus masked, could not cease to be an unjust, barbarous, and unconstitutional exaction. It is unjust, because justice is for one and all, it is equal for all, and tribute oppresses one class in particular, exempting others. It is barbarous, because it preys upon the most miserable and unfortunate class, on which it even imposes the sacrifice of enslavement in order to meet its exactions; it is unconstitutional, because while the Constitution decrees that every tax shall be universal and proportionate, this one snatches the bread from tens of thousands of individuals while respecting the wealth and the prerogatives of the upper classes (Ministerio de Hacienda 1856).

Indigenous tribute was legally abolished at the end of the 1850's leaving this part of the population free of the imposition with which it had been burdened from the moment of the Spanish Conquest and which had continued to exist for thirty-six years after independence.[10]

CONCLUSIONS

We have seen how the imposition of tribute on the Indians was varied and how in great part it provided for the accumulation of capital for the *encomenderos* and for the Crown. Ultimately it was tribute that financed in great part the Treasury during the first years of the Republic.

It is interesting to note the mixture of different forms of tribute practice, the sole aim of which was to convey the surplus value of the indigenous community, first into the hands of the dominant Spanish group and later into those of the colonial nobility.

As we have shown, tribute was not an institution detached from the remainder of economic activities such as agricultural and textile industries. On the contrary, it complemented them, fitting perfectly into

---

[10]   The Minister of the Treasury, referring to native tribute, said: "It is not without pain and shame, yet also hope, that I am about to speak to you of the Indian contribution, seeing that even forty-six years after the proclamation of our independence the most miserable class of our society is still oppressed by all the horrors that were brought three centuries ago by the Conquest, and that in spite of all the sacrifices that have been made, all the reforms that have been undertaken in the name of the people, all the constitutions that have been promulgated and the wealth of republican guarantees, it has been possible for an order dictated by Pizarro to maintain itself. As long as the classes forming our society have not equal rights and duties, as long as there is a class which has duties and no rights, the Constitution is a farce and the Republic a lie. And laws passed in the name of the majority which however do not extend to all are not laws but usurpations (Ministerio de Hacienda 1856:17).

the organizational mechanism of the colonial territories on various levels as a means of extracting surplus value.

In the internal organization of tribute, we observed a certain respect for small areas reserved as communal land where the indigenous family could work and pay tribute. While affirming that certain areas were respected, we must also state that ecologically they were the poorest and that in the hands of *mestizos* and whites they would not have been cultivated nor would they have produced value equivalent to the tribute. The Indian was organized so that he could contribute his work force through the institution of the *mita* and also have his wife and children working on the communal land so as to be able to draw a wage for the payment of the tribute. Such was the procedure for exploiting his physical possibilities in the work of the *mita* and at the same time appropriating a part of the production for his family.

As soon as tribute disappeared legally in the middle of the nineteenth century, the Indians ceased to pay it, yet their rights as citizens of a republic were not fully recognized. Indeed, in a country so racially heterogeneous, one can well understand that the Spanish type of domination created a separation between the white and the Indian on the ideological plane. This pattern of behavior established in the colony and inherited by the Republic meant that, in spite of the disappearance of tribute, the Indian was still an exploited person and that this reality was covered by the mantle of interethnic relations.

Thus while the indigenous population was freed of tribute to the tax office, it continued to pay tithes to the Church; above all release from the obligation of tribute did not free him from the tie of *concertaje* [contract to work as a day laborer] which chained him to the *hacienda*. On the one hand he was discharged from tribute, but on the other he continued on in a position of rural servitude. This position tended to consolidate itself through the creation of involved economic, cultural, and social relationships, the key-note of which is exploitation of the indigenous countryman based on an ideology of interethnic character.

The interethnic tone given to the relationship between the white-*mestizo* and the Indian was an obvious attempt to disguise class relationship, and provides margins for the analysis of ethnic groups, thus shifting the center of the problem, which is no other than that of class relationships, the detection of which is relatively difficult because of the racial nuance which was intended in the first place to veil these class relationships.

REFERENCES

ALBORNOZ, EDUARDO
1971   *Las luchas indígenas en el Ecuador.* Quito: Talleres Gráficos Claridad.
ARCHIVO NACIONAL DE HISTORIA, ECUADOR
1642–1644   "Cuentas de tributos de la Real Audiencia de Quito, tomados al corregidor de Riobamba." Presidencia de Quito Section, volume three, folios 92–167.
1678   "Cuentas de la Real Audiencia de Quito del año 1678." Presidencia de Quito Section, volume six, folios 1–123.
1681–1685   "Cuentas de Tributos del Corregimiento de Quito, desde Navidad de 1681 hasta Navidad de 1685, tomados al corregidor de Quito, General Juan de Orozco, Caballero de la Orden de Santiago." Presidencia de Quito Section, volume fourteen, folios 59–146, 192.
1691a   "Real Cédula para que en los Reynos de las Indias se cumpla, y observe el contenido de la Real Cédula inserta, en cuanto a que los eclesiáticos Seculares y Regulares se abastengan de declaraciones y murmuraciones contra el Gobierno, con lo demás, que se expresa." Presidencia de Quito Section, volume sixty-five, folio 181.
1691b   "Cédula para que en los Reynos de las Indias se cumpla, y observe el contenido de la Real Cédula inserta, a fin de que no se venda al público la obra Incommoda Probabilismi, escrito por Fray Vicente Mas de Casavalle, del Orden de Predicadores." Presidencia de Quito Section, volume sixty-five, folio 179.
1691c   "Cuentas de Tributos de la Real Audiencia de Quito, tomadas al corregidor de Quito, General Pedro García de la Torre, Caballero de la Orden de Calatraba. Años 1691–1695." Presidencia de Quito Section, volume thirteen, folios 67–69.
1750   "Datos de Don Gregorio Cabezas y Doña Antonieta Titizunta Llamoca con don Manuel Velenzuela sobre el cacicazgo de Otavalo." Cacicazgo Section, volume forty-four.
1768   ARNAHIS, volume sixty-five, folio 179.
1786   ARNAHIS, folio 181.
BARBOSA RAMÍREZ, RENÉ
1971   *La estructura económica de la Nueva España 1619–1810.* Mexico City: Siglo XXI.
BAYLE, C.
1968   La vida social en la colonia. *ARNAHIS. Revista del Archivo Nacional de Historia, Quito* 17: 29–40.
CUEVA, AGUSTÍN
1973   *El proceso de dominación política en el Ecuador* (second edition). Quito: Crítica.
GUZMÁN, CARLOS, JEAN LOUP HERBERT,
1972   *Guatemala. Una interpretación histórica-social* (third edition). Mexico City: Siglo XXI.
HARING, CLARENCE
1939   *Comercio y navegación entre España y las Indias.* Mexico City: Fondo de Cultura Económica.

Itinerario
1691–1695 *Itinerario para párrocas de Indias.* Quito.
JÁCOME, NICANOR
1972 "Notas sobre la economía de la colonia ecuatoriana." Mimeograph.
JUAN Y SANTACILIA Y DE ULLOA, ANTONIO
1918 *Noticias secretas de América, siglo XVIII.* Madrid: América.
KONETZKE, RICHARD
1971 *América Latina: la época colonial.* Mexico City: Siglo XXI.
LANDAZURI SOTO, ALBERTO
1959 *El régimen laboral indígena en la Real Audiencia de Quito.* Madrid: Aldecos.
MARINI, MAURO
1972 *Dialéctica de la dependencia.* Quito: Centro de Investigaciones Sociales y Políticos de la Universidad Central del Ecuador.
MARX, KARL
1971 *Contribución a la crítica de la economía política* (second edition). Medellín: Oveja Negra.
MINISTERIO DE HACIENDA DE ECUADOR
1856 *Exposición que el Ministro de Hacienda presenta al Congreso en 1856: colección de Memorias.* Quito.
MINISTERIO DEL INTERIOR Y RELACIONES EXTERIORES
1855 *Cuadro B.I.* Quito.
MONTOYA, RODRIGO
1970 *A propósito del carácter predominantemente capitalista de la economía peruana.* Lima: Ediciones Teoría y Realidad.
MOREANO, ALEJANDRO
1972 *Historia crítica del Ecuador.* Class notes, mimeographed. Quito.
POULANTZAS, NICOS
1969 *Poder político y clases sociales en el estado capitalista.* Mexico City: Siglo XXI.
RAMOS, JORGE ABELARDO
1969 *Historia de la nación latinoamericana.* Buenos Aires: Peña Lillo.
REYEROS, RAFAEL
1972 El "tupu" incaico y sus modalidades. *América Indígena* 32(3): 381–386.
ROEL, VIRGILIO
1970 *Historia social y económica de la colonia.* Lima: Gráficas Labor.
SEMO, ENRIQUE
1972 Feudalismo y capitalismo en la Nueva España. *Comercio exterior de México* 22(5): 449–454.
STANLEY, J., BARBARA H. STEIN
1971 *La herencia colonial de América Latina.* Mexico City: Siglo XXI.
VARGAS, JOSÉ MARÍA
1948 *La conquista espiritual del imperio de los Incas.* Quito.
VELASCO, FERNANDO
1972 Notas sobre la dependencia ecuatoriana. *Economía, Revista del Instituto de Investigaciones Económicas y Financieras* 58: 21–34.
ZAVALA, SILVIO
1935 *Las instituciones jurídicas en la conquista de América.* Madrid.

Danish Colonialism in the West Indies: A Case of Transculturation Failure

POLLY POPE

Although colonialism in the West Indies Islands had much in common, the degree to which native West Indians affiliated themselves with the nation to whom they were in bondage varied decidedly. To speak of the black Englishman of Barbados or the black French citizen of Martinique is not an incongruity, but it is incongruous to talk of black Danes because literary research reveals no mention of them. This is in view of the fact that the Danes ruled the Virgin Islands of St. Thomas, St. Croix, and St. John for nearly 250 years until the islands were purchased by the United States in 1917.

It is our thesis here that the situation is a classic case of transculturation[1] failure from the standpoint of the dominant Danish culture. Gordon Lewis states the proposition well when he speaks of "the myth of Danish culture" (Lewis 1967: 14). The history of the Danes in the West Indies is another example of colonialism and power abuse, which never resulted in war but certainly gave rise to revolts, to the establishment of a Maroon community, and to assorted acts of behavior, which can only be interpreted as responses to an intolerable situation created by the institution of slavery. The hostility felt toward the Danes is still present in the American Virgin Islands today. In 1967, when a black native middle-class businessman from St. Croix was asked about Danish and black relationships, he replied without rancor: "There are some people [black] on this

---

[1]   The word transculturation was first put into use in 1940 by the Cuban scholar Ortiz who preferred it to the term acculturation because "transculturation better expresses the different phases of the process of transition from one culture to another because this does not consist merely in acquiring another culture, which is what the English word acculturation really implies" (Ortiz quoted in Herskovits 1958:475).

island who don't even want a person to mention the names of the 'five royal families'." The families referred to are descendants of Danish whites, residents of the island for generations. Because their family fortunes may have declined in certain cases, they find themselves as a part of the regular workaday world; but some of them still put forth a considerable effort in order to maintain an exclusiveness, largely in their social relationships and club memberships.

In an acculturative situation of long duration between two social groups, there is the expectation that each will borrow from the other, but studies make it clear that individuals may be highly selective in what they choose. As stated by Herskovits:

Contact, therefore, can result in minimal borrowing, with or without external pressure, or it can range to almost complete acceptance of the ways of life of another people. In any given case, the aspects of culture that are transmitted ... are the result of particular historical circumstances which influence the psychological motivations underlying the selectivity that comes into play (1958:482).

Or, conversely, it may be said that what is not accepted from another culture will be a result of the particular historical circumstances and the psychological motivations present.

West Indians in the American Virgin Islands identify themselves as "Virgin Islanders," but in conjunction with this there is also an identification in terms of the individual islands; thus, locals on St. Croix see themselves as "Cruzans" or "Crucians," a reflection of the Spanish name originally given to the island, Santa Cruz. The native-born Cruzans refer to other island subgroups on the basis of place of origin. Thus there are the Puerto Ricans and the "Down-Islanders" (migrants from British and French islands) who do domestic or menial labor; the continentals (Americans, many of whom have retired or work in a professional capacity); and the island whites, largely of Danish origin but also with a sprinkling of French and English. One Danish white, born on the island, reminded the author in 1967, in no uncertain terms, that she, too, "was a Cruzan."

Lowenthal, in discussing West Indian identity, states that West Indians are uneasy about their national identity (although generally I did not find this to be true on St. Croix) and that "The measure of importance is European nationality" (1972:265). He says, quite correctly, that "Identification with Europe is strongest in the French-colonialized Caribbean" (1972:265). "British West Indians are stereotypically less 'anglicized' than the French West Indians are 'gallicized'," declares Lowenthal, who goes on to point out that "fealty more than physiography still makes Barbados 'Little England'. Jamaicans, Trinidadians, and small islanders all emulate

English manners, take pride in Commonwealth status, and pursue British honours" (1972:267).

A search for Danish cultural traits in the course of fieldwork in 1967 on St. Croix showed that there was little if anything remaining of Danish social customs among the Afro-American population. The fact that the Danes were there is revealed by the family names of Danish origin among the native population. This may be attributed largely to the fact that a number of slaves took the surname of the slave owner when freed in 1848 because nearly all were without a surname. Street names such as Strandgade, Kongensgade, and Nygade are visible on signs, but local residents refer to them by the anglicized names, e.g. King Street and the Strand. It is notable that a recent project of the St. Croix Museum and Landmarks League was "redoing the old Danish street signs on local mahogany" (Lewisohn 1964:66). The main towns for the islands, Charlotte Amalie on St. Thomas, Christiansted and Frederiksted on St. Croix, and the names of sugar estates such as Hogansborg give evidence of the Danish presence, as well as the older form of architecture, the heavy massive brick construction found in civic and commercial buildings. A few recipes are said to be of Danish origin. Beyond this there is hardly anything else which could be termed purely Danish.

Of all the islands in the Caribbean, St. Croix is one of the more ideal for the tracing of historical relationships because the island was nearly deserted when purchased in 1733 from the French; probably the only residents were a few Dutch and English. While this study rests heavily on data for St. Croix, it also draws on other material pertaining to the Virgin Islands as a whole. St. Croix lends itself well to a study of colonialism because it was destined to become a plantation-type colony, mainly owing to the flat terrain. From the colonial standpoint, the island was perfect for the growing of sugar, cotton, tobacco, and indigo. In time it was the sugar estate that came to dominate island life, largely made possible by the black population imported from West Africa for the purpose of working the cane fields.

The original purchasers, the Danish West India and Guinea Company, made the grand plan for the colony in 1735. Utilizing Centerline Road as a base for their survey on St. Croix, they mapped out at least 300 plantations, 215 of which were allotted to the shareholders of the West India Company (Westergaard 1917:215).

The plan of the Danes, as well as of the Dutch, English, and French planters who settled on St. Croix, was to assure themselves of a regular supply of cane field and estate workers. Above all, in the early days, the Danish West India and Guinea Company desired to make their overseas venture profitable. Even after the Danish government purchased all three of the islands in 1754, there was to be continuing conflict between government in the home country, who evidenced more sound social concern for those in bondage than slave owners and the political representatives in the Indies.

Taken in historical perspective, the Danes apparently believed that with the establishment of a Free Colored class the nonwhite population would have a model of behavioral propriety to guide them, while the Danes would gain a bulwark against the slave population. Danish colonial authorities clearly occupied the top of the societal pyramid for their West Indian holdings. Although other European ethnic groups had substantial representation, it was the Danes who wielded the political authority, this authority being subject only to the royal government of Denmark. The material available on the Danish plans indicates that they were elaborate.

The Free Colored were divided into three classes, with the first class in turn being separated into three divisions. "Negroes and colored of culture and excellent behavior were allowed in the first class. These individuals might be fortunate enough to get burgher-briefs or licenses to engage in trade. Members of the other two divisions in the first class were presented with a certificate signed by the Governor-General" (Larsen 1950: 165–166). Improper conduct could bring about loss of class membership. Members of the first and most privileged class could be distinguished by wearing a "free-token," a cockade, either of silver of red and white (Larsen 1950: 166). Good behavior and cultural attainment were the means by which Free Colored moved from classes two and three into class one.

As early as 1786, the Free Colored were quite successful in their emulation of the Danes of that period because the government issued an ordinance which restricted the Free Colored in the wearing of gold, silver, silk stockings, and laces. Further repression of their social aspirations was evidenced in another ordinance of 1786, which declared that the firing of shot and the giving of rings at funerals was "harmful expense" (Larsen 1950: 163).

It is difficult to know how blacks, especially those who worked in the fields were to ever become a part of the class system. When the working day for the ordinary slave is examined, it is obvious that the Danish government had no intention of depriving itself of cheap labor. The workday began at 4 A.M. and extended as late as 10 P.M. on the larger plantations for approximately six months of the year with a general work week of five and one-half days. A two-day holiday was given three times a year (Oldendorp 1777: 381–382).

Written permission to travel outside the estate to which he belonged was required for nearly every slave, the single exception to the rule being those "whose wives make their home on a different plantation." Some leeway existed for persons attending church, but they were expected to have written passes (Oldendorp 1777: 391).

The bias of the royal law against the slave took many forms, one of the most notorious being the reimbursement to the slave owner by the Danish government if a slave was given the death punishment. This decree certainly placed the disabled and old in jeopardy; Oldendorp[2] adds that few owners committed this despicable crime (Oldendorp 1777: 393).

Punishment by lashes applied to the bare back ranged from fifty to 100, then to 200, and finally 500 lashes, the equivalent of the death penalty. Punishment could be meted out by a civil judge, but usually was at the discretion of the slave owner. Oldendorp stated, "... if guilt were not admitted willingly, then the procedure is to make him talk by torture" (1777: 391–393).

The punishment, by royal decree, for the slave missing for more than three months was loss of a leg, with the punishment being administered by a public justice of the peace. The penalty for the second offense was removal of the other leg. Such penalties did not prevent blacks from running away and Oldendorp recounts: "I have known such a untameable one who has lost both legs through repeated running away" (1777: 390).

Espousing a special concern, the royal government in Denmark set up a separate commission which was to concentrate on the improvement of slave traffic in both the Danish West Indies and on the Guinea Coast. The commission proposed an end to the slave trade in 1803, nonetheless evincing a concern about the labor supply on the island. The moral concerns of the commission were outweighed by their fears of the planters, hence "The clause relating to the final abolition of slavery ... was concealed from the planters for fear of their opposition" (Larsen 1950: 313).

No statistics are available, but undoubtedly abortion reached alarming proportions because the commission set up to recommend improvement for slave traffic took the topic into consideration in 1791. Among the

---

[2] Oldendorp was a Moravian Missions inspector general who came to the Danish West Indies on 22 May, 1767, and stayed until 23 October, 1768. During this time he recorded the complete history of the Moravian Missions in the three islands, and interviewed the slaves on the details of their lives. In addition, he collected material pertaining to the whites of the islands, especially on the relationships to their bondsmen. Herskovits in commenting on Oldendorp's work states that "... he produced a model report which goes far in enabling the student of today to understand why Africanisms have been forced so deeply underground in the life of these islands, when their inhabitants are compared to the Negroes in other parts of the Antilles" (1958:43–44).

recommendations made by a Hans West, a Danish rector of the Christiansted Lutheran government school, was to seek more freedom and comfort for "mothers who had given birth to five or six children." West proposed a premium for childbearing "in order to check the common practice of abortion" (Larsen 1950:131).

Occasional comments in the literature suggest that the Danes occupied the role of the benevolent slave master. In the words of Lewisohn,

The Negroes were not treated too badly in the Danish islands since the home government set up very strict laws about their treatment, working hours and provisions. These laws were enforced. Nearly every plantation had its "hospital" for the sick workers and lying-in women and retained a doctor on a yearly fee who came regularly. At Beck's Grove ruin there still stands the estate hospital building — a large one of beautiful proportions (Lewisohn 1964: 20).

It is true the Danish government issued ordinances, but, fundamentally, these ordinances changed little or nothing. In 1787, an edict provided for the operation of public schooling for slaves. Four school managers were to be chosen "from the most well-behaved and capable Free Negroes." But by 1789, only two such schools were in operation in Christiansted on St. Croix; the enrollment for one in 1790 was forty-seven children. In addition, there were "several private schools for lighter-colored children" (Larsen 1950:98). Because, the slave population for St. Croix was estimated at approximately 30,000 in 1789, it obviously was not the intent of the government to see that slaves received public schooling even though a royal ordinance so decreed it (Larsen 1950:98).

Most blacks could ill afford to attend the theater on St. Croix. Such social diversions were for whites only, a policy made clear in the *Royal Danish American Gazette*, which stated "No Negro whatever in the house" (Westergaard 1917:248).

The Royal Danish government apparently did not interest itself in getting court representation for the nonwhite population, even though Thorkild Lund, a Danish Lutheran missionary, made the bold attempt to secure some justice by asking for:

... a new court for Negroes with colored as well as white personnel under the supervision of the governor general and other whites — which should adjudge all cases concerning the Negroes. The proposal was rejected (Larsen 1950: 136).

The manner in which the black population regarded the Free Colored is revealed in an account by a brother of the Danish Governor, Peter Von Scholten, who describes how a major of the Free Colored Brand (militia-type corps) was treated on July 2, 1848, when blacks threatened a riot if forced to wait any longer for their freedom:

The Brand major had narrowly escaped with his life. Riding into town from his estate he was attacked by the negroes, a negro woman striking at his neck with an ax, which fortunately glanced off without injuring him (Taylor 1888:129).

Although Von Scholten is often hailed as a hero in Cruzan history because of his general sympathy for the enslaved population he was not permitted to marry Anna Heegaard, his Free Colored consort, because "marriage between white and colored was forbidden by the Danes" (Lewisohn 1964: 49–51).

But the majority of the black Cruzan population, estimated at 20,000 in 1767 to 2,000 whites (Oldendorp 1777:400–401), would never have any such close affiliation with Danish government officials. Most faced a horrendous workday, coupled with callous treatment that led some to form a Maroon settlement, a fact not widely known (Pope 1972). Ordinarily Maroon communities were located only in regions where geography provided considerable isolation such as that in the Jamaica Cockpit country or the Surinam jungle. Nevertheless, on an island approximately fourteen miles long and only six miles wide a Maroon group formed a settlement on a mountain identified as Maronberg, less than 1,200 feet above sea level just a few miles from West End, the present day town of Frederiksted (Oldendorp 1777:394). Both whites and Free Negroes hunted escapees on Maronberg (Oldendorp 1777:395–396).

Failure of the Danes to provide educational facilities has already been noted, but even beyond this one surmises the Danes must have had little personal contact with the black population because there are hardly any traces of the Danish language on St. Croix today.

Whenever a Creole language is present on a West Indian island, it almost always is reflective of the dominant elite who once held power, that is, their language substantially altered through time by local usage and bearing the imprint of West African linguistic patterns. Thus, French Creole, Papiamento, and English Creole are the *lingua francas* on different islands, each dependent on the specific locale. But in the Virgin Islands there is no Danish Creole and never has been. There was a Dutch Creole for a time and later an English Creole, now spoken by nearly every local person, regardless of social position.

In 1967, I questioned whether the word *ja* in a folktale told in English Creole could be Danish. Several of my informants said it was possible, but they really were not certain. An elderly woman told me it grieved her to see the Danish flag taken down in 1917 on Transfer Day, when the United States took possession of the island. A few minutes later, however, she recalled the paltry pay for her work in the cane fields, 20 cents a day in the early 1900's. Then she proceeded to sing with much relish a popular island song, "Queen Mary," that describes a black cane field worker, dubbed Queen Mary, who helped lead rioters in 1878 in the destruction of sugar estates. A favorite line in the song for my informant was "Fan me, buckra [white] missus until the break of day," which refers to the fact that Queen Mary seated herself in the white woman's rocker, where she forced the white woman to fan her.

Espousing the concept of "divide and conquer," Danish colonials on St. Croix managed to rule substantially aided by rigid laws, which in effect seldom gave a slave the right to leave an estate. The Free Colored, as the Danes planned, cast their lot with the whites. However, when the division between the privileged, composed of whites, Free Colored, and Free Negroes, and the slaves is examined, it is clear that the entire socio-political hierarchy was in a state of constant jeopardy.

The establishment of a Maroon community on St. Croix, an eighty-four-square-mile island, attests to that as do the efforts at rebellion. An abortive uprising in 1746 (Westergaard 1917: 51) and again in 1759 on St. Croix (Larsen 1950: 77; Westergaard 1917: 246; 1926: 58–61) is further evidence. The success of the revolt on St. John, where a portion of the slave population, known as the Aminas, managed to hold the island for six months in 1733–1734, is testimony to the blacks' attempt and near success in overthrowing a colonial power. This insurrection, hailed as one of the most devastating of all in the West Indies, was a human hurricane, destructive not only in property loss but in terms of what it did for relations between master and slave in the Danish islands (Westergaard 1917: 168–177; Knox 1852: 71–77). Blacks who received the death penalty for their participation were utilized as an example and "their heads were set upon posts for a long time as a warning to the Negroes" by the Danes on St. Thomas (Oldendorp 1777: 400).

Two uprisings marked the nineteenth century on St. Croix. The first, in 1848, resulted when the "unfree" (a euphemism) decided that they would not wait for freedom promised in 1859, hence proceeded with a rebellion which had been planned "in the most quiet and successful manner" (Knox 1852: 112). Even after the granting of freedom in 1848 the black population, especially on St. Croix, found itself in a state of economic and social servitude. Again inequities reached a climax, this time in 1878, when another revolt, known locally as the "fire-burn," occurred. Today, rows of old slave quarters dot the countryside on St. Croix. There is only a scattering of "big houses" or plantation great houses, especially on the west side of the island, a reminder of the 1878 revolt. The continuing inequities in treatment of cane field workers on St. Croix exploded in the twentieth century with the labor difficulties and strike of 1915–1916.

This time a black leader came to the forefront, D. Hamilton Jackson, a man remembered with fondness and reverence by the Cruzan population today because he was able to stand up to the Danes, made gains for Cruzans in the field of employment, and as one informant said, "He put shoes on my feet."

In reviewing Danish policies and actions, it is clear that the Danes worked at developing social cleavages. There is little evidence that they ever did much to ameliorate the situation of cane field workers on St. Croix. In reference to public services as late as the twentieth century, Lewis states: "... up until the time of the Transfer, sick persons in St. Croix were transported to town on open wooden carts, exposed mercilessly to the sun" (1967: 22).

The list of injustices for Cruzans in the early 1900's was nearly as long as when slavery was in effect:

The *Herald*, valiantly edited by D. Hamilton Jackson in the last years of the Danish regime, fully catalogued the grievances of the Negro masses; police brutality, the numerous petty abuses of the work contract system, the habitual molestation of citizens by arrogant gendarmes, absentee government in both church and state and much else; not to mention a general culture so impoverished that about the only pleasure permitted to the "natives" was the playing of their own colored brass bands (Lewis 1967:22).

Except for an occasional government official and the Lutheran missionaries, the Danes seemingly remained as distant as possible from those at the bottom of the scale.

The Danes were not bent on achieving citizenship, salvation, or education for their subjects; their rule consistently reflected an indifference, which the black population responded to by failing to incorporate Danish custom into their lives. This is noteworthy because Afro-American culture in the New World often borrows freely, however selectively. From the standpoint of transculturation or the acceptance of cultural traits, the Danes failed miserably, especially when contrasted to the English, French and Spanish in the West Indies.

Colonialism and power abuse have left their imprint on the Virgin Islands, visible even today, but a statement of this nature can be made for any Caribbean island. Other factors are involved, and it is but a short step into the realm of national character for further research because the general indifference of the Danes to their subject population and to any others is so clearly conveyed through history. As Trollope remarked in 1858:

To the Danes the island belongs. The soldiers, officials, and custom-house people are Danes. They do not, however, mix much with their customers. They affect, I believe, to say that the island is overrun and destroyed by these comers, and that they would as lief be without such visitors (1858:224).

REFERENCES

HERSKOVITS, MELVILLE J.
1958   *The myth of the Negro past* (second edition). Boston: Beacon.
KNOX, JOHN P.
1852   *A historical account of St. Thomas ... and incidental notices of St. Croix and St. Johns.* New York: Charles Scribner's Sons.
LARSEN, JENS
1950   *Virgin Island story.* Philadelphia: Muhlenberg.
LEWIS, GORDON K.
1967   The myth of Danish culture. *Virgin Islands Review* 3:14–22.
LEWISOHN, FLORENCE
1964   *Divers information on the romantic history of St. Croix.* St. Croix Landmarks Society.
LOWENTHAL, DAVID
1972   *West Indian societies.* New York: Oxford University Press.
OLDENDORP, CHRISTIAN G. A.
1777   *Geschichte der Mission der evangelischen Brüder auf den caraibischen Inseln S. Thomas, S. Croix und S. Jan.* Barby.
POPE, POLLY
1972   A Maroon settlement on St. Croix. *Negro History Bulletin* 35:153–154.
TAYLOR, CHARLES E.
1888   *Leaflets from the Danish West Indies.* London: William Dawson and Sons.
TROLLOPE, ANTHONY
1858   *The West Indies and the Spanish Main.*
WESTERGAARD, WALDEMAR
1917   *The Danish West Indies under company rule.* New York: Macmillan.
1926   Negro rebellion on St. Croix, Danish West Indies, 1759. *Journal of Negro History* 11:50–61.

SECTION THREE

The Latin American Present

Agrarian Reform in Chile and Its Impact on Araucanian Indian Communities

BERNADO BERDICHEWSKY

1. ANTECEDENTS

1.1. *Introduction*

The Chilean population, which is distributed along a thin strip of land in the extreme southwest of South America, totals slightly less than ten million inhabitants. Of these, about 7 percent are Indians, undoubtedly of pre-Hispanic ancestry. Although from a biological point of view these people are largely of an Indo-Hispanic mixture, indigenous characteristics predominate; a large number of indigenous elements have also been preserved in the sociocultural realm, especially language, beliefs, and customs.

Of the various Indian societies which existed at the time of the Spanish Conquest in what is today Chilean territory (from Arica to Magallanes), only two major groups now exist, although with obvious changes and mixtures: the Aymara and Quechua on the high plateau in the extreme north of Chile, and the Mapuche or Araucanians in the lake region in the south. A sparse remainder of the Fuegian Indians can be found in the extreme south, a handful of whom still live in the area of the straits of Chilean Patagonia. The rest of the native population of Easter Island, although not of American but of Polynesian origin, could also be considered Chilean citizens. The latter number less than a thousand and the Fuegians only around fifty. In contrast, the Indians in the north of Chile exceed 50,000 in number and range over two large northern provinces, Tarapaca and Antofagasta. Without a doubt, the most numerous and important Indian community in Chile is that of the Araucanians. There

are more than 500,000 people distributed principally within the immense
territory from the Laja River to the Gulf of Reloncavi in the south of
Chile, which includes seven southern provinces: Arauco, Bio-Bio, Malleco,
Cautin, Valdivia, Osorno, and Llanquihue (Berdichewsky 1970).

1.2. The Demographic Aspect

The majority of existing statistics on the current Araucanian population
in Chile are based on the 1960 census or on even earlier data. While the
1970 census figures and data have recently been tabulated, it has not been
possible to estimate the exact size of the country's total Mapuche population and its geographic distribution. Nevertheless, what we do know
indicates that this population easily exceeds 500,000 persons; however,
we can give only approximate data when we refer to current Araucanian
demography in Chile.

Today more than 50,000 Mapuche, comprising about 8 percent of the
total Mapuche population, live in cities. Of these, more than half live in
Santiago, the country's capital and largest city, and are concentrated
mainly in marginal, populous, and proletarian districts (Munizaga 1961).
Only a small percentage of Mapuche professionals or small-scale businessmen live in lower-middle-class residential districts; the other half of the
urban Mapuche population is distributed over some large- and medium-
sized cities in the south of Chile, e.g. Concepción, Temuco, Angol.
However, about 90 percent of the total Mapuche population continues
to live in rural areas, primarily distributed in the above-mentioned provinces in the south of Chile. More than two-thirds are concentrated in the
provinces of Cautin and Malleco (especially in the first). The Mapuche
population of Cautin exceeds 200,000, of which the majority live in rural
areas, where they comprise 75 percent of the total rural population of the
province. They are concentrated on native reservations of two types:
those divided into family properties and those maintaining communal land
tenure. Of the more than 3,000 Indian reservations which exist in all the
Araucanian areas, two-thirds are found in the province of Cautin. In the
province of Malleco, north of Cautin, there are about 90,000 Indians,
almost all of whom live on some 340 reservations, constituting an even
greater part of the total rural population of the province than the Mapuche
in Cautin (i.e. about 80 to 90 percent). The third most important province
from the point of view of the Mapuche population is Valdivia to the south
of Cautin province. The number of Mapuche there is a little less than
50,000, concentrated primarily on about 450 reservations located in the
northern half of the province; they comprise almost 25 percent of the rural

population. Thus the heart of Araucanian country is currently situated in Cautin province and in the two bordering provinces to the north and south respectively, Malleco and Valdivia, i.e. in the region that extends from south of the Bio-Bio River to the Calle-Calle River. The province of Arauco to the northeast of Cautin follows in numerical importance, after which comes the province of Osorno south of Valdivia. There is an Indian population of less than 10,000 in each province and a total of less than 200 reservations between the two (slightly more than half of which are in Osorno); these groups comprise a little more than 10 percent of the rural population (slightly more than half of which is in Arauco). In the province of Bio-Bio at the extreme north of the Araucanian area, the Indian population is small; and in the province of Llanquihue to the extreme south of the Araucanian area, it is insignificant. From Arauco to Llanquihue the total area occupied by Mapuche during the 1960's was 566,000 hectares, of which more than half (343,000 hectares) were in Cautin province (CIDA 1966: Chapter 7).

This population of about 500,000 Indians is distributed throughout the extensive and important agricultural, cattle-raising, forest region in the south of Chile, in the seven provinces of the Araucanian area (basically concentrated in the three central provinces of this area), and almost entirely in rural zones. While the Indians live primarily on reservations, they can also be found as small independent agricultural landowners, as tenants on small farms and large *haciendas*, as day laborers, or as workers in the reformed areas of the economy on the *asentamientos* and *centros de reforma agraria*, in expropriated *hacienda* lands or "taken" lands. A small percentage live in the urban zones of the Mapuche area, especially in the city of Temuco (this does not include those urban Mapuche who left the Araucanian area, such as those who live in Concepción and Santiago).

1.3. *Ethnic Origin and Social Evolution of the Araucanians*

At the time of the Spanish Conquest, ethnic groups which were located along the central valley of Chile (from the waters of the Aconcagua River toward the south to the Gulf of Reloncavi) and neighboring areas along the coasts and in the mountain ranges could be considered Araucanian; they spoke Mapudungun with different regional dialects. They belonged to an Andean racial variety, with some biological characteristics of their own and with certain minor group differences among the three ethnic groups which made up the Araucanian people: the Picunche, the Mapuche, and the Huilliche. The first group was distributed from south of the Choapa River to north of the Itata River; the second approximately from the Itata River to the Calle-Calle River; and the third in the south to Chiloe Island (Latcham 1928). The Araucanian people of the protohistoric period were basically agricultural and had a simple tribal society. There were a few sociocultural differences among the three groups (for example, the more northern Picunche were slightly more sophisticated and apparently possessed more effective agricultural know-how, the most important of which was the principle of small-scale irrigation).

The origin of these Araucanian groups can generally be traced through archaeological finds, especially through the analysis of the agro-pottery cultural phases of the central and southern parts of the country; emphasis must be given particularly to discovering which cultural phases are related to Araucanian ethnic groups (Menghin 1962). Three prehistoric agro-pottery levels can be distinguished in the central zone of Chile, a region which at the time of the Conquest was the home of the Picunche. These are, from earliest to most recent times, as follows: (1) the Molloide level; (2) the polychrome ceramic level, including the black-on-orange type; and (3) the local Incan level. The three have a broad and uneven distribution, although they existed at different time periods and had different spheres of influence toward the southern zone (that is to say, toward that area which, at the time of the Conquest, was the home of the Mapuche and Huilliche). The last cultural level, the Incan, occurred later and had an indirect influence through the Spanish cultural level (Berdichewsky 1971a).

The first level, with its indications of early cultural influences, seems to correspond to a basic agro-pottery stratum which came about as part of a process of acculturation from the Norte Chico zone. It shows influences from the Molle culture which, it seems, introduced agriculture into the central part of the country in the second half of the first millennium of our era. This influence probably continued toward the south and by the end of the millennium brought agricultural revolution. This was the period in which the first socioeconomic formations of a communal mode of agricultural production occurred in both areas.

In the second cultural level, which arose from this basic agrarian stratum and continued well into the second millennium of our era, all the Araucanian ethnological elements crystallized. This happened first in the central zone and later in the southern zone through local developments and ethnological influences from the Norte Chico, but now from the Diaguita cultural phase and from other more distant influences. Ethnic groups of the Araucanian socioeconomic type evolved in this area (Berdichewsky 1971a).

At the time of the Incan conquest (as is shown as much by archaeological sources as by ethnohistory) a separation and differentiation took place between the northern ethnic group of the Picunche, the conquered group, and the other two more southern groups, Mapuche and Huilliche, who tenaciously resisted conquest by the Incans, maintaining themselves as an independent tribal society. The Picunche, on the other hand, were integrated into the socioeconomic structure of the Incan empire — which corresponded to that of a class society. Because of its character, this mode of production is similar to the type called "Asiatic," i.e. one in which the agrarian and kinship community is not destroyed but is rather incorporated into the socioeconomic and cultural structure in the system of class exploitation in a new state (Marx 1966:70). As a product of the destruction of the Inca empire by the Spanish conquistadors, the separate regions of the former empire — such as the central zone of Chile — remained disunited and, in fact, independent; this resulted in an interregnum of autonomy for decades until the new Spanish Conquest took place in the Picunche area. The Picunche resisted the Spaniards for a long time, but they were eventually conquered when they no longer had a simple tribal society but had developed instead a true tribal confederation with a sociopolitical chiefdom structure. The Mapuche and Huilliche did not go through this process; they were not conquered by the Spaniards, but remained a simple and democratic tribal society with a notable and obvious military orientation, the product of their resistance against the invaders.

The Spanish Conquest subjugated the indigenous peoples of America, liquidating a great part of their populations, destroying their political structures, and ending their independence. It bound them as the principal working force of the new socioeconomic structure which the Spaniards implanted in the New World, and which was the product of the expansion of European society at the dawn of mercantile capitalism before it lost the last traces of feudalism. In Andean America, including central Chile, compulsory indigenous manual labor was used in the initial decades after the Conquest for the extraction of precious metals which went to enrich the cities and capitals of the Old World. This was achieved through the law of *encomienda*, by which the Spanish king granted the right to use Indian labor. Only later was the Indian work force channeled into the agricultural and cattle-raising enterprises which soon supplanted the *encomienda* — the system of *haciendas* or large local landholdings. This evolution is clearly observable among the Picunche in the central zone of Chile.

The socioeconomic structure which the Spaniards imposed on this region during the colonial period was characterized by the coexistence and combination of several modes of production, of which the imposed capitalistic mode of production became increasingly important and dominant, especially after Chile's political independence.

In the Picunche zone there coexisted in varying proportions, particularly in rural areas, capitalist forms of production, feudal or semifeudal forms of production, and even primitive forms of communal production in some indigenous communities. Naturally, this last kind of production among the Picunche did not persist and was integrated into a Spanish socioeconomic form, until the last Picunche indigenous communities in the central zone disappeared at the beginning of the era of Chilean independence.

The social and ethnic evolution of the Mapuche, to the south of Bio-Bio River, was completely different from the tragic and slow disappearance of the Picunche, both as an independent society and as an ethnic group. Toward the middle of the past century, there were practically no more Picunche in Chile.

The so-called *Guerra de Arauco* very quickly became a struggle between the Mapuche and the Spaniards. Some Huilliche groups were integrated into the Mapuche communities and eventually merged with them. Isolated groups and individual Picunche fled from those areas which were occupied by the Spaniards and were also assimilated into Mapuche communities. To this were added the captives, most of whom were women, taken from the Spanish population by the Mapuche during the long and rather sporadic Araucanian War. Many adventurers, criminals, and deserters who reached or fled to the Mapuche regions were similarly integrated into this ethnic group. As for the Spaniards, the prime purpose of the Araucanian War was to obtain captives for replacing or increasing the available manual labor (Jara 1971:42).

It is undeniable that the long Araucanian War, which continued throughout the entire colonial period up to the national republic period, produced a notable ethnic transformation for the Mapuche people and for their socioeconomic structure. A form of contact and cohabitation between the warring sides developed since this war, in spite of its long duration, was limited to a few short periods of total war followed by long years of tacit armistice, intermittently interrupted by small-scale guerrilla actions.

In the course of three centuries, from the middle of the sixteenth to the middle of the nineteenth century, the Mapuche underwent an extraordinary process of territorial and ethnic expansion, as well as one of notable cultural and intercultural contact and ethnic mixture. Excluding those who were assimilated into related ethnic groups such as the Picunche and the Huilliche, as well as those who intermingled with the very different ethnic groups of Spaniards and Creoles, the Mapuche (enclosed on three sides — north, south, and the sea) expanded toward the mountains and beyond. There they struggled against other indigenous groups such as the mountain-living Pehuenche and the Puelche on the other Andean border, and the Tehuelche of the Patagonian pampas, all of whom they "Araucanized" and, more often than not, assimilated. This eastern Mapuche expansion followed the growing commercial cattle trade which developed between the two competing sides, Mapuche and Spaniards, in spite of the tactical movements characteristic of guerrilla warfare.

The Mapuche made frequent excursions to the other side of the mountains, to the pampas, to hunt and rustle wild cattle and horses or to acquire them from the friendly Puelche tribes. Often Mapuche Indians and their armies headed for those areas to attack the colonies and Spanish forts with their *malocas*, at times even approaching Buenos Aires.

The Mapuche spread this new type of economy, and they absorbed and adapted to their own life numerous important features of material Spanish culture such as the horse (used in war, rituals, agriculture, cattle raising, and in trade). They also introduced firearms, metal arms and silverwork, clothing, elements from the Catholic religion, and other Spanish values into their own culture (Zapater 1970).

Up until the middle of the last century, during the republican national period and the development of industrial capitalism in the country, the important Araucanian region continued to be an independent Mapuche territory. Mapuche society managed to subsist successfully through the Araucanian War, and to a large extent it grew even stronger and showed a great adaptability in spite of the changes which took place in that period. Undoubtedly the productive level of the Mapuche socioeconomic structure increased considerably in those three turbulent centuries, making possible necessary changes in their technical relations to production although not in their social relations to production. These continued to be like those of the protohistoric Araucanian society which the Spanish conquistadors found in the sixteenth century. Property continued to be collective, tribal, or acquired by hereditary lineage. Nevertheless, it is possible to perceive the beginning of the breakdown of this system and the first signs of the development of private ownership of the means of production by the chiefs or bosses (except for land, which continued to be collectively owned) especially for cattle raising. Social organization rested on a structure of kinship based on extended family and unilineal lineages having a patrilineal character and based on principles of patrilocal residence (Faron 1961). Political organization went beyond the tribe, evolving into systems of tribal confederations under the direction of several powerful chiefs (Latcham 1922). We can conclude that although the mode of production was maintained in essence as communal or tribal agricultural, it reached a higher level of development, making it possible for a primitive socioeconomic tribal formation to develop into a complex of tribal confederations or chiefdoms which carried the elements of the deterioration of the tribal order itself. This level, which the Mapuche attained by the middle of the nineteenth century (having already begun in the second half of the eighteenth century) was the equivalent of what the Picunche had reached by the middle of the sixteenth century and the start of the Spanish Conquest. In neither of the two Araucanian social formations of these very different historic periods were the internal contradictions directed toward a higher organic action permitting the step toward incipient state and class social structures. In both cases, the external factors were decisive, allowing both tribes to be conquered, dominated, and absorbed by a dominant class society: the Picunche by the semifeudal Spanish social structure and incipient capitalism of the colony, and the Mapuche by the industrial capitalist social structure of the new Chilean nation.

2.   THE INCORPORATION OF ARAUCANIANS INTO CHILEAN SOCIETY

2.1   *Initiation of the System of Indian Reservations*

Toward the middle of the last century, industrial capitalism in Chile increased considerably and brought the agriculture of the central zone into the capitalist market. Large Chilean landholdings were turned into great producers of wheat and cattle destined for domestic and international markets. These large estates, although retaining some structures of enforced labor production in the countryside and developing an extensive although technically backward agriculture, were an important part of the Chilean capitalist socioeconomic structure. The landholding class and the industrial and financial bourgeoisie, in spite of their differences and conflicts, were economically linked through the formation of a political and economic oligarchy that dominated and controlled the country. It was precisely the new sector of industrial and commercial bourgeoisie which impelled and promoted the expansion of these large estates toward the southern zone in the second half of the last century; in the central zone of Chile, the country's largest basic agrarian "bourgeois" expansion of these estates was aggressive; it ended in the conquest and colonization of the Araucanians and was characterized by bloodshed and arson — among many other "legal" or illegal methods by which the lands of the Mapuche Indians were seized. This process coincided with, and was part of, the general expansion of vigorous national capitalism in the first three decades of the second half of the century, which permitted the growth of new economic activities, industrial and financial as well as agricultural, cattle breeding and, particularly, mining. The result was the annexation of new territories and the development of a national market which extended from Arica to Magallanes. A product and an instrument of this expansion was the War of the Pacific, in which Chile defeated the Peruvian-Bolivian Confederation and annexed all the great mining territory in the north. Chile's attempt to open a window to Polynesia with the annexation of Easter Island and its domination in the extreme south of the Strait of Magellan through founding the Bulnes fort and its city of Punta Arenas (which permitted it to acquire the Patagonian pampas and Fuegians for sheep raising) was of a similar nature. The existence of that central and national market formed the basis for the crystallization of the modern Chilean nation.

The last confrontations of the Araucanian War resulted in the final destruction of the Mapuche militant groups, annexation of Araucanian lands as national territory, and the compulsory incorporation, in the form of internal colonization, of Indian communities into the agro-Chilean structure which was characterized by the large expansionist landholdings. The new policy of promoting foreign, especially European, colonists, most of whom settled the "virgin lands" of the Araucanians, was an important part of this national policy of expansion and domination of Araucanian land. Likewise, new cities sprang up which expanded the exchange economy and permitted integration of the whole area into the national market.

As a result of this expansion and colonization, a new sociopolitical structure arose in Mapuche society, imposed by the larger dominant society, which formalized and legitimized the forced domination and incorporation of Mapuche communities into the national society. This structure is what we have referred to as the system of Indian reservations.

In the decade of the 1850's, the Mapuche tribes were divided and captured by the army under the command of the famous Colonel Saavedra. In 1866, the first national law creating Indian reservations (Jara 1956) was passed. Nevertheless, the Mapuche, although already close to defeat, continued a resistance which culminated in the last Indian uprising at the beginning of the 1880's. The action was planned to take advantage of the existence of the War of the Pacific which kept the army busy in the north of the country; but this attempt was not successful, and as soon as the Pacific war turned in Chile's favor, the national government launched a punitive action against the Mapuche "rebels," using "exemplary punishment." Thus ended the final phase of Mapuche resistance and their entire autonomy. As of 1884, the institution of Indian reservations took a definitive, authoritarian form. For four decades, until the 1920's, that process completed and legalized through decress the formation of more than 3,000 Indian reservations. The Mapuche were concentrated on the reservations, which permitted the assignment of most of the best lands in the area to colonists who came from the center or the north of the country or from foreign countries and who became established as great private landowners.

Lands assigned to Indian reservations in the formative phase described above were granted by the government at the same time that lands were assigned to the new colonists. Once these estates in the Araucanian area and the lands "legally" assigned to the colonists (as well as to the newly created reservations) were established in the first decades of this century, their expansion was not arrested. Expansion consumed land which was once the property of the reservations. National legislation reflected this process and, if in the first half-century it was aimed at preserving the existence of collective property of the reservations, in the second fifty-year period it tended more and more to modify legislation in the direction of legitimized individual property in the form of *minifundia*, thus allowing the large estates, or *latifundia*, to acquire or appropriate these properties in whatever way possible (Cantoni 1969). It was under these contradictions that the *Sistema de Reducciones Indigenas* developed.

2.2.   The First Period of the System of Indian Reservations (1866–1926)

With the establishment of the *Sistema de las Reducciones*, the Mapuche remained concentrated on reservations, where the basic source of subsistence was the land; these became communal property and the title to them, called the title of favor, was granted in the name of the chief of the reservation. The chief was generally the *cacique* or *lonko* or his descendant (real or pretender) and had been sanctioned by government authorities. With this act, the political power of the chiefs (greatly weakened during the previous century by the last skirmishes of the Araucanian War which decimated the Mapuche militant groups) partially regained its former status — this time, paradoxically, through conquest and incorporation into a larger society. Moreover, this same society, through the reservation system, preserved the communal holding of land sanctioned by the legislation without leaving a legal opening which might permit the eventual confiscation of lands assigned to the reservations. At first, only a two-thirds approval by the Indian community could permit the sale of these lands, but the most recent laws allowed for a simple vote, making it obvious that previous voting had been characterized by a lack of unanimity in determining the legality of the sale or confiscation of the lands (Berdichewsky 1971b).

This new dominance of the chiefs was sustained partly by tradition, in that the majority of reservation chiefs were descendants of *lonko*, and partly by the new legitimacy of being the possessors or guardians of titles to community lands. Nevertheless, their power was largely fictitious, since they did not have any juridical-administrative powers from the state. All legal problems the Indians faced in the larger society were settled by the distinct powers or institutions of the state, and litigations could only be resolved in special Indian courts of justice in which the chiefs had no authority. For this reason, the chiefs' internal authority in the reservations was very weak and was often supplanted by other persons such as the *machi*, the Mapuche schoolmaster, the Mapuche religious priest, or simply by some natural leader within the community.

The Indian reservations persisted as sociopolitical units which clung to the communal legality that gave them collective landholding for the subsistence of the community. When the reservations were set up they did not always exactly reflect the tribal community or the ancestral lineage which had existed for generations; often two or more neighboring communities — or more often remains of communities — united or were united on one reservation. In other cases, small isolated groups were incorporated into a community to form a reservation. Conversely, one natural community was divided into two or more reservations. In other words, although theoretically the natural community of kinship — whether extended familial by lineage or tribal — was preserved, actual cases show that many natural communities were divided or even destroyed and other new communities were formed in various ways on some reservations. Thus, although the natural communities were not, strictly speaking, maintained as units on the reservations, generally the "Indian community" as such was preserved (although often modified), and within it kinship structures continued to exist as basic elements of the social organization (Faron 1961).

Moreover, the mode of production — obviously modified — of the primitive community was preserved. Subsistence economy continued to play a predominant role on Indian reservations. The means of production used by Indian peasants was not very different from that of their non-Indian counterparts, whether tenant farmers, day laborers for the landowners, independent peasants, or small landowners. The principal difference was in the area of distribution and consumption: the Mapuche sowed wheat and had small farms and some cattle, but only a small part of their products went to market; the rest was intended for internal consumption. They also developed various crafts for their own use and to use in bartering with their neighbors, preferably within their own ethnic group. In this sense we can characterize the Mapuche economy within the reservation system, especially during the first half of the century, as fundamentally (though not exclusively) a subsistence economy. It did not remain at the periphery of the national economy, however; on the contrary, it was incorporated into the latter, and while much of its subsistence form was maintained, greater profit was permitted for the intermediaries, with the result that there was increased exploitation of the Indians. This exploitation was twofold: on the one hand, it maintained a cheap manual labor source in reserve for the large estates, and on the other, it exploited the Indians indirectly through the commercialization of Indian products on the market which were sold at the cheapest possible price. In this way, the selling of wheat and cattle did not generally produce any benefit but instead made Indians sell at prices far below the actual cost, thus increasing their poverty and dependence. While the level of technology of large estate agriculture was low, (except in the case of a few modernized estates), technology in the Indian community was even lower. Thus productivity only permitted the supplying and feeding of the communities. The ratio of inhabitants to land area was not too low relatively, roughly estimated at one man to about six hectares, and although a growing demographic pressure existed on the reservations, this was still reasonable, There was some emigration from the communities, but it was only sporadic since most people did manual labor outside (harvesting, construction etc.) generally returning to the reservation.

The level of scholarship was low and illiteracy common. Primary school instruction was therefore introduced into the Indian communities at this time. This schooling was generally private and supported by the Catholic or Protestant church. This religious influence and that of the private schools were a part of the Mapuche communities even before the reservation system. In certain ways these small communities partly socialized the children to the values of the large society. Nevertheless, the fundamental socialization of Mapuche children and their acculturation to the values of Mapuche culture were generally conducted in their own Mapudungun language and within the family unit. The values of Mapuche culture, although obviously modified, were preserved to a great extent in that period. This was as true for their spiritual values and world beliefs (e.g. their harvest ceremonies of Ñillatun, shaman ceremonies or Machitun, Pewentun, etc.) as for their material culture (expressed in their crafts-manship and technology; in their ideas of work and of cooperation; in numerous traditional customs, habits, and attitudes; and in their familial relationships through mostly traditional kinship structures). But the culture was kept alive most particularly through the preservation of the language.

In the case of other Indian groups, just as with the Mapuche, confine-ment on the reservations contributed to the preservation of Indian communities, even though they remained at the subsistence level. In order to preserve their culture, however modified, the function of group main-tenance was given great importance, and it became a true resistance force against the culture of the larger dominating society. In this way, their ethnic identity, which had been very strong in the past, especially during the long Araucanian War, was strengthened; it became a defense mecha-nism against the racial discrimination of the larger society which facilitated social discrimination and economic exploitation.

Obviously, Mapuche social mobility in the period was minimal, and the social conflict they encountered generally acquired the character of racial conflict: the struggle of the Mapuche against the *huinca* (*mestizo*) as well as against the exploitative class. Although the Mapuche people developed a relatively strong ethnic consciousness, they did not succeed in developing a true social or class consciousness. They were also unable to find an adequate political identity because the political parties of the landholding class were interested in them only as a source of votes. The few Mapuche leaders who functioned on the political level at the end of this period were used by these parties to betray their ethnic group and their class.

2.3. *The Second Period of the System of Reservations and the Beginning of its Breakdown* (*1927–1965*).

The first phase of the system of reservations, the phase in which it began and developed until it assumed the general characteristics indicated above, spanned a period of more than half a century. It had a rather weak beginning in the 1860's, became more generalized in the 1880's, and took its final form in the four following decades. At this point, the second stage began, marked by a new Indian law in 1927 (Jara 1956). This stage (described in the last section) lasted until the middle of the 1960's. It was in this period that all the signs of the breakdown of the reservation system began to appear, emphasizing its internal and external contradictions.

In 1927, many large estates or *haciendas* were firmly established in the southern part of the country. However, the whole Chilean capitalist economy grew increasingly dependent on foreign monopolies, in particular mining and exportation of raw materials. Generally, the landholding class was tied more and more to the importing-exporting bourgeoisie which was increasing in power. Agriculture regressed and became more unproductive, forcing the country to import increasingly large quantities of foodstuffs. Underdevelopment, dependence, economic crises, and the condition of the people gradually worsened. Social conflicts and class struggle sharpened. The worker movement was strengthened, grew enormously, and acquired a strong class consciousness. Social development and class consciousness among the peasants however, were still very weak, although there appeared in agriculture some important social confrontations such as the famous and tragic case of Ranquil in the 1930's. All these factors made the landowner in the south (who was younger and less secure than the landowner in the northern regions) put increasing pressure on the peasant, especially those on the Mapuche reservations. This pressure was manifested in a continued usurpation of land and in modifications of the Indian laws which allowed for more and more legal opportunities for the taking and selling of native land (thus gradually reducing the communal lands of the reservations). Indian communities were tied to the market economy by the exploitation of their labor force as well as by the growing demand for their own agricultural and artisan products. They received a minimal margin of profit for these products, often involving a real loss (especially in the sale of cattle). Thus, this extreme commercialization and the usurious credit extended by landowners and businessmen — to the use of which Mapuche were often obliged to resort — resulted in an indirect and merciless exploitation which increased native poverty. On the other hand, some positive aspects of civilization also reached the Indian communities, although only in a marginal way, e.g. an increase in opportunities for schooling and literacy. Some elements of hygiene and health were introduced which somewhat reduced the high mortality rate and contributed to an increase in the size of the native population. This fact, and the higher birthrate among the Mapuche as compared to the rest of the population, produced, in spite of all their difficulties and miseries, a demographic explosion in the Indian communities: the Mapuche population in this period tripled. This brought about a tremendous demographic pressure on the land, reducing the man-to-land ratio at the end of the period to barely one hectare per person (IREM 1970).

These trends led to a decrease and concentration of communal lands and to overpopulation: they brought about the subdivision of communal lands into small colonies or the subdivision of numerous communities into small parcels of family or individual property. This came about through the seizure or sale of parts of these lands to landowners. Divided communities were thus formed, a trend encouraged by the larger society by imposing its criterion of private property on communal property in the interest of land ownership. But the small properties which arose "legally" in the divided and in *de facto* nondivided communities, influenced by the traditional family system of unilineal heritage and the growth of the population, led in fact (although not legally) to the internal distribution of communal lands among the reservation families and eventually to the end of communal property. Communal landholding was theoretically retained as a legal formality (the precedent was established in the titles of favor granted during the first period of the system of reservations). In actuality, production continued on a fundamentally familial level: each family cultivated a certain number of hectares and only very limited land remained for communal cultivation. Paradoxically, extensive native ownership of land which had been communal property during the first period developed into family property ownership by the end of the second period (1927–1965), and collective land tenure was only retained as a formality. This consequently modified the Mapuche attitude toward the land, changing it from a communal and cooperativist view into the petty bourgeois mentality of small peasant ownership (Berdichewsky 1971b).

Another consequence of this situation was a substantial growth of migration from the reservations to the large *haciendas*, increasing the number of Mapuche tenants and day laborers and the migration toward outside jobs in public works, agriculture, and industries in cities and neighboring towns. This brought about the breakdown of families and the familial system and signs of a disintegration of the traditional kinship structures.

The Mapuche entered into contact with almost all sectors and strata of the rural and urban population. On the one hand, their conflicts and socioeconomic problems increased along with their exploitation and social and racial discrimination. On the other hand, they also began to partici-pate, however slightly, in the social struggles and economic concerns of the exploited classes. Yet their identity and ethnic solidarity did not disappear; indeed they were reinforced by these changes. However, the mobility of the Mapuche population between communities and the effect of contact with and acculturation to the larger society produced changes and conflicts within Mapuche culture.

2.4. *The Third Period of the System of Reservations and the Impact of Agrarian Reform (1965–1973)*

During the second period of the reservation system, the system started to break down (as has been discussed above) because of internal socio-economic contradictions within the Chilean agricultural system and pressure applied by the landowner. The basic factors which promoted this breakdown arose when the economic infrastructure of Indian communities changed fundamentally from that of a communal property system of production to one of small private property. The very subsistence economy was also radically changed and, although not totally undermined, was increasingly tied to the market economy. This hybrid became a specific tool for exploitation of Indians by dominant classes of the region, the landholders and the bourgeoisie, with a sequel of poverty, migration, and proletarization of Mapuche communities. These infrastructural changes also produced schisms in the ideological and social structure of Mapuche society, undermining those aspects based on the kinship system as well as weakening kinship leadership, the effect of which was to bring Mapuche culture and identity values to a point of profound crisis.

This period was also characterized, in general, by increased class struggle in the country and, as a result of this, a greater organization and awakening of peasants' social consciousness, an awareness reflected in the wording of the first law of peasant unionization in 1924 and in the growth of peasant organization through unions, associations, and confederations (Affonso 1971). At the same time, the upper classes tried to obstruct this organization, restricting the terms of laws dealing with peasant unionization, making organization of unions difficult, and persecuting union leaders. Token reforms in agriculture were made by the upper classes to palliate the conflicts without modifying the real structure of the system. As a consequence of this and of the agricultural economic crisis, the first attempts at agrarian reforms were made.

The first set of agrarian reforms effected in this period was of the so-called "expansionist" or *desarrollista* type, similar to that being carried out in the majority of Latin American countries at the same time (with the exception of Mexico and Bolivia and later of Guatemala, Cuba, and

Peru). They were partial efforts, helping the bourgeoisie more than the peasant who, in practice, did not receive any benefit from these attempts. These reforms had two phases: the first began in 1928 with the *Ley de Colonización*, and its instrument was the *Caja de Colonización Agrícola*. It lasted until 1962 and created only 120 communities in a total of 4,779 parcels of land, most of which were small, making up only 2.5 percent of the existing landed property in the country. It did not expropriate land from large landowners but rather bought and sold lots from acquired farms; the consequence was that this land frequently fell into the hands of a new agrarian bourgeoisie which mostly came from the cities. The second phase began at the end of 1962, under pressure from the Alliance for Progress, with the passing of Agrarian Reform Law No. 15,020. This phase lasted until 1967, and the second phase began when Law No. 16,640 was passed by the Christian Democratic government then in power. At the end of 1964 when this political movement took over the government, it could be seen that *desarrollista* type of agrarian reform, after thirty-six years of existence and the passing of two laws, had only slightly benefitted some 5,000 holders of small- and medium-sized farms.

At that time, agriculture had been in a recession since 1920 when Chile's market for nitrate, or natural saltpeter, broke down and the world began to experience the Great Depression. From 1945 on, the population rate began to outgrow the food supply, in spite of an abundance of land and a favorable climate, and importation of agricultural products doubled. In 1964 only a quarter of the work force in Chile was employed in agriculture, one of the lowest percentages in all of Latin America (Barraclough 1971:4).

Agrarian reform only slightly and indirectly affected the Indian communities in its second and last phases. New methods of commercialization, credit, and assignments of land, such as SAG, INDAP and CORA created by Law No. 15,020 in 1962, were the sources of this indirect influence. Only by chance were some Indian communities able to benefit directly from those institutions. Earthquakes in the beginning of the 1960's in the south of Chile also had a tremendous impact on some Indian communities. Several coastal Mapuche communities in the area of Puerto Saavedra suffered severe damage in the catastrophes and had to be moved. Some of the first *asentamientos* created by the *Corporación de Reforma Agraria* in the interior of Cautin province, especially in the county of Cunco, were, therefore, made up of a mixture of peasant groups from that region and groups from those Indian communities which had been moved from the coastal regions affected by the earthquake. With the exception of this unusual case, in neither of the two phases of the *desarollista* agrarian reform were assignments of land made to Indians nor was usurped land returned to communities. On the contrary, many of the new colonists or even new settlers (in the second phase) conflicted legally and in other ways with Indian communities over questions of land; they were also often guilty of usurpation or fraudulent purchase of Indian land.

Sharpening contradictions in the agricultural system during the four decades of the period in question were reflected in the economic and productivity crisis, in demographic changes and migrations, in the displacement of classes and social mobility, in the involvement of the bourgeoisie in the agriculture and landholding sectors, and in the confrontations between those two classes. Likewise, social conflicts were provoked between the exploiting classes and the peasants, and the consequent intensification of the class struggle resulted, on the one hand, in different adjustments and more agrarian reform and, on the other, in an increased organization and social consciousness among the peasants. Besides the changes already indicated in the system of Mapuche reservations, this situation produced a greater assimilation of Mapuche into the larger society, not only through the market mechanism, but also by virtue of their increased integration and partial identification with other peasant strata. The increased social consciousness of the Mapuche took two directions, not necessarily contradictory: a greater ethnic consciousness, and a class consciousness. In 1953, the *Primer Congreso Nacional Mapuche Indígena de Chile* was founded, and in 1961 the *Federación Nacional Campesina e Indígena* was established, in which the National Indigenous Association of Chile was integrated with other peasant organizations.

At the end of 1964, with the beginning of the Christian Democratic government of President Eduardo Frei, and especially during the next two and a half years, the law of agrarian reform began a new phase which we shall call the "reformist" phase. This brought about the last period in the history of the reservation system, a period in which agrarian reform became even more important. This reform somehow gave the *coup de grace* to this system and eventually inaugurated a new epoch in the history of Mapuche society, the current period beginning with the middle of the 1960's.

At the beginning of the Frei government's period of power, the situation of the peasants was disastrous. Per capita agricultural income represented less than half the national average. Seventy percent of the peasants had average incomes of less than one hundred dollars a year. Unemployment was widespread in Chile and it is estimated that one-third of the peasant work force was idle. The poorest sector of the peasant population, numbering 1,250,000, consumed few industrial products, had deficient diets, miserable homes, and a high infant-mortality rate (Barraclough 1971:4). Illiteracy was also very common: almost half the adult agricultural workers and small landowners of central Chile could be classified as illiterate.

More than three-fourths of the cultivatable land remained in the form of large *haciendas* or estates (*latifundios*) which included more than twelve workers, tenant farmers, or cattle herders. Many of the permanent workers received most of their salaries in kind, and principally, in the right to use a small amount of land. These tenant farmers were able to be dismissed at will, depending on the landowners or patrons for credit, for the commercialization of their products, and for the possibilities of work. The unions were almost completely prohibited and peasant political participation minimal. The use of land in the large estates tended to be extensive and not intensive. In spite of their great extension, the *latifundios* employed only 40 per cent of the peasant work force and contributed only 60 per cent of agrarian production. The small landowners or *minifundistas*, who made up one-fourth of the agrarian population, were concentrated on two per cent of the arable land ... thereby increased the proletariat of peasant day labourers without a right to land. Between 1955 and 1965, the number of tenant farmers or fixed workers living on their lands decreased by half. On the other hand the given surface increased by half and the number of small landowners and of workers without land increased vertically (Barraclough 1971:5).

By the end of 1970 the Frei government had expropriated 1,364 landed properties totaling 3,433,744 hectares, approximately 282,473 hectares of which were irrigated. This was about 18 percent of the total agricultural land and approximately 12 percent of that with irrigation. The expropriations benefitted only some 25,000 peasants (Barraclough 1971:6).

New laws of agrarian reform also allowed peasant unionization, a minimum salary for peasants, an eight-hour work day, and represented an attempt at industrializing and modernizing the country. The bourgeois reformism, already well established, was more effective than the earlier *desarrollista* type in introducing modern capitalism into Chilean agriculture. Its aim (which, however, was unsuccessful) was to transform a large number of small and middle-sized properties into diverse cooperatives in which credit and efficient technical assistance could be available (Rivera 1972:6). It more or less ended the existence of the landholding class by expropriating more than one-third of the *latifundios* with more than eighty irrigable hectares.

The Frei government successfully expropriated a little less than one-third of the more than 5,000 holdings (those consisting of eighty hectares or more with irrigation) and the remaining two-thirds were expropriated before the end of the three years of President Allende's Popular Government.

This new government, while continuing agrarian reform with the same laws passed by the earlier government, accelerated the process and ended the *gran latifundio*. "This rapid and massive change in landholding was made almost without violence and without decreasing the planted area of the global agricultural production, a unique case in agrarian reforms of this nature" (Barraclough and Affonso 1973:77). In its third year, the Popular Government found it necessary to pass its own agrarian reform laws. These expropriated small- and middle-sized properties of forty to eighty irrigable hectares, doubling the amount of expropriated land and comprising more than 27 percent of productive land (Barraclough and Affonso 1973).[1]

The character of agrarian reform under President Allende was quite different from that enacted by President Frei. It went from bourgeois "reformism" which attempted to maintain the capitalist structure of the country by introducing agriculture as a counterpart to industrialization to a "revolutionary" kind which attempted to change the economic and social structure of agriculture in particular and the country in general in the direction of a socialist society. This involved structural changes, such as nationalization of basic wealth, expropriation of foreign and national monopolies (creating social ownership of the economy), nationalization of banking, credit, and the redistribution of incomes. Worker participation in development and control and educational reform were planned, all of which would create a social and economic base for initiating socialism.

Peasant participation and social consciousness increased with the growth of peasant unionization and with the creation of peasant county councils. The *asentamientos, centros de reforma agraria,* and *empresas estatales* gave structure to reformed agricultural areas. At this time about 40 percent of the productive agricultural land in the country was involved, to the benefit of about 80,000 peasants. Another basic distinction between this and the former *Reforma Agraria* is that while the former attempted to create a great number of small- and middle-sized private property holdings, the latter established large units of collectivist or cooperative production reducing private property ownership of the land to a minimum. This fundamental change in the basic principle of landholding made a distinct impact on the Indian community.

Both the *desarrollista* government of President Alessandri in 1962 and the reformist government of President Frei in 1967 saw the dissolution of communal landholding on the undivided Indian reservations as objectives of their agrarian reform. Because of this, the Indian law of 1961 was

---

[1]   This was interrupted by the military coup of September 1973.

passed by President Alessandri, which specified that communal holdings were to be dissolved, paving the way for the sale of reservation lands. The Frei government also proposed a law with the same objectives but it was not passed in parliament. Both laws openly sanctioned the indiscriminate sale of Indian lands. Their objective was initially unsuccessful but was later partly accomplished through radical changes (passed by a parliamentary majority in opposition to the Popular Government) which totally destroyed the value of the *le indigena*, presented to parliament by President Allende. Therefore, to a great extent, Indian reservations did not benefit directly from the agrarian reforms of the 1960's although they were clearly affected by the processes of change throughout that decade. A small number of Mapuche were integrated as minority groups or as individuals into the *asentamientos de Reforma Agraria* that were created at this time for the peasants. However, none of the settlements was purely Mapuche nor were reservations transformed into settlements. Likewise, attempts at converting Indian reservations into agricultural cooperatives were minimal. Only in a few of the mixed settlements was there a Mapuche majority and in them an ethnic conflict nearly always occurred between Mapuche and non-Mapuche groups.

Generally, the impact of agrarian reform of that decade on the Mapuche was rather indirect: apart from the general opening up of rural areas preceded by the process of agrarian reform, which was especially pronounced in the second half of the decade (with the decreased power of land holders, greater democratization, the increase in schooling and social mobility, and many other elements of transculturation felt by Mapuche communities), the most profound effects were caused by two particularly significant phenomena.

First, as agrarian reform increasingly introduced the structure and products of modern capitalism into Chilean agriculture, the market economy became more general, especially through state credit organizations and increased commercialization of agriculture. These new manifestations were linked to parallel and proliferating private counterparts. Moreover, there was an increase both in the economic power of the peasant and the introduction of industrial products into the rural area. All this further undermined the semisubsistence economy of Mapuche communities making them more dependent on the market economy. Another considerable area of change was the social order; the reforms of the Frei period were accompanied not only by increased industrialization and spread of the national market toward the rural areas but also by increased peasant organization through the new union laws. Peasant and Indian committees developed a greater social consciousness, and the parallel process of proletarization accelerated. The structure of the *Sistema de Reducciones* was weakened and class struggle in agriculture intensified, leading to social conflicts.

All these occurrences provoked new frustration among Indian communities, and the problems were not solved by the agrarian reforms. This produced a social movement which grew throughout the entire decade and continued to a certain extent during the Allende period. It led to a peasant "takeover" of the land. The Mapuche played an important role in this movement. The effect of agrarian reform on the Mapuche was such that the Mapuche communities were provoked to react and start an active struggle to recover their usurped lands. On more than one occasion, Mapuche peasants were heard to say at this time that the agrarian reform was more for the Chileans and that their usurped lands should be returned to them by the landholders (Berdichewsky 1971b). This attitude did not undermine the social consciousness of the Mapuche although it did give rise to a greater ethnic consciousness when they felt themselves discriminated against by an agrarian reform which did not return their lands. This process of growth of ethnic consciousness can also be detected in the proliferation of a great number of Mapuche organizations of local, regional, and even national character.

The agrarian reform of the Popular Government had a direct impact on Mapuche communities in the sense that within its policy of expropriation of landed estates, provisions were made for restitution of usurped lands to the Indian reservations. The *Corporación de Reforma Agraria* (CORA), in collaboration with the Ministry of Agriculture and the Directorate of Indigenous Affairs (DASIN), echoed petitions for land restitution presented by numerous Indian communities. Many of these lands were taken by Indian peasants, even before CORA took on the responsibility of restoring land from expropriation. But in almost all the cases CORA dealt with, lands were given back to the communities; in some situations, CORA attempted to secure for the reservations more land than had been claimed. The intention of CORA was not only to repair an injustice by recognizing the existence of these usurpations by the landowners but also to attempt to lay the foundation for building larger production units which would enrich reservation lands, would group various reservations or communities into one large unit of co-operative production, or would create settlements on reservations. Between 1960 and 1970, in the decade of the two bourgeois agrarian reforms, the *desarrollista* policies of Alessandri and the reformist policies of Frei, judges of Indian law restored only 1,443 hectares to the Indian communities. By contrast, in the first two years of the revolutionary agrarian reform policies of Allende, there were around 70,000 hectares restored to Indian communities through extrajudicial processes and application of the CORA-DASIN agreement (Allende 1973:312). Various factors obstructed the rapid and total realization of this policy. Often petitions for restitution of Indian lands affected not only large landholding properties but also middle-sized properties (larger than eighty irrigable hectares and therefore liable to expropriation by law), including non-Mapuche small property owners, especially those over whom CORA had no jurisdiction. In some cases CORA simply purchased some of the latter through an agreement with DASIN, but this was not always possible. Sometimes petitions for Indian land restitution pertained to land now held by *asentamientos de Reforma Agraria* which had been based on expropriated farms. Another source of conflict and difficulty was the justifiable suspicion of the Indians, so often deceived, toward agreements: they frequently preferred that the *Instituto Nacional de Desarrollo Agro-pecuario* (INDAP) or the *Banco del Estado* (BECH) simply give the necessary credit to permit each community or family to proceed with its own development, although in the majority of cases, technical help was accepted. Another factor which quickly prohibited the realization of this policy was the petty bourgeois mentality, a product of the problematic system of small landholdings established by the *Sistema de Reducciones*. This factor made many Mapuche reluctant to become a part of units of cooperative production. Moreover, various political groups competed to win over the Mapuche, not only Popular Government groups, the opposition, and the extreme left, but also combination parties within the Popular Government. This competition produced confusion among the Mapuche and made many of them see themselves simply as electoral pawns of the parties. As a consequence, they tried to find some immediate advantage to themselves in this competition.

In spite of the facts that the last agrarian reform was the only one of the four attempts made in the country which proved to be of any benefit to the Indian peasant and that it attempted to find a solution to the extreme situation of the Indian peasant by integrating him organically into the processes of agricultural change, a combination of factors limited the advancement of reform in the desired direction. The economic crisis produced in the country by the great structural changes (including agrarian reform itself), intensifying class struggles, and urban and rural social conflicts, the growth of the black market and "parallel" markets in the rural areas, were among the difficulties obstructing true integration of the Mapuche. The very organs of agrarian reform (CORA, INDAP, SAG, ECA, BECH, etc.) expropriated and assigned lands, granted credit,

opened paths for commercialization, and weakened rather than strengthened the Indian communities by giving priority to existing settlements,
CERAS, and state enterprises. Some results of this contradiction were
breakdowns in many units of production in the reformed area (such as
the appearance of parallel markets, union or functionary bureaucratiza-
tion, problems in the bureaucracy of those state institutions mentioned).
These problems intensified the lack of confidence and skepticism felt by
Mapuche communities. The integration of all agricultural institutions into
a single functional entity of the public agricultural sector partly corrected
some of those defects. In spite of all these difficulties there was an appreci-
able number of Mapuche peasants in the units of production in the
reformed area. Likewise, there were several different types of peasant
cooperatives in the Indian communities. Many reservations received
additional lands, some of which had been expropriated lands which were
returned and some of which were simply new assignments. The mechanisms
of credit and state commercialization were to a great extent opened to the
Mapuche. Mass unionization and peasant organization through establishment of unions and communal councils also included the Mapuche.
Similarly, the proliferation of their own Mapuche organizations; the
creation of the Institute of Indigenous Education (*Instituto de Capacita-
ción Indigena*), legalized by Indian Law No. 17,729 in September of 1972;
the increase in number of student scholarships available to Mapuche
children; the increase in schooling and literacy programs; free entry
granted to Mapuche into political parties; and the slightly increased
numbers of health centers created a new set of perspectives for Mapuche
society.

All this placed the system of Mapuche landholding in a position of
crisis and the abrupt changes involved have resulted in the breaking down
of the social organization of the communities. This can be seen in
deteriorating kinship structures and in the way the Mapuche have increasingly lost control in their own economic as well as social affairs.
They are no longer able to control production and property nor even to
inherit property or acquire it through marriage (Faron 1970). Leadership
and power structures within the community have deteriorated. The
kinship chiefdom has disappeared almost entirely. In the early 1970's,
community leadership among the Mapuche was of a sociopolitical or
economic character. Rather than the familial or kinship chiefs of former
days, the leaders were union directors from political parties representing
county peasant councils, from peasant communities, from the Mapuche
Federation, etc., or they were people in the community who had more
land and/or animals for whom many of the other community members

worked as sharecroppers. Because of this, in the last decade two new situations have developed among the Mapuche. First, there is a slight social stratification, a rising group, still very small, of Mapuche landowners of small- or middle-sized holdings who have a relatively secure future and some capital, which gives them an advantage in comparison to the deprivation of the rest of the people. This is reflected more in properties where cattle are raised than in landholdings. Nevertheless, the greatest proportion of Mapuche, in both divided and undivided communities, are poor, small-scale landowners. Second, there is an acceleration in the proletarization process, especially among the new Mapuche generation of salaried workers, some of whom are already in private businesses or public works or work as members of the associations or centers of agrarian reform. This tendency, more than the contradictions and conflicts described above, has led the Mapuche to an increased social consciousness of an ethnic as well as of a class character. These two processes of parallel consciousness sometimes appear contradictory, although they do not have to be so: on the contrary, ethnic consciousness and ethnic identity can and should go together with class solidarity and the struggle for social and class assertion. This is understood more and more by larger groups both of Mapuche and of non-Mapuche peasants.

The Popular Government, the first government to deal with the restitution of full rights of the Mapuche as Chilean citizens, not only restored more than 70,000 hectares of land in less than two years but also gave the Mapuche access to power and decision making through the opening up of representative peasant organizations to Mapuche groups and through the encouragement of other Mapuche representative groups. Attempts were also made to improve Indian legislation and to find ways of changing and improving the economy. Along with this open and positive policy toward the Mapuche people, efforts were made for improving the schooling of Mapuche children and for creating and making more accessible new schools, including universities, for the communities and Mapuche students. Efforts were also made to improve the literacy of Mapuche adults, not only in Spanish, but also in Mapudungun (Hernandez 1972), along with numerous other initiatives in the field of arts and culture in general. The opening up of the larger society in the last ten or twelve years, especially in the three years of the Popular Government, has hastened and intensified the process of Mapuche transculturation.

When we speak of transculturation here we do not have in mind the traditional anthropological criterion which equates it with an enforced adjustment and conformity for purposes of exploitation. We believe that this process has assumed a conflicting character in Chile because of the way in which structures within the larger society as well as within the Indian community are broken down. In fact, it would be necessary to end this adjustment in order to end the exploitation of Indians and to promote structural changes which would lead to their true liberation. This new process would be directed toward a radical change in the whole Mapuche culture; the changes taking place in the means of production and in social organization in Chile undoubtedly have prepared the country for such a change. These changes within Mapuche culture are not produced in simple or uniform ways, but, on the contrary, are contradictory in form, as are the aspirations and interests of the various levels of the Mapuche people, i.e., the majority of small landowners on the reservations, the more wealthy strata (rural as well as urban), the rural and urban proletariat (including Mapuche peasants of the reformed area), and the growing Mapuche student groups.

Trends toward assimilation into the national culture, which tend to dilute Mapuche culture, do exist and are reinforced by many sectors of the larger society who see this assimilation as an ultimate solution to the Mapuche problem. But generally these trends, although manifested in different ways, tend to affirm Mapuche culture and its ethnic identity. In our judgment they strengthen the ability to accept cultural change and to claim integration in Chilean society, without involving loss of their identity. The search for new outlets can include the revitalization and written expression of their own language, which would then allow the transformation of existing oral literature (Berdichewsky 1968) into a new and vigorous written form, both in Mapudungun and in Spanish. This process is only in its beginning stages and could easily be suppressed. Potentially, however, it is a real possibility. With respect to traditional expressions of Mapuche culture, such as crafts and religious beliefs, most are undergoing a tumultuous period. Some forms of traditional expression will continue, though obviously in a modified form; others undoubtedly will disappear. New cultural expressions are also emerging, such as stage or scenic art, exemplified in the proliferation of theatrical ensembles by Mapuche young people during the short period of the Popular Government.

By 1973, the Mapuche people were experiencing a process of deep, accelerated change in the direction of their real liberation. Although the ultimate outcome is impossible to predict, one fact is certain: their ethnic identity has been affirmed, and their culture is not only alive but shows signs of renaissance and crystallization.

2.5.   *Counter Agrarian Reform and the Indian Communities*[2]

With the military coup of September 1973 and the assassination of
President Allende, the process of radical structural change, which was a
transitional development toward a socialist society led by the Popular
Unity movement, came to an end. A military Junta was installed in power,
parliament was dissolved, political parties suppressed and prohibited, and
democratic liberties suspended indefinitely. The repression of popular
movements and all the progressive groups and persons escalated. All the
structures and mechanisms of popular power, such as parties, CUT (the
national workers trade unions), *Cordones industriales* (industrial sector
worker councils), JAP (neighborhood unions for price control and
supplies), student organizations, county and peasant councils, etc., were
immediately suppressed and destroyed, and local trade unions, although
not dismantled, were deprived of any real power.

    This reactionary and repressive aftermath of the coup also affected the
peasants, including the Mapuche. Those who were more involved in the
process, such as union leaders, activists in political parties or in county
or peasant councils, in Mapuche ethnic organizations, and also those
many Indians who took active participation in the land invasions, were
most affected. How many of these Mapuche were killed, imprisoned, and
tortured is impossible to know, but we must estimate a few thousand. Not
only those slightly involved in the process suffered, but also most of the
Mapuche population was affected by the reaction and by the new process
that could only be called one of counter agrarian reform (Feder 1970).
The new regime stopped the agrarian reform process immediately. No new
expropriation of *fundios* or invasions of land were accepted, and although
most of the institutions related to the former agrarian reform program,
such as CORA, INDAP, SAG, BECH, etc., were maintained, it was only
to control the already existing reform areas without initiating new ones.
Close to 80,000 peasants had already benefitted by agrarian reform, most
of them still living in the *asentamientos*; so, technically speaking, it was
impossible to disrupt what was already done. Nevertheless, the Junta
initiated a process of returning hundreds of *fundios* (to the former landowners), which had not yet been legally expropriated by CORA. Small
plots of land were assigned to a list of about 10,000 peasants already living
in *asentamientos* in order to start a process of changing the land tenure
form of the *asentamientos* of the reformed areas into small peasant

---

[2]   This chapter was written in August 1975, two years after the paper was written and
sent to the IXth ICAES (Editor's note).

properties (Collarte 1974). At the same time, a decree was passed establishing free enterprise, not only in urban areas but also in rural areas, making it clear that anybody could sell or buy land property (*Informe Economico* 1974). If this is not yet a clear counter reform, it is at least the beginning of a process which will lead toward it. There is no doubt that this process is already affecting not only the peasants as a whole, but the Mapuche peasants in particular. They have again begun to lose important amounts of land through returns to landowners. If these counter-reform measures continue, there is no doubt that in a short period of time a neo-*latifundio* system will develop in rural areas of the country and the *minifundio* will multiply with all the consequences of poverty and misery that this means. If we add to this the new burdens imposed on the Chilean popular masses, such as increasing unemployment (about 20 percent) and an abrupt decline of the real income of the people with the sequel of poverty and famine, we could assume that peasants and Indians are retrogressing to the situation of the early 1930's, one of the worst periods in Chilean agrarian history (Winn 1974).

There are, nevertheless, other variables necessary to consider in order to project how the process may develop. In the first place, in that extra-ordinary period of a little more than a decade of constantly increasing agrarian reform, the old *hacienda* system was almost destroyed. It is difficult to imagine that it could be restored. There is no doubt, however, that the countryside is entering a process of counter agrarian reform which is leading to a neo-*latifundio* system, with its counterpart of *minifundios*; but it will be mostly in the form of groups of middle-sized *fundios* under the control of landowner families or enterprises, which will operate in a more capitalistic way with very few tenant-service peasants and many more rural wage laborers, thereby increasing the numbers of the rural proletariat. This and the class solidarity already gained during the agrarian reform process will make the peasants much more socially aware and class-conscious. So we must assume that in relation to the Mapuche, both their ethnic and their class consciousness will not decline but probably will be reinforced. We can also assume that their culture will evolve again toward a culture of resistance against racial discrimination and social exploitation.

The Araucanian people, and especially the Mapuche, have experienced many defeats, but they were never completely defeated or destroyed, and they will emerge in the future when the country changes once more to a just and dignified society.

REFERENCES

AFFONSO, ALMINO
1971   *Trayectoria del movimiento campesino chileno.* Santiago: ICIRA.
ALLENDE, SALVADOR
1973   *Mensaje presidencial ante el Congreso Pleno.* Santiago: Government Printers.
BARRACLOUGH, SOLON
1971   *Reforma agraria: historia y perspectivas.* Santiago: ICIRA.
BARRACLOUGH, SOLON, ALMINO AFFONSO
1973   *Diagnostico de la reforma agraria chilena,* 71–123. Cuad. Realidad Nacional 16. Santiago.
BERDICHEWSKY, BERNADO
1968   "Reseña histórica y cultural de los Mapuches del Calafquén," in *Leyendas del Calafquén de Mayo Calvo G.,* p. 8. Santiago.
1970   "Para una política de acción indigenista en el area araucana." Mimeographed manuscript, (December). Santiago: CORA.
1971a   Fases culturales en la prehistoria de los Araucanos de Chile. *Revista Chilena de Historia y Geografia* 139:105–112. Santiago.
1971b   *Antropología aplicada e indigenismo en los Mapuches de Cautin.* Santiago: CORA.
1966   *Chile: tenencia de la tierra y desarrollo socio-economico del sector agricola.* Santiago: Comite Interamericano de Desarrollo Agricola.
CANTONI, WILSON
1969   *Legislation indigena e intergracion del Mapuche.* Santiago: Centro de Estudios sobre Tenecia de la Tierra.
CIDA
COLLARTE, JUAN CARLOS
1974   New Agricultural Policies in Chile: *LTC Newsletter* 46:1–5. Madison: University of Wisconsin Press.
FARON, LOUIS C.
1961   *Mapuche social structure, institutional reintegration in a patrilineal society of central Chile.* Illinois Studies in Anthropology 1. Urbana: University of Illinois Press.
1970   "El matrimonio entre los Mapuche y el concepto de alianza prescriptiva," in *Continuidad y cambio en la cultura araucana desde la prehistoria hasta la actualidad, Symposium 7.* Edited by B. Berdichewsky. Actas y Memorias del 39 Congreso Internacional de Americanistas, 1970, Lima.
FEDER, ERNEST
1970   "Counterreform," in *Agrarian problems and peasant movements in Latin America.* Edited by R. Stavehagen, 173–223. New York.
HERNANDEZ, ISABEL
1972   "Guia de alfabetizacion Mapuche-Castellano," in *Programa de mobilizacion cultural del pueblo mapuche.* Santiago: Instituto de Desarrollo Indigena.
Informe Economico
1974   Bulletin of the Government of Chile, 19–26. Santiago.

IREM
1970   *Provincia Cautin: estudio integrado de los recursos naturales.* Santiago:
        Instituto de Investigaciones de Recursos Naturales.

JARA, ALVARO
1956   *Legislacion indigenista de Chile.* Mexico City: Instituto Indigenista
        Interamericano.
1971   *Guerra y sociedad en Chile.* Santiago: Universitaria, Cormoran.

LATCHAM, RICARDO E.
1922   *La organizacion social y las creencias religiosas de los antiguos
        Araucanos.* Museo de Etnologia y Antropologia, Publicación 3 (2, 3, 4):
        245–868.
1928   *La prehistoria chilena.* Santiago: Universo.

MARX, KARL
1966   *Pre-capitalist economic formations.* New York: International Pub-
        lishers.

MENGHIN, OSVALDO F. A.
1962   *Estudios de prehistoria Araucana.* Sp. de Acta Prehistorica 3–4. Buenos
        Aires: Centro Argentino de Estudios Prehistoricos.

MUNIZAGA, CARLOS
1961   *Estructuras transicionales en la migración de los Araucanos a la ciudad
        de Santiago de Chile.* Santiago: Universidad de Chile.

RIVERA, RIGOBERTO
1972   "El Campo chileno: ¿donde va la reforma?" in *Punto Final* (Supple-
        ment) 167. Santiago.

WINN, PETER
1974   The economic consequences of the Chilean counter revolution: an
        interim assessment. *Latin American Perspectives* 50 (2): 92–105.

ZAPATER, HORACIO
1970   "Expansión Araucana en los siglos 18 y 19," in *Continuidad y cambio
        en la cultura araucana desde la prehistoria hasta la actualidad,
        Symposium 7.* Edited by B. Berdichewsky. Actas y Memorias del 39
        Congreso Internacional de Americanistas, 1970, Lima.

Jungle Quechua Ethnicity: An Ecuadorian Case Study

NORMAN E. WHITTEN, JR.

The Jungle Quechua

The vast majority of aboriginal peoples living in eastern Ecuador (the Oriente) in 1972 belong to one of two cutural divisions: they are either Quechua, or they are Jívaro. The latter are well known to

This paper is based primarily on five months of preliminary ethnography undertaken during the summers of 1970 and 1971. The research is sponsored by the University of Illinois, Urbana, and the Instituto Nacional de Antropología e Historia, Quito, Ecuador, and is funded by the National Science Foundation (Grant No. GS-2999). I am grateful to the Director of the Instituto, Arq. Hernán Crespo Toral, for his constant interest and encouragement in this preliminary field investigation. Considerable thanks also are due five assistants who worked at various stages of the preliminary project: Cynthia Gillette, Nicanor Jácome, Marcelo Naranjo, Michael Waag, and Margarita Wurfl. Michael Waag also commented critically on an earlier draft of this paper. Confidentiality promised to the subjects of research now prohibits me from thanking those who helped the most — the Quechua and Jívaroan close associates now caught up in the international scheme of "becoming" Indian while confronting cataclysmic changes in their environments.
   The major result of this preliminary research was a proposal to undertake a year of intensive ethnography with the Lowland Quechua, beginning in late August, 1972. This research, a joint project with Dorothea S. Whitten, is also funded by the National Science Foundation (continuation Grant No. GS-2999) and supplemented by funds for research assistance by the University of Illinois Research Board and Center for Comparative International Studies. The study has three basic aspects. In the first, Dorothea S. Whitten, Marcelo Naranjo, and I continue our study of Jungle Quechua ethnicity and adaptive strategies in the face of rapid change in their natural and social environments. In the second, John P. Ekstrom is completing a year's study of colonist strategies of land acquisition between the Pustaza and Curaray River drainages. The third aspect, designed and now being carried out by Theodore Macdonald, involves continuities in Quechua world view and symbolic domains, particularly as they relate to their position in the indigenous shaman system of highland and lowland Ecuador.

anthropology and are regarded as bona fide indigenes. The former
Indians are the largest aggregate, numbering approximately 35,000 or
more (Burbano Martínez, et al. 1964). They speak Quechua[1] as a first
language and live a tropical forest life. Yet they are frequently mentioned only in passing by authors describing the Oriente. Within Ecuador they are often lumped as "Quijos," (e.g. Porras 1961; Ferdon
1950; Peñaherrera de Costales and Costales Samaniego 1961), reflecting their presumed tribal-linguistic origin west of the Napo River
along the eastern cordillera of the Andes; or, they are lumped as
"Yumbos" (Peñaherrera de Costales and Costales Samaniego, et al.
1969; Burbano Martínez, et al. 1964), which suggests that they are
acculturated Highland Quechuas who moved into the tropical forest
and there mixed with other groups (particularly the Záparos). When
compared to the Cofán, Secoya, Siona (Piojé), Huarani (Auca), Awishiri
(Auca), Záparo, and Jívaroans (Untsuri Shuara — see Harner 1972
— and Achuara), the Quechua of east lowland Ecuador are usually regarded as sufficiently assimilated to lowland *blanco-mestizo* culture as to
preclude careful attention. All indigenous people of Ecuador contrast
ethnically with the category *blanco-mestizo* (defined below in the
section on internal colonialism).

The Jungle Quechua of the central Oriente may be linguistically
divided into three major dialect segments:[2] northwest, northeast, and
southern (Orr and Wrisley 1965). The northwest dialect, called Tena,
is found along the upper reaches of the Napo River and its headwater
affluent the Jatun Yacu. The dialect continues through the adminis-

---

[1]   I am using a standard, familiar international spelling for the word "Quechua,"
Ecuadorian usage prefers *Quichua*, or *Kichua*. In Ecuador the term is pronounced
"Keéchuwa."
[2]   Cultural differences between Jungle Quechua of the southern dialect group and
the northern group are extensive, and beyond the scope of this paper to list.
Suffice it to say here that the Quechua speakers of the Bobonaza basin — the
"Canelos Quechua" — are Upper Amazonian peoples who have been adapting for
centuries to the zone best identified with the Bobonaza River north to the Curaray
River and south to the Pastaza River. This is the area carved out as the archdiocese
of Canelos. In spite of their proximity to the Andes and their language, they have
a fundamentally tropical forest way of life, which they have applied in some areas
to *montaña* existence. The Canelos Quechua are, in many ways, more similar to
Jívaroan speakers in cultural content than to the Quijos Quechuas (Tena dialect).
Ethnic derivation is, in historical times, a merger of Záparoan, Achuara Jívaroan,
some Jívaroan proper and more recently, Quijos Quechua cultures. Achuara and
Záparoan are the most important contributors to culture content. Ancient Omagua
and Cocama Tupian influence is probable. The exact origin of the Quechua language in this zone is unknown at this time, but ancient tropical forest derivation
cannot be discounted. A general ethnography of ethnic derivation, world view, and
contemporary adaptation is now in preparation.

trative towns of Tena and Archidona, and on up the Sierra to near the present town of Baeza. It runs down the Napo to the settlement of Ahuano and south to Arajuno, cutting across the Puyo-Napo Road at Santa Clara. The northeastern dialect, called Napo, goes on down the Napo River, and is spoken on such north-Napo tributaries as the Suno and Payamino Rivers. The southern division, called Bobonaza, begins south of Santa Clara and Arajuno and extends to the Pastaza River. Quechua on the Curaray, Bobonaza, Conambo, and Pindo are all of the southern division, though other further dialectical differences do exist. The territory between the Curaray and the Napo is not inhabited by Quechuas — it is exclusively Auca (Huarani, Awishiri) country.

Culturally, the northern and southern divisions of Quechua territories are distinct, and their relationships with highland and other lowland indigenous peoples are also different.[3] The people of the Tena-Napo dialects and Bobonaza dialect regard one another as different; their aboriginal histories and histories of contact are different, and their present socioeconomic status is quite different, though perhaps convergent. The Tena-Napo groups represent expansions around Catholic mission bases from the sixteenth century on to the present (Oberem 1971). Quechua language clearly came from the missions (cf. Steward 1948: 509–515). Their history is one of continuous serfdom to the missions and *haciendas,* and their present socioeconomic position is analogous to that of the infamous highland *Huasipungueros.* They are generally called Yumbos, Napos, and Quijos. For clarity and convenience I will refer to them as "Quijos Quechua." (For a recent monograph on this culture see Oberem 1971.)

Native people of the Bobonaza, Conambo, and Curaray drainages seem to have been buffers between warring groups of Jívaroans, Záparoans, Awishiris, and others from the time of first contact. Missions may have been built in existing refuge areas, and while such missions may have solidified such refuge zones, it may not be accurate to say that the missions created these zones. Throughout southern Quechua territory internal bilingual and bicultural activities between Quechua and Achuara Jívaroan are maintained by marriage. Intermarriage with the Jívaro proper, "Untsuri Shuara," also exists. This pattern of marriage with otherwise warring Jívaroan groups seems to have at least

[3] For example, shamans from the Canelos Quechua are regarded as the most powerful in the world by the Jívaro (see Harner 1972), and highland Indians from near Ríobamba regularly visit Canelos Quechua shamans. But, other highland Indians such as the Salasaca and the Otavaleños generally avoid Canelos Quechua shamans and go directly to shamans and curers in Tena and Ahuano.

a 200-years' time depth. Also, on the Curaray, Corrientes, and Pindo Rivers, Záparo-Quechua bilingualism and biculturalism exist — here people in the riverbank settlements are "Quechua," but many "become Záparo" in the forest. In the latter capacity not only is Záparoan spoken, but aggressive raids against Huarani Auca households have reputedly been made in the recent past. Some Záparo-Quechua bilingualism still exists on the Río Bobonaza. Finally, more profound influences on Quechua life in the southern areas have come from the extension of trade network (for furs, gold, medicines, and cinnamon) and from the rubber boom of the late nineteenth century to early twentieth century than from the establishment of *haciendas* as in the northern case.

From this point on, my paper deals with the southern dialect, with the Quechua of the Bobonaza drainage — the "Canelos Quechua."

The people in this southern area REFER to themselves in Quechua as *runa* [indigenous person]. They also use the term *Alama* "friend" or "mythic brother",[4] among themselves to ADDRESS those who come from the Bobonaza or Curaray drainages and are southern Lowland Quechua speakers. In Spanish they use the term *gente* [People], as a reference for themselves. (When speaking Spanish all Jungle Que-

---

[4] The derivation of the term *Alama* comes from a myth segment, dealing, in various ways, with older brother/younger brother authority and tension. In brief, an older and younger brother were on a huge stone in the middle of a great river, having been placed there by a giant condor. The older brother called a great cayman which came to the rock to help the brothers across, but the younger brother jumped down first, crossed, and by the time the cayman made the return trip for the older brother the younger had disappeared. Walking through the forest, lost, and searching not only for the brother, but also for a lost homeland, the older brother reached out to break off a piece of tree mushroom (*ala*) and as he pinched it the mushroom cried out "ouch, my mythic brother, don't pinch me, real brother" (*aiai alajma ama tiushi huaichu huauqui: aiai* [ouch], *ala* [mushroom, mythic brother], *j* possessive, *ma* emphasis, *ama* [no], *tiushi* [pinch], *hua* [to me], *i* command, *chu* negative complement to *ama, huauqui* [real brother]). On saying this the tree mushroom transformed into the younger brother who rejoined his sibling and they went on to more adventures.

There is more to the *ala* complex than this, for ancient peoples had the ability to send their souls (*aya*) into special rocks and logs when their bodies died, from whence a mushroom would emerge to await a wandering *runa* who, in hunger, would pinch the mushroom and awaken the ancient *runa*. In this way, older and younger statuses can fluctuate, because, although the younger brother was lost, rediscovery of him through this process indicates abilities of soul transformation suggestive of ancient, older status. The term *ala* is used in direct address by all acknowledged male participants in Canelos Quechua culture and is, thereby, a crucial ethnic marker. On being called *ala* or *alaj* one must immediately reciprocate the same term, acknowledging mythic brotherhood, or he must reciprocate a pejorative, negative, ethnic term such as *auca* [heathen] or *mashca pupu* [barley gut, Ecuadorian intruder].

chuas use *gente* in contrast with *blanco.)* There is no term other than *Alama* used to differentiate the people of the Bobonaza drainage from other Quechua speakers in highland and lowland Ecuador. In speaking Spanish, though, the Jungle Quechua of this zone use *gente* for themselves, and from that point distinguish themselves as people from both *runa llacta* (literally, "indigenous land" — which is used as though it were Spanish, when speaking Spanish) and *blancos* (literally "whites" — including Negroes). Jívaros and some colonists who have been in the area for a generation or more designate the Bobonaza Jungle Quechua as *Alama* (and in Jívaro sometimes as "Aram Shuara"), but this is regarded as mildly pejorative by the Indians when used contrastively by any but southern dialect Jungle Quechua speakers. Very few Indians north of Santa Clara on the Puyo-Napo Road even know the term *Alama*, and no one knows its meaning (see Note 4).

When speaking Quechua, the division of ethnic categories and territories is quite clear. The Indians themselves seldom refer to their own referent dialect group, except by implicit contrast, when making the following distinctions. In the west—the Andes—there are two "lands": *runa llacta* and *ahua llacta*. The former is "indigenous land" but is used in the area under study only to refer to highland Indian territory — regarded as all of the Andes. The latter term, *ahua llacta,* is literally "highland" but refers politely to all non-Indian Ecuadorians. The *ahua llacta* term in Jungle Quechua is used as a synonym for the Spanish *blanco.* Neither the designation *gente* in Spanish, nor the designation *runa* in Quechua, is used for the Ecuadorian highland *blanco-mestizo.*

To the north there are two territories of Quechua which correspond to the two dialect areas, called respectively *Alchirona Llacta* and *Napo Llacta* (representing the northwest and northeastern dialect divisions). (Sometimes *Ansuj Llacta* is added to indicate Quechua settlements southwest of the Napo River, on a feeder river to the Jatun Yacu River.) To the north and south lie *Auca Llacta* [heathen lands]. In the north this includes the Cushmas (Cofán, Tetéte, Secoya, and Siona), who are but dimly known by reputation, and the hostile Huarani (called *Llushti Auca* [naked heathens] and *Tahuashiri* [ridge people] in Quechua). On the Curaray River, and recently along the Bobonaza as well, distinctions are made between the Huarani or "true" *Llushti Auca* to the west, now clustered on the Curaray above the mouth of the Villano and the Nushiño River, and the *Awishiri (Tahuashiri) Aucas* to the east, who now live between the Cononaco and Tivacuna Rivers. The legendary (in Quechua legend) *Puca Chaqui Auca* [red leg heathens] of the Tiputini drainage, are said to constitute a third division, and the Canelos Quechua insist that these unknown people speak another language and use bows and arrows. Oil company observations seem to confirm Canelos Quechua insistence on a *Puca Chaqui Auca* group. Also belonging to *Auca Llacta* in the north are Záparo speakers, most of whom are bilingual in Jungle Quechua, and many of whom are trilingual in Spanish as well. Northern Achuara from the Corrientes and Conambo River systems are also part of *Auca Llacta.* (Tessmann [1930], Steward [1948], and Steward and Métraux [1948] give historical data supporting these divisions made by the southern dialect group of Quechua speakers.)

Due east of Alama land, in Peru, live *Andoa Runa* in the most eastern territory of the culture area of the Canelos Quechua. Other *Auca Llacta* are said to exist there, especially the Candochi Jívaroans on the Pastaza, Záparoans from the Marañon River, and Cocama on the Tigre River. Within their own territory the Jungle Quechua identify one another by the administrative center closest to their settlement, unless they actually come from that area, in which case identity is by clan segment and actual residence. From west to east the major identifying settlements are the *Puyo Runa* (sometimes *Pinduj Runa*), which include all people from the Pinduj River south to the Pastaza River, north on either side of the Napo Road for a few kilometers, and northeast to Cabecera de Bobonaza. *Canelos Runa* includes people from east of Cabecera de Bobonaza to Canelos and from Canelos north to the headwaters of the Villano and Curaray River, east to Chambira, and south to the headwaters of the Copotaza River. *Paca Yacu Runa* includes those around the settlement of Paca Yacu north to Villano, and *Sara Yacu Runa* includes all people there south to the Capahuari River, north to the Conambo River, and east on the Bobonaza River to Teresa Mama. *Montalvo Runa* includes the territory north to the Conambo River, east to Peru, and south to the Capahuari. Each *runa* territory is divided into *llactas,* which have recognized living or dead founders and consist of intermarried segments of clans which trek *(purina)* periodically to identified zones, where they encounter other people from other *runa* territories similarly engaged. Sara Yacu-Canelos is seen as the cultural hearth of contemporary Canelos Quechua culture, but the greatest population concentration is between the Pinduj and Pastaza Rivers. The people themselves see their origin area as somewhere around contemporary Yurimaguas, in Peru.

Because of the designation of Canelos as the stereotypic center of

southern Quechua culture, because the people of this zone have so frequently been designated as the "Canelos tribe" in the literature, and
because the designation "Canelos Quechua" is becoming increasingly accepted in Ecuador, I shall hereafter refer to the people of the
southern Lowland Quechua dialect as "Canelos Quechua." The
reader is warned, however, that in the Dominican and administrative
site of Canelos, proper, there exists MORE INTRUSION from Quijos
Quechua and Highland Quechua than in any other area of Canelos
Quechua territory, including Puyo. Figure 1 indicates the major
geographic and ethnic divisions made by the Canelos Quechua in contrastively defining their position *vis-à-vis* other non white ethnic categories in the Ecuadorian Oriente.

Marriage between the Canelos Quechua and both cultural groups
of Jívaroan has taken place for at least two hundred years. The Canelos Quechua have virtually absorbed the Záparo speakers in the
last fifty years, and marriages with highland Indians, occasionally
highland whites, and Indians from both northern dialects today take
place. For the Canelos Quechua, *Indígena* Indian or preferably
nativo [native] is synonymous with their way of life, and they aggressively insist that the appropriate synonym in Spanish for *Indígena* is
gente. Incorporation of Jívaroans, usually classed as *Auca* will be discussed below, when presenting some aspects of the Canelos Quechua
kinship system.

Although the Canelos Quechua are not homogeneous in their ethnic
make-up, they are nonetheles a self-identifying, if highly individualistic,
indigenous aggregate with clear cultural markers; and as an aggregate
they are not merging into *blanco-mestizo* culture. We must understand
the expansion of Lowland Quechua ethnicity as a rational response to
expanding opportunities in the money economy under the continuance
of internal colonialism in Ecuador.

Economically, the staple of lowland life is *yuca* manioc. *Chagras* [cleared fields] cover from one to three hectares. Land is cleared
with ax and machete by a man, his sons, and sons-in-law, more
often than not without help of kinsmen or friends, although *mingas*
[reciprocal labor exchange] may take place. Men plant plantains,
bananas, corn, and naranjilla. The same men carry the manioc stems
to the clearing; then women do the actual planting, keep the *chagra*
clean, harvest the *yuca*, carry it to the house, prepare it, and serve it.
Sweet potatoes and some *yautía* are also grown on the *chagra*, and
these are also the responsibility of women. Palm shoots, *chontaduros*,
yautía, a variety of fruits, peppers, tomatoes, and herbs are grown in

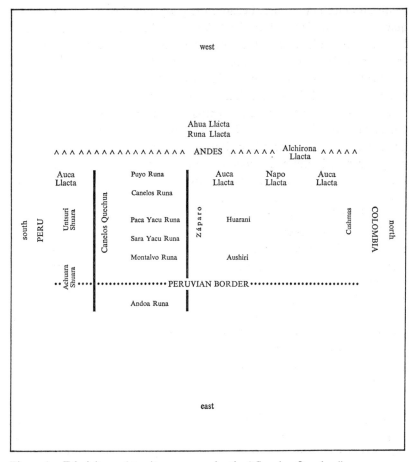

Figure 1.   Ethnicity and territory as seen by the "Canelos Quechua"

kitchen gardens in back of the house as well as on the *chagra*. Near
Puyo the *naranjilla (Solanum quitoense* and several other species) is
grown as a cash crop; otherwise, the Canelos Quechua have few crops
of cash value, though they are ringed on their western and northern
flanks by sugar and tea plantations.

   Manioc beer *(chicha* or *asua)* of very low alcoholic content (more
of a gruel) is a staple of life, and the making and serving of *chicha*
constitute a focal point of symbolic interaction within the household.
The masticated *yuca* is stored in large pottery jars *(tinajas* or *asua
churana manga)* and served in thin, finely decorated bowls *(mucahuas)*. All pottery is made by coiling. Women make their own *tinajas*
and *mucahuas* and guard small secrets pertaining to color, design, and

ways to get the thinnest possible sides and rims. Knowledge and techniques are passed from mother to daughter or from mother to son's wife. The pottery is fired without a kiln. This is the finest pottery made today in the Ecuadorian Oriente, and most, if not all, pottery sold in the highlands as "Jívaro pottery" comes from the Canelos Quechua. Indeed, some Jívaros marry Quechua women and bring them to their own houses in order to have a better pottery than the Jívaro women can provide.[5] Black pottery cooking pots *(yanuna manga)* and eating dishes *(callana)* are also made, sometimes with thumbnail decorations *(sarpa manga)*.

Fine decorated pottery for intrahousehold use is not disappearing with the introduction of metal pots and pans, but the black pottery is rapidly dwindling. People buy the new goods, or trade other things to obtain them, but they maintain at least one or two *tinajas* for *chicha* storage and at least one *mucahua* for serving.

Several fish poisons, such as *barbasco*, are grown in the *chagra* to be used during relatively dry times of the year, when the rivers run quite low and clear. Hallucinogens such as *Ayahuasca* (three *Banisteriopsis* species) and *Huanduj* (several *Datura* species) are grown, together with *Huayusa*, tobacco, and a large variety of medicinal and magical herbs. Men fish with spears, traps, weirs, lines, and nets, and hunt with traps and blowguns. Although many Quechua men make curare poison, using some forty or more plant and other substances, more powerful curare for the blowgun darts comes along trade networks originating in the east. Peruvian Achuara bring poison to Conambo, Montalvo, Copotaza, and Sara Yacu, and Copotaza Achuara or Conambo Achuara carry it on westward. Muzzle-loading shotguns are also used for small game, and cartridge guns are becoming available. Long treks *(purina)* to gather turtle eggs, to hunt for large quantities of meat, to catch and dry large fish, to keep a distant *chagra,* and to buy the appropriate black, red, and white clays for pottery decoration are made by a family once or twice a year, sometimes alone and sometimes with a larger kinship or settlement group.

Travel is frequent among the Canelos Quechua, and it is usually by

---

[5] A crucial aspect of Canelos Quechua cultural perpetuity is bound up with the transmission of knowledge and secrets in pottery making. Three souls go to make up each storage jar and drinking bowl: the clay giver soul, the woman's own created body soul, and the household soul. These souls and the knowledge behind each are transmitted generation by generation through women, just as special knowledge of the clan souls acquired through psychedelic experiences is transmitted generation by generation through males. In my future ethnography I will devote considerable time to analysis of such cultural continuity.

foot. The rivers are too rapid and untrustworthy as far as depth goes (sometimes flooded, sometimes quite low) to provide stable avenues for transportation on the Pastaza east to Ayuy or on the Bobonaza east to Canelos. The Curaray, itself, meanders so much that it is about as efficient to travel on foot from one point to another as to make one oxbow turn after another by canoe. Nevertheless, canoes are used when cargo is to be moved, and the Canelos Quechuas are excellent canoe makers and superior boatsmen.

The nuclear family is a very tightly knit unit with man and woman sharing equally in decision making, in spatial mobility, and in upward socioeconomic mobility in some cases. Residence is ideally matripatrilocal but generally bilocal. There is no term for this unit except the Quechua term *huasi* [house], and the Spanish terms *familia* and *casa* are used synonymously for *huasi*.

The maximal kinship grouping, and segments of this grouping, are referred to as *ayllu*. The *ayllu*, as the maximal clan, is a stipulated descent system from a common animal ancestor, often a variety of puma or jaguar. Each *ayllu* is today identified with a set of surnames and extends through much of Canelos Quechua territory and on into other culture areas, as well. For people in any clan segment, extended clan (also called *ayllu)* reckoning is from father or father's father back to his father's wife. Within the extended clan there are tightly knit stem kindreds, reckoning from an old, founding shaman. These kindreds are also called *ayllu*, but because of the intertwining of *ayllu* membership through marriage with other *ayllu* segments within a territory, the resulting intermarried segments often refer to themselves by the territorial term, *llacta*.

Each *ayllu* (maximal and extended) maintains its special culture, transmitted to intimate residential in-laws. In this transmission special concentrations of knowledge, or culture, concatenate into the territorial *runa*, which expands and contracts with the *purina* system and fissions acros *ayllu* lines in the *llacta* system. In this way shared knowledge embedded in the dispersed *ayllu* of antiquity is transferred repeatedly across *ayllu* boundaries and maintained through conflict and competition in the *llacta* system. *Ayllu* members maintain their *ayllu* ideology, however, through visionary experience, through mythology, and through actual travel. They can reactivate the maximal *ayllu* concept after many generations through the system of shared descent from a common animal ancestor and through shared possession of the souls of the deceased.

In ascending order of kin and neighbor units, a child is born into a *huasi* [household] unit, in which the woman's cultural maintenance through pottery tradition and the man's maintenance through *aya* [soul] acquisition assures each newborn of a place in a maximal clan extending back into mythic time. The *huasi* itself exists within a *llacta,* defensible territory, which was established by a founder in alliance with other founders of *ayllu* segments. These minimal *ayllu* segments within a *llacta* are stem kindreds. Beyond the stem kindred is the extended clan, which includes localized and dispersed kinsmen within and beyond a *runa* territory. And beyond the extended clan is the maximal clan, the everlasting system of stipulated descent into mythic time and structure. The ancient relationships among founders of maximal clans, during the time when all animals were human and humans crawled on the ground like babies, are repeated today as myths and are thought to provide the basis for integration of the Canelos Quechua, long before humans came to dominate their sector of the biosphere.

A developmental sequence exists which ties male *huasi, ayllu,* and *llacta* founders to the knowledge of mythical times. On marriage a male must, by taking *huanduj* datura, converse with the soul-master, *Amasanga,* and have the soul-master cure him of magical darts *(supai biruti)* sent by jealous suitors of his wife. Also, the bride must visit the wife of the *Amasanga,* the *chagra mama* or *Nunghuí mama,* to get her sacred stones and knowledge to make the manioc grow. If a man wishes to head a stem kindred then he must, through a long period of time, acquire the status of *yachaj* or shaman, becoming both curer and potential mystical killer; and when, if ever, he seeks to found a *llacta* he must have made pacts with the various spirits *(supai)* and souls *(aya)* of the territory, in which process he becomes a POTENTIAL *bancu* seat for the souls and spirits. He usually does not serve as *bancu,* however, because retaliation for the evil done by the spirits and souls through the *bancu* leads many people to attempt to eliminate the *bancu*'s social capital — his family, neighbors, and friends — by witchcraft and assassination.

As the process of soul acquisition and making pacts with spirits goes on, something else also occurs due to the constant outward movement of affinally related clan segments: A MAXIMAL CLAN EVOLVES WITHIN A TERRITORY. This maximal clan is often named after a given area. Terms such as Puyo Runa, Canelos Runa, Sara Yacu Runa, etc. then take on another meaning, for not only do the territories exist as interrelated clan segments, but certain clans come to dominate, and knowledge of the *runa* territory suggests the dominating clan. The territorial clans represent a process of "social circumscription" (Carneiro 1970) overlaid with territorial circumscription. Segments of extended clans do cut through these territorial boundaries, however, as do alliances formed through intermarriage. Such cross-cutting of the circumscribed territorial clans suggests an evolution toward an incipient, as yet acephalous, ethnic state of southern Jungle Quechua.

All maximal clans of the Canelos Quechua include Achuara Jívaroans as members of Quechua extended clans. Also, in many of the maximal clans there is one Achuara or even Untsuri Shuara local group *(caserío)* which insures intra-indigenous ethnic contrast (Quechua versus Jívaroan) WITHIN the maximal clan itself. This ethnic contrast between two very different indigenous peoples, together with the countervailing complementarity through cross-cutting intermarriages, is an essential element in the definition of Canelos Quechua ethnicity and social structure and is a key to continuity of indigenous identity during times of rapid change.

The term *ayllu* may refer to the *caserío* when this local group consists of only one segment of the extended clan; otherwise it refers to the speaker's own descent group within the *llacta,* or *caserío.* If the speaker has no descent group members in the *caserío* he will use *ayllu* to mean members of the descent group of his wife, or deceased wife. *Ayllu* is regularly used to denote extended clan and, when involved in territorial disputes with Jívaroans or with colonists, *ayllu* as maximal clan is invoked. In this latter sense indigenous ethnicity is stressed over intraindigenous divisions, and the concept of common, INDIGENOUS DESCENT, together with the acknowledgment of extensive networks resulting from stipulated clan intermarriage, is used *vis-à-vis* outsiders. Such a process of assertion of common descent of otherwise contrastive Indian ethnic identities is well under way in several parts of the Oriente, one of which is the Comuna de San Jacinto, near Puyo.

The Jungle Quechua call themselves Christians, and so distinguish themselves as opposed to all other Indians, except the Highland Quechua. Practices such as genuflecting and kissing the hand of priests and nuns are ubiquitous. There are few churches in the *caseríos,* and where these exist a priest (or evangelist) may visit a few times a year, on the occasion of special fiestas. More generally, the central church for the Lowland Quechua is in a major town, or outlying post (Puyo, Canelos, Sara Yacu, Montalvo, Jesús Pitishca). Everywhere, though, other worlds associated with the sky and an inner earth, and other spirits, creatures and souls associated with the tropical forest and treacherous stretches of rivers, are talked about and visited with the aid of hallucinogens.

THE COMUNA DE SAN JACINTO DEL PINDO

The Comuna de San Jacinto del Pindo was established by executive decree in 1947 by the then national President, Dr. José María Velasco Ibarra. This decree was necessary due to the extreme conflict between colonists and Indians in and around the town of Puyo. Puyo is only nine kilometers east of Shell Mera, the town founded by Shell Oil Company in its explorations beginning in 1937. Indians were inhabiting the area around Puyo (along the Pinduj — now Pindo-Puyo — Rivers) and at the mouth of the Pindo where it joins the Pastaza long before 1899, when a priest (Alvaro Valladares) and some Indians (Jívaroan and Quechua) arrived from Canelos. Long a trading site for furs, gold, cinnamon, and wood, Puyo began to expand rapidly as a national frontier town when Shell Company completed the Baños-Shell Mera Road in the mid-1930's.

There followed about fifteen years of highland colonist settlement in Puyo, which meant squeezing out the Indians, who were apparently vociferous in making their land claims known as more and more settlers moved onto their *chagra* plots and began to raise sugar cane fo rthe production of *aguardiente* [rum]. The 1947 Presidential decree supposedly was made not only due to Indian-highlander conflict, but also due to growing national attention to the Indian plight in this area, stemming from explorers' accounts. One of the most important guides to the Oriente lived near Puyo, and Velasco Ibarra himself was supposedly respectful of this guide and the others of his extended clan (including one of the many powerful shamans of the area — see Eichler 1970: 109). This guide presumably had enough important contacts among prominent Ecuadorians to force some attention to Indian problems among colonists and traders. Also, it seems, many highlanders seeking to exploit the Oriente were sorely in need of Indian guides and labor, and they turned to the Puyo Runa for such help. It benefited all to have a permanent Indian aggregate with marginal dependence on Puyo's money economy but able to subsist on its own when labor was not needed.

Whatever the specific historical causes, the *comuna* was established just south of Puyo. Its 16,000 hectare territory is bordered on the east by the Puyo River, just after its junction with the Pindo-Puyo, and on the west and south by the Pastaza River. The northern pinnacle begins at the Caserío San Jacinto (the oldest official *caserío* on the *comuna*) and runs southwest to where a bridge now crosses the Chinimbimi, a branch of the Pastaza. Today, eleven official *caseríos* of from 25 to

120 people and at least two other dispersed *llactas* ring the *comuna,* and throughout the *comuna* people also live separately, on particular *chagras,* but with identity claimed to one or two *llactas.* The estimated population of the Comuna de San Jacinto during 1973 was 1,600.

The *comuna* is ringed by sugar and tea plantations on all but the eastern flank, and one road cuts the *comuna* en route to the tea plantation south of the Pastaza. This road cuts through a rocky, fertile alluvial plain called *La Isla* [the island] because the Chinimbimi fork and Pastaza River enclose it). Here, along the road, there are more than 150 colonists illegally settled, almost all in conflict with the *comuna* members generally, while many form cooperative dyadic relationships with particular individuals from all of the *caseríos.* At the terminus of the road (Puerto Santa Ana) there is an all-colonist (*colono*) settlement at the base of a hill, with an all-Untsuri Shuara Jívaroan settlement on top of the hill.

In spite of cash cropping around the *comuna,* the *comuneros'* only recourse to cash is the *naranjilla* and sale of forest products (including medicines, wood, furs, and a variety of off-and-on products bringing little cash, such as pottery, tourist lances, beads, and live animals). Basically, the *comuneros* farm their manioc and plantain *chagras* and supplement their diet with poultry, wild birds, fish, and small game. The major change in this has been the impact of cattle during the past eight years.

The *comuna* is loosely governed by a *cabildo,* with elected president, vice-president, secretary, treasurer, *síndico* [lawyer], and a *vocal* [spokesman], from each of the *caseríos.* The election is held annually, and thus far has resulted in officials who are bilingual and bicultural, but who are the children of prominent or high-ranking, extended clans, or the male affines attached to prominent, high-ranking clans. Deals made by the *cabildos* with prominent *colonos,* including the governor of the province, have improved their financial standing; a stratified system of high ranking *cabildos,* having differential access to money through public officials in need of *comuna* land and/or labor, has occurred. However, the intra-*comuna* prestige game involves conspicuous giving (Erasmus 1961), with rank accruing to the giver. Ranking on the *comuna* leads, usually, to uneven access by the *cabildos,* which in turn places them in a position of economic betterment *vis-à-vis* most other *comuneros*; but the need for conspicuous giving within the *comuna* tempers this class system, and suggests one of ranking evolving into stratification (see Fried 1967). Thus far there is no whole clan of Quechuas on the *comuna* with differential access, though in-

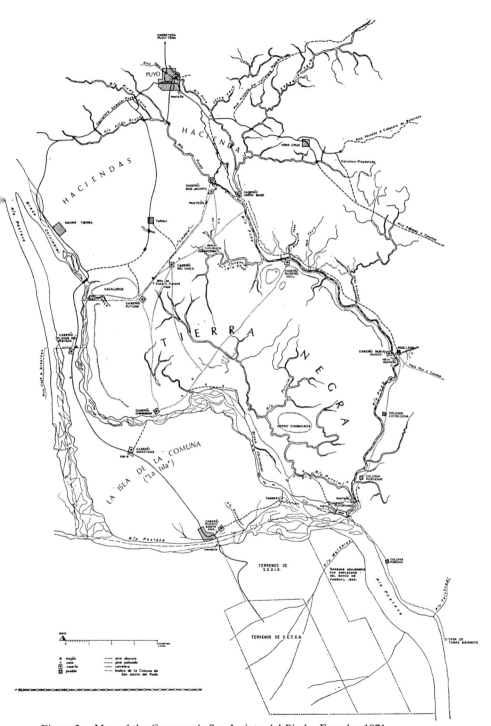

Figure 2.   Map of the Comuna de San Jacinto del Pindo, Ecuador 1971

dividuals from high-ranked clans do manage to place themselves in a position of differential access to local power domains channeling national resources.

Every single *comunero* is concerned with male fertility and female fecundity. Families are generally very large — ranging upward from one or two children when the parents are eighteen or nineteen to a dozen or so by the time the parents reach their forties. Some fathers continue to sire children into their seventies or eighties. This rational serious concern with exploding the population of the Puyo Runa is tied directly to the political economy. The *comuneros* want to totally populate their territory and other territories, knowing full well that this plan depends on gaining increased access to the money economy.

The strategy adopted is to build new *caseríos* only on the border of the *comuna,* as territorial holding units, while at the same time entering into contractual arrangements with colonists who are attempting to gain a foothold on the island. By "renting" land to *colonos,* and using the money to buy cattle off the *comuna,* the people of this area are trying to build capital resources (cattle, marketable land areas) while acquiring new land and at the same time protecting their *comuna* holdings.

In order to do the latter, constant protests are lodged against colonists renting *comuna* lands. This must be done in Quito, at the Ministerio de Previsión Social, for this is the governmental department established to administer the *comuna* system. Since there is no local agent of the Ministerio it is also necessary to depend on local officials, the governor and political heads *(teniente político, jefe político)* of the adjacent administrative units. In dealing on the national level the *comuneros* enter one power domain (Adams 1970), where only conflict with *colonos* is stressed and where superior power and support are sought. In dealing with the local or regional level of the same domain, conflict AND cooperation with officials and colonists must be stressed; economic support and expansion of promised facilities (e.g. a road in another part of the *comuna)* are requested *often with the result of loss of ground on original grievances.*

More will be said about power domains (national and local) in an ensuing section. Suffice it to say at this point that pro tem. transfers of authority from the Ministerio de Previsión Social to the IERAC (Instituto Ecuatoriano de Reforma Agraria y Colonización) are sometimes made in order to bring a local-level competitive domain to the Indians. When this is done, though, *the Indians lose their strategic dual-*

ity of national-regional domain manipulation. They then must cope through a unified national-regional domain — one that has as its charge furtherance of COLONIST EXPANSION and, hence, INDIAN DISEN-FRANCHISEMENT AND TERRITORIAL ENCAPSULATION.

The expansion of *caseríos* on the *comuna* is taking place rapidly, and is accompanied by local-level clamor by the Indians for national facilities on the larger *caseríos*. For example, there is a Catholic church at San Jacinto and a Protestant one at Puyo Pungo. There are now schools at Unión Base, Rosario Yacu, Río Chico, Chinimbimi, Puyo Pungo, Amazonas, and Playas del Pastaza. Children are taught or preached to in Spanish. In the schools, teachers are recruited from various parts of the nation. They live in the schoolhouse, and teach there for about eight months of the year. The sixth grade is the highest, from which some children go on to school in Puyo, this being paid for by their families.

The experience of the Comuna de San Jacinto del Pindo is being copied by a number of other people in definable *runa* territories that are becoming bounded by colonizing non-*runa* from the highlands. East of the Puyo-Napo Road there are two other *comunas* (San Ramón and Arajuno), and still more are talked about. The *comuna* at Canelos has now become quasi-official by executive decree, and there is talk all down the Bobonaza of establishing *comunas* at the sites of the various administrative towns. In fact, the term *comunero* is being increasingly applied to all Indians, whether or not they live on the *comuna*, and many, if not most, *blanco-mestizos* knowing anything at all about the residence of Indians think that *comuna* means *caserío* and are surprised, or even bewildered, to find that *comuna* refers to the grouping of maximal clan segments in a given area. The Indians always explain their social-territorial structure to non-Indians in kinship terms, noting the intersection of extended clans in the past. When pushed, for example, by curious *blancos* in Puyo as to why there are many families from different backgrounds and with different origins, the reply is that such families were previously related in grandparental generations through marriage, so that *all present comuneros are descended from a common, ethnically diverse, breeding population.* By invoking this rule of stipulated ethnic descent the *comuneros* become, in their own eyes, a distinctive race — different from all *blanco-mestizos* and generally related to, but nonetheless distinct from, all other Indians.

I will say more about the Comuna de San Jacinto after setting forth more of the relevant social environment of the Jungle Quechua by reference to internal colonialism, expanding infrastructure, colonization, and the relationships between power domains in this frontier cultural ecological setting.

INTERNAL COLONIALISM

Internal colonialism refers to situations "... where an independent country has, within its own boundaries, given special legal status to groups that differ culturally from the dominant group, and created a distinct administrative machinery to handle such groups" (Colby and van den Berghe 1969: 3). The plural nature of Ecuadorian society has been documented repeatedly (see Jaramillo Alvarado 1936; Whitten 1965; Burgos 1970). What is usually assumed, though, is that expanded economic opportunities will result in the breakdown of plural segments and the establishment of a "mixed" or "*mestizo*" national ethnic category. Pareja Diezcanseco sums up a prevalent intellectual view on contemporary Ecuador:

Ecuador is not a country inhabited by white folk, for as an ethnic minority they only add up to scarcely one-tenth of the total population. Neither is it a country of Indians, for in that case its history would be one of regression, or else, of stratification ... the nation is *Mestizo* ... Once the Indians enter civilized life ... *the Mestizo part of the population will be more homogeneous* (1970: 88. Emphasis added).

The swelling of the "*mestizo* part" of the country is seen by many, within and outside of Ecuador, as part of a growth of ethnic homogenization and a basis for the cultural and social revolution that will do away with a caste system where political and economic control rests with the very few *blancos*. But a large percent of the nation is Indian, and a small, but concentrated, percent is black (not mulatto). The national concept of *mestizo* contains a denial of *blanco* (white) supremacy and affirms roots to Indian and (sometimes) Negro, or at least Moorish-mulatto, ancestry. Such an IDEOLOGY OF MIXTURE allows for considerable EXCLUSION OF THE NONMIXED, including highland and lowland Indians, and ethnically distinct black communities in northwest, north, and southwestern districts. Furthermore, economic and political integration of Ecuador is taking place through internal colonization, particularly through an expansion of highland *mestizos* to lowland areas inhabited primarily by Indians in the east and blacks in the northwest (see Whitten 1965, 1968, 1969a, 1969b, 1974).

Casagrande, Thompson, and Young (1964: 281–325) and Gilette

(1970) give preliminary analyses of colonization in Ecuador. The former state:

The theoretical interest in studying colonization lies both in the processes whereby an already established sociocultural system is extended, replicated or reintegrated ,and in colonization as a CREATIVE PROCESS, since colonists frequently must accommodate themselves to a new ecological situation, and to novel sociopolitical and economic arrangements (Casagrande, Thompson, and Young 1964: 282).

In an earlier work (Whitten 1965), I also took this approach to the predominantly black population of San Lorenzo, a northwest coastal rainforest town. I gave primary attention to the internal social and political structure of black *costeños* and thought of colonists as having to adapt to the new, local scene. But, in the view taken here, another important creative process must be stressed. This is the process of colonization from the high Andes to tropical lowlands. The process is characterized by a transposition of *blanco* ethnic values, reinforced through demographic shifts, causing local peoples classed as *negro* or *indio* to face a socioeconomic environment with an effective, continuing, ideational blockage to strategic resources exploited within their territories.

As highland *mestizos* descend the Andes they enter zones which lack members in the contrasting, upper-class, *blanco* category, and, it seems, in the absence of such *blancos* they assume membership in the *blanco* category themselves. As a consequence, those who would be *choo* or *mestizo* in the Sierra become *blanco* on the coast and eastern slopes. "*Blanco*-ness" is reinforced by generalizing the non-*blanco* ethnic contrast — lumping black *costeños* into one pejorative category and lowland Indians into another. In eastern Ecuador, Indians have again and again had their residences forced completely out of the commercial and administrative towns, while their economic dependence on these towns continued to increase.

It seems to me that the process of breaking up specific Indian linguistic-ethnic units ("tribes") is leading not to increased assimilation of Indians to "*mestizo* ways" but rather to an expanding generalized category "Indian" *(Indio)* to which *mestizos contrast themselves for virtually all purposes, when new opportunities in the money economy arise.* National and labor policies designed to speed up change in the *mestizo* sector, then, increasingly retard opportunities for those classed as *Indio*.

The crucial environmental factor for the contemporary Lowland Quechua is the expanding, contrastive ethnic category *blanco,* which includes the *mestizo* in the absence of upper-class *blanco* culture-bearers. *Blanco-mestizo* ethnicity forces Quechua ethnicity to intensify, and the strategies played in the arena of expanding and generalizing ethnicity have powerful economic consequences for both ethnic categories, *particularly when one ethnic category (the Jungle Quechua) is encapsulated by national policies of "Indian protection" while the other* (blanco-mestizo) *is given wide powers through the national policy of colonization.*

By "ethnicity" I mean *patterns of human interaction which form the basis for categorical social relations with observable, or projected economic consequences.* Categorical social relationships are characterized by stereotypic criteria, as distinct from structural relations which are characterized by group membership or network relationships which are characterized by extant exchange patterns between interacting individuals (see Southall 1961: 1–46; Mitchell 1966: 52–53; Banton 1967; Whitten and Szwed 1970: 43–48; Whitten and Wolfe 1972). Land access is intimately tied to the economic consequence of ethnic status.

In Ecuador today, Indian lands can only be legally protected from invasion by colonists with the formation of *comunas Indígenas* [native communes]. The information of *comunas* is Indian-initiated but depends for administration on the Ministerio de Previsión Social; special laws pertain to the actions of Indians (and colonists) on the *comunas* (see Peñaherrera de Costales and Costales Samaniego 1962). The Instituto Ecuatoriano de Reforma Agraria y Colonización (IERAC), by contrast, is established not only to do away with *latifundia* holdings in the highlands, but also to encourage as rapid a penetration as possible of colonists into the Oriente, particularly in the zones where oil exploration is underway and where the pipeline and access roads are being built. Colonists are by definition *blanco* in the Oriente in contrast to all people classed as *Indio*.

All Oriente people classed as Indio *or* Indígena, *fall into a national power domain which is essentially static. It must await Indian protest before it will even investigate infiltration and invasion of legitimate Indian land. All people classed as* colono (blanco) *in the Oriente fall under a domain of national expansion and dynamic bureaucratic manipulation aimed at opening new land claims for non-Indians.* More will be said about the domains in the ensuing section.

In terms of oil exploration, Indians are generally regarded as "hunters" of the interfluvial zones and so are hired primarily to set up camps, to stay in the forests, and to work only "on the line" for the oil companies. *Blancos*, by contrast, are seen as new potential agriculturalists, are employed near camps and near towns, and are regarded as the proper spokesmen for all workers (including the Indians).

Quechua has long been the national trade and work language for communicating with all lowland Indians, while Spanish has been used primarily for the *blancos*. Today special bilingual line bosses (mostly recruited from the Summer Institute of Linguistics school teachers) are hired to deal with real and potential "Indian problems," while problems of labor organization, minimal wage, etc., are regarded nationally as a strictly *blanco-mestizo* concern.

EXPANDING INFRASTRUCTURE AND POLITICAL ECONOMY

An infrastructure is the network of transportation facilities enabling economic expansion, together with the administrative and educational apparatus, which establishes a bureaucratic information system facilitating the expansion based on transportation networks. Hegen (1966) provides a good base for the study of infrastructure expansion in the Upper Amazon up to the mid-1960's. In his study Hegen makes a dramatic, if unrealistic, statement related to colonists (pioneers), which draws our attention to the nation as a whole:

Pioneering creates sociocultural demands and establishes a tax source which in turn will supply funds to satisfy these demands. It will stimulate the establishment and growth of trade, manufacturing and service industries, and the general exchange of goods, based upon a money economy. It will lead to regional specialization, fulfilling thereby the requirements of the demand-supply complex. Above all ... pioneering will revolutionize the static social and political life of the people by integrating them into the responsible, decision-making processes of a modern democracy (1966: 36).

Although apparently writing his conclusion prior to the events themselves and making enormously overgeneralized statements about a political economy which is now in the hands of foreign companies and a national military dictatorship, Hegen does direct attention to the expanding infrastructure itself and its importance in opening previous frontier zones to national bureaucratic controls. The official, national expanding infrastructure "follows" the *blanco* settlements, which mark the first results of the colonization programs. Pioneer settlements are not distributed willy-nilly around the jungle, nor are they necessarily first established in the best riverbank agricultural zones. They tend to cluster in areas where resources of value to international commerce exist, at a given time, as well as in the areas already targeted for national development. Not surprisingly, the two areas — those designated for development and those of special interest to foreign concerns for resource extraction — often coincide.

Regardless of the strategic importance of *colono* settlement to national planning, however, one inescapable need must be met — the colonists must find a stable food supply. And they are usually totally ignorant of tropical agriculture. Where Indian settlements exist, the *colono* food supply becomes the native *chagra*. To understand the informal aspect of an expanding infrastructure, we must put native peoples of the Oriente into the picture and carefully note the cycle whereby new lands are "opened" by *blanco* pioneers muscling into Indian *chagras*. By the time an official agent of a responsible bureaucracy arrives via plane or helicopter to an area to investigate alleged irregularities, the colonists are in control of major manioc plots, planted by Indians but claimed by colonists, and the stereotype of Indians as hunters is used to force the natives away from their own productive agricultural lands. This forces the Indians to open new territories to be later exploited in the same manner, unless effective counterstrategies are concurrently enacted. The Lowland Quechua seem remarkably effective in devising counterstrategies that are peace producing and accommodating in terms of warding off destruction of their population.

Good land for growing crops within any given *runa* territory is limited, and the Jungle Quechua often opt to remain near enough to the national infrastructure tentacles to press early claims during times of invasion. This gives them more opportunity for social network maintenance within a known geographic zone than is characteristic of other Indian groups. The Lowland Quechua are particularly effective in losing one thing to gain something else *vis-à-vis* colonists and in maintaining strength *vis-à-vis* various quasi-sympathetic and relatively helpful brokerage agencies (Catholic and Protestant missions, military bases, powerful *hacendados*, land speculators, and even some Peace Corps volunteers). This allows them to not only survive in such a situation of replacive colonization, but to actually expand under such an impress. But the price of their expansion is often peonage, in one form or another, to one of the patronage "helpers."

If we were dealing with nineteenth-century and early twentieth-century exploitation of natural resources (as we are when dealing with the history of the Jungle Quechua), we might by now be able to construct an adequate model of Indian-*blanco* relationships. Steward

(1948: 507–512) did just this, though the many new data turned up will demand a reexamination of his model sequences. But the penetration in the last five years of foreign oil companies (Texaco-Gulf in the north, Anglo and Amoco in the central Oriente, together with subsidiary exploration companies and subcontracting companies) and their new technologies make it clear that the frontier itself falls within an expanding technological sphere superior to, and guided by, agencies more powerful than Ecuador's political economy. *Blancos* and Quechua alike fall into power domains of national bureaucracies and, also, supranational domains reflecting new levels of politico-economic integration (Wolfe 1963). These latter domains are most productively considered as competitive to national interests.

Richard N. Adams (1970) presents us with an exhaustive and highly productive model and methodology for the study of dynamic structure of power in contemporary nations. He defines "power domain" as

... any arrangement of units wherein two or more units have unequal control over each other's environment. Wherever there is a distinctive difference in the relative power exercised by two units with respect to each other, there is a domain, and the two units pertain to different levels of articulation. Units in confrontation at one level will usually pertain to distinct domains (Adams 1970: 56).

Regarding the expanding infrastructure itself, a bit more needs to be said. The Puyo-Napo-Tena Road has moved to Cotundo east of Tena, and the Papallacta-Baeza Road (from the Sierra toward the Oriente) opened in 1971. The Baeza-Cotundo section is underway. The oil pipeline constructed by Texaco-Gulf in late spring, 1972, runs from just south of Esmeraldas up the western Cordillera and moves from just south of Quito to Papallacta and follows the Papallacta-Baeza Road. It swings north from Baeza following the Quijos River and Coca River northeast to the Agua Rico River and then due east to Santa Cecilia and south to Coca. The Coca-Santa Cecilia section is completed, with access road, and oil is now being pumped for foreign consumption. The construction of this roadway virtually obliterated the Cofán, Secoya, and Siona Indians in this area (see Robinson 1971).

REFUGE, STRATEGY, AND ETHNIC
DISENFRANCHISEMENT

In the area around Puyo the infrastructure expansion is taking place in large part by foot and by plane. From a small airport at Shell Mera, which used to see a maximum of two flights a week, there were over 100 per day until around February, 1973. Most of these fly cargo to the oil camps, but many flights fly colonists and food for colonists. Neither the Jívaro nor the Quechua of this zone intend to let *blancos* invade their territory or take over their land. But they are perfectly willing to exchange usufructory rights to land on a temporary basis for cash that will allow them to expand their own territories. Quechua and Jívaro, as well as *colonos,* want to be near the loci of national interaction — the airports, the proposed roadways, and the basic walking trails. Because the terrain along the Pastaza and Bobonaza is very rugged, it is not clear that there will be roadways in the foreseeable future, though many are on the planning boards. This means that the Indians have a temporary refuge area from Puyo due east, even though the Puyo area is itself the most developed in the current Oriente.

But this refuge area will not last for long. Recently an airport has been opened at Canelos, and Montalvo appears to be the central Oriente analog to Santa Cecilia in the north. The Canelos Quechua are increasingly hemmed in, and maximal clan segments and *purina* treks are cut in their fringe areas by *blanco* penetration settlements. Their rational, firm desire to participate in the expanding Ecuadorian economy results in dynamic adaptive strategies which are contingent on national acceptance for success. Practically, I think, they must be "allowed" to continue their legal *comuna* formation, while at the same time fully participating in *colono* expansion.

This mixed strategy, which insists on both boundary establishment and land acquisition, also demands a duality of ethnicity — Indian and bicultural. The former stresses communal ownership of property and the latter individualism. Such a mixing of survival requirements and their strategic presentation to representatives of different national bureaucracies may seem paradoxical, but from the Quechua perspective it is the only way to avoid being further hemmed in and bounded by "protective" measures which establish rigid *comuna* boundaries. The national concept of *comuna indígena* suggests a reservation complex governed from afar as a total institution. It is supposed to be locally maintained by internal primitive democracy through total agreement by all indigenous members, themselves ideally living in blissful, child-like, ignorance of their treacherous external social environment. Since, of course, no such group of Indians exists on or off any *comuna,* it is easy for developers and those seeking patronage roles to decide that the Indians are too disorganized to maintain "their" *comuna* structure and to use such a rationale to take an even heavier hand in rigidifying Indian territorial boundaries.[6]

The national concept might even now be transformed to reflect the Lowland Quechua notion of *comuna* as a corporate HOLDING COMPANY. By this perspective the corporation allows for the carrying out of united extended clans' subsistence pursuits, while at the same time allowing people variously to employ their individually and familistically held land and social "stock" to give backbone to expansionist, colonizing functions of their own, eventually increasing the assets of the *comuna*-holding corporation. I frankly doubt that Ecuadorian non-Indians will allow this to happen. They will probably continually seek to contain indigenous expansion. Indians themselves will probably continue to attempt to use the *comuna* corporation established through *blanco* containment strategies to break out, economically, politically, socially, and symbolically, unless all their energies are taken up in simply protecting their *comunas* from very real *blanco* invasion.

The well-known international process of Indian disenfranchisement and exploitation, as a complement to ethnic annihilation, rushes on in the Ecuadorian Oriente. The fixing of blame on the disenfranchised by the invocation of an "Indian problem" exacerbates Lowland Quechua territorial consolidation and leads to heightened ethnic awareness, to *blanco* discrimination against Indians, and to *blanco* patronage of those people who are socially and politically disenfranchised.

A pamphlet on Ecuadorian ethnocide (Robinson 1971) is receiving some justifiable attention in Latin America. The very real annihilation of surviving native groups in countries such as Ecuador cannot pass without such attention, concern, and hopefully remedial action. The focus here of my own preliminary report on Jungle Quechua ethnicity seeks to anticipate the complementary problem of total disenfranchisement and structural confinement of the survivors of national ethnocide.

---

[6]   One floundering United States Peace Corps project recently gave "motivational training" to a valiant group of *comuneros* fighting for their very lives to hold their territorial boundaries against a massive onslaught of territory-hungry land-grabbers. At the same time, the Peace Corps saviors helped land-grabbers from the highlands to formalize their land claims on institutionalized Indian territory and even offered courses in new agricultural skills to the exploiters. The rationale behind the motivational training was that the Indians had not yet learned to live "communally" on their *comuna*!

POSTSCRIPT, AUGUST 1973

From our work over the past year, I see the following as unfolding. As the pressures from the militaristic Ecuadorian government, Gobierno Nacionalista Revolucionario del Ecuador, working with the ideology of a "political culture *(cultura politica),*" increase on the Canelos Quechua, these valiant people seek more and more ways to adapt their lifeways to new exigencies in their environment. At one level, they enter a domain of rapid change, but at another they intensify traditional beliefs and practices which give the only meaning possible in a biosphere experiencing chaotic stimuli. As national planners observe the rapid change they assume that the Canelos Quechua are plunging toward *mestizo*-ship in the political culture. But the Indians are increasingly expanding their self-identification system at one level, and becoming more and more "Indian conscious" at another level.

It is apparent to any Ecuadorian or foreign planner, evaluator, or administrator that the Canelos Quechua have a dynamic set of lifeways which is puzzlingly nonnational. But because these people show fewer and fewer overt signs of stereotypic Indianness (they wear clothes, eschew face painting and feather wearing in the presence of *mestizos,* and speak a language which many Ecuadorians understand), differences are attributed not to cultural continuity but to disorganization resulting from rapid change. Our thesis that people who survive, expand their population, and consolidate their social system in the face of chaos have a clear, nonanarchistic, social structure is generally dismissed, perhaps because it is too destructive of national and international ideology aimed at simplistic models of how the poor should behave.

I think the following two complementary positions regarding jungle peoples are the only allowable ones in Ecuador today: (1) We must mourn their passing, make great noises about ethnocide, condemning those who destroy indigenous peoples, and do much self-searching to see if, somehow, we are all guilty of the destruction of native life, and (2) We must respect the *mestizo* all the more, for he is the last living embodiment of nativeness; the native has become a national with civilized *blanco* values, and in the new *blanco-mestizo* lifeway lies both the future and the past of national consolidation.

Again, the complementarity of ethnocide-mourning, plus heightened *blanco-mestizo*-ness, establishes a basis for considering the contemporary Jungle Quechua as a flagrant contradiction to national ideology. Perhaps this is why so much contempt is heaped upon these people, even by those nationals and nonnationals who cry loudly for Indian rights. I suspect that all over the world there is a complementarity in the expansion of ethnic culture and its denigration by those who seek to mourn the passing of other traditional cultures and to "help" the expanding ethnic cultures reach a new, "nondifferent" position within the nation. The problem with such help, given the rationale sketched above, is that it is probably a force equally as destructive as planned ethnocide, for it grows from the same source and serves the same national purpose.

REFERENCES

ADAMS, RICHARD N.
1970   *Crucifixion by power: essays on Guatemalan national social structure, 1944–1966.* Austin: University of Texas Press.
BANTON, MICHAEL
1967   *Race relations.* New York: Basic Books.
BROMLEY, RAYMOND J.
i.p.   Agricultural colonization in the upper Amazon basin: the impact of oil discoveries. *Tijdschrift voor Economische en Sociale Geografie.*
BURBANO MARTÍNEZ, HÉCTOR, LUIS ANTONIO RIVADENEIRA, JULIO MONTALVO MONTENEGRO
1964   "El problema de las poblaciones indígenas selváticas del Ecuador." Paper presented at the Quinto Congreso Indigenista Interamericano, Quito, Ecuador, October, 1964.
BURGOS, HUGO
1970   *Relaciones interétnicas en Ríobamba.* Instituto Indigenista Interamericano Ediciones Especiales 55. Mexico.
CARNEIRO, ROBERT L.
1970   A theory of the origin of the state. *Science* (August 28): 733–738.
CASAGRANDE, JOSEPH B., STEPHEN I. THOMPSON, PHILIP D. YOUNG
1964   "Colonization as a research frontier: the Ecuadorian case," in *Process and pattern in culture: essays in honor of Julian Steward.* Chicago: Aldine.
COLBY, BENJAMIN, PIERRE VAN DEN BERGHE
1969   *Ixil country.* Berkeley: University of California Press.
EICHLER, ARTURO
1970   *Snow peaks and jungles.* New York: Crowell. (Reprint of 1955 edition with new introduction by Alfredo Pareja Diezcanseco.)
ERASMUS, CHARLES J.
1961   *Man takes control: cultural development and American aid.* Minneapolis: University of Minnesota Press.

FERDON, EDWIN N., JR.
1950   *Studies in Ecuadorian geography.* Monographs of the School of American Research 15. Santa Fe.

FRIED, MORTON
1967   *The evolution of political society: an essay in political anthropology.* New York: Random House.

GILLETTE, CYNTHIA
1970   "Problems of colonization in the Ecuadorian Oriente." Unpublished M.A. thesis, Washington University, St. Louis.

HARNER, MICHAEL J.
1972   *The Jívaro: people of the sacred waterfalls.* Garden City: Doubleday, Natural History Press.

HEGEN, EDMUND E.
1966   *Highways into the upper Amazon basin: pioneer lands in southern Colombia, Ecuador, and northern Peru.* Center for Latin American Studies Monograph 2. Gainesville: University of Florida Press.

JARAMILLO ALVARADO, PIO
1936   *Tierras del Oriente.* Quito: Imprenta Nacionales.

MITCHELL, J. CLYDE
1966   "Theoretical orientations in African urban studies," in *The social anthropology of complex societies.* Edited by Michael Banton. New York: Praeger.

OBEREM, UDO
1971   *Los Quijos.* Memorias de Departamento de Antropología y Etnología de América. Madrid.

ORR, CAROLYN, BETSY WRISLEY
1965   *Vocabulario Quichua del Oriente del Ecuador.* Mexico City: Instituto Lingüístico de Verano.

PAREJA DIEZCANSECO, ALFREDO
1970   "Introduction," in *Snow peaks and jungles.* By Arturo Eichler. New York: Crowell.

PEÑAHERRERA DE COSTALES, PIEDAD, ALFREDO COSTALES SAMANIEGO
1961   Llacta runa. *Llacta* 12. Quito.
1962   Comunas juridicamente organizadas. *Llacta* 15. Quito.

PEÑAHERRERA DE COSTALES, PIEDAD, ALFREDO COSTALES SAMANIEGO, *et al.*
1969   *Los Quichuas del Coca y el Napo.* Escuela de Sociología de la Universidad Central, Serie de Documentos y Estudios Sociales 1. Quito.

PORRAS G., P. PEDRO I.
1961   *Contribución al estudio de la arqueología e historia de los valles Quijos y Misaguallí (Alto Napo) en la región oriental del Ecuador, S. A.* Quito: Editora Fenix.

ROBINSON, SCOTT S.
1971   *El etnocidio ecuatoriano.* Mexico City: Universidad Iberoamericana.

ROBINSON, SCOTT S., MICHAEL SCOTT
1971   *Sky Chief.* Thirty-minute color documentary film.

SCHEFFLER, HAROLD W., FLOYD G. LOUNSBURY
1971   *A study in structural semantics: the Siriono kinship system.* Englewood Cliffs: Prentice-Hall.
SOUTHALL, AIDAN
1961   "Introductory summary," in *Social change in modern Africa.* Edited by Aidan Southall, 1–82. London: Oxford University Press (for the International African Institute).
STEWARD, JULIAN H.
1948   "Tribes of the Montaña: an introduction," in *Handbook of South American Indians,* volume three: *The tropical forest tribes.* Edited by Julian H. Steward, 507–534. Smithsonian Institution Bureau of American Ethnology Bulletin 143. Washington, D.C.
STEWARD, JULIAN H., ALFRED MÉTRAUX
1948   "Tribes of the Peruvian and Ecuadorian Montaña" (sections entitled "The Jívaro," "Zaparoan Tribes," and "The Quijo"), in *Handbook of South American Indians,* volume three: *The tropical forest tribes.* Edited by Julian H. Steward, 617–656. Smithsonian Institution Bureau of American Ethnology Bulletin 143. Washington, D.C.
TESSMANN, GÜNTER
1930   *Die Indianer Nordost-Perus: grundlegende Forschungen für eine systematische Kulturkunde.* Hamburg: Cram, De Gruyter.
WHITTEN, NORMAN E., JR.
1965   *Class, kinship, and power in an Ecuadorian town: the Negroes of San Lorenzo.* Stanford: Stanford University Press.
1968   Personal networks and musical contexts in the Pacific Lowlands of Ecuador and Colombia. *Man: Journal of the Royal Anthropological Institute* 3(1):50–63.
1969a Strategies of adaptive mobility in the Colombian-Ecuadorian littoral. *American Anthropologist* 71(2):228–242.
1969b The ecology of race relations in northwest Ecuador. *Journal de la Société des Américanistes* 54:223–235.
1974   *Black frontiersmen: a South American case.* Cambridge: Schenkman.
WHITTEN, NORMAN E., JR., JOHN F. SZWED, *editors*
1970   *Afro-American anthropology: contemporary perspectives.* New York: Free Press, Macmillan.
WHITTEN, NORMAN E., JR., ALVIN W. WOLFE
1972   "Network analysis," in *Handbook of social and cultural anthropology.* Edited by John J. Honigmann. Chicago: Rand McNally.
WOLFE, ALVIN W.
1963   The African mineral industry: evolution of a supranational level of integration. *Social Problems* 11(2):153–163.

Jívaro Head Hunters in a
Headless Time

HENNING SIVERTS

1.   The Jívaro Indians of the Ecuadorian and Peruvian Montaña have
for a long time attracted the attention of anthropologists and laymen alike
due to their warlike practices and their habit of shrinking enemy heads
into miniature trophies.

This paper is an attempt at viewing Jívaro warfare and head hunting as
the core of "jívaroness" and source of ethnic maintenance. More precisely,
one could argue that the ideology underlying head hunting represents the
basic value orientation of the Jívaro and that the head-hunting itself is one
of the diacritical features exhibiting the Jívaro life-style.

Together, the ideological underpinning and the head-hunting war
complex constitute the cultural content that the Jívaro as an ethnic group
encloses (cf. Barth 1969: 14). The important point, however, is not so
much what is enclosed as the process of enclosing, i.e. how ceremonial
head hunting becomes the "source of ethnic maintenance." Thus, inter-
tribal warfare, including resistance against the white intruders, was and is
considered a totally different undertaking from intratribal head-hunting
raids.

2.   Probably more than 40,000 Jívaro inhabit an area comprising some
60,000 square kilometers.[1] The region is difficult of access, characterized
by rugged mountains and steep hills covered by dense tropical forest and

---

[1]   These figures are estimates based on various sources (Guallart 1964, 1970; Uriarte
1971, 1972; Varese 1970). It is further assumed that the Ecuadorian Jívaro groups
occupy a territory about the same size as the Alto Marañon region, i.e. some 30,000
square kilometers (Uriarte 1971).

crisscrossed by swift-flowing rivers and brooks in an intricate fluvial net. Some of the rivers and tributaries are navigable by canoes and balsa rafts but, as Harner (1968) points out, travel by means other than foot is difficult in large portions of the territory, where hardly visible trails and paths tie settlements together.

Subsistence activities involve shifting horticulture, combined with hunting, fishing and collecting of wild fruits and plants. The chief garden crops are yucca or sweet manioc (*Manihot esculenta*) and various species of plantains and bananas.

Although they form a linguistic and cultural entity—an ethnic group—they do not constitute a TRIBE if we take tribe to mean a permanent political group or corporation. The Jívaro are rather an aggregate of neighborhoods, called *jivarías* in Ecuador and *caseríos* in Peru, whose members consider each other as ceremonial foes or temporary allies within an all-embracing kin and affinal network. As head-hunters, they recognized only Jívaro heads as worth taking and shrinking into /¢án¢a/ to be displayed and celebrated at the great victory feast following a successful head-hunting expedition. In other words, a Jívaro is a potential /¢án¢a/ while all others, including the white people are just foreigners.[2]

At present when head-hunting is no longer feasible and the victory feast cannot be performed, many Jívaro, reared as warriors, feel that their identity is being threatened, that their hallmark as a people is being lost. In spite of the fact that war parties are no longer organized and the concomitant ceremonial reassurance of commonness is a thing of the past, the fundamental values on which these activities were based are still shared by the majority of the Jívaro whether they live in Ecuador or Peru.

The implication of this observation seems to be that the Jívaro are aware of some "ethos," or, rather, a style of life, which they consider exclusively Jívaro. During fieldwork among the Aguaruna Jívaros on the Peruvian side of the border, the subject of Jívaro unity and diversity was brought up repeatedly, even by the informants themselves.[3] For obvious reasons they showed concern for the future and wondered what would become of them all now that the military had got a foothold in their territory. They had no organizational means by which to mobilize all Aguaruna, not to speak of other Jívaro groups, in order to resist the invaders and the colonists pouring into the area.

---

[2]   Transcription of Aguaruna Jívaro words corresponds to phonemization proposals suggested by Pike and Larson (Pike and Larson 1964; Larson 1963).

[3]   Fieldwork was conducted in the Alto Marañon area between August 1970 and April 1971 and was supported by the Norwegian Research Council and Smithsonian Institution (Urgent Anthropology Program).

It is common knowledge that the Jívaro, until the recent past, have been able to unite in large and effective military operations, repelling attempts at conquest both on the part of the Incas, the Spaniards, and later the Peruvians and the Ecuadorians. The Jívaro themselves know this for a fact. That is why they are concerned; and that is furthermore why it seems pertinent to speak about the Jívaro as an ethnic group which is biologically self-perpetuating, shares fundamental cultural values, makes up a field of communication and interaction and, finally, has a membership which identifies itself, and is identified by others, as constituting a category distinguishable from other categories of the same order (cf. Naroll 1964).

The Jívaro do recognize the overt cultural forms signifying unity such as language, dress, house types and technology. But, what is more significant, they assume existence of a set of common value orientations: "the standards of morality and excellence by which performance is judged" (cf. Barth 1969: 14).

The concept of /kakáham/ is a case in point. A /kakáham/ is a man who has killed several times, a *valiente*, and the Aguaruna still distinguish between the /kakáham/ and other persons. The former is likely to be an influential local leader. According to Harner, "the personal security which the Jívaro believe comes from the killing has some social reality. A man who has killed repeatedly, called the *kakaram* [i.e. /kakáham/ in Aguaruna] or 'powerful one', is rarely attacked because his enemies feel that the protection provided him by his constantly replaced souls would make any assassination attempt against him fruitless" (1962). According to Aguaruna informants the /cimpuí/ or special chair is reserved for the /kakáham/ and the /nágki/, the war lance, should be touched only by a person belonging to this category.

In other words, /kakáham/ provides us with a focal concept by which the Jívaro classify human beings and their actions. As an achieved status, /kakáham/ represents a valued end and a measure of success. Not all Jívaro became /kakáham/ but they certainly aspired to become one, and indeed a young man was marriageable only after he had proved his ability as hunter and warrior (cf. Stirling 1938: 110). Thus a Jívaro man is by definition a warrior, and the ideal career involves the recognition as /kakáham/ and later /wáhiu/, leader of men and organizer of war parties. The designation /kúhak/, derived from the Quechua-Spanish *curaca*, was probably reserved for those influential men who could muster a following among several local groups.

Thus the typical social categories refer to excellence of performance within a pattern of behavior which is focused upon warfare and trophy making. These activities are still emphasized and until recently were made organizationally relevant. But the warrior ideal cannot be maintained much longer as the primary concern of men. The presence of troops, white settlers, merchants and missionaries prevents the Jívaro from realizing in actual life the most important aspect of the Jívaro male role: the enacting of the warrior. Consequently individual men may consider themselves as only "part-time Jívaros," implying a gradual blurring of the image of virility and manliness assumed to underlie Jívaro behavior. "Since belonging to an ethnic category implies being a certain kind of person, having that identity, it also implies a claim to be judged, and to judge oneself, by those standards that are relevant to that identity" (Barth 1969: 14). According to the Jívaro way of arguing, social order is based on moral order, and the latter is composed of a series of demands and obligations derived from a set of beliefs about souls and esoteric power and the way to obtain it. Only Jívaro own the souls and control the power, and killing another Jívaro is a means by which power is attained, hence a claim to be judged as Jívaro is to kill another Jívaro, or in Karsten's words:

It is characteristic of the Jivaros that they especially wage war against tribes belonging to their own race and speaking the same language. To such an extent has this been the rule for centuries that the word *shuara*, "Jivaro Indian," has become synonymous with the word "enemy." "My enemy" in Jivaros language is *winya shuara* (1935:276).

Vengeance and blood feuding, then, is the logical outcome, war parties are a natural tactical device, head trophies the overt and highly dramatic symbol of performance according to standards of morality, and military alliances are the long-term strategic solutions by which one may hope to maintain a reasonable balance between peace and war.

It is not clear whether the Kandoshi were included among Jívaro foes. They waged war on each other, but there is no evidence of head taking. Nevertheless, the Kandoshi are reported as fierce warriors and apparently showed great similarity in their war pattern and beliefs (Wallis 1965). In case Jívaro heads were severed and displayed among the Kandoshi and vice versa, we may assume, according to the argument pursued, that the Záparo-speaking Kandoshi and the Jívaro considered each other as participants in the same raiding game, sharing fundamental values about souls and power, i.e. "the assumptions about reality upon which they [the Jívaro] predicate" their warlike practices (Harner 1962). The implication of such a reciprocity would be the inclusion of the Kandoshi in a Jívaro-Kandoshi ethnic group.

One of my young Aguaruna informants offered a simplified "history" of the area to the effect that in the beginning all Jívaro were united against different foreign tribes, including eventually the white people. Then the Huambisa and Aguaruna started warring against each other and ultimately the Aguaruna split up into feuding units. Speculating over this version for a while, without grasping its meaning, it suddenly occurred to me that my friend was actually conveying a message, the interpretation of which might be the following: Formerly all Jívaro were potentially united, but, as we can all see, now they are separated in smaller groups. In other words, he tried to reconcile the facts relating to the present situation and the oral tradition referring to the great alliances of the past. A further indication of relative distance in time and space corresponding to some real or fictive alliances is found in the "tribal" designations handed down from an earlier period. All the people beyond Río Santiago were called /patúk/, comprising both the Huambisa and the Ecuadorian Untsuri Shuara. However, the Huambisa reserve the term /wampís/ for themselves and apply /patúk/ to describe the Ecuadorian Jívaro. The Achual are named /acuág/ by the Aguaruna.

Clearly this selection of "names" for peoples may reflect a particular alliance constellation or some vague notion about territorial groups. Dialect differences may also be involved. Indeed, we can expect a proliferation of names as long as every little *quebrada* [river valley] has its name by which also the group of people living there is known.

A temporary grouping of allies was given the name of the war leader or of the river on which he was residing. Thus the Antipa may well have been an Aguaruna group distinguished from other Jívaro on account of a powerful leader by the name of Antipa. Today, nobody seems to remember the Antipa, but in 1899, when Up de Graff braved the Pongo de Manseriche, the Antipa were a powerful group which had joined forces with another Aguaruna group in order to attack the Huambisa further up on the Santiago River (Up de Graff 1923: 241ff.).

According to Up de Graff fifty-five canoes containing some two hundred men were heading up-river "bent on a common mission (which needs no explanation)" (1923: 242). Not all raids counted such formidable forces, but apparently the Jívaro of those days were politically rather active, forming alliances and organizing war parties of considerable size. From Stirling's description we get the impression that the extension of influence assigned to any one *curaka*, or war leader, varied from time to time, implying the waxing and waning of alliances between smaller units:

The number of households under the influence of a given curaka is subject to a great deal of fluctuation. It frequently happens that a strong curaka will build up a fairly powerful group of warriors about him. A weak curaka or capito may have a blood-revenge killing to attend to but will find himself outnumbered by the enemy to such an extent that he is afraid to attempt a killing with his own group. In this event he is likely to call upon the strong curaka to arrange the killing for him with a gun or a woman. Often, too, a weak curaka, fearing that his group would not be able successfully to defend themselves against an attack from enemies, will voluntarily place himself and his group under the influence of the strong curaka in a loose sort of alliance. In this way the strong group tends to grow and to become even stronger until one curaka may have 8 or 10 lesser curakas more or less under his control. This state of affairs is usually not very permanent. Owing to the loose organization and lack of any real power on the part of the head curaka, the large group becomes unwieldy or develops diverse interests and it tends to split up again into independent units. Consequently, in as little as 2 or 3 years' time, the original head curaka may find that one or more of his former lieutenants are now stronger than he (Stirling 1938:39).

Neither Up de Graff nor Karsten are specific in their treatment of alliance-forming and social organization generally. We have to rely on the work of Stirling from the thirties and Harner's from a more recent period. Fortunately Stirling does go into some details on this point, documenting his generalized description of the political process by citing two cases of regional fusion and fission which he personally had encountered during fieldwork in 1930–1931. The first example illustrates how military strength is related to personal power and, by implication, the physical and mental fitness of the leader or strong man:

Four or five years ago there was a strong chief on the Upano River named Tuki, known to the Ecuadoreans as José Grande. In the manner previously described, all of the curakas from Macas on the Upano River to Mendez on the Paute River became subchiefs under him until he was generally recognized as the strongest of all of the Jivaro curakas. However, he was beginning to grow old by this time and some of his subcurakas were strong men in their own right. About 2 years ago, Ambusha, who had been gradually gaining in power and becoming famous for his headhunting activities, split off with his own group, taking several curakas and their men with him. A little later Utita did the same thing. At the time of the writer's visit (1931), although Tuki was recognized by the Government of Ecuador as being head chief of the Macas-Mendez region, actually he had lost all power excepting that over his own family group and was in reality no more than a capito. These divisions of the organization, if it may be termed such, took place apparently without any ill feeling or formal announcements (Stirling 1938:40).

The second case illuminates the demographical question in a warring society, by simply showing the repercussion of success:

In 1925 the Canga River and the upper Yaupe was very populous and prosperous. The Indians were a warlike group confident of their own strength and

much feared by all of the Indians in the neighboring regions. The curaka of the
Canga Jivaros was a well known warrior called Cucusha. Anguasha ... another
warlike leader, was head of the Yaupe group. The two had always been close
friends and companions. During a period of 10 or 15 years they compiled a
notable war record, each being credited individually with more than 50 heads
during this time. Their raids extended to all of the tribes in the district and some
quite distant, until they became the terror of the region. However, these constant
raids under two such aggressive leaders began to take their toll of men. Although
many victories were registered, they were constantly losing warriors, until
eventually their numbers were appreciably reduced (Stirling 1938:40).

The flexibility of organization which these excerpts suggest, is amply
demonstrated in my own material on Aguaruna local groups and the
process by which they are established and maintained. Just as the military
alliances were subject to a developmental cycle, the house clusters (*caseríos*)
and larger neighborhoods change through time in composition and
numbers, corresponding to or reflecting ecological and demographical
circumstances, individual mobility and independence being concomitant
features. Genealogical data reveal that single persons and families have
changed house sites several times not only within a settlement, they have
also moved from one *caserío* to another far away. In so doing they have
attached themselves to relatives and avoided traditional "enemies."

As I have argued elsewhere (Siverts 1971, 1972) the habitat requires
mobility, and this moving about in search for suitable house sites, yucca
gardens, hunting grounds and hunting partners is made possible by the
linking of houses and settlements through genealogies. This linking of
genealogies or rather fragments of genealogies constitutes an underlying
framework of organization which, by extension, embraces all Jívaro in a
kin-and-affinal network. Apparently the Aguaruna consider all other
Jívaro, whether foe or friend, as somehow related. Personal experiences,
implicitly shown in a statement such as, "my mother was a Huambisa,"
corroborate this notion.

The alliances of *caseríos* (or *jivarías*) were expedient activations of more
or less extensive portions of the genealogical network, a measure which,
by implication, established relative peace within an area. The lack of
persistence of any particular alliance provided for constancy of the
genealogical network itself which thereby was left unbroken as an organizational potential: new constellations of *caseríos* could always be established.

In view of this flexibility of organization, permitting the establishment
of impermanent corporations, Jívaro invincibility in the past makes sense.
The question has been asked how the Jívaro, preoccupied with the taking
of each other's heads, could possibly muster an effective resistance against

intruders. And the answer must be one that takes account of the strategic advantage offered by the habitat itself as well as the military strength presented by the Jívaro as an ethnic group.[4]

It is this latter theme that is intimately related to the main problem of this essay, viz., the process by which "jívaroness" is maintained and the cultural boundary defended. From the Jívaro point of view this boundary is essentially one which separates /¢án¢a/s from non-/¢án¢a/s, and its territorial counterpart is recognized only insofar as the head-hunting pattern or the conditions for pursuing this activity is threatened. Thus, the Jívaro make no territorial claim and they did let foreigners visit them and establish contact without showing hostility.

It was when they first felt that Spanish settlement and Spanish rule interfered with their own way of life and its esoteric basis that they acted; and they were able to act in concert since the underlying framework was all-encompassing, and potentially permitted the emergency mobilization of all able-bodied men in a grand alliance transforming the Jívaro ethnic group into a corporation.

3.   Such a complete fusion of antagonistic, feuding units may be seen as the automatic result as long as blood revenge and war were parts of daily life, the shifts in power continuous, and the alliance forming an ongoing, cyclical process.

Even as late as the thirties, when Stirling visited the area, the following statement was probably appropriate:

The alliance between nature and the Jivaros has enabled these Indians success-fully to repulse for 400 years the most determined efforts of the white man to establish himself in their territory. The many-faceted account of this prolonged struggle against military, theological, commercial, and territorial aggression constitutes one of the most colorful chapters in aboriginal American history (1938:28).

The bulldozer and the machine gun have changed the situation. It is no longer possible for the Jívaro to control the area by watching the mountain passes or attacking isolated and vulnerable outposts.[5] The highway and the garrisons have put an end to the endless feuds, and prevented the most

---

[4] How strong the striking power was is illustrated by the famous Jívaro revolt of 1559 when perhaps as many as twenty thousand warriors under the leadership of Quiruba annihilated the town of Logroño, terminating Spanish rule in the Jívaro territory. Not even the Peruvians or Ecuadorians succeeded in making headway in this area some fifty years ago. At least they never won a decisive victory.
[5] In 1915 a Peruvian garrison on the upper Morona was routed and practically everybody killed; and in 1925 the village and mission of Cahuapenas on the Apaga River were wiped out (cf. Stirling 1938:28).

dramatic expression of "jívaroness." A further consequence of this state of affairs is the retention of old grievances between former opponents without the natural outlet, leaving the underlying framework obsolete for corporation-forming purposes and hence leading to a situation of political inactivity and indecision.

And this indecision, combined with the distrust of fellowmen, has made it easier for the respective governments to launch their colonization projects, forcing the Jívaro, one by one, from their *chagras* [yucca gardens] and hunting grounds. It is symptomatic that the Aguaruna of Alto Marañon are so paralyzed that they have permitted the Peruvian authorities to back a figurehead, hated by everybody.

There is only one case on record showing signs of political activity and a will to act *in corpore:* a group of armed men gathered in the Cenepa district in order to resist another round of DDT fumigation. For the first time, the "DDT gang"[6] met resolute and concerted action. They fled, and news about the success spread all over the region. Today, the "malaria agency" people find it difficult to continue working in the area, which means one nuisance less to cope with.

However interesting this instance appears under the circumstances, it may not necessarily herald a new drive or revival of political activity on a large scale. It takes more to unite head hunters when there are no heads around to be taken; and in addition the prospects offered for Jívaro survival as an ethnic group are rather gloomy under the auspices of a "headless" minority policy.

REFERENCES

BARTH, FREDRIK, *editor*
1969   *Ethnic groups and boundaries: the social organization of culture differences*. Bergen-Oslo: Universitetsforlaget; London: Allen and Unwin.
GUALLART, JOSÉ MARÍA
1964   *America Indígena* 24:315–331.
1970   "Magia y poesía aguaruna: poesía magica y poesía lírica entre los aguarunas." Unpublished manuscript.
HARNER, MICHAEL J.
1962   Jívaro souls. *American Anthropologist* 64:258–272.

---

[6] The "DDT gang" is short for the employees of the *Servicio Nacional de Eradicación de Malaria* (SNEM) (see Siverts 1972).

1968   Technological and social change among the eastern Jívaro. *Proceedings of the Thirty-seventh International Congress gf Americanists*, 363–388. Buenos Aires.

KARSTEN, RAFAEL
1935   *The head-hunters of western Amazonas: The life and culture of the Jívaro Indians of Eastern Ecuador and Peru.* Helsinki: Societas Scientarum Fennica, Comentationes Humanorum Litterarum.

LARSON, MILDRED L.
1963   *Emic classes which manifest the obligatory tagmemes in major independent clause types of Aguaruna [Jívaro].* University of Oklahoma Summer Institute of Linguistics, Norman, Oklahoma.

NAROLL, RAOUL
1964   On ethnic unit classification. *Current Anthropology* 5:283–312.

PIKE, KENNETH L., M. L. LARSON
1964   "Hyperphonemes and non-systemic features of Aguaruna phonemes," in *Studies in languages and linguistics.* Edited by A. H. Marckwardt, 55–67. Ann Arbor: University of Michigan Press.

SIVERTS, HENNING
1971   "The Aguaruna Jívaros of Peru: a preliminary report." Mimeographed manuscript, University of Bergen.
1972   *Tribal survival in the Alto Marañon: the Aguaruna case.* IWGIA-Document 10. Copenhagen.

STIRLING, M. W.
1938   *Historical and ethnographical material on the Jívaro Indians.* Smithsonian Institution of Washington D.C. Bureau of American Ethnology, Bulletin 117.

UP DE GRAFF, FRITZ W.
1923   *Head-hunters of the Amazon: seven years of exploration and adventure.* London: Herbert Jenkins.

URIARTE, LUIS M.
1971   *Situación de genocidio, etnocidio e injusticia entre las tribus aguaruna u huambisa del Alto Marañon.* Comisión Episcopal de Acción Social, Cuadernos de Documentación 2. Lima.
1972   "Algunos datos preliminares del censo aguaruna-huambisa." Unpublished manuscript, Chiriaco.

VARESE, STEFANO, *editor*
1970   *Estudio sondeo de seis communidades aguarunas del Alto Marañon.* Division de Communidades Nativas de la Selva, Dirección de Communidades Campesinas. Series de Estudos e Informes 1. Lima: Ministerio de Agricultura.

WALLIS, ETHEL
1965   *Tariri, my story.* Translated from Kandoshi by Lorrie Anderson. New York: Harper and Row.

The Fiesta of the Indian in Quibdó, Colombia

NINA S. DE FRIEDEMANN

The conceptualization of the "Indian problem" as a structural problem arising out of the linkage of the Latin American economies and the international capitalistic system is presently shared by many social scientists. The continual loss of Indian lands over the past four centuries has been the mechanism by which the Indian groups have been reduced to their present state of social inferiority, exploitation, poverty, and lack of education (Frank 1969: 36). This present state renders them incapable of manipulating new circumstances which the dominant society elaborates in order to maintain their subordination.

Mariátegui's analysis (1934: 27) of the problem of loss of Indian lands is that administrative measures such as building rural schools or opening roads in or near Indian territories become acts of political demagoguery and thus superficial and extraneous attempts to solve the problem. Other scientists assert that the cultural defeat in which the Indians have lived for four centuries would cease only if they could in turn defeat the dominant economic system, a task which no one is inclined to do for the Indian (Frank 1969: 141).

On the contrary, cultural mechanisms of subordination are continuously generated by the dominant system to counteract any means of defense that the Indian groups may adopt. There is evidence that these mechanisms are generated nationwide by governmental and religious institutions.

The data for this article are part of the body of data from the research *Studies of black peoples in the Pacific Littoral of Colombia* which the author started in 1969.

The author expresses her gratitude to Coleman Romalis of York University, Toronto, for his comments and suggestions, and to Ronald J. Duncan of Universidad de Los Andes, Bogotá, for his suggestions and revision of the English version.

A cultural mechanism of subordination is the bringing of Indians into contact with the urban "white" population of the regional city which represents the dominant national society. The regional city in an intercultural zone is an instrument of domination in the economic relations of the Indians with the national society, as defined by Wolf (1955: 456–467) and by Stavenhagen (1970: 253, 256).

Under the pretext of encouraging intercultural relations, and with the benign aloofness of the national society, overtly amicable contacts with the Indians are attempted by the encroaching national groups. These usually take place in non-Indian territory, in the context of celebrations and events organized by government and other national institutions. In this manner, asymmetrical cultural situations are created in which non-Indian groups reinforce their socialization to the national image of the Indian, his life-style, and his universe. This "intercultural" contact is administered with the notions of the colonialist cultural heritage. This cultural heritage, still rooted in the nationwide educational system, maintains a stereotype of the Indian as a "savage, irrational, incomplete, uncivilized being, without intelligence, without religion, without culture, etc."

In Colombia, ethnographic evidence continues to confirm the above statements. At the same time, the evidence shows destruction is being perpetrated by the national society against the tribal groups in many different regions. Contacts between the national society and the Indian populations have continuously resulted in disaster for the Indians. The "intercultural" contact events continue to be a fertile field for the cultural and physical extinction of the Indians. Groups and cultures are disappearing rapidly, often in bloody circumstances. The overall program for the "integration of the Indian into national life" rather than solving the "Indian problem" has led to their continuing disappearance.

The Catholic Church, a major Colombian institution, played an important role in the so-called "pacification of the Indians" during the Spanish Conquest, and today continues to play the chief role in the extinction of Indian cultures. Since 1824 its activities have had the sanction of governmental laws which, according to Arango Montoya (1971: 33), have given a legal basis to missionary agreements between the Colombian government and the Church, *which have as their special object the Christian civilization of our Indians.* Their ideology of converting and civilizing Indians includes integral elements of the "integrationalist" policy mentioned above, which is being actively pursued in territories at present inhabited by Indians. These lands are legally considered to be waste lands or unoccupied lands. Their natural resources are available for commercial exploitation by national and international big business. The fiestas held in the honor of saints in the regional cities have been converted into socializing mechanisms that effectively perpetuate the stereotype of the Indian. The Easter week festivities in Quibdó furnish a case study of interethnic relations on the Pacific Littoral that shows the asymmetry of this neo-colonial situation of exploitation and domination.[1]

Quibdó is a regional city on the Atrato River; it is the capital of the Department of Chocó. It has a population of about 60,000 inhabitants who are for the most part civil servants, employees, and merchants. It is situated in an intercultural zone of black, white, and Indian populations.[2] Indians live in the forests remote from the city, near the headwaters of the rivers. They are being driven further inland by the pressure of the growing black population with concomitant loss of their lands.

The cultural mechanism of subordination used to bring Indians into contact with the people of the regional city of Quibdó is the "Fiesta of the Indian" which takes place in Easter week. The Emberá Indian group accepts an invitation to the fiesta and defenselessly enters a territory foreign to their habitat and culture. Their reception by officials and public has been organized for the past forty years with the object of "civilizing the Indians" by dressing them and persuading them to enter the Catholic Church. Both blacks and whites do their best to make Indians drunk. The public posture of the white Catholic priests, both Spanish and Colombian, is expressed in the condescending charity of old clothes and public dressing of the recipients in the street. Finally, they select one or two of the Indians who are dressed to be part of the group that acts out

---

[1] Other regional fiestas of a similar nature are:
1. FIESTA DE LA CANDELARÍA (Candlemas) in Orocué, on the Meta River, Department of Boyacá. Sáliva and Piapoco Indians. February 2 (Jon de Landaburu, verbal report).
2. CORPUS CHRISTI FIESTA in Barbacoas, on the Telembí River, Department of Nariño. Cuaiquer Indians. June. Since the group has been pushed back to the headwaters of the rivers the Indians no longer come to Barbacoas. However, in recent years the blacks in the riverport have been symbolically representing the Indians who formerly participated in this celebration (De Friedemann, field notes).
3. DAY OF THE INDIAN in Caño Mochuelo, on the Casanare River. Department of Boyacá. Cuiva Indians October 12 (Francisco Ortíz, verbal report).
4. INDIAN WEEK in Mitú and other regional centers on the Vaupés River. *Comisaría* of Vaupés, Tukano, Cubeo, Barasana, Wanano, and other Indian groups. December (Horacio Calle, verbal report).
5. CHRISTMAS FIESTA in Puerto Leguízamo on the Putumayo River. *Comisaría* of Putumayo. Witoto Indians. December 24 (Horacio Calle, verbal report).
[2] "White" and "black" are categories with complex definitions in the Pacific Littoral of Colombia. The majority of the population of Quibdó is phenotypically black. Many of these people and other people of white phenotype form the group culturally "white" who behave according to the standards of the dominant social class in Colombia.

the scenes of the Last Supper of Jesus Christ and the twelve apostles in the cathedral.

The Indian becomes a comedian who amuses children and adults alike. His personal adornment, his language, his physical traits, his obvious ignorance of the Catholic ritual, which pervades the life of Quibdó during Easter week, become the factors that structure the stereotype of the Indian. The fiesta takes place in a context of general drunkenness in which the blacks and the whites do violence to the dignity, rights, and cultural identity of the Emberá people. It is also the opportunity for reinforcing and spreading attitudes in favor of the cultural ethnocide which occurs in these fiestas.

In other areas of the nation such events support the physical ethnocide of Indians. Evidence of the effect of this socialization complex upon the behavior of Colombian citizens was demonstrated in the declarations of eight "white" colonists who killed sixteen Cuiva Indians with revolvers, axes, and machetes in Hato de la Rubiera, in Arauca, on December 27, 1967.

The colonists' candid explanations for what they had done illustrate two very important points: (1) they had been taught to hate Indians as being dangerous people, and (2) they had been taught that it was not wrong to kill Indians. Private citizens and government employees had done so with no punishment. Moreover, the colonists considered it a praiseworthy deed to kill an Indian. One of them had killed six Indians before.

Following are quotes that appeared in the course of their trial which closed in July of 1972. The jury found the colonists NOT GUILTY (Castro Caycedo 1972: 29–41).[3]

LUIS MORÍN: In Arauca we consider the Indians as wild animals. I was a little boy when I was taught that they were different from us in dress and in every way. I thought it was like a joke to kill them, and that it was not punishable.

RAMÓN GARRIDO: The only thing I did was to kill a little Indian girl and two Indian men .... When I was a child I realized that everyone killed Indians; the police, the DAS [Administrative Department of Security] and the Navy. Over there, on the Orinoco, they killed Indians and no one took note of it!

MARÍA ELENA JIMÉNEZ: I think that Indians are like us, because they are people. Only they lack brains. They are not equal to us in intelligence.

---

[3] The verdict is being appealed in spite of statements by authorities such as Carlos Gutiérrez, the Chief Prosecutor of Justice in Villavicencio, site of the trial, who concluded: "The condemnation of these people would not solve a problem that arose in the beginning of our history."

PEDRO RAMÓN SANTANA: They taught me this: to hate them, and since out there, there is no civilization ....

EUDORO GONZÁLEZ: I killed those Indians because I knew that the Government wouldn't make me pay for it nor punish the crime committed.

ANSELMO TORREALBA: Before this, I killed six Indians in 1960 and buried them in a place called El Garcero.

CUPERTINO SOGAMOSO: I didn't think it was wrong to kill them, because they were Indians.

The violence that traditionally is used in dealing with the Indians is displayed in Colombia in the plunder of Indian lands, through economic exploitation and the extraction of natural resources. Félix Cisneros, a former colonist of the same area in Arauca (Castro Caycedo 1972: 40–41), states this clearly:

It is true that colonists who settle here kill Indians to protect their cattle. They kill and pursue the Indians because the Indians are thieves and treacherous .... The lands that formerly belonged to the Indians — like the Hato de la Rubiera — are still considered by the Indians as their property.

On the other hand, the Fiesta of the Indian in Quibdó is a joint effort on the part of government institutions and the merchants to attract Indians, who are withdrawing further and further into the tropical rain forest. Their increasing distance has led to a shortage of hunting and gathering goods from the jungle in the Quibdó market. For example, there is a scarcity of otter and ocelot skins which supply an important leather industry in the neighboring Department of Antioquia. Raw rubber, balata, bananas, maize, and basket-work goods are also becoming scarce. The latter articles are used for both the national and international markets in handicraft goods.

It is well known that the Indians drink heavily, so the townspeople offer free liquor to the Indians as a part of the Catholic celebration of Easter to attract them to closer ties with the town. In 1971 the government of the Department of Chocó allotted a sum of money for the organization of the fiesta and approved the use of CARE food for the farewell lunch for the Indians on Easter Sunday. The police and fire-brigade loaned vehicles for a special parade of the effigy of Judas, accompanied by Indians. When the black family who organized the festivity appealed for financial support, the businessmen responded with money and clothes and paid the cost of a band of black musicians who were to enliven the parades of drunken Indians dancing through the streets.

During the first years of these fiestas the main feature was an event sponsored by the Church in which an effigy of Judas Iscariot was given to the assembled crowd of Indians to be torn apart, hanged, and finally burned. In recent years, the Church has withdrawn from active participation allegedly due to the "debauched" quantity of alcohol consumed during Easter week. Now the Church officially ignores the fiesta, although the priests still use the occasion to dress the Indians in the streets and make them enter the cathedral.

On Palm Sunday, Indian families come down the rivers, tie up their canoes, and unload the goods they have brought to sell. Many who come to the fiesta belong to the Emberá group which is one of the largest ethnic groups in Colombia (Reichel-Dolmatoff 1960: 73–158; Faron 1962: 13–38). While they are in Quibdó, some of them stay in the homes of black *compadres* to whom they give presents of forest products. In Quibdó and in the forest the black merchant-entrepreneur is the link between Indians and the outside world. Deluz (1970: 4) asserts that the black is a barrier between the Indians of Chocó and the whites. At the same time, the whites use the blacks as instruments and as intermediaries for their domination and exploitation of the Indians.

The chief organizer of the fiesta is an old black merchant who, like many others now, used to go up and down the rivers in Indian territory trading cloth, pots, and machetes primarily for animal skins which he then sold to white businessmen in Quibdó. He is also the man who makes the effigy of Judas which is mutilated in the celebration.

The climax of the fiesta is reached on Saturday and Easter Sunday, after the Indians have been drinking all week in the various bars and cantinas. Often the Indian families fall asleep on the sidewalks or in the doorways of houses. When drunken quarrels occur between Indians, the townspeople urge them on in the hope of enjoying a foot and fist fight. Other people load the Indians into jeeps and trucks and drive them through the streets of the town. A high-ranking white government official once condescendingly commented, "... these poor Indians simply love to ride in cars."

On Saturday of Easter week, Judas is given to the Indians. The Judas is over six feet tall, with a wooden face, blue eyes, blond hair, and moustache. The body is stuffed with sawdust and dressed in a brightly colored outfit of satin and cotton and leather shoes.

Then the parade begins. Judas is seated in a chair and carried on the shoulders of the Indians in caravan-chair style like that in which the Spanish colonists had themselves carried by Indians in parts of America. The parade passes with jubilant crowds through the main streets of

Quibdó to the beat of a black band playing popular coastal tunes of the Pacific Littoral. The band is playing trumpets, drums, flutes, and cymbals. The Indians who dance in the parade become foolishly drunk with the *aguardiente* and rum freely given to them by the organizers and other people. The onlookers enjoy the "ridiculous" spectacle made by the Indians. The parade ends only when the exhausted Indians abandon Judas until the next day, when the fiesta reaches its climax with the "burning of the Jew."

A second parade precedes the "burning of the Jew" on the morning of Easter Sunday. In 1971 this second parade included police cars, fire engines, and sirens. Judas was seated in one of the trucks among the Indian women and children who hesitatingly crowded in against the sideboards of the truck. As the truck paraded through the streets of Quibdó, the band and black townspeople who wanted to dance followed the crowd of Indians who were again dancing and drinking. Crowds of spectators lined the balconies and sidewalks up and down the streets. About noon, the Indians were gathered together in the central plaza of Quibdó in front of the great cathedral. Policemen helped to hang the effigy of Judas by rope from the top of a utility pole. With the force of the hanging the body burst open and the sawdust began to fall over the crowd. The black band and the shouts of the crowd enlivened the square. According to custom, the Indians then received the body of Judas and tore it to pieces, amusing themselves by putting on the costume and shoes and dancing with the torn-up pieces of the head and body.

The crowds of townspeople stayed, enjoying the spectacle until the organizers decided to begin the last act of the fiesta and ordered lunch to be served to the Indians. They sat down on the ground in the same plaza and each received a plateful of rice and beans. The whites and the blacks then left the plaza, and Easter week with its Fiesta of the Indian was over.

The evening of the same day and the following morning, Indian men, women, and children began to leave the town for the banks of the Atrato River. In silence they stowed their provisions aboard. Standing in the prow of the canoes, the men used their paddle tips to push off the sandy beaches and slip into the water. Their destination was the peaceful jungle.

Deculturation as a part of the ethnocide that has occurred among American Indians can be seen in the circumstances described above. The victims find themselves in conflict with their normal way of life, they become ashamed of their own image and traditions, and they may take any one of many roads to extinction. Some of the Emberá Indians who participated in the Fiesta of the Indian in Quibdó live on the banks of the Munguidó River. One of them, Lucio, related to Eric Isakson (personal communication)[4] the dream he had on his return from the fiesta:

I dreamed I was in a great city, on the other side of the river. It was a city with cars and White people. I myself was no longer an Indian. I was White and dressed in trousers, a shirt and an Antioquian hat [Antioquian businessmen dominate commerce in Quibdó].

The dream of the Indian, Lucio, brought to my memory the sight of him and other Indians abandoning the town streets for their canoes. On the bank of the Atrato River, they also abandoned the old shirts and trousers that the priests and businessmen had made them put on during Easter week.

REFERENCES

ARANGO MONTOYA, FRANCISCO
   1971   *Los indígenas en Colombia: ayer y hoy de los indígenas colombianos*
          26–38. Bogotá.
CASTRO CAYCEDO, GERMÁN
   1972   La matanza de la Rubiera. *Antropológicas* 1:29–41. Bogotá.
DELUZ, ARIANE
   1970   "Emberá. Relato de actividades de investigación." Bogotá. Mimeographed copy.
FARON, LOUIS C.
   1962   Marriage, residence and domestic group among the Panamanian
          Chocó. *Ethnology* 1(1):13–38.
FRANK, ANDRE GUNDER
   1969   *Capitalism and underdevelopment in Latin America*. New York:
          Monthly Review Press.
MARIÁTEGUI, JOSÉ CARLOS
   1934   *Siete ensayos de interpretación de la realidad peruana*. Lima.
REICHEL-DOLMATOFF, GERARDO
   1960   Notas etnográficas sobre los indios de Chocó. *Revista Colombiana de
          Antropología* 9:73–158. Bogotá.
STAVENHAGEN, RODOLFO
   1970   "Classes, colonialism, and acculturation. A system of inter-ethnic
          relations in Mesoamerica," in *Masses in Latin America*. Edited by
          Irving Louis Horowitz, 235–288. Oxford: Oxford University Press.
WOLF, ERIC
   1955   Types of Latin American peasantry. *American Anthropologist* 57(3):
          452–471.

[4] Eric Isakson is affiliated with the Department of Anthropology, University of Uppsala, Sweden.

Crosses and Souls

ALICJA IWAŃSKA

In the concepts of "functional" and "dysfunctional" anthropologists have overemphasized gratifications derived by the individual from a smoothly functioning, integrated society; they forget about individual happiness and self-realization and that people are sometimes harmed rather than helped by such an ideal entity.

Inspired by the concerns with individual happiness and self-realization of such nonprofessional social scientists as Freud and Bertrand Russell,[1] I would like to explore those unfashionable but always desirable "human conditions" in two Mazahua communities of central Mexico which have the same cultural past, a similar sociopolitical structure, and strongly contrasting magico-religious cults.

I studied one of those communities, El Nopal, in the early 1960's (Iwańska 1971); another one, San Simón de la Laguna, was studied from 1967 till 1969 by the Mexican anthropologist Efrain C. Cortés Ruíz and is described in detail in his conscientious and intelligent book (1972).

The term "happiness" may be defined for the purpose of this article as (a) an objectively assessed minimum of somatic well-being (sufficient food, safety, shelter, etc.) and (b) a subjective sense of well-being (lack of anxiety, suspicion, some *joie de vivre*).

The term "self-realization" (and, maybe one should speak only about possibility of self-realization) will be understood here as the possibility of living according to one's goals and values. If, for instance, a typical person from a given community believes that in order to be a self-respecting human being one should hold (i.e. subsidize) at least some public offices

---

[1] I have in mind Sigmund Freud's book *Civilization and its discontents* and Bertrand Russell's *Conquest of happiness*.

during his lifetime, and he cannot afford it because of lack of means, such an individual is deprived of the opportunity for self-realization. Societies which force women into choice between marriage and career obviously deprive them of an opportunity for self-realization.

In this article I will try to analyze the relationship between beliefs (religious and magical) and the chances for happiness and self-realization of a typical Mazahua villager in the two communities in central Mexico.

Both villages (San Simón with 1275 inhabitants in 1969 [Cortés Ruíz 1972:35] and El Nopal with around 1120 inhabitants in the early 1960's) are well-integrated, corporate communities, governed by traditional politico-religious Indian governments. San Simón, however, is much more isolated geographically and more traditional. This isolation and traditionalism are strengthened by the lack of a school, by the type of land tenure (private *minifundias* of about five hectares per family) and an almost below-subsistence farming which does not force villagers into contacts with the larger world and does not make them open to innovations.

El Nopal is much less isolated. There is a Pan-American highway less than one mile from the village. The population since early 1930 has been organized into an *ejido* [an organization of the recipients of land distributed in consequence of Agrarian Reform] with the local *mestizo* population from the county seat, Las Animas, situated about two miles from El Nopal. Since 1962 El Nopal has had its own school as well. The contacts of these villagers with the larger world (with local *mestizos* and even with Mexico City) are much more frequent than those of the villagers from San Simón.

In both San Simón and El Nopal three administrative systems operate: (1) the national administrative network represented at the community level by so-called *delegados* [representatives of the county elected from among the villagers]; (2) a Catholic Church organization which at least in El Nopal is only occasionally served by a parish priest; and (3) traditional Indian government.

Those last two administrative systems, though formally separate, are in both communities (as in many other Mexican Indian villages) represented by one and the same group called sometimes *autoridades* [authorities], sometimes *gobierno*, as in El Nopal or sometimes *junta* as the villagers from San Simón call it.[2]

Efrain C. Cortés Ruíz (1972: 58–60) documents conscientiously and analyzes very well indeed the complicated processes which have resulted in this still changing strange politico-religious structure known as "traditional Indian government." This government actually governs in

[2] It seems that in San Simón the network of national authorities is integrated into the *junta*, the village government (see Cortés Ruíz 1972: 69–77).

both villages in question. The other two administrative systems (that of the Catholic Church and the network of national delegates) though backed by powerful national and international institutions respectively appear rather pale, powerless, or even nonexistent in comparison with the village government. In San Simón for instance the network of national *delegados* (quite strong numerically because it is composed of as many as nineteen persons) (Cortés Ruíz 1972: 69), seems to be almost absorbed by the traditional Indian government. In El Nopal on the other hand a very small network of national delegates is truly nominal and its existence is explained by the villagers as a necessary compromise with local *mestizos.*

Because the church at least in El Nopal (but probably in San Simón as well) is used mainly for Catholic-pagan services performed by Indians themselves (in El Nopal for instance every night the headman of the village [*cabezilla del pueblo*] has to ring the church bells and every second afternoon or so he has to conduct the rosary) it would be easy to conclude that the Catholic administration simply does not function in such villages. Such a conclusion would have to be promptly rejected however, at least for El Nopal where the complex Mazahua marriage ceremony is not only dependent upon but even strongly controlled by the Catholic administration. Because the Mazahuas from El Nopal believe that their Mazahua weddings should be preceded by a religious Catholic ceremony, they are forced to do it "properly," i.e. to confess and take communion (which they usually do not do) and to rent Western clothes for the church wedding.

Most of the important and enjoyable social roles performed by the villagers of both communities and contributing greatly to their prestige, happiness, well-being, and self-realization are connected with the functioning of the traditional Indian government in which they have their *cargos* [offices] held jointly by married men and their wives.

In spite of the common precolonial culture, the identical cycles of their Catholic-pagan festivities, and the very similar structure of their contemporary Indian governments, the content of the religious beliefs and rituals is very different in the two villages.

Mazahuas from San Simón have singled out as main objects of their cult dangerous crosses located in their small and carefully locked family chapels (*oratorios*), and they spend a great deal of their energies appeasing those malevolent deities.

Among Mazahuas from El Nopal the ritual of appeasement of a malevolent cross (placed in an open chapel at the entrance to the village and decorated every Wednesday with fresh flowers) has played only a minor role.

While in San Simón all people fear the blackmail and vengeance of their crosses, the cross from El Nopal is dangerous to little boys only. ("It makes them sick if it is not well attended, or when the boys approach it, or for no reason whatsoever.") Even this belief, however, so mild in comparison to beliefs in the malevolent powers of the crosses in San Simón, has been disappearing from El Nopal.

While the malevolent cross seems to be the main cultural symbol in San Simón, the main cultural symbol in El Nopal is the full-of-flames-but-also-full-of-hope purgatory where the souls of Mazahua ancestors and all other souls of deceased villagers reside (only the souls of little children, *angelitos*, go directly to heaven according to the villagers from El Nopal). Life is seen as very difficult by those villagers but full of hope; it is very much like their purgatory through which everybody has to pass but from which everybody will be rescued eventually. This outlook on life perhaps could be called "optimistic fatalism" because nobody, even the worst human being, according to those Mazahuas from El Nopal, is condemned to hell; everybody (without special prayers or favors from the saints) who serves his term in purgatory eventually will reach heaven.

Mazahuas from San Simón live in constant anxiety as they try to appease their malevolent and irrational crosses, and they are never sure whether their frantic appeasement rituals will really help, because the crosses are malicious, whimsical, and hard to understand.

Mazahuas from El Nopal are free of such anxieties. Their beliefs do not terrorize them into costly and uncertain rituals. In fact their anxieties are largely secular (mainly related to health, communal identification, and economic problems). Their religious beliefs (though expressed in rituals costly in time and money as are all Indian rituals) give them a great deal of moral support in the difficult realization of their communal goals such as preservation of their Mazahua identity and introduction of such selected elements of *el progreso* [progress] as education, electricity, and running water.

There are two identical seats of religious cult in San Simón and El Nopal. There is a communal church inhabited by various Catholic saints and attended by *cargueros* [office-holders in the traditional Indian government]. The Christ on the cross (which is not malevolent like the crosses of family chapels) is found in the communal church of both villages, and in in El Nopal (I do not have information for San Simón) there is also a picture of *Las animas*, representing the souls of Mazahua ancestors in purgatory, usually nude, with fair complexion, and often with blue eyes — a physical type contrasting with that of Mazahua Indians — placed together with various other images at the main altar.

The second seat of the religious cult common to both villages is the household altar. On these altars — little wooden structures attached to the walls — villagers accumulate various saints and often (as in El Nopal) other sacred objects, e.g. such cherished and "sanctified" things as alarm clocks, little Mexican flags, pictures of metal biscuit cans from newspaper clippings, etc. The picture of *Las animas* [souls in purgatory] usually occupies the central place on such a home altar in El Nopal. I observed that during the two-day All Souls' Celebration, the image of the ancestral couple is taken out of the home altar and placed on the floor in a corner of the room where it is appropriately illuminated and attended.

In San Simón in addition to the two seats of religious cult described above, there is a third seat of religious cult, family chapels (*oratorios*), miniature windowless houses, carefully locked and opened on occasion of the cult only. Efrain C. Cortés Ruíz describes in detail the cult of the crosses (the only ritual objects located in the *oratorios*) and through the description of the rituals of appeasement of those crosses he shows us the whole complex family, kinship, and lineage structure of this isolated and traditional Mazahua village.

Otomi and Mazahua *oratorios* were, so far as I know, described first by Jacques Soustelle (n.d.); these, however, are not inhabited by malevolent crosses. Rather, like El Nopal home altars, they house various saints and cherished objects and probably the images of the ancestral couple as well. I did see personally such images in two of the visited *oratorios* in a village studied by Soustelle, San Bartolomé del Llano. The images of *Las animas* in San Bartolomé del Llano were very similar to those in El Nopal and the villages in both communities claimed that they were painted by Mazahua painters in the old days; the explanation is highly improbable because of the non-Mazahua physical type of the ancestral couple and because of the availability of such images at various antique markets in Mexico City. It is quite possible, however, that the old Catholic cult of All Souls' Days got fused at some point with the Mazahua cult of their ancestral couple — *Padre Viejo* [Old Father] and *Madre Vieja* [Old Mother] (Carrasco Pizana 1950: 133–134) venerated probably throughout the whole Mazahua (García Payón 1942).

On the second visit in San Bartolomé del Llano I invited a few of my Mazahua friends from El Nopal in order to show them those family *oratorios*. Only then did I learn that El Nopal used to have similar family chapels which were abandoned only a generation ago. On the basis of this information I hypothesized (Iwańska 1967) that the images of an ancestral couple "emigrated" (along with other saints and objects) from their family chapels to home altars, and their cult diminished, giving way to a more "modern" (and less ritualized) belief emphasizing the dwelling place of the ancestral couple, the full-of-flames-but-also-full-of-hope purgatory. It is possible that this shift coincided with the increased secularization of communal life in El Nopal, stimulated by the land reform occurring at that time and the incorporation of the Mazahuas from this village into the completely new, future-oriented secular organization of *ejido*.

So far as I know there were never any malevolent, dangerous crosses inside the *oratorios* of El Nopal, as they did not exist and do not exist in the area of Ixtlahuaca investigated by Jacques Soustelle. But there were other malevolent crosses in El Nopal and there still is one such cross, as I already pointed out, which is, however, becoming less and less dangerous. This is what the people from El Nopal have to say about their crosses:

> Years ago everybody had a cross in his house made of wood or stone. According to our grandfathers, if the cross was not paid attention to, if it was not brought its branch of flowers, and candles were not lit for it, the cross became angry and seized boys who would become sick with fear (Iwańska 1967: 204).

The same dangerous characteristics are still being attributed to the cross placed at the entrance to El Nopal, this cross being definitely a close relative of malevolent crosses from San Simón.

The relationship between the increasing modernization of the people from El Nopal and the diminishing of their belief in malevolent crosses is well illustrated by the following account of the villagers from El Nopal:

> But now we know that this is not so, the cross cannot do anything and that only God can punish a child. If the child is sick the best thing to do is to take him to the doctor because it is certain that it is sickness which is bothering him and that this has nothing to do with the cross (Iwańska 1967: 207).

Efrain C. Cortés Ruíz has argued very convincingly that the crosses have probably acquired their malevolent, dangerous characteristics in Mazahua Catholic-pagan cults because they became associated with the Conquest. It was the cross which was first imposed upon the conquered Indians and only later were such deities as *Virgen María* and other saints introduced. The crosses were placed on the flags of Spanish ships, they were immediately erected in place of destroyed Indian idols (Cortés Ruíz 1972: 93–94), and one should add that the monks who did convert Indians carried on them their large crosses and sometimes they preached with a large crucifix in hand.

There are numerous examples from contemporary life which help us to understand such "guilt by association" acquired by objects. Since injections were used in Nazi concentration camps to kill prisoners (Iwańska 1957) and later less powerful Evipan injections were used by Soviet

Russians during political investigations, it is no wonder that there was some reluctance among those who remembered those times to the use of Evipan as anesthetic during operations. It is possible that the Japanese of Hiroshima would have reacted at first with a similar reluctance if atomic energy had been presented to them for peaceful uses shortly after the atomic bomb had destroyed their city.

In both San Simón and El Nopal there are, however, good, benevolent crosses side by side with the malevolent ones. There are such good crosses in the church of San Simón (Cortés Ruíz 1972: 96) and there is such a cross on the top of the mountain in the area of El Nopal, the cross venerated by the people from the whole region every May 3.

Because the symbol of the cross was known in pre-Hispanic America, we need much more prehistorical research to find out whether it was known by the Mazahuas as well. Much more research also should be done on the details of the cult of ancestral couples throughout the Mazahua area. This belief, as I hypothesized, was fused through Christianization with the Catholic cult of All Souls' Days, a hypothesis which should be checked through even further inquiry into the processes of Christianization. Christianization apparently was conducted in the Mazahua region by the Franciscan Order (Cortés Ruíz 1972: 96).

It is possible, however, even without such further research to return to the question of happiness and self-realization of a typical Mazahua in the two villages.

If we consider the Declaration of Human Rights as a document formulating the minimum conditions for human happiness and self-realization, the people of San Simón and El Nopal (like those of similar rural communities of the underdeveloped areas) do not have most of those minimum conditions (adequate diet, shelter, medical help, education, etc.) though Agrarian Reform implemented in this particular area in the early 1930's greatly helped in rescuing some of those rural people from the worst misery. It seems that people from El Nopal have profited much more from Agrarian Reform than people from San Simón. Both communities have integrated corporate social structures and because their inhabitants are all poor (no great economic differences exist even in El Nopal where a few of the "wealthiest" families have mules and painted houses) they all have more or less equal access to the system of traditional Indian government offices (*cargos*) so essential to their self-realization. The sense of usefulness and the amount of social participation are, maybe, even stronger in San Simón than in El Nopal due to the frequency of frantic magico-religious rituals performed in family *oratorios* whenever the malevolent crosses begin to "behave strangely." Word about such "strange behavior" spreads quickly among the members of the extended family, throughout kinship groups and often increases to the level of communal paranoia.

Unlike the other communal festivities which have their exact dates, the cult of *oratorios* depends on a variety of signals given by the crosses (such as cracking, sickness in the family, or a message given in dreams) and maintains the people of San Simón in a constant alert. Whenever they think that the cross is dissatisfied with something they mobilize all their energies and resources to appease it. They buy expensive food, candles, and fireworks for the fiesta given for the cross; sometimes an exigent cross even demands a godfather from a neighboring village, and once it "gets used" to him the godfather has to be begged to continue forever his attentions to the capricious cross.

In El Nopal all religious and magical rituals not only produce social solidarity but also help to maintain high morale among the villagers.

In San Simón some of such rituals (those related to the functioning of traditional Indian government) are morale maintaining, while others (related to the cult of *oratorios*) though no doubt maintaining the kinship and communal solidarities, are at the same time so morale destroying and energy draining that they impede or even prevent villagers' sense of well-being.

Though, apparently, most of the villagers in San Simón believe in malevolence of their crosses and live in constant anxiety and terror, some individuals have already abandoned this belief and "nothing has happened to them whatsoever." About a person who is not afraid of his family cross and does not pay attention to it any more, one says in San Simón: "That man does not want to cooperate [in the cult of *oratorio*] since if something happens to him he can go to cure himself elsewhere" (Cortés Ruíz 1972: 110).

In El Nopal, too, the belief in the capacity of the village cross to make little boys sick has disappeared with the availability of medical help in a nearby county seat.

This type of substitution of scientific for magical beliefs is rarely sufficient, however, in such Indian communities as San Simón and El Nopal. If the belief in malevolent crosses had disappeared suddenly from San Simón, through the establishment of a village clinic for instance, some painful social vacuum probably would have taken the place of kinship solidarities maintained by frantic and anxious cults. And such a social vacuum with its lack of norms and confusion could turn out to be even more damaging to San Simón villagers than their strong but specific anxieties and terror.

I strongly suspect that it was not only the availability of the doctor in the neighboring village which helped almost completely eliminate the belief in the dangerous village cross in El Nopal, but also the basic restructuring of the village which occurred with introduction of *ejido* (Iwańska 1965) and later with the inauguration of the school (Iwańska 1963).

Participation in *ejido* probably distracted the energies of adult Mazahuas from the maintenance of the extended family solidarities, made them abandon family *oratorios*, and replaced their kinship solidarities with a new communal *esprit de corps* so indispensable to their survival in that period of change.

What the *ejido* did for Mazahua adults, inauguration of the school did for Mazahua boys. Involved in their demanding and interesting school activities and boys' club organized by the social worker they forgot about dangers coming from the village cross, and their parents did not remind them about those dangers either.

In spite of the loud assertions of the villagers in El Nopal that the cross cannot harm anybody, and the increased awareness of modern medicine, the cross has been decorated nevertheless with fresh flowers every Wednesday. It is quite possible that when with time the belief in the dangers of this cross disappears completely those decorations will remain anyway, acquiring a different meaning. Because the cross is located at the entrance to the village, maybe the villagers will start believing that it protects rather than harms them, thus allowing Christianity to enter their village this time without sword and fire. Or, maybe the cross decorated with fresh flowers will become a symbol of hospitality greeting the guests to an increasingly open and modern Mazahua village of El Nopal.

REFERENCES

CARRASCO PIZANA, PEDRO
  1950 *Los otomies.* Mexico City: UNAM Instituto de Historia, with the collaboration of the Instituto Nacional de Anthropología y Historia.
CORTÉS RUÍZ, EFRAIN C.
  1972 *San Simón de la Laguna.* Mexico City: Instituto Nacional Indigenista.
GARCÍA PAYÓN, JOSÉ
  1942 *Matlacincas y pirindas.* Ediciones Encuadernables. Mexico City: El Nacional.
IWAŃSKA, ALICJA
  1957 "Values in a crisis situation." New York: Columbia University. On microfilm.

1963 New knowledge. *Sociologus* 13(2).
1965 The impact of agricultural reform on a Mexican Indian village. *Sociologus* 15(1).
1967 Mazahua purgatory: symbol of permanent hope. *America Indígena* 27(1).
1971 *Purgatory and utopia.* Cambridge, Massachusetts: Schenkman.

SOUSTELLE, JACQUES
n.d. Le culte des oratoires chez les Otomies et les Mazahuas de la région d'Ixlahuaca. *Mexico Antiguo* 3(58).

Chinantec Messianism: The Mediator of the Divine

ALICIA MABEL BARABAS

This article forms part of a more extensive study which I carried out with my husband, Miguel A. Bartolomé, over a period of ten months, among the Chinantecs of Ojitlán in the state of Oaxaca, Mexico.

Although the phenomenon that we are endeavoring to analyze has been in existence only a short time, we believe a knowledge of it to be of great importance because of the events that led to its appearance. We have had the opportunity to observe these events from their earliest stages.

We shall not expatiate on traditional and contemporary Chinantec culture; a lengthy description would go beyond the objectives of this study. This will be the subject of a later and more complete analysis.

BRIEF SURVEY OF CHINANTEC CULTURE

The region of Chinantla, assigned to the state of Oaxaca, occupies an extensive territory running northwest to southwest, on the borders of the state of Veracruz. To the north it runs into the Mazatec region and into a small Mixtec enclave, toward the west it comes into contact with the Cuicatecs and the Zapotecs, and in the south with the Zapotecs and the Mixes. The Chinantec habitat combines mountainous zones with ravines and valleys. The soil, suitable for every type of crop, is especially fertile on the river flats, yielding two harvests in the year — *temporal* [summer harvest] and *tomamil* [winter harvest] — with traditional methods of cultivation.

The Chinantec language, which is a member of the Otomanguean family (Olivera and Sánchez 1965:30–31), is fragmented into numerous dialects, some of which are mutually unintelligible.

For this reason, when festivals bring natives together from places far apart, the bilingual population uses Spanish as the *lingua franca*. At present the monolingual speakers of the Chinantec dialect of *ojitlán* constitute about 57 percent of the total population. Of the 43 percent remaining about 25 percent is bilingual (Chinantec-Spanish), in the majority of cases only a rudimentary Spanish is spoken, and 18 percent monolingual in Spanish.

As Agustín Delgado says (1956:29), originally the Chinantla was a collection of villages which about A.D. 1300 divided into two domains: Great Chinantla and Pichinche Chinantla,[1] of which Ojitlán was a part. This self-division into domains has now been lost, and the villages of which they consisted have been broken up to form territorial units (municipalities, districts, etc.[2]) and parishes which have little or nothing to do with the distribution and connections of the Chinantecs as an ethnic group.

As Nahmad says (Nahmad 1972:225): "One of the features of colonialism from which the native groups suffered was that they were not permitted their organization as ethnic groups, in the way they existed before colonization." These divisions, created in colonial times with the aim of disorganizing the ethnic groups and facilitating domination, still exist. Under the present system of internal colonialism they have been strengthened so as to prevent those interconnections between communities which might, through self-organization, form a barrier against the intrusion of the national system.

Therefore, a series of small communities surround a "ruling center," which receives the civil status of "capital of the municipality" and assumes the direction and control of internal affairs. Such is the case of the borough[3] of San Luís Ojitlán, for instance, which is rapidly becoming *ladino* and controls its "constellation" in every department, while depending in turn on the fully *ladino* city of Tuxtepec.[4] Even if contacts exist between Ojitlán and Valle Nacional or Ojitlán and Usila, they are only occasional, and arise through economic dependence (in the case of Usila) on the ruling center, a dependence created by the expansion of regional society and not of ethnic identity.

[1] Chinantla Grande: the domain formed by the villages of Valle Nacional, Zacatepec, Chiltepec, etc. Chinantla Pichincho is the domain formed by the villages of Ojitlán, Usila, Nayuktianguis, Tlacoatzintepec, etc.

[2] Mexico consists of villages, and a municipality is a certain number of inhabitants under one legal authority, the *ayuntamiento* [local council]. The district is the next authority below the state; it is comprised of several municipalities. — Translator.

[3] "Villa," the category of Mexican village above the "pueblo." — Translator.

[4] San Juan Bautista Tuxtepec, in the state of Oaxaca, is situated on the flats of the river Papaloapan and is the capital of the municipality of Tuxtepec. — Translator.

Economy

The basis of the Ojitlán economy is agriculture, complemented by the breeding of domestic animals and livestock, market gardening, and fruit growing, and occasionally eked out by fishing, hunting, and food gathering. In recent years the making and selling of hand-worked articles (*huipils*[5]) has become important as an aid to the family budget.

The principal cash crops and source of income for the acquisition of manufactures are rice, maize, sesame, and tobacco. Maize, kidney beans, and condiments are produced for personal use, but do not in many instances completely cover a family's needs because more land and attention are being given to cash crops. Maize and kidney beans then have to be bought at a much higher price, and recourse is had to the killing and eating of domestic animals, which together with livestock constitute the domestic assets, and to the gathering of forest plants. Without entering into detail on the agricultural techniques and tools employed, we may say that in spite of their rudimentary nature the average returns are fairly high, owing to an excellent ecological adaptation and to the quality of the soil.

It is principally on the commercial and credit side of production that the peasant sees every possibility of free and just dealing frustrated. The system locally developed by regional society is known as "outfitting" (*habilitación*); it involves loans of money or seed which the rich merchants and monopolists (Indian and *mestizo*) grant the peasant in return for his promise to hand over the harvest to the "outfitter" (*habilitador*) at a price fixed by the latter, and, in addition, to pay interest (varying with the type of crop) on the total amount of the loan. This system creates continuous indebtedness for the Indian, since the price paid by the outfitter never quite covers the debt contracted, and he thus remains dependent, the process repeating itself when the next season comes around.

Often the outfitters of Ojitlán are in turn dependent on those of Tuxtepec and on the industries of Córdoba (Veracruz), thus functioning as intermediaries of outfitting. Outfitting is available only for cash crops and obliges the peasant to cultivate in accordance with market demand, with resulting soil impoverishment, to mention only one of the losses incurred.

Moreover, bank loans are rare, ill-timed, and accompanied by bureaucratic paraphernalia that the Indian cannot understand. Apart from that, they are apt to result in commercial failure for want of finding out what

---

[5]   *Huipil:* traditional women's garment woven on the loom and richly embroidered.

new crops are on the market; at the same time the peasant is burdened with the debt incurred. These and other reasons generally oblige the Indian to accept the offers of the outfitter or "intermediary outfitter," who in both cases functions as a middleman.

Thus it is evident that the neglect or abandonment of subsistence farming in favor of a market economy and the eagerness to acquire consumer goods as indicative of status, especially evident on the *ejidos*[6] which are close to the ruling center and have better communications, are but the consequences of the economic and social pressures of regional society. These pressures tend to control not only the production, but also the means of production of the Indian. The capitalist penetration of regional-national society transforms the *ejidatario* [member of an *ejido*], who theoretically is in possession of the means of production, into a wage-earner, through the control exercised over his land, the *ejido*. This usurpation is sufficiently disguised for him to believe that at least he possesses the land, which is the thing he values most.

Sociopolitical Organization

According to Balandier (1969:183), "the colonial situation imposes the coexistence of a strongly sacralized traditional system, which establishes relations of direct subordination of a personal character, with a modern system based on bureaucracy, which institutes less personalized relationships."

Lucy Mair (Balandier 1969:53) establishes, on a basis of differentiation and concentration of power, the existence of three types of government. She says: "On the lower level we find 'minimal government', and near to it 'diffused government'." According to her,

... this latter issues in principle from the adult masculine population as a whole, but certain institutions (such as classification by age) and certain office bearers (enjoying the corresponding authority) are responsible, as of right and in fact, for the administration of public business. The most elaborate type, established on a clearly different and more centralized power, is that of "State government" (Balandier 1969: 53).

---

[6] The *ejido* is a system of land tenancy, set up at the time of the Agrarian Reform (1915–1916), which grants perpetual usufruct of the land and is transmissible only by heredity. In accordance with the stipulations of the laws of Agrarian Reform, the *ejido* is a collective endowment. In present practice, the *ejidatario* [member of an *ejido*] possesses an individual parcel of land which comes to function as private property. This prevents the granting of state credits and facilitates the intrusion of outfitters.

In our view, this classification constitutes a convenient point of reference since the traditional government of Ojitlán — which followed the Conquest — appears to situate itself between what Mair calls diffused government and state government, and presents the characteristics noted by Balandier of "marked sacralization" and "relationships of direct subordination," while the institution of national government "based on bureaucracy" creates "less personalized" relations of subordination. The governmental bureaucracy, in the case of Ojitlán both a regional and national bureaucracy, is not established directly, so as to dislodge ancient structures, but instead creates (through the expansive dynamism which animates the system in all its parts) an internal bureaucracy, Indian as a rule, that is linked to the municipal system. Little by little this bureaucracy displaces and limits the authority of the traditional leaders, and weakens existing organizations.

The native bureaucracy, (recruited in the bilingual, economically superior sector) adopts the dominant bureaucratic model, separating those political and religious roles which before were combined in one single system of government. To this Indian bureaucracy is added a growing *mestizo* bureaucracy; relations with it develop on the level of economic and political rivalry, and imitation (of the second by the first) as regards those cultural patterns which further "raise" acquired status.

The new local bureaucracy which today has the power (supported by the internal colonialism of the country), rarely succeeds in separating itself from the political roles established by the state (in this case Oaxaca) of which it is part, and its representatives act as "political mediators" between those official levels and the Indian population. At the same time it recruits from the Indian mass new elements ready for a change, to whom it assigns the role of "secondary mediators" between the two sub-systems.

This internal dynamism of colonization generates direct and indirect attacks on the traditional system, for it facilitates a multiple-direction penetration on the part of the regional-national society and the rise of new models of stratification which erode the validity of the traditional order.

We now pass on to a description of the present system of government, giving at the same time a brief history so as to show its development.

The official system of political organization implanted in the native community has its roots in a territorial division based on a certain number of inhabitants per unit. Thus we have a MUNICIPALITY whose capital is the borough of San Lucas Ojitlán which has jurisdiction over lesser communities, such as the *ejidos* and police stations. The municipality as a whole forms part of the DISTRICT of Tuxtepec, and this forms part of the STATE of Oaxaca.

The authorities elected through the national electoral system correspond to the state (the governor), to the district (the district president), and to the municipality (the municipal president), with their corresponding administrative bodies. The authorities of the *ejidos* are appointed by the municipal authorities, or theoretically elected by the community, although in reality these appointments are decided by previous party loyalties, and do not represent the interests of the *ejidatarios*. Normally the commissioners for the *ejido* are those we have called secondary mediators, their function being to mediate between the native people of the *ejidos* and the municipal authorities. At the same time principal political mediators mediate between the Indian communities and representatives and the superior levels of government.

Municipal political posts are in the hands of those Indians whom Hunt (1968:597) calls *revestidos*, i.e. those who have a relatively high economic status and whose social group differs from their ethnic group. These culturally *mestizo* Indians combine the roles of political and economic mediators, and eventually come to compete for these posts and activities with the *mestizos* who have lived for a long time in the area.

The traditional system of government was in the hands of a council of elders, each member of which was the head of one of the five wards of the borough (and after a fashion the representative of a certain number of dependent *ejidos*). The council's functions are political as well as economic and religious. The *cargo* system by which one acceded to the council of elders included the following categories in ascending hierarchical order: *Soterotopil, fiscal, contribuyente* (married) *diputado, mayordomo, mesero o semianciano*, elder and principal elder. To these categories were added those of *rezanderos* [professional prayers] and of shaman, but to belong to these did not imply scaling the pyramid of social stratification represented by the system of offices; these were terminal grades of absolute value. On the first rungs of the ladder the system of offices ran parallel to the system of age-grades, but from the grade of delegate on they separated, and the system of offices coincided explicitly with the religious system. Levels of participation (and position in the ascending hierarchy) within the system of offices were determined by (1) economic position and social prestige joined to age and "ceremonial expenditure," and (2) merits accumulated by participation in public events. An office with its title, as Balandier says (1969:102), carried with it ceremonial and ritual adjuncts that led to the acquisition of new social identities (festivals of the confraternity are a case in point) and determined the type of authority and power conferred by the society.

This social, political, and religious organization, which gave every individual access to a ladder of religious and political participation based on prestige and age, was firmly implanted and had little to say to the later (and for a while parallel) desacralized bureaucracy. As soon as contact was made with the national institutions and the new system of internal government appeared, the *cargo* system began to lose its force as a method of economic, religious, and political stratification. With the disappearance of confraternity membership, the focal point of the system, the source of prestige was secularized and shifted toward the imitation of alien cultural patterns, with a resultant widening of the gap between the *revestidos* and the Indian conservators of the traditional social order. They are also spatially divided. The former occupy the borough, especially the central streets and the *ejidos* with better communications, while the latter remain in the remote *ejidos*, near the hills, where they have less to put up with from continual innovation, although in fact they are included in the modified systems.

The expansion of regional society and of the negative wedges of penetration also affected in various ways the kinship system, traditionally of patrilineal descent and virilocal residence. Its basis was the extended family, which acted as an economic unit (production, distribution, and consumption). Each domestic group participated on a certain level in the prestige conferred by the *cargo* system, and this family prestige extended to the ward or *ejido* of which it was part. From one of these domestic groups emerged the elder representative of the ward and dependent *ejidos* and from time to time of the community if he transformed himself into a principal elder.

The growing instability of domestic groups, because of the impossibility of acquiring more land, was added to the breakdown of the system of offices as a source of family prestige. The scarcity of parcels of land for work within the paternal *ejido* — which has no room for numerous children — and the lack of additional land, monopolized as it was by private property, eroded the laws of residence and prepared many changes in family relationships, the life cycle, and the processes of socialization. In some cases the man took up part of the lands of his wife's father (if the latter had not many brothers) or made a contract with a neighbor for use of land.[7] Through the intensification of the market economy, the individualistic characteristics of the *ejido*, and the insufficiency of the income drawn from it, which, if not absorbed in ceremonial expenses, was destined to procure consumer goods, the

---

[7] An *avecindado* [neighbored] is a man without any part in the *ejido* who asks a neighbor for permission to use part of his land in exchange for money or work.

extended families ceased to function as economic units and broke up into nuclear families. It should be noted, however, that such modifications in the kinship organization are much more frequent in regions inhabited by the *revestidos*, and that more isolated *ejidos* preserve the form of the traditional organization.

The Spiritual World

We shall not linger over this theme; nevertheless, for the purposes of the analysis of the movement which is to follow, it is interesting to note the importance and vitality of certain elements, such as streams, caves, and hills in the cosmic vision of the Chinantecs. The process of popular acceptance of the Catholic religion and the significance that certain "saints" have in popular devotion will likewise be discussed.

As we know, the power of the council of the elders, which before was absolute, was reduced to the institution of shamans (with its consequent level of political and social control), and through its ambivalent nature this institution continues to be feared and respected on all social levels of the community. Within this institution figure the sa^2 $m'ui^1$, a generic term applied to wizards (which at times are the elders themselves). They possess (are) the *nahuals*, thus distinguishing themselves from ordinary people who possess (are) a *tona*, or double. Thus while some have the capacity to be transformed into "an animal creature" (*nahual*), others have a double, an animal creature of their own into which they cannot transform themselves, which they do not know and do not remember, but to which they are united by a common destiny. Hermitte says (1970: 379–380) that "conscious knowledge is the control of one's own *nahual*, the capacity to dominate one's own animal and celestial co-essences at will, and to attack by supernatural means." It is in this capacity to "know" and to "transform" oneself at will that we believe the *nahual* differs from the *tona* and that the supernatural status of ordinary people is distinguished from that of the wizard.

Wizards are recognized at birth by certain physical characteristics that disappear rapidly, one being to have the upper part of the body in human form and the lower part in that of an animal which is the principal *nahual* (they can have up to seven). In these parts the wizard, or the *nahual*, is entirely an animal. These wizards have ambivalent powers (of harm and of cure). As it seems, the "harm" is worked through the *nahual*, and the cure through the separation of the spirit ($ju^3gn'ia^2$) from the body and communication with the world of magic.

When the enemy, the one to be harmed, is also a *nahual*, a struggle ensues. The result is the death of the loser's *nahual* and the subsequent decomposition of the human body with which it coexisted. Death occurs only when the principal *nahual* dies; the death of one of the secondary ones entails a passing illness or debility. When it is a case of inflicting a harm as punishment for some infraction of the established political or social order, i.e. a harm as a species of social control, the elders have recourse to a wizard (or they may put themselves into action) to whom they give the order. A PETITION for a harm can also be made to an elder or a wizard by an ordinary person. In either case the *nahual* carries the sickness to the house of the accused's family. When the man to be punished or one of his family (he who has weaker doubles) becomes ill, he resorts to the elder of his ward and the latter calls the council together. There a judgment is passed as to whether the punishment is just or unjust. If it is just, the harmed person will die when his double dies. If it is unjust, the elders order the wizard to revert the harm to the person who petitioned it.

At the same time these wizards have the ability to "cure" sicknesses by means of their link with the world of magic to which they have access through the potency of their spirit. The wizards' powers of cure extend to sicknesses not produced by natural agents, such as harms, "frights," "bad winds," etc. Natural sicknesses belong to various medicine men (herbalists, snake men, bone men, etc.) initiated through the revelation or instruction of another medicine man.

When a wizard diagnoses an illness, he does it by means of a "cleansing" with an egg and shoots of plants that are considered to be powerful. The signs formed by the egg when broken after the cleansing indicate the source of the infirmity. Immediately the wizard goes to the spring taking with him the garments of the sick man and the offerings for the spring. Once there he recites a formula, takes some water, gives it to the sick man to drink, and rubs him with it. This practice has its origin in the belief that all the Chinantecs have a spirit living in the spring. Indeed at birth every one of them drinks its water and is rubbed with it by the wizard, and from that moment on they are bound to that spring.

In the spring dwell the "eddies," ambivalent forces which look after the spirits dwelling in the spring and which can also do injury when they escape the control of the "master or lord of the spring." When two or more spirits inhabiting the stream fight in it, one of them may be expelled, thus bringing about the bodily sickness of the possessor of that spirit. The wizard will then petition the lord of the spring to accept this spirit again; if the petition is unsuccessful, he will go to another spring until the sick man's spirit is accepted and cured. In all cases of sickness not produced by natural agents, the spirit of the wizard enters the spring in order to communicate in the world of magic with the lord of the stream while at the same time his body recites a formula ("Jesusa, Jesusa ...") from without and offers gifts to flatter the "lord."

The other category of wizards, one of higher supernatural status (and to which the elders also may belong), is identified by bodily characteristics which promptly disappear, but which do not involve the manifestation of the animal *nahual*. Instead it involves signs such as nightcaps, berets etc. which indicate that the principal phenomenon is a celestial phenomenon such as a thunderbolt, a gust of wind, a comet or a ball of fire.

Some of these wizards also possess an ambivalent power (for harm or benefit) even though they do not cure or cause infirmities. They foresee dangers that lie in wait for the community, protect inhabited sites, and cause harm to revert to the village of the attacker or attackers; others are exclusively maleficent.

Among the first are the so-called "guardian spirits of the borderline" (the frontier lines of the villages) or the "gentlemen" or the "men of the hill." Among the second are the "blood-suckers" and the "hermaphrodites" whose principal *nahuals* are balls of fire, and whose only function is to produce harms and kill persons or animals.

The power of wizards in the first category is highly important, for it can be utilized against enemies (wizards) of rival villages. The guardians of the borderline are thunderbolt or wind *nahuals* which prevent other spirits outside the borderline from introducing sicknesses or threats to the security of the village when returning harm to the causers of it. The men of the hill or spirits of the hill, whose *nahual* can also be the thunderbolt, dwell in the neighboring hills and caves and in great cities within the hills that shelter springs, animals, and precious metals. (The *cerro de oro* [hill of gold] is an example.) At the same time, there are the "masters and lords of the animals," whose function is to look after the springs and the caves, and to prevent the animals that live in the hills from becoming the prey of uncontrolled hunting, especially because many of them are doubles or *nahuals*, while a number of others are human beings transformed into animals as a punishment for not accepting Christian baptism.

Catholicism has led to a structure of religious syncretism, which combines the aforesaid beliefs and practices with the Catholic ritual instituted upon first contact with the church. Sometimes the importance of Catholicism consists in its being counted as a ceremonial center (sacred space) which offers the people new forms of protection in their relations with the sacred and the universal, sometimes in its sacred personages (saints and virgins), who likewise afford protection to the ward, the family, and the individual. Of these sacred personages the most important is the Virgin of Guadalupe, in whose honor the most important sodality celebration takes place.

The image of the Catholic priest is always foreign and even rejected when he intervenes to modify the forms adopted by popular worship, but as his dominion over the sacred is in a fashion recognized, his approval, and even his mediation, is sought.

The native bureaucracy, which knows and fears but as a rule does not participate in this syncretic religion, weakens it through its secularizing activity. For this purpose it can count on the help of the priests who think that Catholic worship is being "imbued with paganism and thereby deformed."

THE PRESENT CHINANTEC PROBLEM

Owing to the importance of hydraulic control in Mexico as the principal factor in socioeconomic development (Barabas and Bartolomé 1973:2), a number of commissions dependent on the Secretariat of Hydraulic Resources (SRH) were appointed which took control of the most important river basins in the country.

In 1947 the Commission for the River Papaloapan was appointed, which had as one of its objectives the planning and execution of a program of integrated development that would bring a backward area into line with the national economic growth. This area is of 46,517 square kilometers, comprising the south of the state of Veracruz and parts of the states of Oaxaca and Puebla.

Central to the activities of the Commission was the construction of two great dams to regulate the rise of river levels and to protect against the flooding of the river Papaloapan. It was also concerned with the distribution of electric current and the bringing of districts under irrigation.

The first dam (Miguel Aleman) on the river Tonto was completed between 1949 and 1955, removing 20,000 Mazatec Indians from their lands (Barabas and Bartolomé 1973:3–4). Toward 1972, the project — which had long been postponed — of constructing the Cerro de Oro Dam on the river Santo Domingo was resurrected. The necessity of preventing the floods which regularly affected the lower Papaloapan (in the state of Veracruz), of providing the new modern industries that were being started with electric current, and of forming an extensive irrigated area argued in favor of its rapid construction.

In order to construct the Cerro de Oro Dam about 20,000 Chinantecs (mostly of Ojitlán) were to be dislodged, and some Mazatecs (all residing in the state of Oaxaca), because their lands would be at the bottom of the waters of the artificial lake formed by the dam. Two questions pre-occupied the Indians: why should they be the ones to be affected, seeing that the floods did not harm Oaxaca but Veracruz and that they would not be the beneficiaries of any of the works following on the dam? And, if they were dislodged, what lands would be given them in compensation for those they had lost, and what kind of a living would they get from these lands?

In these circumstances and because of these two questions there began to develop in the affected zone a complex political process which now courses along many channels. Participating in this process, offering various kinds of alternatives, are the Indians concerned, the political mediators, and regional and national society.

PRESSURES OF REGIONAL AND NATIONAL SOCIETY ON THE CHINANTECS

We thought it convenient to divide the power groups to which we shall refer as follows:

1. OFFICIAL POWER GROUPS (regional and national): the Government of the district, state and nation as well as the institutions which in one way or another participate in the project, banking institutions, the National Indigenist Institute (INI), the Secretariat of Hydraulic Resources (SRE), the Commission of Papaloapan, the Department of Agrarian Affairs and Colonization (DAAC), agrarian groups such as the National Rural Confederation (CNC) and the Independent Rural Confederation (CCI), the representatives of political parties such as the Institutional Revolutionary Party (PRI) and the Authentic Party of the Mexican Revolution (PARM), and influential regional personalities supported by one or another of the official power groups. Although different in many respects, we think that as it now stands these groups might be considered together from two distinct viewpoints: (1) the LEVEL OF INFORMATION they manipulate, and (2) the CAPACITY FOR DECISION on a regional and/or national level (although varying in degree).

2. LOCAL POWER GROUPS: constituted by municipal authorities and rich tradesmen, stock-breeders, and Indian or *mestizo* outfitters. Although these groups are economically and politically dependent on one or the other of the official power groups, and are in fact their political and economic MEDIATORS, they also defend the particular and local interests in

which they would be affected by the construction of the dam. In that case their ambivalent position will have as much weight as the level and quality of the information they obtain and with which they must mediate, and their capacity for decision on the problem.

The pressures of the regional-national society began to be seriously felt in 1972, although the break-up of the traditional system of authority which we have noted was one of the means of avoiding later conflict. Now more than ever it was necessary to prevent the formation of internal groups of resistance to the decisions of the power groups, and to distract the Indian population by multiple alternatives which would make it forget its own organization. In order to effect this, the highest political levels of national and regional society, through the institutions, bolstered their already known political mediators insofar as these corresponded to the (contradictory or antagonistic) interests brought into play by each power group in relation to the monumental project.

The antagonisms of the official power groups centered on the choice of the region of reaccommodation, though certainly their interests went far beyond that. While some were inclined to favor the future irrigation district to be created by the dam, others wanted to reaccommodate the Indian population in a distant region unsuited to agriculture, while still others decided in favor of the free areas that would remain within the catchment area. Still others selected regions not even included in the limits of the Papaloapan basin (Barabas and Bartolomé 1973:12–17). A decision in favor of any of these alternatives would have prejudiced the interests of one or another set of groups. It was obvious that there would be a good deal of discussion and that subtle tactics would be deployed before a final decision was reached. In such a situation, the MEDIATION of the local authorities is employed; but as the very considerable political program needed every available force to avoid "inopportune demands" from the Indian masses, a new category of middlemen appeared on the scene to complement those already there.

To the culturally *mestizo* native middlemen and the *mestizo* middlemen are now added the TECHNOCRATIC MIDDLEMEN, hitherto rare or non-existent. These take up their parts in the Chinantec scenario either directly or through the national and regional institutions or organisms dependent on these institutions. The engineer, the university graduate, the local representative of such and such a commission vie with one another for primacy and efficiency in the manipulation of the native.

Evidently the intrusion of this new category of mediators, better informed and without specific local interests, was bound to bring about conflict among the already existing ones. But this precisely was the overall strategy. In the creation of different SOURCES and KINDS of messages in answer to the same questions (construction of the dam and region of reaccommodation), messages which, being contradictory and proceeding from the mediators, would be attributed it was believed only to these and would provoke dissension among local power groups and confusion among the Indian masses until one of the official power groups would impose its solution.

It was a covering strategy designed to prolong the subordination of the native, and the mediators were the transmitters of the manipulatory messages. Occasionally the replies of the Indian people appeared to be aimed directly at the upper levels of power, but always they were misguided or distorted by the mediators; inversely, the official power groups established "direct" communications, counting on the previous preparation and intervention of their mediators.

We believe that the channels of communication opened up by the mediators were a one-way traffic only, that of messages directed to the natives, while their real responses to the conflict situation were not considered but rather distorted or fabricated by the mediators before reaching the official power groups. The power groups then competed against each other "in the defense of the authentic opinion of the people," given out by the respective mediators as the one and only opinion.

Under these circumstances the Indian population began to realize that its representatives, whether elected or voluntary, were not properly considering its fate. If they themselves did nothing, their land, their hills, and their springs would be lost. Many old men would die of grief if removed, and families would be still more split up. There had not been even a reply to their initial inquiries. Mediation had given clear proof of its intentions. The validity of the mediation was not discussed, nor its fundamental role in the matter. It was clear only that the mediators had not listened to what the people had to say. They had been transmitters solely of the messages of one of the parties: the government. If they managed to smash the established intercultural media of communication they themselves would be the transmitters of their own messages and would confront the social chaos, now reaching a climax, with their own powers.

THE MESSIANIC RESPONSE

The texts which we reproduce below were handed to us by the recipient of the messages about the middle of April 1973. The messages were received by Andrés Felipe Rosas in the Ojitlán-Chinantec dialect. Since he does not speak Spanish he repeated them to his daughter, Rosa Felipe Montor, who had asked the schoolmaster of Potrero Viejo to type what was said. They then made copies of the text and distributed them to the authorities of Ojitlán and to some visitors who did not understand the dialect.

Even if this is considered to be the first organized response of most of the Indians to the problem, we must take into account certain incidents (known to all the villages) that occurred a short time before the first message became known. It was said that some engineers of the Papaloapan Commission had disappeared into the Cerro de Oro, and that the Cerro would soon open up and engulf all who were working for the dam. At the same time the elders told the wizards (the guardians of the borderline) to send their *nahuals* to kill the President of the Republic. The latter was identified as a wizard whose *nahual* was endeavoring to bring calamities and misfortunes to "this side of the borderline" (Ojitlán). The wizards were unable to comply with this request, seeing that, as was said later, the President was much protected by his guardian spirits, whom they identified as guardians of the borderline of another town (Mexico City).

Text of the Messages

The text is as follows:

a. Andrés Felipe Rosas is an *ejidatario* of Potrero Viejo in the municipality of Ojitlán, district of Tuxtepec, state of Oaxaca. He was born on the *ejido*, and is forty-six years old. He was married civilly and by the church; he has twelve children by his wife María Montor. No one has ever testified that he was not a truth-teller.
b. He was working on the afternoon of September 10, 1972 around five o'clock, when an unknown person appeared before him and said to him: "Listen! Do you see how many paths have been trodden out between here and the Cerro de Oro? Do you think that the work of the Cerro de Oro dam will be completed?"

    Andrés answered, "I don't think so for this river has a strong current." Andrés asked the unknown, "Where do you come from?"

    The unknown answered, "My name is The Great God Engineer. I live here."
c. On September 15, about nine o'clock in the morning, this Lord returned and said to Andrés, "Jesus Christ a little while ago wished to open and divide with a thunderbolt the Cerro de Oro so that all the water below inside the Cerro might come out. It was not divided because the Virgin of Carmel intervened and forbade it in the interest of all her children, of

innocent childhood, and because the whole region of Tuxtepec and Veracruz would be lost. Jesus Christ will respect the prohibition of the Virgin of Carmel and will leave another Virgin, she of Guadalupe, above the place where one meets the Virgin of Carmel, so that in this way there is more strength."

d. On September 17, near midday, the Great God Engineer appeared and said to Andrés, "Ask yourself where the people will stay if the dam is built by the caprice of the Government." Then he asked Andrés, "Dost think it would be a good thing to set up the village on the hill?"

Andrés said, "There is no water on the hill."

The Great God said, "Yes, there is water." He said also, "Do not go away for you and your people are in great danger."

e. On November 10, 1972 the Great God Engineer said to Andrés, "Mr. President Echeverría has pledged himself solemnly, and if he accepts that the dam be not built, everything will turn out well, seeing that the President made a mistake in paying attention to the state of Veracruz and not taking this region into consideration. Mrs. Echeverría has given much thought to the Mexican family." And he added, "I approve of the credit that has been opened for the peasants."

f. On November 20 Andrés went to see his tobacco seed-plot on the hill. The Great God Engineer was there when he arrived at that place and said to him, "I have been looking for you since yesterday. How is the affair going, has it been noted down?" The Engineer again insisted, "See that you tell the authorities of Ojitlán about this business for the good of the village in which we live. Does the government not remember that an old man once defended Mexico with a standard of the Virgin of Guadalupe?"

Andrés says that the Great God Engineer wears a Virgin of Guadalupe on his back and when he goes away it disappears from sight at about fifteen meters every time he speaks with Him on the hill.

g. On January 5, 1973 it was not the Great God Engineer that appeared, but the Virgin of Guadalupe herself. She said, "Speak to Diego, and tell him that as he wanted proof, I have come. He must try to speak with the Municipal President of Textepec so that the dam is not built, for it will not withstand the Cerro and in a short while it will burst and many children will perish. That will give me great pain, that is what I do not want. For that reason I name Diego to avoid the catastrophe." She also said, "Don Benito Juárez made laws that the Mexicans were not to be molested nor to go elsewhere. So did Don Lázaro Cárdenas who divided the land that the country folk might not be ousted from their homes nor have water poured on them." And she added, "You must see the President of the Republic so that the dam is not built; and if it cannot be avoided you must see the President of Tuxtepec and get him to erect a barrier from the house of Emilio Patatuchi to the ward below, so that when the dam gives way that whole part of the state of Veracruz and Tuxtepec is not lost. For this reason Hidalgo the parish priest, to win the fight, first brought out the standard for the defense of the Mexicans and went with generals and soldiers when he fell in Mexico."

At that point her foot bled (of the Virgin of Guadalupe) and she showed the blood to Andrés Felipe and said, "It gives me great pain that not a child is born in a month that does not cost its mother much time and travail, for this I am doing what I do." Then the Virgin began to weep and said, "If the President of the Republic has any consideration for me, I myself will save him, and the Municipal President of Tuxtapec if he pays attention to me, and this can be published in the Tuxtepec periodical *Action*."

h. On March 8, 1973 the Great God Engineer arrived and said, "The President of the Republic has said the same thing as Benito Juárez: 'Between individuals and nations respect for the rights of others is peace', for he said when he came here on his election campaign and was not in the presidency, that there was to be 'no dam'. He also said, 'I must help you with highways, electric light, drainage, drinking water, etc'."

And the Great God Engineer said to Andrés, "You people need have no fear, nothing will happen to you. If the competent authorities put you in prison, I promise to help you by order of the Virgin of Guadalupe. The Virgin told me that she agrees with everything that is being said up there, only with the business of the dam she is not in agreement." And he added, "Forget not what I told you on the day when I came to show you the place where a bridge is being built to bring out the products of the poor from this side of Santo Domingo between the high hills of Las Pochotas and Potrero Viejo."

i. On March 30 the Lord again appeared to Andrés in his house about eight o'clock at night, and said, "Give no proof, for the parish priest has said, 'he wants to be bigger than I'." And he said, "Be not troubled, if the priest does not want to come, she herself (the Virgin of Guadalupe) will seek a way to make him come. It is for the priest's own good that he should come to the cave. Force is not needed."

Analysis of the Messages

Many of the explanations and interpretations that appear here were given or suggested to us by Don Andrés Felipe through his son. They show the element of disguise in the messages and the assimilation of the personages of the Catholic religion to those of the traditional religion.

a. The first part presents the recipient of the messages, whom it is necessary for us to know, as the Great God Engineer had indicated. In it he is identified as an ordinary member of the Chinantec group, a country-man, respectful of the laws and of the Catholic religion. These are important qualities if his mediation was not to encounter obstacles.

The recipient of the messages is not a $sa^2m'ui^1$, but his mother-in-law is, and she lives on the same *ejido*. As wizards and witches are always known outside their village, and by the elders of Ojitlán, the family name of his wife is mentioned in order to establish indirectly the link between Andrés Felipe and the institution of shamanism, a link which will be very important in the development of the movement since his mother-in-law is the person entrusted with the cure of the maladies of the "faithful."

b.   The first apparition was in the *milpa* [maize field] on the hill. The reply of Andrés Felipe represents the opinion of practically the entire Indian population. They see the attempt to control the forces of the river and of the Cerro de Oro, an area controlled by magic forces, as doomed to failure. Their conception of the relationship "human force to natural force" is fundamentally different from that of the technological society. The presence of the Great God Engineer, therefore, is seen as a confirmation of their own beliefs as opposed to those displayed by the engineers of the Commission of the Papaloapan. The Great God Engineer, a personage in possession of technical knowledge, comes to inform the natives of what they do not know, and to confirm their opinions. The new elements of the modern world with which they are coming into contact will serve their interests if they come to be a part of the known and guaranteed religious structure, on terms favorable to themselves.

In secular reality, the engineers are personages of high status, who in their role of technicians or technocratic mediators are frequently in touch with the Indians, and their influence — especially in this situation of conflict — is seen as decisive. These personages acquire ambivalent characteristics (harm-benefit); sometimes they help the natives by showing them how to increase their crops or make water available for dwelling houses. At other times their advice causes the loss of harvests, and they deny the needed water. They build bridges and roads that connect the *ejidos*, but at the same time they build dams. To the engineers, especially in their capacity as mediators, is attributed the power of preventing the construction of the Cerro de Oro Dam; nevertheless, it is clear to the Indians that they have supported the project.

To the "malefic" role of the engineers in secular reality, they oppose the "benefic" one of the Great God Engineer in sacred reality. Engineers being personages of such great importance, their decisive participation in the religious manifestation goes without saying. This time, the engineer is a supernatural being (of greater power, therefore, than even the other engineers) who presents himself in defense of the Indians and to prevent their being deceived. For the traditional cultural code accepts new figures drawn from a reality that the Indians cannot manage in accordance with their traditional action patterns, and confers on them a divine character that enables them to supplant the secular mediation they have smashed.

The presence of the Great God Engineer implies the beginning of a new epoch, this time favorable to the Indians. As his dwelling is the hill, he is a "man of the hill" (especially through the control he exercises over that area and which he manifests in other apparitions), and at the same time he is God (the Christian God), which is not at all in contradiction with the syncretic religious structure that has been built up.

c. The second apparition of the Great God Engineer brings the first message (though the previous apparition in itself implies a message). In the domain of the sacred it appears there are no defined hierarchies, seeing that Jesus Christ as well as the Virgin of Carmel and then the Virgin of Guadalupe present themselves as absolute powers and at the same time relative to other powers. In this message the Great God Engineer appears as the transmitter of messages sent by Jesus Christ and the Virgin of Carmel to those who are being wronged. Jesus Christ sends a direct threat, implying a break with the established system of conciliation. Being linked with the thunderbolt, he is converted into a wizard of the guardian of the borderline type, whose function is to prevent the coming of harm to his village (the dam) and to return this harm to the one who causes it. By means of his *nahual* he wants to split the Cerro de Oro and pour out the water it contains, thus bringing about the avenging cataclysm immediately. The Virgin of Carmel appears as a moderating influence, offering a possibility of peaceful coexistence between the Indians and the inhabitants of Tuxtepec and Veracruz, who in this case are castigated by Jesus Christ, together with others responsible, whose destiny it would be to disappear beneath the waters.

At this point the intermediate position occupied by the messages manifests itself, a position oscillating between the reform or readjustment of the established order, and the smashing of that order and the creation of a new one in which those responsible for the conflict will have ceased to exist. This is the only message that restricts salvation to the Indians and radically separates the "just" from the "unjust."

The menace of destruction gives way to a reinforcement of divine power which while it warns is destined to give confidence to the elect and to disturb the guilty. The Virgin of Guadalupe (whose protective virtue is fundamental) is accompanied by another "guardian" on Santa Rita hill. At this psychological moment the Great God Engineer transported Andrés Felipe (without his noticing it) to the Santa Rita hill, on the Potrero Viejo *ejido*, and showed him a cave that up to that time had been unknown. On the walls and floor within were figures of the Virgin of Guadalupe, the Virgin of Miracles, and Saint Rosa. From that moment on began the daily pilgrimages to the cave, known to the faithful as "the church" (*ru*[1] *'kua*[3]), where the ritual of salvation that we shall describe later developed.

d.   In the following revelation the Great God Engineer appears directly as the giver of the message. As man of the hill he has dominion over these areas and knowledge of their secret riches. The message contains the explicit PROMISE OF SALVATION, represented by land (the land of the ancestors) and by sustenance, for there they can add to their maize fields and get the water which will be given them by the Great God, in order that his people may live and maintain their traditional way of life away from foreigners. The basic problem of life on the hill is water; therefore the "Engineer" is the right person to solve it. As man of the hill he controls the springs and as technician he is entrusted with the distribution of water.

The promise of salvation upsets the established order. Even if the dam is constructed the Indians will survive the cataclysm and will gain an independence from the decisions of the government. The solution does not come from profane reality but from divine reality; rapidly it acquires strength. In anticipation many of the Indians of the municipality of Ojitlán began to build canoes and collect arms and food for the move to the "promised land" (Potrero Viejo hill) chosen by the Great God Engineer, there to remain until after the cataclysm (the bursting of the dam and the flooding of the earth) when they might venture to descend into the valley. Together with the promise of salvation goes the warning of danger, which abandoning their lands will mean to the Chinantecs, a danger not only to physical but to cultural survival.

Here the Great God Engineer acquires the full character of a messiah who comes to restore justice and save his people from the destruction of its identity. In this case, which is different from the others, the messiah is sacred and remains within sacred reality without entering into direct and permanent contact with the faithful or with the terrestrial world. He chooses as his terrestrial representative an individual who is not a shaman (although connected with the institution of shamanism), or an ancestor returning to save his people, or a cultural hero. He reveals his own messages to him so that he may transmit them. Although this individual serves as a liaison between the natural and the supernatural world, it is not he who is to institute the new society. He cannot be confused with the messiah.

e.   In the following revelation there is a renewed attack on the dam. There are veiled threats against the person responsible for the conflict, threats the faithful understand as a harm that the wizards will bring about, especially the harm the Great God Engineer will inflict upon the President of the Republic if he insists on inundating the land of the Chinantecs. Nevertheless, the punishment does not extend to his wife, who gave her support to the creation of a cooperative of *huipil* makers, thus benefiting family economy. Reference is made to Veracruz which would benefit most directly from the dam because it will prevent the usual floods. At the same time there is confirmation of the renewal of official agricultural credits which were suspended from the beginning of 1972 because of official indecision regarding the dam. The peasant is thereby obliged to have recourse more than ever to outfitters.

The close link between secular events and various points of the sacred message demonstrates the sociopolitical character of the movement. As Bastide points out (Pereira de Queiroz 1969:11), "religion is a metaphor for social life," expressed in a religious language that gives scope for all ideas.

f.   The next apparition is on the tobacco seed-plot. Then the Great God Engineer transported Andrés to "the church." The reference to writing down the message proves the parallel development of the movement, for Andrés had the messages copied in order to distribute them among the local and regional authorities who did not understand the dialect, while the faithful received them from Andrés himself. Thus, the mediator role of the recipient of the messages is evident, a role assimilated to the model prevailing in the political process, since solution by mediation — except in the allusions to destruction — is continually sought.

The sacred personages are simultaneously transmitters, mediators, and executives; they are messiahs who approach the power groups through Andrés Felipe, the MEDIATOR OF THE SACRED. In our opinion we have here an inversion of the channels of communication existing on the secular-political level. The divine personages have in their hands the ultimate decision; the natives carry it out on earth by approaching the regional and national government through the mediator of the sacred. Normally the political process is secular; here it is sacred, and as such guarantees triumph to the natives and puts them on a plane of equality and even superiority *vis-à-vis* the power groups.

In this message reference is made to a historical personage (possibly identified with Hidalgo, the parish priest) who participated in the movement that generated Mexican independence, hoisting a banner of the Virgin of Guadalupe as a symbol of national unity.

The figure of the Virgin of Guadalupe which the Great God Engineer carries on his back when he appears in "the church," and which disappears as he goes away, is proof that the Virgin, "the Guardian," dwells in this place; in it are the symbols that create ritualization.

g.   The apparition of the Virgin of Guadalupe is the consequence of pressure from the Ojitlán and Tuxtepec authorities and of the Catholic priest to produce proof of the authenticity of the messages. The Virgin, always present in the church, now appears in a tree (twenty meters from the entrance to the cave) in front of Andrés Felipe. Proof is the impression of her image left on the tree. The Virgin asks Andrés Felipe to show this proof of her apparition to Diego Lorenzo, municipal president of Ojitlán, so that he may communicate it to Tuxtepec and that, once the authenticity of the messages has been corroborated, the dam may be given up and the destruction of the world outside Cerro de Oro avoided.

In this message there are a number of historical references linked to personalities best known to the Chinantecs. Like the previous one it is not placed against a historical background, but one present and active (through their acts and words) outside historical time, in the contemporary reality, thus forming one syncretic time. Usually the mention of historical personages (Benito Juárez[8] and Lázaro Cárdenas[9]) is tied to the Virgin of Guadalupe, whereby their sacred character and their ahistoric essence are reinforced. The messages recall ancient happenings, recovering them from the past and creating a plane of extrahistoricity that makes possible a repetition of these happenings. The extrahistorical personages, highly sacralized, furnish the elements of a social criticism; they make possible the identification of present necessities and objectives with those of other situations and reveal to these necessities and objectives the revolutionary aspect of their action. They serve as an actualized model for them, so as to form with other peasants and natives likewise placed on an extrahistorical plane one single vindicatory group. We believe that this message is a resuscitation of the events of the Mexican Revolution, whose sign (blood on the foot of the Virgin) indicates the timelessness of events in the domain of the sacred and the possibility of a recreation of the struggle in the present. Without instigating — either openly or covertly — the natives to rebellion against the established power, the message recalls that the past may return to punish the guilty, although at the same time this may be avoided if it is heeded by the government.

Joined to this ultimatum, with its violent overtones, is the evident recurrence of the categories of mediation established by the political process, since the message must pass through the "political mediators" to get to the President of the Republic who is considered to be responsible for the conflict. It is mediation that offers a new possibility of salvation. However, this time it is not a case of salvation for the Indians (THEIR salvation is unquestionable and is on the hill Potrero Viejo) but for the

---

[8]   Benito Juárez was a Zapotec native who rose to become President of Mexico.
[9]   Lázaro Cárdenas was President of Mexico from 1930–1936 and instituted laws in accordance with agrarian reform.

non-Indian peasants who, without being responsible for the construction of the dam, would disappear beneath its waters if it were to be built. For that salvation it recommends the construction of a containing wall to hold back the waters when the dam bursts.

As aforesaid, the traditional cultural code assimilates new reality in a syncretic structure wherein the mass media are utilized (by publication of the messages in the newspaper) in order to make known the divine decisions, thus combining secular and religious media for the solution of a sociopolitical conflict. The resolving of the conflict, as the messages show, is a divine prerogative. The Indians do not take salvation into their own hands through action, if by action we mean massive rebellion. The only thing that concerns them is compliance with the ritual of salvation, and the only thing that concerns Andrés Felipe is the guidance of ritualization and the mediation between the sacred and the secular, a mediation that is always directed by the divine personages. Participation, restricted in the secular reality, becomes active in the sacred through ritual, which goes on molding the actual messianic manifestation into a movement that agglutinates a great part of dispersed Chinantla.

h. In this message the reasons of the Indians for opposing themselves to the dam are strengthened, for it alludes to previous promises made by the present president which secured for him the political support of the Chinantecs. These promised benefits are the only ones that the Indians wish to receive from the government.

The Great God Engineer appears once more, in response to the apprehensions of the mediator of the sacred and also of the faithful, to guarantee the invulnerability of his followers in face of the pressures of the authorities.

i. The last of the messages — as far as we are acquainted with them — assumes a less conciliatory tone. In view of the fruitlessness of mediation the pact is broken, and the Virgin decides to provide proof of her apparition.

It is probable that as the messages continue, their characteristics become more clearly defined, though it may be that the established model of mediation persists.

Even though we consider the Great God Engineer to be the sacred messiah who will establish a new society for the Indians, it should be noted that the Virgin of Guadalupe, as announced by the Engineer, also plays a messianic role, whether in showing the way to salvation to non-Indian peasants or in guiding personally the process of mediation which is continually being obstructed by the civil and ecclesiastical authorities. In her role of guardian, of guide, and of symbol of social justice when she is linked up with extrahistorical personages, she is a messiah who will bring back the justice and order lost in political conflict.

The Movement

Although contained and guided by the messages, its concretion in ritual has achieved a certain independence.

Almost immediately in the first message, the religious manifestation extends beyond the limits of the *ejido* Potrero Viejo, attracting other *ejidos* (some of them traditional rivals) of Ojitlán, of Usila, and of Valle Nacional. From that moment on large numbers of the faithful went to the house of Andrés Felipe to hear the message, and a short while afterward began to make preparations for going to live on the hill chosen by the Great God Engineer when he should give the signal. When Andrés Felipe discovers the church the ritual begins to develop. Revelations are received by Andrés alone, but confirmation of them is in the church. Beginning 15 September 1972, more than a hundred faithful arrive here every day. Andrés Felipe remains in the church the whole day with his daughter and son, awaiting the arrival of new faithful who, so popular are the messages, now come even from Veracruz. Most, but not all, are Indians, peasants of the region who come to be cured in the church, and to pray that the dam may not be built. It is evident that a conflict which until now did not worry them, inasmuch as they did not feel themselves involved, has been revealed to them through the divine messages, warning them that they also are in peril and pointing out the way of salvation.

The group of the faithful most attached to Andrés Felipe goes to the church two or three times a week to hear the messages again and to take offerings which they place before the "altar." Many remain there day and night praying to the Virgin and the Great God Engineer to bring happiness and justice to the Chinantecs, to save them from the cataclysm, and to guide them to the promised land. From the beginning the sa^2 $m'ui^1$ held curing sessions within the church, performing cleansing operations with shoots of plants gathered on Santa Rita hill and believed potent because they belonged to the extensive sacred area, and tracing crosses of holy mud on the affected parts of the body while reciting the sacred traditional formulas.

IDENTIFICATION OF THE SACRED SYMBOLS   The sacred symbols left by the divinity within the church were identified during the first pilgrimages. They are the figures of the Virgin of Guadalupe, the Virgin of Miracles, and Saint Rosa, which appear on the rocky walls of the cave and on small heaps of stones.

Personal identification of these symbols by which divinity manifests itself — or identification of other new ones — is the principal form of adhesion to the group and the movement. He who "sees" is immediately imbued with a sacral character and becomes part of the collectivity that expects salvation.

This first and definitive test passed, the faithful purify themselves so that they, having been stripped of their imperfections, may pass from the profane to the sacred state. Purification is indispensable if one is to become part of the group of "the just," or those who will be saved. At first the rite of purification consisted in washing oneself and drinking the water of a small spring within the cave, where the altar stood. When the "holy water" dried up because many took it home in bottles to give it to those relations who had not gone to the church to drink, purification was achieved by rubbing the body with the mud that had remained and which internal humidity constantly maintained.

The just are defined as much by identifying the symbols as by purification, and participation in the group (as for instance in shamanic cures) is accorded to all those who comply with both requirements, whether they be Indian, peasants, or *fuereños* [temporary residents of the city of Mexico].

The acceptance of the latter (visitors and technocrats from Mexico City) is accounted for by the necessity of getting backing for the mediation. It is known that their participation in the group is accidental and generally short-lived, but if they comply with the aforesaid rules the messages are transmitted to them and they are allowed to enter the church. The hope is that this diffusion will gain greater acceptance among the authorities who will listen with more interest to a resident of the capital than to an Indian.

As for the peasants of Veracruz and Tuxtepec who feel themselves in danger if the dam is built, their support is very important for the Chinantecs, for they see in them a source of backing and even mediation in their interests. These countrymen do not form part of the same group as the Indians and do not share the same expectation of salvation, but find themselves more involved in the ritual than the visitors. Some visitors are admitted temporarily if they show themselves favorable to the solutions offered by the messages; others, the non-Indian peasants, share a conflict and a salvation feasible only if the mediation of the sacred triumphs.

A very important fact, in our opinion, is the combination of forces which involves, on the one hand, extensive reinforcement of the ethnic identity of the Chinantecs, achieved by the messages and their concretion in the movement and, on the other, adhesion of the peasants to the struggle in the interests of justice — in this case perhaps the first stirrings of class-consciousness. For the Indians the chief thing is to bring the sacred mediation to a successful conclusion, for the peasants to reinforce the demands of the principal beneficiaries of divine care, and by joint action with them to attain their own salvation.

THE SACRED AREAS   The areas in which ritual develops have different degrees of sacredness, with corresponding differences of attitude on the part of the faithful.

The Road   This area of preparation begins at the crossing of the river, i.e. on the *ejido* of Potrero Viejo. On the way (which is two-and-a-half kilometers) faithful pilgrims from different places join one another. All that has happened from the beginning of the revelations is the topic of conversation. There are conjectures about the destruction of the dam and the punishment of the guilty, plans for Chinantec life on the hill, and enumeration of cures that have taken place in the church. Each repetition of these facts — frequently commented on by the same persons and with the same words — is a reenacting of them as an experience of the sacred, a kind of litany that unites the pilgrims in their shared hopes.

The Cross   At the end of the road is the cross. This is the first threshold. Beyond it the air is charged with sanctity which increases in intensity as the church draws near. At that cross, which is permanently surrounded by flowers and lighted candles, each person stops to make the sign of the cross and, if he wishes, leave some object that he is carrying. From that point on, say the faithful, "anyone can leave anything and it will not be touched."

It is important to note the high degree of purity and sanctity with which each of the faithful is imbued (even the pilgrim who has not yet been incorporated into the group) as he crosses the threshold, and how this creates an atmosphere of justice and honor in the group. From that moment men cease to be individuals. They become a part of a collectivity whose goal is salvation.

Ascent of the Hill   During the climb, which lasts from one to two hours, the faithful remain silent, forming small groups that go forward together, helping and waiting for one another. Preparatory to entering the church the solidarity of the group intensifies. Separation by sex, age, ethnical affinity ceases to exist, thus underlining the difference from daily customs outside the sacred area. Yet the links between the faithful created within it persist outside of it, marking them off from the rest, "the others," those who will not be saved by the divinity.

In each hollow space along the roadway candles and flowers are placed. These also are sacred precincts before which the faithful pray and make the sign of the cross. In every little cave the man of the hill is present, the messiah.

The Church   This is the precinct that has the highest degree of sanctity. Within the faithful burn copal and offer candles and flowers which they bring every day and place in front of the altar. The latter is a small rocky structure which before was the spring and around which appear the images. There also is the *sa²m'ui*[1] surrounded by other old women who assist her in the ritual. Within the church the faithful pray silently for hours. The faithful would say, "This is not like the church of the parish priest where everything is chatter and gossip. This is serious."

Just outside the church there is a big open space where Andrés Felipe retails to the faithful the details of the revelation.

The Tree Trunk   On it the Virgin of Guadalupe appeared, leaving as proof of her appearance an impression of her image on the trunk. This place also is surrounded with flowers and candles, and the faithful approach it to pray.

Under its aspect of ritual as well as of mediation, the movement has provoked different reactions among Indian and *mestizo* mediators as well as among technocratic ones. The latter refuse to accept the genuineness of the revelations and attribute the messages to political manipulation by some sector. They call the Virgin of Guadalupe, "the virgin of politics," and try to belittle the figure of Andrés Felipe, the recipient of the messages. However, they view the excitement of the Indians as a serious menace to the continuance of their political domination. Although repeatedly invited to do so, neither they nor the Catholic priest are willing to approach the church, whether from fear, incredulity, or the desire not to confirm the validity of the messages and the movement by their presence.

The local technocracy and the regional-national government ignore or appear to ignore the politico-religious movement that has grown since the delivery of the messages, as well as the threats and petitions addressed to the power groups. This "not interested" attitude in face of the part played by religious manifestations in response to sociopolitical conflicts frequently brings them to the boiling point.

Attempt at a Theoretical Characterization

Many authors have formulated concepts and elaborated typologies of religious movements. Among them are Linton (1943), Voget (1956, 1959), Wallace (1956), Clemhout (1964), Lanternari (1965), Ribeiro (1968), Balandier (1969), Hobsbawn (1968), Schaden (1965), Wolsley (1967), and Pereira de Queiroz (1960, 1969, 1971). These authors have tackled the question of religious movements from different points of view — according to the context of the manifestations — and have established categories and typologies whose aim in many cases is to agglutinate different types of religious movements, whether it be under the name of "nativistic," "revivalist," "liberating," "prophetic," "millenary," or "messianic."

Such being the case, we take as our basis the contributions of María Isaura Pereira de Queiroz, and will clarify those concepts developed by her which in our opinion are not applicable to the movement engendered in Chinantec society.

According to Pereira de Queiroz (1969:20),

... millenary movements are defined by the belief that in a future age, secular and yet sacred, terrestrial and yet celestial, all wrongs will be righted, all injustices removed, and sickness and death abolished. It is in the nature of millenarism to be at the same time religious and sociopolitical, and to intertwine the sacred with the profane. Messianic movements constitute a branch of millenary movements, and are characterised by the presence of a messiah who formulates the millenium that will have as its mission the establishment of the perfect society.

The Chinantec movement can be characterized as messianic in the sense that there is a formula for a reparative millennium, and that this is not a hope indefinitely postponed, but present in the messiah who formulates it. It is his mission to repair the injustices, solve the conflicts, and reorganize the society.

Its sacred and, at the same time, profane characteristics do not come under discussion, for it is clear that messianic movements all have earthly goals. They formulate socioeconomic and political objectives while availing themselves of religious language. As Pereira de Queiroz says (1960:71), "supernatural means not only guarantee the so-called renewal but render the new created world transcendental. The catastrophes foretold announce the transformation of the world ..." The division between sacred and profane ceases to exist in this type of movement. The content of the messages, the collectivity that will be saved, the ritual of entry into the group of the elect, and the areas shared by the faithful and the promised new society are all imbued with the sacral, as are the objectives and the actions performed to remedy the conflicts. Within the movement the mediation is a sacred mediation.

Another aspect is that, as Pereira de Queiroz says (1971:389), "the genetic situation seems to combine with the reformist and revolutionary dynamism adopted by the movement" and she adds, "just as some movements are a response to cultural disorganisation and anomie, others are a response to a 'colonial situation', i.e. the situation of a previously autonomous society brutally integrated into Western society." Concerning the former, she thinks movements will be reformist and will merely endeavor to improve the existential situation; in the latter, which is a case for structural transformation, they will be revolutionary, and will endeavor to found a third society, inclusive of all the old and the new, and therefore different from both. Colonial situations, she says, generate movements of liberation, while situations of cultural anomie give rise to movements of reform. In both cases the style of response to the crisis is essentially religious, though the direction it takes is determined by the social situation in which it originates (Pereira de Queiroz 1971:389).

In our opinion a colonial situation is not in any way independent of the situations it generates internally throughout the period of domination, and subjection (whether brutal or gradual) brings in itself social disorganization and cultural anomie. Therefore it is not possible to separate these two genetic factors, nor in consequence their functional dynamism.[10]

As we pointed out in the first part of this article, Chinantec society is an example of internal colonialism, and the mode of domination implanted by this system (supplanting of traditional forms of government, disruption of the ethnical group, economic exploitation, dismemberment of the family, manipulation by power groups, etc.) has given rise to a state of anomie and disorganization that embraces all levels of native society to a greater or lesser degree. Thus we find ourselves confronted by the two genetic factors of Pereira de Queiroz, but forming in this case one single context, and we see that the movement develops alternatively on the plane of "reform" and "revolution." As the messages indicate, the aim is to improve the existential situation, but at the same time (if the divine mediation fails) a structural transformation of the existing order is foreseen through the cataclysm. Implicit is an attempt to found a third society (for the natives) on the action model established by historical personages and situations which are given a character of extrahistoricity and sacredness: a third society that includes the just and their traditional form of life, and at the same time the group of the just is widened to

[10] Pereira de Queiroz establishes the distinction between any genetic situation and functional dynamism mainly on the basis of the Guaranis' messianic movements.

make room for the non-Indians and the goods of the dominant society that are necessary for them.

In our judgment, therefore, this movement corresponds to one single genetic situation (for it merges domination and anomie) and oscillates between reform of the existing order, and establishment of a new order. It is at one and the same time a movement of liberation and of social reorganization whose language is religious and whose tactics sacred mediation.

As we have seen, we are dealing with a syncretic movement, linking shamanist personages and traditions (implicit in the messages) with explicit personages of the Catholic religion. The former are assimilated into the latter and take in hand the salvation of the group. At the same time they announce catastrophes and provide the collectivity with a safe-conduct to salvation through ritual, which likewise is syncretic in that the cave is "the church," the spring "holy water," the flowers and candles "offering," and prayer and making the sign of the cross adequate signs of passage from the profane to the sacred area.

Moreover, the rite of purification, the identification of symbols and the shamanist cure initiating an era of health are elements peculiar to many of these movements, and permit a definite separation of the just and the unjust. The theme of the just, the faithful who have succeeded in transcending the common order and placing themselves in the sacred sphere, and of the unjust, the violators of the established order, exhibits special characteristics in this movement. The unjust does not include all non-Indians, but only one part of the other society, the power groups and the Indian bureaucracy. Hence it is that the movement, as we said before, accepts non-Indian countrymen, as poor and as wronged by the dam as the Indians, and not responsible for the conflict. It is an ethnic movement in that it has reassembled members of a stock that were arbitrarily separated by the dominant society, and it has unified the natives of Ojitlán in face of a common problem, in spite of internal divisions created by political mediation. Yet it includes also all those recognized as wronged irrespective of their ethnic identity. Clearly there is discrimination in the form of salvation offered to certain sectors of the oppressed collectivity. Some will have a "promised land"; their salvation is beyond question. Others will be saved only if the sacred mediation has positive results, and they will remain in the land that they now occupy.

It is our belief that the movement, though concerned with ethnic reintegration, has extended its frontiers and given rise to an incipient class-consciousness which will increase in this particular case if the allied peasants manage to exert enough pressure on the power groups. Until now the sole intention has been to secure backing, by means of the sacred messages, for the mediation.

The movement also oscillates between reacculturative and acculturative tendencies. It is reacculturative in postulating the separation and isolation of the Indians, the return to the traditional culture and to self-sufficiency; it is acculturative because it accepts, as the alternative, the goods and benefits of the dominant society and seeks coexistence with it through mediation.

To sum up, it can be said that these oscillating characteristics of the movement (reformative, revolutionary, acculturative, reacculturative, etc.) cannot be understood as a function of previous categorization, but of the historical moment and the particular conjunction of relationships existing between Indian, regional, and national society, i.e. the total societal situation.

On another aspect Pereira de Queiroz states:

... in messianism someone — a hero, a divine messenger — will have the function of founding the perfect society ... it will not be messianic if it is not led by a sacred chief in direct contact with the beyond. Messianic belief not only imagines the future world, but above all describes the sacred chief who must come to establish it, so that the faithful may recognise him and follow him ... (1969: 21–22).

She says further that:

... divinity does not enter into direct contact with the faithful, it uses the messiah for this. The messiah is the indispensable intermediary who brings together divinity and the believer, his function is always that of intermediary of the gods ... (1969: 136).

Chinantec messianism does not exactly comply with this idea of considering the messiah as a divine messenger who comes and remains on the earth in order to establish the new world by the will of the gods. As a rule the messiah is an envoy of the gods to the earth. His role is eminently active although it is guided, and his person is sacred because the gods have so decided.

In this case, however, the messiahs are sacred personages in themselves who always remain in the supernatural world. They are messengers of their own messages and mediators one of another, but they exist on an extraterrestrial plane. They are simultaneously messiahs and gods, they both decide salvation and effect it. The messages fully describe the messiahs who will save the just. Recognition of them procures the elaboration of the ritual and their separation from the interpreter, who participates in their sacral quality like all the faithful but is not sacred in himself.

Of the two messiahs, the Great God Engineer and the Virgin of Guadalupe, the man of the hill and the guardian, the former appears to address himself more to the Indians seeing that he takes in hand their salvation on the hill, while the Guadalupian embraces the entire group of the just and links herself to extrahistorical personages and indicates, sometimes through the Great God Engineer, the path which sacred mediation has to follow.

As was noted, the recipient of the messages is not confused with the messiah, although he alone receives the messages, for the establishment of the new society is not in his hands, nor is the redemption of the collectivity. In this sense he might be called the prophet of the messianic group because he announces the presence and the designs of the messiah, indoctrinates the faithful, and guides the ritual of salvation through his knowledge of the divine symbols; and he is a mediator of the sacred when he recites the messages to the power groups. We believe that these double-faceted functions of the recipient of the messages are linked to the other peculiar characteristics of this movement, although certainly the keynote of the process is mediation, whether notably political and secular or politico-religious.

As Balandier says (1969:139), "religious movements make political rivalries brilliantly manifest, providing them with a language and means of action." Attachment to the land being one of the active elements in the gestation of a messianic movement, the disrupted Chinantec society, in face of the now certain menace of dispossession, makes use of its traditional means of action, which are religious, to oppose the dominant political powers. Not represented in secular mediation, they have recourse to sacred mediation, reinterpreting this model and endowing it with a new social life.

The dynamics of social change imply a reelaboration of changes in function of one's own socioreligious organization. Very remote from the "symbolic paralysis" that results from social domination and disorganization, this movement demonstrates the mechanisms of a society struggling against ethnocide.

REFERENCES

BALANDIER, G.
1969   *Antropología política*. Barcelona: Ediciones Peninsula.

BARABAS, A., M. BARTOLOMÉ
1973   *Desarrollo hidráulico y etnocidio en México: el caso de los mazatecos y chinantecos*. International Work Group for Indigenous Affairs Documents. Copenhagen.

CLEMHOUT, SIMONE
1964   Typology of nativistic movements. *Man* 64(7).

DELGADO, AGUSTÍN
1956   La arqueología de la Chinantla. *Tlatcani* 10(2): 29–33.

HERMITTE, ESTHER
1970   "El concepto del nahual entre los mayas de Pinaloa," in *Ensayos de antropología en la zona central de Chiapas*. Edited by N. A. McQuown and J. Pitt Rivers, 371–390. Mexico City: Instituto Nacional Indigenista.

HOBSBAWN, ERIC
1968   *Rebeldes primitivos*. Barcelona: Ediciones Ariel.

HUNT, ROBERT
1968   Agentes culturales mestizos: estabilidad y cambio en Oaxaca. *América Indígena* 28(3).

LANTERNARI, VITTORIO
1965   *Movimientos religiosos de libertad y salvación de los pueblos oprimidos*. Barcelona: Editorial Seix Barral.

LINTON, RALPH
1943   Nativistic movements. *American Anthropologist* 45: 230–240.

NAHMAD, SALOMÓN
1972   Gobierno indígena y sociedad nacional. *Estudios Indígenos. Cenapi* 2(2): 225–232.

OLIVERA, M., B. SÁNCHEZ
1965   *Distribución actual de las lenguas indígenas de México 1964*. Mexico City: Instituto Nacional de Antropología e Historia.

PEREIRA DE QUEIROZ, MARÍA ISAURA
1960   Aspectos gerais do messianismo. *Revista de Antropología de São Paulo* 8(1): 63–74.
1969   *Historia y etnología de los movimientos mesiánicos*. Mexico City: Siglo XXI.
1971   On materials for a history of studies of crisis cults. *Current Anthropology* 12(3): 387–390.

RIBEIRO, RENÉ
1968   Movimientos mesianicos no Brasil. *América Latina* 11(3).

SCHADEN, EGON
1965   Aculturação indígena. Ensaio sobre os fatores e tendencias indias en contacto con o mundo dos brencos. *Revista de Antropología de São Paulo* 13: 1–317.

VOGET, FRED
1956   The American Indian in transition. *American Anthropologist* 58: 249–263.

1959   Toward a classification of cult movements: some further contributions. *Man* 59.

WALLACE, ANTHONY
1956   Revitalization movements. *American Anthropologist* 58: 264–281.

WOLSLEY, PETER
1967   "Millenarium movements in Melanesia," in *Gods and rituals*. New York.

The Role of Peasant Organizations in the Struggle Against Multinational Corporations: The Cuban Case

GERRIT HUIZER

In some of the so-called underdeveloped countries, the struggle against multinational or transnational corporations has gradually evolved from relatively weak efforts to gain certain concrete benefits to outright revolutionary action. This kind of evolution was not the result of a clear theoretical consciousness of peasants and workers of the role of such corporations, but was a reaction to the rigid and crude forms of exploitation and domination maintained by these corporations at all costs. Examples are the struggle of the peasant workers in the Laguna area in Mexico in 1936 against the Anderson Clayton and other cotton-producing and trading companies, leading to the almost complete expulsion of these companies from the region; the land invasions organized by the Union General de Obreros y Campesinos de Mexico (UGOCM) in 1958 against the Cananea cattle company in Sonora; and the actions of the *comunidades* of Pasco and Junin, Peru, against the Cerro de Pasco Corporation (Huizer 1972a). A particularly clear example is the gradually escalating struggle of the Cuban peasants against national and foreign large landowners and plantation companies.

In the developing countries, the ill effects of transnational corporations have often been felt more strongly in agriculture than in other fields of the economy. In the mining, and particularly in the manufacturing and oil industries, the transnational corporations can claim that certain or even considerable benefits accrue to the countries where they operate, in spite of the huge profits made by these corporations. In agriculture, however,

The author is heavily indebted to the Asociación Nacional de Agricultores Pequeños Havana, which supplied him with data on the Cuban peasant struggle through interviews and training material (e.g. Regalado 1973).

the exploitation of the host country and its population is more clear-cut and brutal. Protest against inhuman working conditions in the mining, manufacturing, or oil industries, can often be neutralized by giving in to certain material demands, such as wage increases or higher taxes or royalties. This is more difficult in the plantation economy. Although simple wage demands can be met, the demand for land by peasants whose forefathers or who themselves have been evicted by the plantations when these were introduced cannot be fulfilled unless the agrarian structure as such is radically changed. There are numerous cases where the demand for land has aroused the population of developing countries to strong resistance movements against the transnational corporations. A main reason for this fact is that in the past or even recently the transnational corporations have displaced or evicted the indigenous peasant population in order to get good lands to create the plantation system. The initiation of the plantation economy has often been felt as an intrusion and, in fact, often consisted of simple usurpation of lands originally belonging to local peasants or communities.

Thus from the start many plantation corporations have been a source of frustration for the local population, and on the whole they have done very little to compensate for this. On the contrary, they have often aggressively continued the trend set at their initiation. Formerly independent peasants who were forced to work on the plantations were badly paid and housed. If more lands were needed, because of the profitability of the plantation agriculture, the same rude means of usurpation or similar doubtful approaches were used to get these lands from neighboring peasant communities. Whenever movements to correct these practices were initiated by the victims or those who were interested in helping them, the counterreaction of the corporations was out of proportion. Thus the moderate efforts of the Guatemalan government in 1953 to expropriate some of the unused lands of the United Fruit Company (UFC) for distribution among landless peasants led to international action to defend the UFC's interests, going as far as overthrowing the Guatemalan government and installing a military dictatorship which has caused the deaths of numerous peasant and labor leaders until today. In several developing countries the plantations are a strongly dominating force, virtually unchallenged.

The influence of transnational agricultural corporations in some of the smaller developing countries comes out clearly in Table 1 from Beckford (1970:448).

In some cases resistance to change by the corporations and their increasingly violent reaction against legitimate demands has led to an esca-

Table 1. Big companies and small countries: a comparison of company activity data and national aggregates for selected plantation economies 1967–1968 (million dollars U.S.)*

| | Company | | Country | | |
| | Annual sales | Net income | National income | Exports | |
				Total	Plantations[a]
Booker	198.6	11.5			
Guyana			162.5	108.2	31.8
Tate & Lyle	549.2	27.1			
Jamaica			787.2	219.5	44.9
Trinidad			569.0	466.2	24.2
United Fruit	488.9	53.1			
Panama			634.0	95.2	55.6
Honduras			649.0	181.4	85.4

* *Source:* all country data from International Monetary Fund, International Financial Statistics, January 1970. Company data are from respective company annual reports.
[a] plantation exports refer to exports of the commodity produced in the particular country by the relevant metropolitan enterprise.

lation of the peasant and worker resistance against them. The resistance of the peasants organized by Viet-minh against Michelin and other foreign powers is probably the most notorious, but also certain peasant movements, e.g. in the Philippines and Cuba, which later became more or less violent revolutionary movements should be mentioned. The way through which moderate, legalistic peasant interest groups, in their demand for justice and recognition of rights became an outright revolutionary movement as a reaction to the intransigence of the established elite and the corporations is well illustrated with the case of Cuba.

As in several other Latin American countries, in Cuba the struggle of peasants against large estates and corporations has a tradition which goes back to the colonial period. In Cuba it started particularly after the introduction of railways around 1830 made the cultivation of sugar cane profitable. The owners of sugar estates then started to extend their lands aggressively at the cost of the small tobacco-producing farmers, through eviction and usurpation.

Peasant resistance was initially sporadic and isolated. When, however, the armed struggle for independence started in 1868, the peasants joined this movement. Although this struggle was repressed, many peasants participated again in the Mambi army, in the revolution of 1895 against the Spanish regime. As a counteraction the peasants were "concentrated" by the colonial regime in villages; because they lost even more lands through this form of eviction, they joined more massively the liberation struggle until it ended because of the American intervention. The Americans took more and more power in Cuba, replacing the colonial forces. Instead of institutionalizing the armed forces of the liberation as a national army, as was proposed by the Cubans, they created the Guardia Rural [Rural Guards] with elements which were not identified with the peasantry. Supported by this Guardia Rural the process of eviction of peasants from communal lands and small private plots went on, creating more and more plantations in the hands of American companies or individuals. By 1905 there were 13,000 American properties in Cuba, covering almost 10 percent of the total surface of the country. The estates were dedicated to sugar cultivation or cattle. Moreover the promises made to those who struggled in the liberation war to get uncultivated land were not kept. Many of the veterans went to the Oriente province and took idle lands. Officially this was made possible by a law in 1904, but in fact large landowners took away those lands from the peasant occupants. Protest against these activities was initially sporadic.

Between 1910 and 1920 the peasant struggle in Cuba became somewhat influenced by the growing urban labor movement and by socialist and communist ideas. A greater effectiveness and increasing radicalization of the peasant struggle was, however, particularly a reaction to the rapid expansion of large estates which took place between 1915 and 1925, mainly in Oriente province and Camagüey. Thousands of peasants were evicted and pushed into the mountains or forced to work as laborers on the estates or in the large sugar factories, often owned by foreign companies. There was a close collaboration between the companies and the Cuban government. President Garcia Menocal, for example, was linked to the Cuban American Sugar Company, the second largest American sugar enterprise in the country. In 1923 there was a massive mobilization of peasants against the usurpation manipulations of an American company in Caujeri, Oriente province. Peasants were willing to defend their lands by armed force. The same happened in Sagua de Tánamo.

Although peasants often had started to defend their rights through legal action in the courts, they were able to use more radical means since many of them were veterans of the Independence struggle. Unrest went on for years in one or another part of the country. In 1928 the peasants mobilized to get back lands or prevent usurpation by the United Fruit Company, which received help from the Guardia Rural, in several places at the north coast of Oriente province. By 1933–1934, however, the peasants had become more formally organized and were able to struggle more effectively in a coordinated way. One outstanding leader, a veteran of the 1895 revolution, was Lino Alvarez. His strategy, particularly at the beginning, was to try all the possible legal means to defend the peasants' lands. More radical leaders denounced his "excessive legalism," but it gave time to organize the peasants effectively and mobilize them into big demonstrations when it became clear that the legalistic approach dismally failed. The peasants then felt better prepared to initiate more radical and extra-legal actions such as invasions of land.

During the twenties and thirties the sugar workers also had been organized through the Confederación Nacional Obrera de Cuba (National Workers Confederation of Cuba) oriented by the Communist Party which had been created in 1925. Sugar workers and cane-cultivating peasants worked together in the struggle against the owners of plantations and sugar mills, such as the United Fruit Company. This struggle became particularly acute when the repressive Machado regime was overthrown through a general strike in 1933. The peasants had their own demands, increasingly radical, such as "land to the tillers," and "school for the children." At the Second Congress of the Communist Party of Cuba in April 1934 the slogan "Agrarian and anti-imperialist revolution" was launched, and mass meetings of peasants, at times supported by rallies or movements in the towns, were organized around this slogan. Trade union leaders and Communist Party cadres who went out into the rural areas were surprised by the force of such peasant movements as those in the mountainous areas of Oriente province.

In some areas, such as Camagüey, the peasant struggle initially took the form of the creation of pro-school committees. The joint efforts as such and the difficulties encountered had a solidifying and radicalizing effect on these groups. These committees from Camagüey, supported by the Communist youth organization, initiated a First National Peasant Congress in 1937, to coordinate peasant activities all over the country. After this congress in Havana many peasant committees and associations were created in different provinces, where they did not yet exist.

Elsewhere they were brought together regionally. Thus in 1939 the Peasant Federation of Oriente was created at a peasant congress there. The struggle everywhere for concrete and moderate demands encountered such a rigidly negative reaction from the landowners and companies that the peasants realized that these were practically their class enemies. As a result of this awareness the small local groupings saw the need to become more strongly and rationally organized and to give a more radical content to their demands. Thus, a more or less organized struggle emerged gradually. At the Second National Peasant Congress in Havana in 1941, in which over 800 peasant delegates participated, the Asociación Nacional Campesina (National Peasant Association) was created. The main struggle of the Association and its affiliates all over the country was against the numerous evictions of peasants by the large owners or companies. In the following years the efforts of the estate owners or companies to evict peasants and usurp their lands became increasingly violent. Many peasant houses were destroyed, several peasant leaders who led the resistance against such activities were assassinated, such as Niceto Pérez García in 1946 and Sabino Pupo Pillán (leader of the struggle against eviction by the Manati Sugar Company) in 1948. By 1944 the Asociación Nacional Campesina denounced the fact that altogether about 40,000 families were threatened with eviction. Mass meetings and demonstrations were organized in several parts of the country against the eviction threat.

The need to demand such fundamental changes in the rural social structure as agrarian reform rather than small gains was felt increasingly by the peasant associations. Under the governments of Grau San Martin and Prio Socarrás promises about land reform were made and some action, though weak, was taken in that direction. Efforts to neutralize the radicalization of the peasant movement and the increasing demands for structural change were also made through the creation of an alternative organization, the Confederación Campesina de Cuba (Peasant Confederation of Cuba), led by persons related to the government. Also, the Banco de Fomento Agrícola e Industrial de Cuba (BANFAIC, Agricultural and Industrial Development Bank of Cuba), created in 1950, tried, with some success, to give the impression that a new reform-oriented policy had been initiated. Another institution created with that purpose was the obligatory membership of producers of certain products, such as tobacco, into a corresponding national organization, such as the tobacco growers. Although at the village level these organizations were sometimes led by small farmers, nationally they were dominated by the large producers. Members of the radical Asociación Nacional Campesina tried to take over more and more leadership in these organizations, rather than struggling against them.

After the coup d'état which brought Batista to power as president in 1952, the struggle of the peasants again became more outspoken because large landowners and companies started to increase their demands. The Asociación Nacional Campesina organized many meetings, and pro-land-reform committees were created in many sugar areas. The attack on the Moncada barracks by young revolutionaries headed by Fidel Castro on July 26, 1953 had a considerable impact on the militancy of the peasants and workers. The sugar strike of 1955 which paralyzed over a hundred sugar mills was an expression of the radicalization trend. So was the confrontation of the peasant associations with the King Ranch (from Texas) when it tried to usurp lands in Adelaide, Camagüey province in 1954, and against the Francisco Sugar Company which tried the same in 1958. After the men were imprisoned when they tried to prevent these companies from taking their lands, women took over and tried to halt the bulldozers that came to destroy their houses and crops. Similar activities were permanently taking place in Oriente province. When the small group of revolutionaries headed by Fidel Castro started a guerrilla struggle in Oriente province after their landing with the Gramma in December 1956, they found the peasantry ready for insurrectionary action. The tradition of resistance against the violence of the large landowners and companies had radicalized the peasants to such an extent that they were prepared to support or even to join the guerrilla forces.

The repressive action of the Batista regime, trying to concentrate the rebellious peasants in areas where they could give no support to the guerrillas, only radicalized their resistance. The careful way in which the guerrilla forces approached the peasants in the areas they dominated, and the reform measures they encouraged, found immediate support from the local peasant associations. In particular, Law No. 3 of the Rebel Forces, promulgated October 10, 1958, giving the land to its cultivators free of charge (up to twenty-six hectares) helped to mobilize the peasantry behind the revolutionary forces, which gained a victory on January 1, 1959.

Soon after the revolutionary regime came to power a land reform law was promulgated (May 17, 1959) which prohibited the possession of land beyond the size of thirty *caballerías* (about 390 hectares). More than 100,000 tenants, sharecroppers, and other precarious cultivators became proprietors of their plots.

The large company-owned estates were expropriated and transformed into cooperative or state farms. Efforts to turn the clock back, by overthrowing the government, as was done in Guatemala in 1954, were undertaken in 1961, through the invasion of Playa Girón. This effort failed and Cuba became the first Latin American country to eliminate drastically the influence of multinational corporations.

The next country to take serious steps in this field was Peru. The 1969 land reform, introduced by a "revolutionary military government," dealt in the first place with the huge sugar estates of such multinational corporations as W. R. Grace, Gildemeister, and others in the northern coastal regions. It should be noted that the military forces which made up the Peruvian Government from 1968 onward, in earlier years had been made aware of the serious problems created by the large estate system, when they had to confront massive peasant movements and land invasions involving over 300,000 peasants (including the occupation of the estate of the Cerro de Pasco Corporation).

In the struggle against the increasing influence of multinational corporations peasant resistance movements have played a crucial role and will probably continue to do so in the future. As clearly demonstrated by the Cuban case, the intransigent reaction of the companies and large estate owners to the reasonable and legitimate demands of the peasants and workers led to a radicalization of the peasantry in demands as well as means of struggle. This process of escalation introduced by the established powerholders eventually led to their own destruction.

REFERENCES

BECKFORD, GEORGE
1970 The dynamics of growth and the nature of metropolitan plantation enterprise. *Social and Economic Studies* 19(4):448. University of West Indies, Jamaica.
HUIZER, GERRIT
1972a Land invasions as a non-violent strategy of peasant rebellion. *Journal of Peace Research* 3.
1972b *The revolutionary potential of peasants in Latin America.* Lexington, Massachusetts: Heath Lexington.
REGALADO, ANTERO
1973 *Las luchas campesinas en Cuba.* Havana.

The Cultural Dependency of Rural Communities and Peasant Guerrillas in Latin America

ZBIGNIEW MARCIN KOWALEWSKI

> From the countryside ... a peasant army, which is pursuing the great objectives for which the peasantry must struggle (the first of which is the just distribution of land), will occupy the cities. Upon the ideological base of the working class, whose great thinkers discovered the social laws which guide us, the peasant class of America will provide the great liberating army of the future, as it has already done in Cuba.
>
> ERNESTO CHE GUEVARA[1]

This article is intended to elicit a response among that minority sector of anthropologists who represent radical social science, or the anthropology of liberation, especially those who are occupied with research on Latin American social reality. It is also directed at those who are doing scientific work on the social formations of peripheral capitalism in other areas and who believe that the results of research devoted to Latin America may contribute important theoretical insights to a knowledge of the whole, unfortunately named "Third World."

I consider it necessary to specify those whom I hope will be receptive to this study. The IXth International Congress of Anthropological and Ethnological Sciences, for which this article was originally prepared, was organized as a world forum of a professional group. The professional divisions of its social groups, however, have so far played a secondary role in social life, both national and international, with regard to the

---

[1] In *Obras 1957–1967*, page 411.

divisions created by the fundamental reality of society: the modes of production of material goods and the corresponding class structure. Independently of the degree to which the social sciences are autonomous from ideological structures, we anthropologists do not, by participating in in a professional meeting, thereby cease to represent scientific activities which serve different and even antagonistically opposed social classes. In other words, we retain our status as scientific workers from one or another specific social class, because politics and class ideology intervene in conditions determined by the scientific practice of anthropology. And anthropology in turn intervenes in conditions determined by political practice and class ideology.

Just as I was preparing the final text of this article, I received a letter sent by one of the Congress participants to some of those regarded as militants of radical anthropology. The author opened with an analysis of the Congress's program and a résumé of its contributions, as provided by the organizing committee. He then denounced the predominance of anthropological currents which directly or indirectly serve the social class under whose hegemony and in accordance with whose interests this science appeared in history and became an integral part of social knowledge. "Anthropology is born from the discovery of the non-Western world by Europe and the development of the various forms of Western colonial domination over the world, from the first contemporary forms of the birth of capitalism to the world imperialism of the twentieth century" (Godelier 1973: 28). (According to an expression by Lévi-Strauss anthropology is, at a scientific level, the daughter of imperialist violence exercised over colonized ethnic groups.)

I fully agree with the appraisal of the nature of the predominant class of the Congress made in the above-mentioned letter. Moreover, I adhere to the belief that it is absolutely necessary to acknowledge the force of the social polarization of classes; this aspect has been intervening with increasing strength in the conditions determined by the scientific practice of anthropology from the moment one sector started to dissent from the influence of its historical roots. This polarization is causing a radical break with (or is freeing it from) the ideological mystification which has traditionally informed it and which has fixed its historically formed class bonds. The result is that anthropology is being placed at the service of knowledge and the emancipation of the social groups dispossessed by capital.

My objective here is to define the anthropology of liberation as a new and important field of scientific activity, an object of investigation which is constituted by a certain social phenomenon incubating among the peasant masses of some Latin American mountain regions. I refer to the emergence of insurgent peasant armies and revolutionary sectors. They, in accordance with the forecasts with which we introduced this article, are being called upon to discharge a basic role in the coming period of a revolutionary transformation of the Latin American continent.

Since the middle or end of the 1960's communities in certain rural zones of Latin America have been changing their position within, or have begun to break with, the traditional framework of political and cultural relations corresponding to the social relationships of production and dependency. These communities, constituting that specific sector of Latin American society which has been formed by the modes of production inherent in dependent, peripheral capitalism, are exceeding the objectively narrow limits characteristic of agents of a small mercantile production. They are using the autonomous historical initiative of the peasant to provide human elements, not only as a base, but also as a vanguard for revolutionary movements which are emerging from their midst. And they are planning the conquest of State power by the peasantry in alliance with the working class.

We are witnessing the appearance of sectors of the peasantry which have begun to adopt new forms of social awareness. They are practicing a new ideology and politics which would have been unheard of in earlier periods. They are establishing themselves as a social group "in and of itself." No longer are they proposing simply a change in land-ownership relations within the localized compass of their microcosms, nor only at a regional or even at a national level, as occasionally occurred in the most important peasant mobilizations of earlier decades. On the contrary, they see the seizure of the modes of production within the perspective of seizing political power and abolishing capitalist productive relations. And at the same time they identify the long road towards the birth of the new society under worker-peasant revolutionary power with an armed violence which is methodically developed and exercised.

The pilot centers of this extraordinary peasant awakening are located primarily in the mountains of Santander Department, in Colombia, where on 4 July 1964 the National Liberation Army began to operate under the command of Fabio Vázquez Castaño; and also in the Sierra of Guerrero State, in Mexico, where on 18 May 1967 the armed struggle of the Party of the Poor (Partido de los Pobres) and its Peasant Execution Brigade (Brigada Campesina de Ajusticiamiento) started under the command of Lucio Cabañas Barrientos. (A third center, which remains outside my consideration here because I have little information about it, seems to have been developing since April 1972 in the forests of Pará

State in Brazil and concerns the activity of the Guerrilla Army of the Araguaya River.) In recent years, the two insurgent peasant armies have become the most important and successful rural guerrilla forces of Latin America. In fact, within their framework and around their mobile armed focal points, new sectors of the revolutionary peasantry are forming and growing. For the first time they are culturally and politically independent of traditional bourgeois hegemony.

These are two of the more important epicenters. However, the new phenomenon is not limited to these because in some cases the movement is developing on a scale which extends far beyond the rural regions directly controlled by guerrillas exercising their armed struggle. In order to understand the more generalized and observable dimensions at broader levels, it seems fitting to refer to one of their more public expressions: the sensational address of the illiterate peasant Jair Londoño. He is a militant based with the National Association of Peasant Concession Holders (Asociación Nacional de Usuarios Campesinos) of Colombia, and on 3 December 1971 he addressed the Latin American Seminar on Agrarian Reform and Colonization held in Chiclayo, Peru. Here are a few paragraphs from his speech, through which a new peasantry, with a clearly revolutionary profile, revealed itself to Latin American public opinion:

I have been taken away from the mountain. I have suffered violence and exploitation, persecution, everything! I have all too recently been wounded, which is why they have permitted me, though they lack respect for anyone ... to say to you in Bogotá: Dear masters, you who believe that you are putting the situation of the peasant to right, here from an office, without being aware of the life he is living, you will fail till hell freezes over! You don't know anything about it! And when one speaks — they have told me that I am subversive because I speak in these terms. Subversive ... yes? ... when the professionals speak, that is democracy, when the politicians and important men speak, the masters, that is democracy, and when a peasant expresses his pain, his situation, that is subversion ... In my country, where some political parties exist, what is the position of us peasants in the face of political parties? We know all too well that not one of the political parties in my country is capable of carrying out agrarian reform. Not one is capable. Why? Because the leaders of the political parties are nothing less than its principal enemies, the principal landholders and large estate owners are the leaders of the political parties and to carry out agrarian reform one would have to begin with them ... to expropriate their large estates ... their properties ... and as they are the ones who make the laws, it is very difficult for them and we already know this, we the peasants are already aware of this, that the parties, not one of them, at least in my country, I repeat it again so no one misses it, I repeat again that in my country there are some parties and that we peasants are already aware of this — it'd be ridiculous if we weren't aware of them by this time; we are aware that not one of the parties is capable of carrying out agrarian reform as we need it.... When we fully discussed and approved a document sacred to us, which is called the first peasant mandate, and published it, how frightened were the politicans and even more so the landholders and large estate owners! When we said in the mandate that we must seize the land, without paying a peso, not a single peso because land is a public right, God made land for the service of humanity, so what would humanity do without land? When man came into the world the land already existed for him to use. God did not deed the land to anyone, the land is a communal right like water and air. It is simply that some who were more shrewd took possession of it and then legislated to legalize that position with deeds and legal codes and swords. But land is a common good, God made the land so that man, so that humanity might live from it — what does not come from the land? What ever could? Everything comes from the land, we are part of creation, man is part of creation, and land appeared so that man might use it; thus it is a common good. It should not be deeded out to anyone, so that we might all have access to it. But we peasants are only entitled to dig the ground, to work, and to make some other wretch rich at the expense of our labor and our hunger. We are entitled to *that*, and that is what our laws allow us so we don't get in the way ... We say to the peasants, to our comrades: Comrades, learn to recognize your enemy, learn to locate him, to know where he is, what his name is, who he is, how he acts, how he keeps you suffering hunger and misery; do not resign yourself to this; we aren't going to do what some priests do who say to the peasant: Resign yourself, my child, because it is the will of God. That's not how it is! That's wrong! The peasant can't be deceived in the name of Christ, nor can he be told that he should be submissive to some wretches who exploit him, who keep him hungry. We don't give a damn for that sort of virtue! No! The peasant must be told where his enemy is, who keeps him in that position, how he operates, who he is and what his name is and where he is entrenched, so he can learn to know where he is ... The same large estate owners are the senators who make the laws which govern the country; the same large estate owners approve agrarian reform, what a dis-graceful business! The same large estate owners are governors and ministers, it is the Congress of our Republic which makes the laws, and there we find all our principal estate owners and landholders, entrepreneurs, large-scale merchants, and industrialists ... The trade union movement struggles and struggles and fights, and goes on strike for a miserable extra peso in wages. Once it gains that peso or two, or ten or twenty or whatever the amount, the struggle has ended. We peasants are not fighting for that, not struggling for that. We shall struggle for a change of structures, for the overthrow of a capitalist, oligarchical, persecuting government. Those are the goals of a peasant movement, to achieve a government which is truly of the people (Jair Londoño 1972: 95–108).

The emergence of insurgent peasant armies has tremendous political and cultural significance in terms of the prospects for social emancipation and for the formation of the peasantry, together with the working class, into a revolutionary State of the working masses. Its significance may be appreciated by referring this phenomenon to two distinguishable types of dependent — though relatively autonomous — positions of rural communities and peasant movements which have been recorded in Latin America. Proceeding in this manner, we may observe what insurgent or subversive potentials of the rural masses are expressed by the peasant guerrillas. And we may see how their political-military practice and ideology, granting a focus for these potentials, overcome objective limitations; how the peasantry becomes not a secondary political force or a follower of one of the two basic capitalist modes of production (constituted by the polarization and antagonistic contradiction between industrial capital and salaried labor), but rather the principal factor in the class struggle. We shall call the first type of dependent, autonomous position "dependent marginalization" and the second "dependent participation."

For a schematic analysis of the first position, it seems appropriate to concentrate our attention on those rural communities found on the rural periphery which are to a considerable degree marginalized, under-developed, and in general submerged in what Frank (1969a, 1969b) suggests calling passive capitalist involution. According to Frank, this type of involution results from the weakening of the links between rural satellite peripheries and their dominant centers, or metropolises. The participation of these peripheries in the capitalist development of their centers (international, national, or regional) gave them the typical structures of underdevelopment of an export capitalist economy and a peripheral commercial capitalism. This occurred in their period of greatest dependent development. When the market for their exportable products became limited or disappeared, whether temporarily or perma-nently, the metropolitan centers abandoned them to their own fate, forcing them to fall back on themselves. At the same time, their structures of productive forces and production relationships, as well as their political relations and cultural forms, were prevented from generating their own autonomous economic development. These structures forced upon them a passive involution towards a subsistence economy with regionalized or localized markets, relatively isolated from the developed centers. Basically, the greater and more solid the links between the center and the periphery and the dependent development of the latter in the past, and the weaker these links are at present, the greater is the underdevelopment of that periphery today (Frank 1969a:13–15; 1969b:148).

On the underdeveloped and marginalized rural periphery, ample areas of operation for a peripheral commercial capital are left by the following: large industrial, financial, and corporate capital of the principal societies of the international capitalist system (basically the monopolistic capital of the United States); the capital of subsidiaries of transnational corporations operating in peripheral societies; and satellite native capital (i.e. dependent national capital) of peripheral societies. The peripheral commercial capital, merged or in cooperation with profiteering and self-serving capital, speculative or otherwise, dominates local and regional markets and involves the masses of direct agricultural producers in dependency relationships. It also exercises a monopolistic control over trade relations — and often over the principal means of production (the land). Moreover, it organizes distribution and consumption relationships and, frequently, the production relations themselves. Certain other contradictions arise as a result of capitalist dependency relationships — internal colonial polarization between trade centers and the small mercantile economy of the peasant, for example, and the dominant position of these commercial centers as local or regional components of the capitalist system within the peripheral region (in spite of the weakening of its links with the external centers). These further contradictions involve the expropriation/appropriation of economic surplus and the polarization into metropolises and satellites. Furthermore, we see in operation the law of unequal and combined development characteristic of the capitalist system and the phenomenon of polarized accumulation of wealth and poverty, development and underdevelopment.

Owing to these dependency relationships, the commercial bourgeoisie establishes monopoly and monopsony. It sets itself up as an obligatory intermediary between direct producers of goods and the market; it limits barter between peasants, intruding among them like a parasite; it appropriates arable land and leases it out to the peasantry; it then appropriates their production with exclusive rights and makes use of these very rights to satisfy their demand for the use values which they themselves do not produce. This makes it impossible for domestic peasant industries to create the products which constitute use value, since they are offered to them by the commercial bourgeoisie. In this way the development of the productive, material, and intellectual forces of the local peasant periphery is curbed. The commercial bourgeoisie obtains the products of peasant labor which created exchange and use values and appropriates part or all of the potential profits created by peasant labor.

All relations of exploitation experienced by the most marginalized peasant peripheries would not be conceivable without a complete integration of these underdeveloped rural zones into the capitalist system. This occurs through the relationships of dependency in which they are placed with respect to their centers of predominance. It is only because of this integration that commercial capital (and any other kind of capital which does not appear in opposition to salaried labor) maintains a permanently dominant position on the rural periphery of the capitalist system. In a precapitalist environment, this capital could only have been introduced into the intervals of the social structure and only sporadically have extracted profits from a hybrid system of commercial exploitation. Independent of the solidity of its bonds with the dominant forms of capital in society and in the world capitalist system, commercial capital constitutes — even when undergoing a passive involution — a subordinate form which is dependent on industrial capital (as such or integrated into financial or corporate capital). Industrial capital is the dominant existing form of exchange value in the capitalist mode of production. The only thing guaranteeing commercial capital its dominant position on the periphery is its dependent relationship with the dominant industrial capital in the center of the capitalist system, under which the former in turn incorporates the periphery in the form of commercial capitalism.

In the same way, mercantile production (defined by the identity of labor as creator of use and exchange values) can only predominate in the rural periphery as a result of the integration of the periphery within the capitalist system. This system demands the maintenance of a dependency relationship with the centers, in which an industrial, capitalist production (defined by the identity of labor as creator of use and surplus values) predominates. Small-scale mercantile production can only predominate in the periphery on the basis of a dependency relationship with the dominant center, which determines the form of labor (with respect to salaried labor) and the corresponding form of production modes (with respect to industrial capital). Moreover, this small-scale mercantile production is defined not only by the identity of labor as socially useful and as creator of exchange values, but also by labor as creator of economic surplus. Thus it is the dependency of peripheral commercial capital with respect to central industrial capital (financial, corporate) which causes commercial capital to abandon or to retrieve the periphery according to the needs of the predominant centers. It is the dependency of peripheral production with respect to central production which makes the subsistence economy on the periphery undergo change along with the mercantile economy, in accordance with the needs of the predominant centers. In short, it is the dependency of the periphery with respect to the center of the capitalist system which forces the periphery to be incorporated into development from the underdeveloped state or to be abandoned to the passive involution of underdevelopment, always in accordance with the requirements of the predominant centers.

Once the economic and political resources of a specific rural periphery lose importance for the dominant international and national centers of the capitalist system, as well as for its dominant international and national class, there is a weakening of the political and cultural control exercised over that periphery by the dominant national centers and by the dominant sector of the dependent national bourgeoisie. This leads to a falling back of the periphery onto (or a passive involution toward) its underdeveloped political-cultural rear guard (cf. Wolf 1966).

However, that is not the only cause of the marginal position — culturally, economically, and politically — of peripheral rural communities. The degree of incorporation or marginalization (and other aspects of dependency relationships with the dominant centers and with the central class structure) varies in forms which are basically determined by the structure and development of the capitalist system at national and international levels. Nevertheless, as Frank points out, these relationships also result from the partially successful efforts of the peasant sectors in defending themselves against certain effects of exploitation which are regarded as particularly onerous or undesirable (Frank 1969a: 63). The most important of these effects is a permanent threat of separation of the peasant from his means of production, the land, as well as from his working tools. The economic structure of the capitalist system (within whose framework the rural communities of Latin America function, and whose dynamics determine the fate of these communities) is the result of the combination of production relationships with dependency relationships. On the one hand, production relationships (the contradiction between capital and labor and class polarization), and on the other hand dependency relationships (the contradiction between dominant centers and satellite peripheries and colonial polarization), are the forces which interrelate and determine, interpenetrate and oppose, and attract and reject in a dialectic relationship in both dominant industrial centers of the capitalist system and in their dependent rural peripheries.

At this point I wish to return to certain observations I have made in an unpublished study dealing with the nature of colonized peasant cultures.

An objective basis for the existence and reproduction of social groups which preserve (in the form of possession or property) their organic link with the land as direct producers is constituted by the fact that the private exchange of goods, while developing between rural communities and urban centers and/or estates, does not completely affect the internal life of these groups. It does not dominate all their production and distribution relationships, nor does it give them the form of exchange value for all goods produced as immediate use value. The predominance of exchange value and the production of exchange value imply that the labor force itself is an exchange value, that it is separated from its objective working conditions; that is to say, that it behaves with regard to its own objectivity as with regard to an alien property. This is in fact precisely the relationship of capital. The reduction of all products and activities to exchange value presupposes the dissolution of all relationships which link the worker with his means of production and existence; it also signifies the dissolution of social relationships between persons and the appearance of a social relationship between objects, which would itself be expressed as exchange value.

This phenomenon does not occur completely in the rural communities of Latin America: the power of things over people, or the fetishism of goods, is only partial; merchandize, although it constitutes the basic economic cell of global society and tends to become a unique social cell, i.e. to destroy all other cells (including the rural community), nevertheless coexists with the rural community. It penetrates it, but at the same time encounters its opposition. Capitalism, though it involves rural communities in relationships of exploitation, does not therefore necessarily convert its constituent elements into the salaried workers of industry. This is because the production relationship between industrial capital and salaried labor in its framework is fundamental and dominant, but not exclusive: unequal, combined development constitutes a general law of capitalism. In order for that law to function, capitalism (at the levels of development achieved up to the present time) needs to abandon an important segment of human labor to exploitation by forms of capital which do not appear in opposition to salaried labor. In order to act and discharge their functions, assuring the capitalist system of unequal development under the dominance of industrial capital, those forms of capital which do not appear in necessary opposition to salaried labor must have available a social environment in which colonial relations (i.e. of dependency) and polarizations between centers and peripheries prevail over class relations and polarizations between capital and labor. For this purpose they produce this environment, make it persist, and create the conditions for it to reproduce; and one of its component parts is precisely the rural community.

The community may be defended (at times successfully) by peasant groups because its existence is necessary for the operations of its own capital. It must be defended for it to exist, because one of the forms of this capital is that which appears in opposition to labor converted into exchange value, and the condition of the appearance of this labor is the destruction of the rural community and the dissolution of the peasant's organic link with the land.

The ideological control exercised by the bourgeoisie is weak where economic resources are exploited by a simple mercantile production of small agricultural owners, tenants, partners and coowners, laborers, and native joint owners and where these participants have a marginal, peripheral importance for the dominant sector of the dominant bourgeois class in the dominant centers of the system and nation. This weak control makes it easier for the peasantry to cultivate cultural values which are not reducible to exchange values. These exchange values supersede the worker's organic link with the land and restrain the development of the relationship of capital in rural communities, i.e. restrain the development of his proletarization, or rather his *Lumpen* proletarization. For land to be property, individual or communal, but not merchandize; for it to be a mode of production, but not capital; for it to be a source of income, but not rent; for the peasant to fulfill himself and safeguard his social identity, working the land which he owns or at least possesses and enjoys the use of (Stavenhagen 1969: 219); for these conditions to prevail, then a cultural pattern must correspond to his bond with the land. This bond is opposed to the "materialized" bond expressed in exchange value. The cultural pattern intervenes on the level of the peasant's social condition, strengthens it, and exercises a preserving action over it. In other words, he must have a cultural activity which is not reducible to a general thing: the value which represents a suppression and negation of all individuality and originality. It must not become a culture of social groups which are defined more by their position in the class structure and shaped more by the polarization and contradiction of capital and salaried labor than by their position in the colonial structure; such a culture is precisely the result of such suppression and negation, that is to say, reduction to a general thing: exchange value.

The peasantry thus needs to have an effective cultural material at hand which escapes in part from the cultural control of the bourgeoisie and which, by a creative act on the part of the group, can be transformed into a cultural structure which is more or less compact and durable. This culture must be resistant both to brutal aggression and to a subtle traffic of cultural elements proper to the bourgeoisie and its whole ideological practice. Such an effective material in a social group, which by devoting itself to a small and simple production of goods in a localized and marginalized microcosm has only a limited autonomous historical initiative, is provided basically by tradition. This is an allusive and illusive representation of the historical past, the image of everything that previous generations did on the level of social organization, economic activity, interpersonal relations, beliefs, language, clothing, norms of behavior, moral values, etc.; it is what ensured previous generations their peasant identity, the possession of lands, and partial protection in the face of the capital relationship (Kowalewski 1973b).

A passive capitalist involution of the rural periphery (to which corresponds the falling back of rural communities on their own cultural resources) greatly favors the persistence of peasant cultural traditionalism. And therefore not only does the capitalist system tend to marginalize rural communities, but the communities themselves tend to become marginalized in order to have recourse to their culture. Moreover, this marginalization develops in order to oppose any internal tendency for social relationships between individuals or groups and the means of production, or relationships between individuals and groups, to become predominantly relationships between objects, to be expressed in exchange value opposing, in sum, the total separation of the peasant from his land.

Thus, we may say that peripheral rural communities constitute underdeveloped and dependent counterpoints of the city, the *hacienda*, or any other type of dominant center — local, regional, and national — which has colonial relations with its peasant satellite periphery. And at the same time these relations and the poles they link are penetrated by, as well as opposed to, class relationships and their corresponding cultural forms. On the level of unity and the struggle of cultural rivals in ideological class relationships, their unity prevails over their struggle. This is why the cultural forms which correspond to the class structure are necessarily structured to bourgeois dominance. In colonial ideological relations between the rural periphery and its dominant centers, on the other hand, the struggle of cultural rivals prevails over cultural unity. And this gives the peasant culture its own characteristics and strongly accentuated, distinctive features. It involves it in a relationship of dependency, but at the same time it is one of extreme contradiction with the cultural resources which ensure the dependent national bourgeoisie of its cultural domination over the sum total of other parts of society.

Rural communities constitute the weakest link in the bourgeoisie's chain of ideological domination, and a chain, as is well known, is only as strong as its weakest link.

The marginalized cultural position of the peasantry changes with the emergence of rural movements identified and jointly involved at a supralocal and supraregional level, i.e. those which go beyond the limits of the localized microcosm of rural communities. The peasantry mobilizes in the struggle against the monopoly of land and trade exercised by the dominant bourgeoisie at a local, regional, or national level, and against the expropriation of potential economic surpluses by said bourgeoisie and by the centers which exercise their dominance over the peripheral rural communities. It does so in conditions under which (and because of which) the traditional dominant sector of the bourgeoisie that was engaged in agricultural commerce and commercial export is displaced from power by the modern sectors of the financial-industrial bourgeoisie. The marginalized microcosm of rural existence is affected, at least indirectly, by the economic, political, and cultural effects of the new form of dependency: the technological-industrial dependency of world society.

The peasant, entrenched in his local microcosm, initially offers arduous and silent resistance to all change which would involve the penetration of the contradictions between capital and labor, class polarization, domination of exchange value in social relationships, and separation of the peasant from his means of production and subsistence. This resistance is transformed, however, once the peasants are mobilized, identified, jointly involved with other peasant conglomerates; the peasants then become a pressure group. This new unity is directed to the struggle to share to a larger degree in the access to basic resources and in the distribution of earnings and other goods, both material and spiritual, available in world society. It is directed, on the one hand, to school construction; to the buying of a portable radio; to the promotion of leaders not between the sectors which used to provide a traditional leadership of the community, but between the people with greatest horizontal mobility and greatest knowledge of the outside environment, particularly urban; to marches to the city; to assistance offered by legal advisers, workers' trade unions, urban parties, and an intelligentsia of the new middle class, etc. And on the other hand, there is the search for a regional and even national articulation of the peasant movement as a pressure group. This occurs under conditions in which communities and rural zones are isolated from each other and may interact exclusively or basically through their urban metropolises. Also, then, the peasantry becomes vulnerable to, and pursuant of, the politics and culture of the dominant centers. It does not matter if one is dealing directly with bourgeois politics and culture, or rather (and this is happening increasingly) with the petty bourgeois and workers' currents of such politics and culture. These are the currents which complete the picture of bourgeois domination in urban metropolises. In following them (and it cannot help following them once they are mobilized as a pressure group), the peasantry tends to become liberated from its marginalized position through a dependent participation.

Historical initiative, as I have already said, is limited politically and culturally because of its status as an agent of a simple and small mercantile production; and it does not leave any alternatives to the peasantry other than to occupy a dependent marginal position or a position of dependent participation in the structure of society as a whole. In both positions it is not difficult to observe basic conditions which would favor the emancipation of the peasant; in both positions, however, he is frustrated by their dependent structural nature.

The phenomenon which presages the emergence of the guerrillas of the National Liberation Army in Colombia and the Party of the Poor in Mexico consists essentially of a peasant mobilization which takes advantage of the favorable basic conditions for emancipation existing in these localities. The peasants make a radical break, constituted in insurgent armies, from their structurally dependent system.

Among the traditional peasant movements which abound in the contemporary history of Latin America (Landsberger 1969; Quijano 1969; Huizer 1971), these guerrillas are distinguished because they do not emerge spontaneously from the peasant masses; they are not an expression of a spontaneous peasant uprising. Of the many rural guerrillas who appeared and suffered reverses in Latin America in the decade of the sixties, they are distinguished because they do emerge and develop organically with the peasant mass, while still preserving a relationship of relative autonomy with respect to the rural communities to which they are linked and which serve as their base and support in subsequent development.

In order to define the two rebel peasant armies on a theoretical plane, three elements must be taken into account: (1) the ideology of the working class; (2) the peasant movement; and (3) the political-military practice of the revolutionary class struggle to seize power. At the present time, the union of these three elements seems to be the axis (not exclusively but without a doubt basically) around which the resolution of the essential contradiction of Latin American peasant life may take place. His existence fluctuates perpetually between dependent marginalization and dependent participation and may give rise to a revolutionary peasantry capable of discharging the role of the base and vanguard elements in the political-military struggle for national liberation and socialism.

In relation to the rural communities which serve as a supportive base for these guerrillas and which are the object of their radiating action, both insurgent armies constitute a new dominant center, both politically and ideologically. This center stands in radical class opposition to the centers of bourgeois dominance and to the subordinate currents (i.e.

petty bourgeois, worker, and peasant currents) which complete the picture of this bourgeois domination in the city and country. Both insurgent armies encompass the combination of two contradictions: the contradiction of labor with capital, characteristic of capitalist production relationships, and the contradiction of the peasant satellite periphery with its dominant centers, characteristic of capitalist dependency relationships, which are merged into a united drive for a revolutionary break.

The relationship between these rebel armies and their peasant supportive bases is extraordinarily specific in the sense that it does not involve a worker-peasant alliance in which the latter would be a subordinate group and follower of the working class. In spite of the fact that the guerrilla armies of whom we speak do in fact constitute political-military focal points of the revolutionary worker-peasant alliance, the peasant groups which comprise them nonetheless occupy an independent position: they do not follow the working class, either politically or ideologically, but they proletarianize morally through the exercising of the political-military class struggle. They appropriate the proletarian ideology and carry out a proletarian policy. This involves, within the general trend of the class struggle in the capitalist system, one of the specific forms of undertaking the socialist revolution in the social formations of peripheral capitalism.

According to Stavenhagen (1973:42–43), one of the outstanding militants of radical anthropology, an understanding of this phenomenon consists of relying on the analysis of present trends and dynamic forces as they emerge from historical processes; one can then propose possible alternatives open to a society. Stavenhagen maintains that the greater or lesser viability of future social evolution depends not only on the validity of the analysis which precedes it but especially on the conscious action of men dedicated to transforming the conditions of their existence. In order to understand and constructively confront this problem of social evolution in Latin America, it is no longer sufficient to limit oneself to repeating the orthodox theses (even the most audacious versions) on the revolutionary potential of the peasantry. According to these theories, it is necessary to attribute

... to the proletariat the key role in the advent of socialism, less because of the misery which it has suffered than because of the position it occupies in the production process and the capacity it has to acquire from that fact a talent for organization and cohesion of action unmatched by all the oppressed classes of the past. It is not a matter of questioning the revolutionary capacity of the landless peasantry of the countries of the Third World nor of disputing the fact that the latter has provided the largest number of participants to the revolutionary struggle, on a world scale, in the past twenty years. Nevertheless, two considerations must be added to this assertion so that it does not become a false reflection of world reality. First, that this peasantry, as the Marxists have predicted, is in itself incapable of acquiring power and founding new states; it lacks for this purpose a leadership of proletarian origin, composition, and inspiration. Second, that this poor peasantry is incapable in itself of constructing a socialist society in the sense that Marx understood it, that is to say, a society which guarantees a full and complete development of all human potentialities (Mandel 1972:19).

What was not possible in the earlier periods of development of the world capitalist system appears as an objective possibility in the present period of imperialism. In this period, under the form of proletarian ideology, "consciousness acquires worldwide characteristics" because it is "the product of development of all the productive forces of the world" and of the existence of the socialist states (Guevara 1970: 324).

The poor peasantry of Latin America, still cast in a marginal position with regard to access to basic resources, has, because of its peripheral location in the social structure and because of its position as a last link in the chain of capitalist exploitation, taken upon its shoulders the lion's share of misery and underdevelopment. It is these shoulders which, at distant opposite poles, both international and national, have been the sources of wealth and development. The economic surplus expropriated from dependent societies, on the one hand, and from their rural peripheries on the other, has realized extraordinary profits which, redistributed partially among the working class of international and national metropolises, have become the source of the reformist opportunism of the worker movement. "The workers in imperialist countries are losing their international class spirit under the influence of a certain complicity in the exploitation of dependent countries" (Guevara 1970: 370). The search for extraordinary monopolistic profits explains the imperialist nature of capitalism. But it also explains the phenomenon of internal colonialism, observable in the dependent societies of Latin America. There is a link not only between imperialism and the opportunism of the worker movement in world metropolises, but also between internal colonialism and the opportunism of the workers' movement in Latin American national metropolises. Therefore, the industrial working class in the overwhelming majority of societies of Latin America has never exercised a role of political class leadership with respect to their principal ally: the peasant masses. Many economic and social victories of the working class have been financed from resources formed by extraordinary profits which the bourgeoisie extracts from exploiting the country. Many crises in the relations of capital and salaried labor have been avoided by the bourgeoisie's knowing how to export these contradictions, or their consequences, from the industrial plants to the countryside.

What we have said does not suggest that the industrial proletariat has lost its revolutionary role in the capitalist system. For in Latin America itself, in certain societies, it has adopted measures of great importance to exercise this role. We only wish to indicate, in outline form, the most fundamental structural causes which with greater or lesser force, according to the opportunities, curb the discharging of its historical mission. At the same time, we cannot forget that seen from this angle, an insurgent army assumes the task of eliminating, through the exercising of a proletarian policy, those structural causes and their effects and of organizing the working class. It does this precisely in order to pave the road to assuming a position of revolutionary leadership which objectively belongs to it, based on its position in the capitalist modes of production.

In Marx's theory on capitalism, the proletariat is not always necessarily revolutionary. It was not revolutionary in the period of manufacturing, becoming so only as a consequence of the introduction of machinery during the Industrial Revolution. The long-term effects of the use of machinery, nevertheless, are different from their immediate effects. If one does not take advantage of the opportunities of the initial period of modern industry, the proletariat of the country which is being industrialized tends to become less and less revolutionary. This does not mean, however, that Marx's argument, to the effect that "capitalism produces its own grave diggers," is mistaken. If we regard capitalism as a world system, which is the only correct procedure, we see that it is divided into a handful of exploiting countries and a much greater and more populous number of exploited countries. The masses of these exploited dependencies constitute, in the world capitalist system, a force which is revolutionary, in the same sense and for the same reasons that Marx believed that the proletariat is revolutionary in the initial period of modern industry (Sweezy 1972: 164–165).

The peasantry of peripheral rural communities has the advantage of being at the edge of the perimeter in which the bourgeoisie exercises its strongest ideological control and develops its most important political activities; it has been placed in this position by the very structure of the capitalist system. At the same time, however, capital has not completely stripped the peasantry of its means of production and subsistence, since its labor force does not revolve completely around exchange value. As a result, it has been involved in an intricate network of devices of extra-economic coercion in order to effectively and systematically exploit the peasantry and in order to multiply capital without having recourse to the conversion of the peasantry into a salaried mass. Therefore, if we omit a few doubtful exceptions, almost every attempt, no matter how timid and insignificant, to acquire greater access to basic (and even secondary) resources or to appropriate the goods and services which have long been guaranteed as a natural right to the industrial working class (even of the underdeveloped Latin American metropolises) has encountered brutal resistance and drastic repression on the part of the agro-commercial bourgeoisie. And this resistance and repression have been solidly supported by other sectors of the commercial-exporting, industrial, and financial bourgeoisie. This is why almost every attempt to change or improve working conditions, education, medical services, communication, and, of course, relations of ownership and terms of commercial exchange becomes a potentially political action, an act of the class struggle, and raises the problem of state power.

When elements of proletarian ideology are introduced into the peasant environment from urban centers, the peasantry perceives that no social change which it regards as beneficial and indispensable for its subsequent subsistence is possible without changing the social class exercising political power. Some sectors (of course, still in the minority) of the Latin American peasantry now attribute greater importance to the question of who exercises political power and what class he represents than do the social groups which, because of being involved in the contradictions between capital and labor, should be, theoretically, the propelling forces in the struggle for the seizure of power and the expropriation of the bourgeoisie.

A constant danger hangs over the peasantry, the danger of being absorbed by the capital relationship as salaried manpower, or becoming part of the lumpen proletarianized structural marginality without land and fixed employment. This would in fact oblige it to assume an attitude of resistance to capital. That is its specific means, though only marginal, of participating in the contradiction between capital and labor. The limitations of its revolutionary potential, which are due to the fact that it is not a direct participant in the production relationship between capital and labor (which engenders the basic antagonistic class contradiction in capitalist society as a whole), are overcome by the insurgent army. This army, supported by peasant resistance to the relationship of capital and to the ideological effects of a weak development of this relationship in rural communities, involves the peasantry in its revolutionary action. It also gives the peasantry the opportunity to exercise and appropriate the proletarian ideology and to carry out a proletarian policy. That is to say, to become a participant, ideologically and politically, in the antagonistic contradiction of class which is basic to capitalist society, in spite of being far removed from it on the economic plane.

To express this in another way: although the political and ideological effects of the main contradiction in the structure of capitalist production relationships do not constitute a revolutionary force in the place where they occur with greatest force, they do not fail to intervene outside this place, at its edge. This is where they encounter more suitable conditions for intervening and basing this revolutionary force, to wit: the insurgent peasant army.

The basic contradiction which causes the capitalist modes of production to disappear is not, however, the one which exists between the two antagonistic elements which combine and oppose each other within the structure of production relationships (i.e. between capital and labor). Instead it is the contradiction which appears on the outside, although it has its foundation within it. And that is the contradiction between productive forces and production relationships.

If the rate of growth of productive forces in the period of monopolistic capitalism is more rapid than in any previous period of capitalist development, it is erroneous and dangerous to forget that this rate implies at the same time the under-use and even the destruction of immense possibilities for economic and social development at the level of the world capitalist system: in short, that the present-day lack of correspondence between productive forces and production relationships is translated into a huge loss, quantitatively and qualitatively, of productive forces on the level of the world capitalist system (Godelier 1973: 238).

The rural peripheries of the social formations of peripheral capitalism in Latin America do, in fact, constitute zones in which this contradiction (which takes the form of a huge loss of productive forces) is sufficiently acute to involve the revolutionary army (and the peasantry which the army directs politically) in the two antagonistic contradictions constituted by the evolution of the capitalist modes of production in a society where the guerrilla operates. This involves not only the internal contradiction of the structure of production relationships, whose political effect is represented by the guerrilla and in whose ambit he intervenes through his political-military practice, but also the contradiction which tends to cause the said modes of production to disappear.

Dispersion and isolation of families or communities, which impair the peasantry as a potential political force, disappear once it is integrated into the insurgent army; or these disadvantages are weakened, if not altogether nullified, once the peasantry is embraced by the organization which the guerrillas establish in the countryside. Habits of collective activity, the talent for organization, the cohesion which industrial labor tends to form, as well as the knowledge of techniques and theoretical training, are also acquired by the peasant in the insurgent army.

Thus, in order to consider the role of the peasantry in the shaping of emerging revolutionary alternatives to the social formations of peripheral capitalism in Latin America, especially as a continental whole, it is not sufficient at the present time to limit oneself to an analysis at the level of production relationships. Such an analysis only permits one to know the limits of political initiative proper to the peasantry. On the contrary, attention must be shifted to an analysis at the political level of the class struggle and, concretely, at the level of new facts which in the political field are constituted by the presence of the revolutionary peasant armies. Such an analysis would envisage the conditions of breaking those limits. There can no longer be a correct focus on the revolutionary role of the peasantry in Latin America which does not embrace and emphasize the presence of the emerging insurgent armies. This does not mean that the orthodox theoretical concept of peasant revolutionary ability is useless or must undergo revision. It only means that in the face of a new reality, understanding of which has not been established, it is necessary to use this concept in the only possible way: as a means of producing an understanding of that reality.

As Fabio Vázquez Castaño, Commander-in-Chief of the National Liberation Army, maintains (1972), the working class plays a basically passive role in the revolutionary process, which is constituted by the following aspects: the strategically decisive role of the insurgent peasant army in the revolutionary struggle for the seizing of power; its independence with regard to the working class; the role of a vanguard exercised in the revolutionary movement by the peasantry, which appropriates the proletarian ideology and puts proletarian policy into practice by means of its armed struggle; the functions of the clandestine urban apparatus in the training of a proletarian political cadre for the rural guerrillas; and the beginning of the shifting of the guerrilla war from the country to the city. These conditions, he points out, result from

.. the ideological influence which the bourgeoisie exercises over our working class, which is undermined by reformism and for this reason has no ability to direct the struggle at the present time ...; far from being able to exercise a leading role at this time, the working class has to be pulled along to effective participation and ... this is only achieved through a deepening of the armed struggle from the country. ... Only through the action of the rural guerrilla is the revolutionary awareness of the people, and specifically the peasantry, generated and channeled. ... It is in the mountains where the emergence, consolidation and development of the revolutionary army are best guaranteed, since in the city the enemy has greater maneuverability, channels of communication, supplies of money and material resources, etc. It is less difficult for him to get in a good blow against the organization, since the latter very quickly loses the tactic superiority used in action. The rural guerrilla cannot depend on the success of the urban action for his emergence and consolidation, particularly when experience has shown that in Latin America only the strengthening of the country can guarantee the development of the urban organization. ... Experience shows that under our conditions, the political-military leadership has to lie in the guerrilla ...; the role which belongs to the city in the revolutionary process in our Continent ... is basically one of political development which leads to the training of men who are cast as revolutionary cadres and who join the guerrillas so that they may give their contribution there in the construction of the revolutionary army (Vázquez 1972).

It is ... for the tactical reasons of knowing the land and adapting to the hard life lived in the mountains that the peasantry goes on to occupy the vanguard in this struggle. It is in the mountains where it must undergo its first test; there it must be polished, there it must purify itself until it achieves its consolidation as a revolutionary force and wins over other sectors of the masses: workers, students, professionals, and intellectuals, consistent with the reality of our stage. It must organize them, place them in the struggle, gradually develop the organization, learn from errors, propose tasks which are not outside the real scope of their forces. It must attain a third stage in the revolutionary struggle, that of matching forces with the enemy and preparing for the assault on the government. The assault on the government must start from the mountains. That is to say, the struggle for national liberation must go from the countryside to the city (Menéndez 1967: 33–34). (For a full discussion of the theses of Fabio Vázquez, see Kowalewski 1973a.)

With respect to the social awareness of the revolutionary peasantry, different ideological levels, structured hierarchically, are combined and dominated by the ideology of the revolutionary vanguard, whose organ is the insurgent army. In the first part of this article, we examined an address by a peasant who expresses aspects of the ideological structure which lays the foundations of the revolutionary peasantry and its movement. For this structure to subsist and to continue to embrace increasing numbers of peasants, it must be under the leadership of the revolutionary ideology of the army, since it finds itself strongly influenced by the political-military practice of this revolutionary army. The ideology, in turn, constitutes a result of the intervention of the scientific theory of history, under conditions determined by the ideological practice of the guiding organ of the armed peasant movement. Such a theory explains the conditions of the reproduction, transformation, and disappearance of the capitalist means of production and the whole code of social relationships which constitute a specific social form of peripheral capitalism, in which the armed revolutionary struggle is developed.

Proletarian ideology has been appropriated by the vanguard organized in its political-military organ, the peasant insurgent army — which has assumed a dominant role in the peasant movement — and has become a revolutionary ideology. It has summed up the program of its ideology in the "Ideario del Partido de los Pobres [Principles of the Party of the Poor]" (Partido de los Pobres 1973: 6–8). This document, the fruit of some six years of theoretical work and ideological training carried out in the guerrilla camps and mountain huts of the insurgent peasantry, was drawn up in the Sierra de Atoyac in March 1973. I have decided to reproduce it in its entirety in the Appendix, convinced that it constitutes an eloquent proof of the radical change taking place among peasants in Latin America. The "Ideario" sets forth the theoretical conditions for the disappearance of the modes of capitalist production in the society in which the Party of the Poor is developing its armed action. We are now becoming aware of the operation of peasant revolutionary vanguards, organized as guerrillas in a strategic mobile force.

The Latin American peasantry has never before had a greater opportunity to become the prime agent for revolutionary change and the vanguard for the struggle for national liberation and socialism. The present time is the most favorable, given the new political and ideological conditions which are emerging thanks to the presence and action of the insurgent peasant armies.

Scientific practice is inevitably to meet with the revolutionary movement and armed struggle developing under the form of guerrilla warfare from the countryside; it is to meet with the polarizations — and with the antagonistic colonial and class contradictions — of dependent, peripheral capitalism. Anthropology, for which the rural community traditionally constitutes an object of privileged and consecrated knowledge, cannot avoid these influences, which necessarily tend to polarize it in accordance with the class contradictions which are characteristic of nations and of the world system whose reality it studies and inhabits.

Once again, and perhaps more than ever, anthropology is at a turning point, as are all the social sciences. At one pole, an anthropology of counterinsurgency is taking shape. The task for an incipient anthropology of liberation is not only that of denouncing and revealing its latent links to public opinion, but also that of recovering it and becoming fully aware of its own latent class bonds, acknowledging them as obvious and necessary. That is, to explain in language stripped of euphemisms, to regroup and form around an opposite pole, in a counter anthropology of insurgence, as long as the international and national class struggle requires it.

Objectivity and the taking of sides are not excluded, because they do not constitute a pair of opposites. Objectivity is indispensable in order for anthropology to be a science and not an ideology; the taking of sides is inevitable because being a science does not imply that anthropology ceases to be a social fact. There will be no disagreement where one seeks to reject the taking of sides instead of taking the opposite side.

The present emergence of the revolutionary peasantry, the insurgent peasant armies, and the guerrilla war from the countryside are a Latin American phenomenon whose cause has to be taken up by the anthropology of liberation which in turn must bring it to maturity.

APPENDIX: PRINCIPLES OF THE PARTY OF THE POOR

To the People of Mexico.

To all workers.

The Party of the Poor, an organ which has come from the deepest affections of the Mexican People and which is daily preparing itself, consolidating and developing in the armed struggle and revolutionary war of the exploited against the exploiters, herewith sets forth in general terms the principal and essential objectives which form the basis of its *raison d'être*, conduct, and action.

Our essential principles and objectives are:

1. To struggle inevitably with arms in hand alongside all armed revolutionary organizations and alongside our working People, in order to bring about the socialist revolution; to take over political power; to destroy the exploiting and oppressive bourgeois state and form a government of all the workers; to construct a new society without the exploited and their exploiters, without the oppressed and their oppressors.

2. To destroy the capitalist system; to abolish private property, which is the basis and essence of man's exploitation by man; to annihilate the bourgeoisie as a privileged, exploiting, oppressive class, since its capital and its accumulated and concentrated wealth have been created by the blood, sweat, and labor of the working classes, peasants and laborers. Therefore, the historical justice which belongs to the working class, to the peasantry and to the many generations of laborers, will be reclaimed. What has been created by the labor and sacrifice of the People must belong to the People themselves.

3. Consequently, after the armed triumph of the Socialist Revolution and the seizure of political power by the People, the structure of the exploiting economic-social system will be destroyed and economic power will be taken over; for this purpose, the industrial, commercial, and agricultural enterprises and the financial institutions, etc. which are now in the possession of the bourgeoisie will be expropriated and nationalized. After the expropriation and nationalization of the modes and instruments of production, natural resources, banks, etc., they will be administered by the workers themselves and by the proletarian state. Foreign and internal trade will be under the control of the state of all the workers; and economic, political, and social relations with all Countries will have to be based on the fundamental interests of their Peoples, on equality and mutual assistance.

4. Exploitation and oppression in the countryside will end; the large estates, *haciendas*, and all properties of the capitalists of the countryside will be expropriated. Land will be collectivized and administered by those who work it; the state of all the workers will give to the entire peasantry the machinery, techniques, means, and resources sufficient to raise the production and level of life of all peasants; land and production will belong to those who work it.

5. Large property owners will have their homes expropriated, and they will only be allowed what is necessary to live with dignity. Luxurious mansions, hotels, motels, and vacation centers which are today in the possession and service of the bourgeoisie, will pass to the hands of the workers.

6. Large sanatoria, clinics, pharmacies, laboratories, health centers, and hospitals will be expropriated and placed in the service of the people to guarantee health and avoid death through lack of medical attention.

7. Air, maritime, and land transport, and communications (telephone, telegraph and post) will be nationalized and placed in the service of society as a whole.

8. The bourgeois culture, because it is counterrevolutionary and incompatible with the interests of the workers, will be destroyed. The People will develop and create their own culture. The techniques and science used by the capitalist state to increase exploitation, oppression, and the death of the working masses will pass on to the service of the People in order to transform the country and raise production and the level of life of society. Education, culture, technical knowledge, and science will lose their commercial character in the new society. Education will be given and administered free by the revolutionary state to all the People in order to make a radical end to the illiteracy, ignorance, and cultural backwardness which the capitalist regime has fostered; education will be scientific, that is, it will be based strictly on truth, the material nature of the universe, the world, and society.

9. The press, radio, and television will be expropriated, since they constitute bourgeois instruments for subjecting and alienating the People, deforming truth, creating false moral and cultural values, and increasing its own profits and wealth. When the press, radio, and television are expropriated, the revolutionary state and government will be in charge of transforming the orientation and contents of those mass media of information and communication, whose fundamental aim will be to guide, educate, and raise the revolutionary conscience and morality of the People and assist in the training of the new man.

10. The laws and the entire bourgeois juridical system which guarantee private property and legitimize the bourgeoisie's exploitation of the workers will be abolished. The army and all police bodies which comprise repressive and criminal machinery — the defenders and basic support of the state and the bourgeois order — will be destroyed. The proletarian state will create laws, principles, and courts which will express, represent, and authentically defend the rights and interests of all workers and all society. The fundamental basis of society will be socialist democracy, which will entitle all workers to enjoy full rights and obligations and will place women on a level of equality with men with regard to work and society. The revolutionary state will consolidate and develop its own army and will arm all of the People; the house of every worker will be transformed into a trench for combat, and every worker will be converted into a revolutionary soldier to defend the country against its internal and ex-

ternal exploiters. The People will not lay down their arms until the last redoubt of exploitation and the last enemy of the revolution have been eliminated.

11. Man's labor will be free from all exploitation and oppression; it will cease to be a commodity and will no longer be regarded as a curse or a punishment, but as the rational and fundamental activity of man on the road to infinite self-betterment, the transformation of nature, the creation of the moral and spiritual values of society, and the production of material goods. Production and wealth will be distributed fairly, taking into consideration the basic interests and needs of all workers.

12. The struggle of the Mexican People for its full emancipation is an integral part of the international revolutionary movement for the total liberation of humanity; the artifical boundaries which have been set up and imposed by the exploiters to separate Peoples must be swept away by the struggle, by revolutionary internationalism. To carry this out, we identify fully and join with all exploited peoples, with all men and women who are fighting throughout the world against the common enemy: capitalism. We are in deep harmony with all peoples who have achieved their political, economic, and social emancipation and who therefore constitute a revolutionary example to us.

To attain and achieve the objectives indicated, the workers must inevitably wage an irreconcilable war to the death against the bourgeoisie, against the capitalists; it becomes necessary to develop, deepen, and generalize the war of uprisings and rapid decisions and extend the guerrilla war to the whole country. The guerrilla war will carry the whole People to increasingly superior forms of struggle, to general insurrection and the seizing of power, until the bourgeoisie is destroyed and buried together with its exploiting and oppressive capitalist system.

The historical, economic, political, and social conditions necessary to organize and develop the socialist revolution in our country have been produced. The immediate task of the exploited is to group into clandestine organizations and to act. Revolutionary theory and practice will have to generate the general revolutionary organization of the vanguard, politically and militarily capable of directing the war and coordinating revolutionary actions.

The consequent revolutionary practice will have to define and unite the revolutionaries and separate them from the opportunists, renegades, traitors, and agents of the bourgeoisie within the revolutionary movement.

We call upon all workers to unite, organize, arm, and struggle against the bourgeoisie and against all means and instruments which are used to exploit and maintain its control.

We call upon the workers to liquidate the trade union charade, politically and physically to take over the factories, to transform them into centers of insurrection, and to struggle for their historical objectives.

We call upon the poor peasantry to take over by force of arms the estates and lands in the possession of the rural capitalists and therefore to integrate themselves with the armed struggle.

We call upon the militant student body and revolutionary intellectuals to convert the schools and working centers into combat trenches for the socialist revolution.

We call upon all the People to fight against the rich capitalists, wherever the latter are found, to attack their wealth and goods, and to destroy their

police/military forces and their exploiting and oppressive system.
The duty of every revolutionary is to carry out the Revolution with weapons in hand:

Conquer or Die.

PARTY OF THE POOR

The Mountains of Guerrero State
March 1973

REFERENCES

FRANK, ANDRÉ GUNDER
  1969a *Latin America: underdevelopment or revolution.* New York and London: Monthly Review Press.
  1969b *Capitalism and underdevelopment in Latin America.* New York and London: Monthly Review Press.
GODELIER, MAURICE
  1973 *Horizon: trajets marxistes en anthropologie.* Paris: Maspero.
GUEVARA, ERNESTO CHE
  1970 *Obras 1957–1967*, volume two. Havana: Casa de las Américas.
HUIZER, GERRIT
  1971 "Peasant unrest in Latin America." Mimeograph. University of Amsterdam.
KOWALEWSKI, ZBIGNIEW MARCIN
  1973a *Guerrilla estratégica: vanguardia y método de movilización campesina.* Caracas: Salvador de la Plaza.
  1973b "América indígena: condición de una cultura colonizada." Unpublished manuscript.
LANDSBERGER, HENRY A., *editor*
  1969 *Latin American peasant movements.* Ithaca and London: Cornell University Press.
LONDOÑO, JAIR
  1972 Habla un campesino de Colombia. *Economía y Desarrollo* 11.
MANDEL, ERNEST
  1972 *La formation de la pensée économique de Karl Marx.* Paris: Maspero.
MENÉNDEZ RODRÍGUEZ, MARIO
  1967 *Fabio Vázquez Castaño. Sucesos 1778.*
PARTIDO DE LOS POBRES
  1973 Ideario del Partido de los Pobres [Principles of the Party of the Poor]. *¿Por Qué?* 253.
QUIJANO, ANÍBAL
  1969 Los movimientos campesinos contemporáneos en América Latina. *Pensamiento Crítico* 24.
STAVENHAGEN, RODOLFO
  1969 *Las clases sociales en las sociedades agrarias.* Mexico City: Siglo XXI.

xico and the Hopi, Pueblo, and Chippewa in the U.S. He is Founder
e Asociación Mexicana Albert Schweitzer. His publications include:
:ido y absurdo de la misión cristiana entre los Indios de la Selva"
eedings of the International Congress of Americanists, 1970) and
te tropigues o país de esperanza?" (Amaru, Revista Escuela de
iería, Lima, 1970).

RUDE DUBY BLOM (1901–) was born in Switzerland and was
ied to the late Frans Blom, the Maya archaeologist. She received
mas as a horticulturist and as a social worker. She worked in
Fascist organizations and as a journalist in various countries. Her
work in Mexico, where she arrived in December of 1940, was as a
selor for the Labor Department in developing cultural programs for
en working in backward industries. She then studied the role of
en in the agrarian revolution, writing reports about famous women
rs. The Governor of Chiapas assigned her to an expedition to the
forest in Chiapas in order to study the conditions of the isolated
ans living there. Her publications include a book about the Lacandon
ans and another about the problems of race discrimination (both
ished by the Ministry of Education) as well as several works with
is Blom, with whom she worked in the Maya ruins. Her photographs
been published and exhibited in many countries. She is the President
he Patronato Fray Bartolomé de Las Casas and member of the
inario de Cultura Mexicana de Mexico D.F., of CEDAM (Club de
loraciones y Deportes Aquáticas de Mexico and of the Academía
ional de Historia y Geografía. For her work in Mexico, especially in
areas of helping Indians and conserving the forests, President
everria gave her Mexican nationality in 1971.

N H. BODLEY (1942–) was born in Eugene, Oregon. He received his
., M.A., and Ph.D. (1970) from the University of Oregon and con-
ted fieldwork in the Peruvian Amazon. He is presently at Washington
e University. Recent publications include: Victims of progress (1975)
Anthropology and contemporary human problems (1976).

A S. DE FRIEDEMANN (1934–) was born in Bogotá, Colombia. She
died at the Instituto Colombiano de Antropología, Hunter College, and
University of California. Appointed Permanent International Research
ociate at Emory University, Atlanta, she worked in 1967 and 1968 as
earch Member in their Center for Research in Social Change. She is
fessor in the Department of Anthropology, Universidad Nacional de

1973   El futuro de América Latina: entre el subdesarrollo y la revolución.
        S.C. Libre 14.
SWEEZY, PAUL M.
1972   Modern capitalism and other essays. New York and London: Monthly
        Review Press.
VÁZQUEZ CASTAÑO, FABIO
1972   La guerrilla rural no ha fracasado en América Latina. ¿Por Qué?
        213, 214.
WOLF, ERIC
1966   "Kinship, friendship, and patron-client relations in complex societies,"
        in The social anthropology of complex societies. London: Tavistock.

Biographical Notes

ALICIA M. BARABAS (1948–   ) was born in Buenos
education in anthropology at the Buenos Aires Natio
From 1969 to 1971, she was Researcher at the Bu
logical Institute. She has been a resident of Mexic
searcher at the National Institute of Anthropology a
since 1973. Her recent publications include: "Hydra
ethnocide: the Mazatec and Chinantec people of O
Miguel Bartolomé, 1973), "Profetismo, milenarisr
las insurrecciones Mayas de Yucatán" (1974), and
los Mayas de Yucatán" (1976).

BERNARDO BERDICHEWSKY (1924–   ) was born in Sa
in 1956 from the University of Chile and did postgr
universities of La Plata, Argentina; of Saarland
Madrid, Spain (where he received his Ph.D. in 196
seventies, he did research for the Agrarian Reform
situation of the Mapuche Indians in the Agrarian Ref
He was Professor of Anthropology at the Universi
military coup of September, 1973, when he left the cou
Visiting Professor of Anthropology and Sociology
Texas, Austin, Texas. He has published extensively c
archaeology of South America.

TEODORO BINDER (1919–   ) has specialized in the foll
medicine and mythology among the Amnesha, Sl
tribes; the rights and chances of ethnic minorities, inc

Colombia. She has written numerous publications on black populations and interethnic relations in Colombia. Her recent publications are: *Minería, descendencia y orfebrería. Litoral Pacífico* (1974); *Indigenismo y aniquilamiento de Indígenas en Colombia* (coauthor) (1975); *Tierra, tradición y poder en Colombia* (editor) (1976). She has also produced the following films: *Güelmambí* (1973), *Villarrica* (1974), and *Tierra Es Vida* (1974). She is presently Research Associate at the Instituto Colombiano de Antropología, Bogotá, Colombia.

GERRIT HUIZER (1929–) studied social psychology at Amsterdam University and has been active in community development and peasant organization since 1955. He worked as a volunteer in a village in Central America and later with Danilo Dolci in Sicily. From 1962 to 1971 he worked with different agencies of the United Nations (particularly ILO) in Latin America and Southeast Asia in field projects and action research. He has written numerous articles in literary and professional journals and readers and a book, *The revolutionary potential of peasants in Latin America* (1972, Lexington, Mass.: Heath Lexington Books) which came out also in Spanish and a Dutch version and in an abridged edition (*Peasant rebellion in Latin America*, 1973, Harmondsworth: Penguin). He has been Visiting Professor at the Institute of Social Studies, The Hague, and Fellow of the Institute of Development Research in Copenhagen and has been Director of the Third World Centre, University of Nijmegen, Netherlands, since 1973.

ALICJA IWAŃSKA (1918–) was born in Poland. She received her M.A. in Philosophy from the University of Warsaw in 1946 and her Ph.D. in Sociology from Columbia University in 1957. She has been Professor of Sociology and Anthropology since 1965 at the State University of New York, Albany, and has done fieldwork in Mexico, Chile, and the United States. Her recent publications include: *Purgatory and Utopia: a Mazahua Indian village* (1971); "Without art" (1970); "Emigrants or commuters: Mazahua Indians in Mexico City" (1973); and "Indianscy Intelektualiści" (1974).

NICANOR JÁCOME (1945–) studied sociology and political science at the Universidad Central del Ecuador (Quito) and is currently Sociologist with the Junta Nacional de Planificación and Professor with the Faculty of Economics at the Universidad Central de las Cátedras. He does research in the socioeconomic formation of Ecuador and the methodology of scientific investigation in the Escuela de Ciencias de la Información.

Published works include: *El metodo en la investigación social, El Diseño de la investigación social,* and *El manejo de algunas técnicas.*

ZBIGNIEW MARCIN KOWALEWSKI (1943–   ) is Researcher at the Inst. Historii Kultury Materialnej in Warsaw. His interests include: peasant culture and social change in Latin America, corporate rural (peasant) communities, and social organization and evolutionary potentials studies in their interaction with revolutionary movements in Mexico, Guatemala, Peru, Vietnam, Indonesia, Kenya, and Zaire. Among his publications are: "Wspolnoty rolne chkopow andyjskiego altiplano [Peasant agrarian communities of the Andean altiplano]" (*Łódzkie Studia Etnograficzne* 9: 359–371; 1967) and (with M. Sobrado) *Antropología de la guerrilla* (Caracas: C. M. Nueva Izquierda; 1971).

INÉS LLUMIQUINGA (1942–   ) studied sociology and political science at the Universidad Central del Ecuador (Quito) and is currently Sociologist at the Ministerio de Agricultura y Ganadería. She has published "La mujer ecuatoriana en el proceso laboral."

SIDNEY DAVID MARKMAN (1911–   ), Professor of Art History and Archaeology at Duke University, Durham, North Carolina, has devoted the major part of his professional career to the study of the architecture and urbanization of colonial Central America. He is the author of *Colonial architecture of Antigua Guatemala* (Philadelphia: American Philosophical Society, 1966), a definitive monograph on the architecture and urban history of the former capital of the Reino de Guatemala. He has also published a number of articles in the *Journal of the Society of Architectural Historians* and the *Boletín del Centro de Investigaciones Históricas y Estéticas* (Caracas, Venezuela) as well as a short monograph, *San Cristóbal de las Casas, Chiapas* (Seville: Escuela de Estudios Hispano-Americanos, 1963). Since 1966 he has been a participant in the symposia on urbanization held at the biennial International Congress of Americanists. *Colonial Central America: a bibliography* is due for publication in 1976 by the Arizona State University Press.

POLLY POPE was educated at the University of California and the University of Southern California in anthropology and journalism. She is now an Associate Professor and Chairperson of the Department of Anthropology, California State College, Dominguez Hills. She has written several papers on folklore and warfare.

ELIAS SEVILLA-CASAS (1942–) was born in Colombia. He received his Ph.D. from Northwestern University (Evanston, Illinois) in 1973. He is currently Professor of Anthropological Research at the University of Los Andes, Bogotá, Colombia and Permanent Consultant to three *Cabildos* [Indian councils] among the Paez peoples of Tierradentro, Cauca, Colombia. His major areas of research are rural organization and development, political education of minority groups, "action research," and peasant/Indian communities of southwestern Colombia.

HENNING SIVERTS (1928–) received his doctorate in 1959 at the University of Oslo and is now Senior Curator at the University of Bergen. In 1953–1954, 1961–1962, and 1964, he did fieldwork in Tzeltal and Trotzil of the Highland Chiapas, Mexico, and in 1970–1971 he worked among the Jívaro (Aguaruna) of the Montaña in North Peru. Other research interests include political systems, ethnicity, ecology and human adaptability in tropical forest regions, and language in society (cognitive systems and ethnographic procedures). Publications on the above topics include "The Aguaruna Jívaro of Peru: a preliminary report" and *Tribal survival in the Alto Marañon: the Aguaruna case.*

NORMAN E. WHITTEN, JR. (1937–) is Professor of Anthropology at the University of Illinois, Urbana. He took his Ph.D. in 1964 at the University of North Carolina, Chapel Hill. Besides fieldwork with the Lowland Quechua of Ecuador, Whitten has worked extensively with black cultures in Nova Scotia, Canada, the southern United States, Colombia, and Ecuador. He is author of two books: *Class, kinship, and power in an Ecuadorian town: the Negroes of San Lorenzo* (Stanford: Stanford University Press, 1965), and *Black frontiersmen: a South American case* (Cambridge, Massachusetts: Schenkman, 1973) and senior editor of *Afro-American anthropology* (New York: Free Press, 1970). He is currently writing a book on Lowland Quechua social structure and cultural adaptation in the face of massive changes in the Amazonian Lowlands.

Index of Names

Index of Subjects

1973 El futuro de América Latina: entre el subdesarrollo y la revolución. *S.C. Libre* 14.

SWEEZY, PAUL M.
1972 *Modern capitalism and other essays.* New York and London: Monthly Review Press.

VÁZQUEZ CASTAÑO, FABIO
1972 La guerrilla rural no ha fracasado en América Latina. *¿Por Qué?* 213, 214.

WOLF, ERIC
1966 "Kinship, friendship, and patron-client relations in complex societies," in *The social anthropology of complex societies.* London: Tavistock.

Biographical Notes

ALICIA M. BARABAS (1948–) was born in Buenos Aires. She received her education in anthropology at the Buenos Aires National University (1971). From 1969 to 1971, she was Researcher at the Buenos Aires Anthropological Institute. She has been a resident of Mexico since 1972 and Researcher at the National Institute of Anthropology and History of Mexico since 1973. Her recent publications include: "Hydraulic development and ethnocide: the Mazatec and Chinantec people of Oaxaca, Mexico" (with Miguel Bartolomé, 1973), "Profetismo, milenarismo, y mesianismo en las insurrecciones Mayas de Yucatán" (1974), and "Identidad etnica de los Mayas de Yucatán" (1976).

BERNARDO BERDICHEWSKY (1924–) was born in Santiago. He graduated in 1956 from the University of Chile and did postgraduate studies at the universities of La Plata, Argentina; of Saarland, Germany; and of Madrid, Spain (where he received his Ph.D. in 1961). During the early seventies, he did research for the Agrarian Reform Corporation on the situation of the Mapuche Indians in the Agrarian Reform process in Chile. He was Professor of Anthropology at the University of Chile until the military coup of September, 1973, when he left the country. He is presently Visiting Professor of Anthropology and Sociology at the University of Texas, Austin, Texas. He has published extensively on the ethnology and archaeology of South America.

TEODORO BINDER (1919–) has specialized in the following areas: ethnomedicine and mythology among the Amnesha, Shipibo, and Coribo tribes; the rights and chances of ethnic minorities, including the Mazahua

in Mexico and the Hopi, Pueblo, and Chippewa in the U.S. He is Founder
of the Asociación Mexicana Albert Schweitzer. His publications include:
"Sentido y absurdo de la misión cristiana entre los Indios de la Selva"
(*Proceedings of the International Congress of Americanists*, 1970) and
"Triste tropigues o país de esperanza?" (*Amaru, Revista Escuela de
Indeniería*, Lima, 1970).

GERTRUDE DUBY BLOM (1901–) was born in Switzerland and was
married to the late Frans Blom, the Maya archaeologist. She received
diplomas as a horticulturist and as a social worker. She worked in
anti-Fascist organizations and as a journalist in various countries. Her
first work in Mexico, where she arrived in December of 1940, was as a
counselor for the Labor Department in developing cultural programs for
women working in backward industries. She then studied the role of
women in the agrarian revolution, writing reports about famous women
leaders. The Governor of Chiapas assigned her to an expedition to the
rain forest in Chiapas in order to study the conditions of the isolated
Indians living there. Her publications include a book about the Lacandon
Indians and another about the problems of race discrimination (both
published by the Ministry of Education) as well as several works with
Frans Blom, with whom she worked in the Maya ruins. Her photographs
have been published and exhibited in many countries. She is the President
of the Patronato Fray Bartolomé de Las Casas and member of the
Seminario de Cultura Mexicana de Mexico D.F., of CEDAM (Club de
Exploraciones y Deportes Aquáticas de Mexico and of the Academía
Nacional de Historia y Geografía. For her work in Mexico, especially in
the areas of helping Indians and conserving the forests, President
Echeverria gave her Mexican nationality in 1971.

JOHN H. BODLEY (1942–) was born in Eugene, Oregon. He received his
B.A., M.A., and Ph.D. (1970) from the University of Oregon and conducted fieldwork in the Peruvian Amazon. He is presently at Washington
State University. Recent publications include: *Victims of progress* (1975)
and *Anthropology and contemporary human problems* (1976).

NINA S. DE FRIEDEMANN (1934–) was born in Bogotá, Colombia. She
studied at the Instituto Colombiano de Antropología, Hunter College, and
the University of California. Appointed Permanent International Research
Associate at Emory University, Atlanta, she worked in 1967 and 1968 as
Research Member in their Center for Research in Social Change. She is
Professor in the Department of Anthropology, Universidad Nacional de

ELIAS SEVILLA-CASAS (1942–) was born in Colombia. He received his Ph.D. from Northwestern University (Evanston, Illinois) in 1973. He is currently Professor of Anthropological Research at the University of Los Andes, Bogotá, Colombia and Permanent Consultant to three *Cabildos* [Indian councils] among the Paez peoples of Tierradentro, Cauca, Colombia. His major areas of research are rural organization and development, political education of minority groups, "action research," and peasant/Indian communities of southwestern Colombia.

HENNING SIVERTS (1928–) received his doctorate in 1959 at the University of Oslo and is now Senior Curator at the University of Bergen. In 1953–1954, 1961–1962, and 1964, he did fieldwork in Tzeltal and Trotzil of the Highland Chiapas, Mexico, and in 1970–1971 he worked among the Jívaro (Aguaruna) of the Montaña in North Peru. Other research interests include political systems, ethnicity, ecology and human adaptability in tropical forest regions, and language in society (cognitive systems and ethnographic procedures). Publications on the above topics include "The Aguaruna Jívaro of Peru: a preliminary report" and *Tribal survival in the Alto Marañon: the Aguaruna case.*

NORMAN E. WHITTEN, JR. (1937–) is Professor of Anthropology at the University of Illinois, Urbana. He took his Ph.D. in 1964 at the University of North Carolina, Chapel Hill. Besides fieldwork with the Lowland Quechua of Ecuador, Whitten has worked extensively with black cultures in Nova Scotia, Canada, the southern United States, Colombia, and Ecuador. He is author of two books: *Class, kinship, and power in an Ecuadorian town: the Negroes of San Lorenzo* (Stanford: Stanford University Press, 1965), and *Black frontiersmen: a South American case* (Cambridge, Massachusetts: Schenkman, 1973) and senior editor of *Afro-American anthropology* (New York: Free Press, 1970). He is currently writing a book on Lowland Quechua social structure and cultural adaptation in the face of massive changes in the Amazonian Lowlands.

Index of Names

Index of Subjects